Islandica

A Series in Icelandic and Norse Studies
Cornell University Library
PATRICK J. STEVENS, MANAGING EDITOR

VOLUME LXIV

Wisdom of the North
Proverbial Allusion and Patterning in the Icelandic Saga
RICHARD L. HARRIS

Wisdom of the North
Proverbial Allusion and Patterning in the Icelandic Saga

Richard L. Harris

ISLANDICA LXIV

CORNELL UNIVERSITY LIBRARY
ITHACA, NEW YORK
2023

All rights reserved. Except for brief quotations in a review,
this book, or parts thereof, must not be reproduced in any form
without permission in writing from the publisher.

Copyright © 2023 by Richard L. Harris

Design and composition: Jack Donner, BookType
Illustration on book cover:
Chapter 36 (chapter 42 in the Íslenzk fornrit edition) of *Brennu-Njáls saga*.
Detail from manuscript AM 163d fol., 14r.
Used by permission of Stofnun Árna Magnússonar í íslenskum fræðum.

A complete version of this book is available through open access
at https://ecommons.cornell.edu/handle/1813/55752
ISBN: 978-0-935995-29-9

Hardcover printing 10 9 8 7 6 5 4 3 2 1

To my mother,
Elizabeth,

and to my wife,
Michelle,

I dedicate this analysis,
with much love and gratitude.

Contents

Preface	ix
Acknowledgments	xii
Abbreviations	xvii

CHAPTER 1.
Introductory: Reading the Sagas Against a ... 1
Paroemial Background

CHAPTER 2.
Paroemial Patterns of the Mythic and the ... 31
Legendary Backgrounds

CHAPTER 3.
Paroemial Strategies, Apophthegmatic Scenes, ... 85
and the Heroic Ideal in *Gísla saga*

CHAPTER 4.
Paroemial Thematic Signaling in *Njáls saga* ... 107

CHAPTER 5.
Grettis saga and the Paroemial Delineation of Character ... 163

CHAPTER 6.
Various Uses and Variant Forms of Proverbs in the Sagas: ... 197
The Proverbial Foolishness of *Hrafnkels saga Freysgoða*

CHAPTER 7.

Proverbial Echoes and the Point of *Hœnsa-Þóris saga*: 221
"Ek ætla þar vándum manni at duga sem þú ert"

CHAPTER 8.

Fóstbrœðra saga, *Sverris saga*, and Narratives of the Will: 245
"Jafnan segir inn ríkri ráð"

CHAPTER 9.

Concluding Discussions and Directions of Research 275

Bibliography
   Primary Sources 287
   Secondary Sources 294

Preface

Although I took up work specifically on the present volume only a few years ago, Icelandic proverbs themselves had come to my attention long before—when I was a graduate student in Iceland in the mid-1960s. On my first visit there, I had asked the Icelandic Tourist Bureau to place me in a professor's home, as was sometimes possible then. While no homes with professors were available, I was sent to Ásta Jónsdóttir, who kept a bed-and-breakfast at Ránargata 21 in Reykjavík and who had studied in France. She knew many languages, and was of course intimately familiar with her country's artistic and literary culture. My friendship with her developed over a number of years, during which she helped me adjust to, and come to a deeper understanding of, Iceland's unique society and the past that made it what it is.

Among the numerous topics of our evening conversations over coffee were discussions of proverbs, one of which comes to mind on this occasion: "Sólin handa öllum er, en ekki jafnt til gleðis" (The sun is for everybody, but not for their equal pleasure). She did not mention, and until recently I did not know, that this text constitutes two lines from a poem among the *Ljóðmæli* of Steingrímur Thorsteinsson. I was finally able to discover the source only a few years ago, thanks to a Google search, although Icelanders with whom I had previously shared the quotation did comment on the likelihood that the lines came from a poem. As will be clear in chapter 1 of this volume, people persuaded of the traditional definition of the term "proverb" might hesitate to accept this as an authentic artifact, but they would surely be less reluctant to acknowledge the legitimate, authenticated proverbial force of its first clause, similar in its intent to established texts such as "Sólin er allra skepna yndi" (The sun is the delight of all creatures), or "Sólin lýsir öllum eins, illir og góðir njóta" (The sun shines on everyone, the evil and the good enjoy it).[1] Steingrímur's innovative continuation of this formula, whose roots lie in Iceland's communal repository of wisdom, might not in itself have such traditional validity, yet the value of its own wisdom is obvious and places it among Iceland's formulaic sentences of advice. Equally challenging in significance is another proverb I learned at that time: "Fjarlægð gerir fjöllin blá og mennina mikla" (Distance makes mountains blue and people large). *Orð að sönnu* identifies this proverb as coming from the play *Fjalla-Eyvindur*, by Jóhann Sigurjónsson, and it shares, in its second part, the same sort of surprise that we find in Steingrímur's lines.[2]

I have cited these particular texts here, so early in my book, to give readers a glimpse into how proverbs as we think of them can change with their users, in form as well as intention, and also to provide the briefest witness to a body of wisdom that seems to me as alive in Iceland today as it was so many centuries ago, when the country's ancestral stories first came to the written page. It was to this fascinating world of formulaic wisdom that Ásta introduced me in my student days, and I have long cherished her contribution to my perceptions of life and its conduct, as my friends and my Old Icelandic students know very well.

Before starting this book I had spent nearly a decade compiling an online Concordance to Proverbs and Proverbial Materials in the Old Icelandic Sagas and using its data to study how our understanding of this literature could be enhanced by our literary critical awareness of the proverbial presence in these narratives. Based in large part on that research, the present volume could, perhaps, have been limited to a technical study of saga proverbs in their contexts, and that would have also served a legitimate purpose, though perhaps one of less general interest and attention. However,

---

[1] Jón Geir Friðjónsson, *Orð að sönnu: Íslenskir málshættir og orðskviður* (Reykjavík: Forlagið, 2015), 531. Hereafter referred to as JGF. Quoting from Steingrímur Thorsteinsson, *Ljóðmæli*, 2nd ed. (Reykjavík: Sigurður Kristjánsson, 1910), 195.

[2] Bjarni Vilhjálmsson and Óskar Halldórsson, *Íslenzkir málshættir*, 2nd ed. (Reykjavík: Almenna bókafélagið, 1982), 86. Quoting from Jóhann Sigurjónsson, *Rit*, 2 vols. (Reykjavík: Mál og menning, 1940-42), 1:117; JGF 151.

it seemed to me more useful to a greater number and wider circle of readers to provide students of this medieval corpus with a set of extensively detailed literary critical examinations of several sagas, and to base this set on an awareness of how the proverbs were used in various ways by their respective composers to indicate and to reinforce the meanings they intended their narratives to convey.

The title of this volume, *Wisdom of the North: Proverbial Allusion and Patterning in the Icelandic Saga*, thus defines the parameters of the discussion I have established for my undertaking: to study how and for what purposes proverbs were used by the composers of the sagas; and to demonstrate by example how our awareness of proverbial occurrence in these narratives can enable us to reach more productive literary critical views of such works than we could do otherwise. The methods I use here can be, and in some cases already have been, applied to the reading of other medieval texts and, in particular, those originating within societies where the presence or persistent influence of preliterate culture can be found.

The book is structured so that, after establishing the operative terms and definitions in chapter 1, I discuss, in chapter 2, ways in which our interpretations of saga narratives are enriched by an awareness of the proverbial legacy of the Eddic corpus. I try to show there how medieval Iceland's communal memory retained a large repository of social wisdom, actively informing the conduct of its members as well as its judgment of their fellows—both of their character and their behavior—and applying to this phenomenon the term *paroemial cognitive patterning*.

The following chapters, 3 through 5, study how three of the most finely written *Íslendingasögur* make explicit use of proverbs in quite different ways, respectively, in order to imbue the fabric of their texts with ethical and moral value. Since the start of recording proverbs in writing, they have been represented by sometimes quite brief allusion, as well as by their full texts, and in chapters 6 through 8 I show how the meaning of several sagas seems clarified when we observe and analyze such allusive processes.

Chapter 9, in drawing these discussions to a conclusion, begins by exploring potential investigative parameters in the matter of paroemial cognitive patterning. This is followed by a few suggestions for avenues in which proverb studies of medieval Icelandic literature might be productively directed over the coming years.

I hope this book will be useful to readers of the sagas who seek to understand these texts and their composers' purposes more fully than might be likely without attention to the proverbial element. Much remains to be discovered through paroemiologically based literary critical approaches to the Old Icelandic corpus using methods such as those demonstrated here.

Acknowledgments

A full acknowledgement of my indebtedness to others for the completion of this volume would make a chapter in itself, but I should mention first the inspiration gained from my Old Icelandic students of former years, in particular Shelley LePoudre, who pointed out to me the patterned disposition of repeated proverbs in *Njáls saga*. Robert Cook, when he learned of my conviction that these repetitions had intentional artistic purpose, sent me all his notes on paroemial material in the saga, which he was translating at that time. Susan Deskis was among the first to urge making the Concordance to the Proverbs and Proverbial Materials in the Old Icelandic Sagas available online, and she has provided ample help with founding, and furthering the interests of, the Early Proverb Society, and thus spreading the influence of paroemiological study through many sessions of the International Congress on Medieval Studies at Western Michigan University. I owe much to her also for her long supportive following of my proverb studies over the last decade and for her suggestions regarding improvements in the book.

When I first visited Cornell University in 2004 in connection with work on my Concordance, I met and was welcomed into the local saga-reading group by Jeffrey Turco, who has been a source of much encouragement and informative conversations these past years. My debt to him is too large ever to be repaid, for years of kindly support and generous sharing of his wide knowledge of the literature, sometimes challenging my thinking with subtler questions of reading that might otherwise have escaped my attention.

xiv   Acknowledgments

In 2008 I began attending the annual Fiske Conference on Medieval Icelandic Studies at Cornell, where I have benefited from many discussions with fellow lovers of the sagas in an ideal setting, fostered by Tom Hill's generous hospitality at his acreage. Norsestock, as it is affectionately known by its loyal participants, was in various ways the ultimate source of a great deal of the content of this book.

Patrick J. Stevens, Curator of the Fiske Icelandic Collection in the Cornell University Library's Division of Rare and Manuscript Collections and managing editor of the Fiske's monograph series, Islandica, took a kindly interest in my work and encouraged me in its pursuit, devoting eventually a great deal of painstaking editorial effort to its wording and form.

Tom Hill and Megan Gilge read the original manuscript with its many problems and helped me improve its overall presentation before its submission to the publisher. And Megan subsequently spent considerable time reshaping large portions of the manuscript, making the thread of the argument more coherent. Most recently, Gabriel Bartlett undertook copy editing of the completed work, and its precision of expression and annotation owes much to him.

Adam Oberlin most obligingly read Chapter 1 with a view to ensuring that my use of ideas from the discipline of linguistics had legitimate applicability to my argument for the proverb's existence as a syntactic structure in a Chomskyan sense. And many other people helped in so many ways as I brought this book to fruition, too many to be named here. In the end, however, the work's flaws are truly mine, and much of what is good in it is the result of generous help from others.

My home institution, the University of Saskatchewan, awarded me several sabbaticals, which provided the time crucially needed to bring this project to fruition. And my professional account there provided partial funding for editing the work. A number of my local colleagues were supportive of these studies over a long period of time, and I am especially grateful to Yin Liu, Corey Owen, and Michael Cichon for many useful conversations about proverbs and their uses. As well, our departmental Chair, Brent Nelson, kindly made allowances for extra time spent in Savannah with my books and notes there. This generosity of spirit made a great difference as I was finishing the volume.

Of my family I must ask forgiveness for those long self-isolated periods when I was compiling the Concordance, the foundation of textual data for the present analysis, over a decade ago now. To my wife, Michelle, I owe most for making work on this book possible through these last years of repeated seasonal migration, from teaching in Canada to writing in Savannah. Without her loving support there would have been no book.

Abbreviations

CSI = *The Complete Sagas of Icelanders: Including 49 Tales.* Edited by Viðar Hreinsson. 5 vols. Reykjavík: Leifur Eiríksson, 1997. Abbreviated as *CSI*, with volume and page numbers.

C-V = Cleasby, Richard, and Gudbrand Vigfusson. *An Icelandic-English Dictionary*. 2nd ed. Oxford: Clarendon Press, 1957. Abbreviated as C-V, with page number and column designation.

FJ = Finnur Jónsson. "Oldislandske ordsprog og talemåder." *Arkiv för nordisk filologi*, 30 (1913–14): 61–217. Abbreviated as FJ, with proverb word number and page number.

FSN = *Fornaldar sögur norðurlanda.* Edited by Guðni Jónsson. 4 vols. Reykjavík: Íslendingasagnaútgáfan, 1954, 1959. Abbreviated as *FSN*, with volume and page numbers.

GJ = Guðmundur Jónsson. *Safn af íslenzkum orðskviðum, fornmælum, heilræðum, snilliyrðum, sannmælum og málsgreinum, samanlesið og í stafrófsröð sett af Guðmundi Jónssyni prófasti í Snæfellsnessýslu og presti í Staðarstaðarsókn.* Copenhagen: Hið íslenzka bókmenntafjelag, 1830. Abbreviated as GJ, with page number.

ÍF = Íslenzk fornrit. Hið íslenzka fornritafélag. Abbreviated as ÍF, with volume and page numbers.

JGF = Jón Geir Friðjónsson. *Orð að sönnu: Íslenzkir málshættir og orðskviðir*. Reykjavík: Forlagið, 2015. Abbreviated as JGF, with page number.

TPMA = Kuratorium Singer, eds. *Thesaurus Proverbiorum Medii Aevi: Lexikon der Sprichwörter des romanisch-germanischen Mittelalters*. 13 vols. Berlin: De Gruyter, 1996–2002. Abbreviated as *TPMA*, with volume and page numbers.

Published translations that I have modified slightly are noted accordingly in the footnotes. All translations of Old Icelandic without attribution to earlier publication are mine.

CHAPTER 1
Introductory
Reading the Sagas Against a Paroemial Background

In this chapter, readers will find a brief background for the discipline of paroemiology—that is, the study of proverbs and their uses in human communication—with particular reference to reading the Old Icelandic sagas. Discussion of the earliest known proverb inscriptions and the regard for wisdom texts by those who first studied them can help us understand their traditional treatment through more than twenty centuries of Western civilization. We will then consider terminology and definitions originating in recent linguistic theory that may facilitate more precise and systematic approaches to this discipline.

Our immediate purpose is to enable a discussion of aspects of proverbially based approaches to literary critical analysis of the Old Icelandic sagas in the following chapters, utilizing linguistically informed perspectives on the nature, formation, and recognition of the proverb. More generally, we will see how sentential strings that might previously have been excluded from data considered proverbial may be regarded as having a legitimate place in such inventories, and how their inclusion greatly benefits our paroemiological investigations. With such shifts in theoretical perspective, the study of how proverbs are used in literature, including the sagas, will acquire a more comprehensive field. This chapter will conclude with a brief survey of proverb collection and compilation in Iceland to the present time, as well as of Icelandic proverb studies—in particular, those of Hermann Pálsson.

The Ancient Paroemial Traditions

There could be no useful paroemiological discipline without the arduous and painstaking labor of the paroemiographers who compile our collections of proverbs and who have undertaken their task since the earliest years of literate cultures. In fact, to judge by what is available to us from the dawn of literacy, these traditional wisdom texts were among the first things people wanted to write down after they learned how to express by inscription concepts more complex than statistics of kingdoms and inventories of royal wealth. Among the earliest extant Sumerian cuneiform inscriptions, dating back almost five millennia, we find compilations of proverbs, often in abbreviated form. Such inscriptions indicate that their scribes had sufficient oral familiarity with the proverbs to be able to record them laconically and interpret them through allusion.[1]

Therefore, whatever the functional or intellectual reasons may have been for these circumstances, proverbs originating in the preliterate cultural background constitute a part of our earliest literary knowledge. It will prove of elemental concern to our understanding of the nature of the proverb that among the very first paroemial texts extant are proverbial allusions, rather than the complete proverbs themselves.

* * *

The sentence forms we recognize as proverbial were used by their earliest speakers to convey communally accepted world views and the wisdom of social behavior. The book of Proverbs is the compilation that universally comes to mind in the West when proverbs are mentioned in general conversation. This recognition arises from the important role that the biblical compilation and similar works once had in Western civilization, as well as the Old Testament environment's continuing message and recommendation of the acquisition of wisdom as a salvific function in the Judaic and Judeo-Christian

---

1. This early tendency is examined by Gary Beckman, "Proverbs and Proverbial Allusion in Hittite," *Journal of Near Eastern Studies* 45 (1986): 19–30. See the passages in Bendt Alster, "Proverbs from Ancient Mesopotamia: Their History and Social Implications," *Proverbium: Yearbook of International Proverb Scholarship* 10 (1993): 1–20. See also Jon Taylor, "The Sumerian Proverb Collections," *Revue d'Assyriologie* 99 (2005): 13: "Proverbs can often be heavily abbreviated, leaving just an elliptical rump."

worlds: "The fear of the Lord is the beginning of knowledge; fools despise wisdom and instruction."[2] Extolling the erudition of this book's reputed maker, the writer of 1 Kings describes Solomon as a man of

> wisdom, discernment, and breadth of understanding as vast as the sand of the seashore ... [who] surpassed the wisdom of all the people of the East, and all the wisdom of Egypt. ... He composed three thousand proverbs, and his songs numbered a thousand and five. He would speak of trees, from the cedar that is in the Lebanon to the hyssop that grows in the wall; he would speak of animals, and birds, and reptiles, and fish. People came from all the nations to hear the wisdom of Solomon; they came from all the kings of the earth who had heard of his wisdom. (1 Kings 4:29-33)

The context of royal intellectual accomplishment in which the book of Proverbs is situated places such wisdom among the most valuable forms of knowledge in the culture, although its ostensible spiritual agenda, which is similar to narrative pretexts for the background of other, later, compilations, was in fact secondary to the earlier purposes of its teachings. Indeed, some passages in the book were assimilated from sources external to Judaic society. It is also significant that the writer of 1 Kings mentions, in the context of Solomon's knowledge and accomplishments, the proverbial wealth of neighboring civilizations, of which he and his audience were well aware. Other Middle Eastern texts included in Proverbs have been noted by many scholars.[3] Of particular interest is the *Wisdom of Amenemope*, from the eighth century BC, which is reflected in Proverbs chapters 14, 22, and 23.[4]

---

2. Proverbs 1:7. All biblical citations are from *The New Oxford Annotated Bible with the Apocryphal/Deuterocanonical Books*, ed. Michael D. Coogan, 3rd ed. (Oxford: Oxford University Press, 2001).

3. For a discussion, see Bruce K. Waltke, "The Book of Proverbs and Ancient Wisdom Literature," *Bibliotheca Sacra* 136 (1979): 211–38.

4. The similarities between these two texts, first noticed in 1924, have been the subject of a long and complex discussion of the direction of influence, with the consensus favoring indebtedness of Proverbs to Amenemope. For detailed coverage, see Glendon F. Bryce, *A Legacy of Wisdom: The Egyptian Contribution to the Wisdom of Israel* (Lewisburg: Bucknell University Press, 1979). For an English rendering of the Egyptian work, see Miriam Lichtheim, *Ancient Egyptian Literature: A Book of Readings*, vol. 2, *The New Kingdom* (Berkeley: University of California Press, 1976, 2006), 146–48.

In Western European culture as well, paroemial texts make an early appearance with the development of literacy. Among the earliest Greek poetry to be written down, thus originating at the beginning of a literate culture, are two works by Hesiod, a late eighth-century BC poet of central Greece who wrote in hexameters of the Ionian style and dialect otherwise associated with the contemporaneous Homeric poetry of heroic narrative. From his writing we learn that Hesiod lived in the village of Ascra, in Boeotia, where his father had come from a maritime trading occupation in Aeolian Cyme, in an area now part of Libya. Called by the Muses while tending sheep on Mount Helicon, he first sang of the gods in his *Theogony*, discussing their origins and relationships and explaining the creation of the world.

Succeeding the *Theogony*, Hesiod's *Works and Days*, of a moral-didactic nature, is addressed to his brother Perses, with whose behavior the poet is in some ways dissatisfied. He admonishes him, among other things, to work. Hesiod has directions for farming and seafaring, and also rules for behavior in society, religious taboos, and the favorability or otherwise of particular days of the month for various undertakings. Hesiod's writing, like other poetry of the time composed in his tradition, is didactic, of a moral and practical nature, and his *Works and Days* contains some of the first compiled paroemial content of Western literature. Both books show influence from Eastern thinking, and his poetic wisdom follows traditions that can be traced back at least as far as 2500 BC in the Egyptian, Semitic, and Sumerian cultures, where paroemial literature, so far as we know it, finds its roots.[5]

A parallel circumstance in medieval Iceland might also be noticed here, with early writers in that country showing similar interest in the preservation of proverbial wisdom arising from their culture's ancestral past. In particular, the so-called "Gnomic Poem" of *Hávamál*—that is, its first ninety-five strophes—is regarded as having originated in pre-Christian Norway, expressing the communal views of that culture, yet it was included with the larger collection of wisdom found in the great mid-thirteenth century Eddic compilation known as the Codex Regius.[6] In addition, the Eddic

---

5. Peter Walcot, *Hesiod and the Near East* (Cardiff: University of Wales Press, 1966).
6. *Hávamál*, ed. David A. H. Evans, Viking Society for Northern Research Text Series 7 (London: Viking Society for Northern Research, 1986); see 3, "The Gnomic Poem," 9–23.

trilogy *Reginsmál*, *Fáfnismál*, and *Sigrdrífumál*, the last especially imbued with gnomic content, all date from pre-Christian times and are probably of Norwegian origin.[7]

Early Terms and Definitions

For some scholars, the pursuit of the paroemiological discipline has changed direction radically in recent decades. This transformation has resulted from shifting perspectives on the nature of the proverb, from its identity as a cultural artifact to its perception as a linguistic construct. It may prove helpful to consider how the more familiar, traditional views were formed and how recent changes came about in our thinking.

Paroemiologists seeking early evidence of this subject in the West refer to a citation of Aristotle by the Neoplatonic philosopher Synesius of Cyrene (ca. 370–ca. 413), who eventually became bishop of Ptolemais in Cyrenaica. In one of his lighter essays, *A Eulogy of Baldness*, which is addressed to Nicander, he alludes to Aristotle's opinion that proverbs are remnants of an ancient philosophy which thanks to their brevity and pertinence survived the great catastrophes that had befallen mankind in the past."[8] At several places in his works, Aristotle touches on this earlier, preliterate body of wisdom. It was his theory that knowledge in human culture had a cyclical existence, with that from earlier phases being partly preserved in later ones, though often in obscure ways. In his *Metaphysics*, for instance, he considers how, regarding the stars, "A tradition has been handed down by the ancient thinkers of very early times, and bequeathed to posterity in the form of a myth, to the effect that these heavenly bodies are gods, and that the Divine pervades the whole of nature." Expanding on this individual example, he then continues in a more general vein:

> As for the mythology built upon this concept, the entertaining stories of how these gods are human in shape or are like certain

---

7. *The Hávamál: With Selections from other Poems of the Edda, Illustrating the Wisdom of the North in Heathen Times*, ed. D. E. Martin Clarke (Cambridge: Cambridge University Press, 1923).
8. Synesius of Cyrene, *In Praise Of Baldness*, trans. George H. Kendal (Vancouver: Pharmakon Press, 1985), 36.

other animals, ... if we separate these statements and accept only the first, that they supposed the primary substances to be gods, we must regard it as an inspired saying and reflect that whereas every art and philosophy has probably been repeatedly developed to the utmost and has perished again, these beliefs of theirs have been preserved as a relic of former knowledge. To this extent only, then, are the views of our forefathers and of the earliest thinkers intelligible to us.[9]

Aristotle's concern with the study of remnants of earlier civilizations was probably the motivation for his compiling a collection of proverbs, now lost. For practical purposes, Bartlett Jere Whiting summarized Aristotle's understanding of the proverb as "a short saying of philosophic nature, of great antiquity, the product of the masses rather than of the classes, constantly applicable, and appealing because it bears a semblance of universal truth."[10] Most paroemiologists since Aristotle have adopted this traditionalist view, identifying if not defining such texts by proof of their usage in earlier written sources and by evidence of their currency in living usage.

In other circumstances, our thinking about the nature of the proverb could have gone in a different direction altogether, considering its functional value as its ultimately defining characteristic, and bringing focus more productively on *how* proverbs were used as speakers and writers employed them. Aristotle had vaguely approached the nature of the proverb in such terms in his *Rhetoric*:

> Proverbs also are metaphors from species to species. If a man, for instance, introduces into his house something from which he expects to benefit, but afterwards finds himself injured instead, it is as the Carpathian says of the hare; for both have experienced the same misfortunes. This is nearly all that can be said of the sources of smart sayings and the reasons which make them so.[11]

---

9. Aristotle, *Metaphysics X–XIV*, trans. Hugh Tredennick, Aristotle 28, Loeb Classical Library 287 (Cambridge: Harvard University Press, 1935), 163.

10. Bartlett Jere Whiting, "The Nature of the Proverb," *Harvard Studies and Notes in Philology and Literature* 13 (1931): 47–80; repr. in *When Evensong and Morrowsong Accord: Three Essays on the Proverb*, ed. Joseph C. Harris and Wolfgang Mieder (Cambridge, MA: Harvard University Press, 1994), 51–85.

11. Aristotle, *The "Art" of Rhetoric*, trans. John Henry Freese. Aristotle 22, Loeb Classical Library 193 (Cambridge: Harvard University Press, 1926), 417.

Despite Aristotle's functionalist musings, however, it was the traditionalist view of paroemial texts that would preoccupy Western culture over the next 2,300 years.

Aristotle's interpretation of the nature of proverbs found further support in the very terms that had come to be used for them—*paroemia* in Greek and *proverbium* in Latin. The former has roots that might be interpreted as "words by the road," while the latter signified "words put forth"; in both cases the words imply the traditional currency of proverbs in speech communities. Such terms were therefore resonant with Aristotle's emphasis on the currency and traditionality of the proverb as prerequisites of its authenticity, and this resonance must have reinforced the dominance of his views. Bartlett Jere Whiting's essays of the 1930s focused on such features, concerned as he was, like traditionalists before him, with the proverbiality of a text in terms of its use "by the road," as the etymology of the old Greek form had suggested. Problems inherent in this approach, however, included ascertaining standards of measure to assess currency and traditionality. How often, and for how long, must a proverb be in use for it to achieve such critical currency as to authenticate its status? There were no clear answers, and after Aristotle, little useful progress was made toward a precise definition of the proverb beyond the unresolved limitations of these imprecisely defined traditionalist terms.

Archer Taylor's Dilemma: "the Incommunicable Quality"

It was Archer Taylor who, in 1931, inadvertently moved paroemiologists toward a new, potentially more useful understanding of what they were working with. Humorously annoyed that "the definition of a proverb is too difficult to repay the undertaking," he identified it for practical purposes as "a saying in popular use, remarkable for some shrewd and novel turn." Influenced by the Aristotelian mindset, he declared: "Let us be content with recognising that a proverb is a saying current among the folk."[12] Such thinking has persisted to the present day, with Wolfgang Mieder stating in his most useful *Proverbs: A Handbook* (2004) that currency and evidence of traditionality are necessary for a phrase to be considered a true

---

12. Archer Taylor, *The Proverb* (Cambridge, MA: Harvard University Press, 1931), 3.

proverb.¹³ Later twentieth-century developments in the field of folklore and in applications of linguistic theory pointed, however, toward a resolution of the Aristotelian problem, and a restatement of definitions, first anticipated by Taylor, who, after expressing his frustration with the prestructuralist definitions, had observed most significantly, "An incommunicable quality tells us this sentence is proverbial and that is not."¹⁴ Taylor himself never explicitly analyzed this quality, but developments in linguistic theory in succeeding decades brought paroemiologists to a point where it was possible to arrive at some understanding of what he had perceived.

* * *

Below, we will review highlights in linguistic theory by which our understanding of this "incommunicable quality" that signals proverbiality came about. This linguistically focused pursuit of the paroemiological discipline by no means precludes earlier, more traditionalist forms of proverb study. Rather, this volume attempts to test how useful the implications of recent theoretical, linguistically founded models of the proverb may prove for reading the Old Icelandic sagas, especially in some textual passages that have in the past received little if any attention. If this reading is judged successful, then paroemiologically engaged students of Old Icelandic, as well as of other medieval literatures, may see fit to apply methods tried here to their own fields of interest.

Ferdinand de Saussure's "Object of Linguistics"

Students of pre-Chomskyan structural linguistics in the United States in the 1930s found useful delimitations of the field in the published lectures of Swiss linguist Ferdinand de Saussure (1857–1913). Although de Saussure was known during his lifetime for his *Mémoire sur le système primitif des voyelles dans les langues indo-européennes* (1878), which was written as a contribution to the then-fashionable

---

13. Wolfgang Mieder. *Proverbs: A Handbook* (Westport, CT: Greenwood Press, 2004), 3. Quoting himself from a previous publication ("Popular Views of the Proverb," *Proverbium* 2 [1983]): 119), he says the following: "A proverb is a short, generally known sentence of the folk which contains wisdom, truth, morals, and traditional views in a metaphorical, fixed and memorizable form and which is handed down from generation to generation." And yet, he adds (*Proverbs*, 4), "It is my contention that not even the most complex definition will be able to identify all proverbs. The crux of the matter lies in the concept of traditionality that includes both aspects of age and currency."

14. Taylor, *The Proverb*, 3.

Neo-Grammarian school of comparative historical study, his most significant contribution for subsequent linguistic theory was these lectures on aspects of general linguistics. Some of his ideas have particular applicability for our study of paroemiology today. Noticing the lack of consensus on the most productive purpose and direction of linguistic research, he drew a distinction between what he called internal, as opposed to external, linguistics:

> In internal linguistics the picture differs completely. Just any arrangement will not do. Language is a system that has its own arrangement. Comparison with chess will bring out the point. In chess, what is external can be separated relatively easily from what is internal. The fact that the game passed from Persia to Europe is external; against that, everything having to do with its system and rules is internal. If I use ivory chessmen instead of wooden ones, the change has no effect on the system, but if I decrease or increase the number of chessmen, this change has a profound effect on the "grammar" of the game. One must always distinguish between what is internal and what is external. In each instance one can determine the nature of the phenomenon by applying this rule: everything that changes the system in any way is internal.[15]

Ultimately, the rules of the game of chess hold an importance for players that is similar to the rules that a language's grammar holds for the speakers of that language, or for linguists attempting to understand its processes. Nothing matters except the details of how the game is played, or how a language is used to produce and comprehend mutually intelligible signals between human beings: "the true and unique object of linguistics is language studied in and for itself."[16] As will be seen below, de Saussure's observations, when applied to the discipline of paroemiology, make it possible to consider proverbial segments of speech as part of the system of natural language, with reference to the rules by which they are generated and their segments transformed into utterances, or surface strings, that are recognizable as paroemial in their nature for reasons still beyond precise description.

---

15. Ferdinand de Saussure, *Course in General Linguistics*, ed. Charles Bally and Albert Sechehaye, trans. Albert Riedlinger, with notes and introduction by Wade Baskin (New York: Philosophical Library, 1959), 22–23.

16. de Saussure, *Course*, 232.

One might study where a proverb came from, its meanings in various contexts, and other matters having more to do with what could be termed its archaeological situation, rather than its useful existence in human speech communities. It may be difficult, however, to be confident of one's conclusions on such questions without a clear understanding of the nature of proverbs themselves. That clarity would come from a careful, rigorous analysis of the sort made possible by certain developments in linguistic theory that started in the 1950s.

Noam Chomsky's Concept of Grammaticality

Further illumination of paroemiology has come, indirectly, from Noam Chomsky's theory of generative-transformational grammar. In 1957, in *Syntactic Structures*, Chomsky examined the notion of "grammaticality" separate from the semantic concept of "significance." Thus, while in the English language the string "Colorless green ideas sleep furiously" is grammatical, semantically it is nonsense, just as is the string "Furiously sleep ideas green colorless," which, in addition, is ungrammatical.[17] Since neither statement makes sense, and since only statement one adheres to the rules of English grammar, it follows that grammaticality is a quality whose existence does not depend on the meanings of words or of the constructions in which they occur. "I think we are forced to conclude," says Chomsky, "that grammar is autonomous and independent of meaning."[18] For both speaker and auditor, a grammatical sentence of English is recognizable by its syntactic structure, devoid of any reference to its meaning. These ideas have had a profound impact on our notion of what constitutes a proverb, suggesting that we question the definition of previously accepted features, such as traditionality and currency, as lying in the sphere identified by de Saussure as external linguistics, and as having no bearing on the rules of language generation. Rather, it seemed more reasonable that our ability to create and recognize the utterances we call proverbs lies also in the syntactic structure of those segments, not in their meaning or accepted usage. This perspective has enabled the theoretical background for a completely new examination of what proverbs are and how they might be studied most effectively.

---

17. Noam Chomsky, *Syntactic Structures* (The Hague: Mouton, 1957), 15.
18. Chomsky, *Syntactic*, 17.

Structurally Based Paroemiological Theory

Several paroemiologists who have been influenced by, but who have little reliance on, the generative-transformational movement have approached the definition of the proverb in terms of syntactic structure. For example, G. B. Milner's "What is a Proverb?" briefly described his theory of "quadripartite structure."[19] For Milner, a proverb consisted of four quarters, or minor segments, grouped into halves, or major segments. Such proverb structures could be analyzed, in each half, according to the attachment of binary features, derived and reassigned by Chomskyans from phonological methods of the Prague School, to significant words in each minor segment. Although Milner's approach soon revealed its limitations, other scholars also utilized linguistic structural analysis as a means of understanding what a proverb might be.

Alan Dundes, remarking in 1975 on the directions in which paroemiological research had been developed, complained of the traditionalist status quo in proverb studies, observing the persistence of an earlier historical emphasis where "commonly the goal is to discover proverb cognates among peoples with related languages or to propose possible places and times of origin for individual proverbs."[20] Thus scholars might be interested in the origins of a particular saying, devoting themselves to what we might term "paroemial archaeology." They could indeed trace a proverb from its presumed source, in Greek for instance, or even in the ancient wisdom collections of Sumerian culture, showing the steps by which it had made its way from a first inscription to its use in a modern context. Such endeavors tended, in the best circumstances, to lead to a clearer understanding of the proverb's significance in its successive cultural contexts. Although often producing interesting results, these pursuits required vast scholarly breadth and tireless investigation, which led to conjectural conclusions. Interest in this diachronic approach to proverb study

---

19. G. B. Milner, "What is a Proverb?" *New Society* 332 (1969): 199–202. His thesis is more succinctly stated in "Quadripartite Structures," *Proverbium* 14 (1969): 379–83. For later discussion, see Theodore A. Perry, "Quadripartite Wisdom Sayings and the Structure of Proverbs," *Proverbium: Yearbook of International Proverb Scholarship* 4 (1987): 187–210.

20. Alan Dundes, "On the Structure of the Proverb," *Proverbium: Yearbook of International Proverb Scholarship* 25 (1975): 961. Reprinted in *The Wisdom of Many: Essays on the Proverb*, ed. Wolfgang Mieder and Alan Dundes, Garland Folklore Casebooks 1 (New York: Garland, 1981), 43.

came, toward the end of the twentieth century, to be replaced in large part by the investigations of proverbs in social contexts or synchronically in the work of a specific author.[21]

Dundes, though he cites theoretical shortcomings of work in this area, was concerned with what he called folkloristic markers rather than with seeking specifically linguistic features to identify a proverb: "The question is rather whether there are underlying patterns of 'folkloristic structure' as opposed to 'linguistic structure' which may be isolated."[22] In this context, Dundes perceived, as had others before him, "a close relationship between proverb structure and riddle structure," which he analyzed in some detail.[23] While "the proverb appears to be a traditional propositional statement consisting of at least one descriptive element, a descriptive element consisting of a topic and a comment," and riddles are similarly constituted, in the latter "the referent of the descriptive element is to be guessed whereas in proverbs the referent is presumably known to both the speaker and the addressee(s)."[24] He noticed further that neither the structure of riddles nor that of proverbs depended "upon whether the [utterance] was a literal or metaphorical description."[25] Dundes did distinguish between different groups of proverbs by the application of contrastive features, a concept he borrowed from linguistics. Two such groups were what he called "oppositional" and "non-oppositional," the former represented by such utterances as "Man works from sun to sun but woman's work is never done," the latter by "Like father, like son."[26] This insightful study was productive in categorizing some proverb structures in a way that parallels linguistic analysis, and its conclusions may still prove useful in further investigations.

---

21. I draw these distinctions also from de Saussure, who identified and explained in theoretical terms the synchronic/diachronic dichotomy in the discipline of linguistics. See Susan E. Deskis, "Proverbs and Structure in Maxims I.A," *Studies in Philology* 110 (2013): 667–68, for a terminology that combines traditionalist definitions with a linguistically based approach. Her more recent and very useful work is diachronic in its approach. See *Alliterative Proverbs in Medieval England: Language Choice and Literary Meaning* (Columbus: Ohio State University Press, 2016), especially chapter 1, "Alliterative Proverbs in Time," 19–61.
22. Dundes, "On the Structure," 962; Dundes, *Wisdom of Many*, 46.
23. Dundes, "On the Structure," 965; *Wisdom of Many*, 50.
24. Dundes, "On the Structure," 970 and 965; *Wisdom of Many*, 60 and 50.
25. "On the Structure," 965; *Wisdom of Many*, 50.
26. Dundes, "On the Structure," 970; *Wisdom of Many*, 60.

Of particular interest to our study at this point, Beatrice Silverman-Weinreich in "Towards a Structural Analysis of Yiddish Proverbs," observed in 1978 that "to set it apart from ordinary utterances, the proverb, as an indicator of a rule, appears to be cast into certain linguistic molds, and to be characterized by certain formal markers. These markers serve as a kind of oral quotation marks, making the proverb easier to remember and to transmit for those who know it, while intimating to those who do not know it that it is a proverb, when heard for the first time."[27] Her markers fell into the following categories: grammatical, identified by types of sentences; semantic, including allegory or metaphor, as well as riddle patterns; and phonic devices, such as rhyme, alliteration, and metrical patterning. Approaching grammatical patterns, she remarked that the subject of proverbs was "abstract, generic or symbolic," while the verb was in the present or future tense.[28] The patterns themselves included conditional and comparative sentences, as well as imperatives, interrogatives, and negatives. She considered also less common syntactic constructions, such as the "riddle pattern" that includes a phrase where a riddle question has been turned into a statement, followed by an explanation.[29] Parallel constructions, using "better than," "worse than," as well as ellipsis, parataxis, and emphatic word order, were also observed.[30]

Among semantic markers, the author viewed what she called allegory but what others might call metaphor as "one of the clearest semantic markers of a proverb"[31] Semantic parallelism is also noticeable: "Outright repetition, synonyms and contrasts occur mainly in compound declarative proverbs"[32] "The logical connection between the parallel elements can be: (1) antonymy or contrast, . . . (2) equality or identity, . . . (3) synonymy . . . or (4) cause and effect"[33] "Paradox, irony, sharp contrasts, surprising comparisons—these are all devices which are apparently found in

---

27. Beatrice Silverman-Weinreich, "Towards a Structural Analysis of Yiddish Proverbs," *Yivo Annual of Jewish Social Science* 17 (1978): 6–7, reprinted in *The Wisdom of Many*, ed. Mieder and Dundes, 71.
28. Silverman-Weinreich, "Structural Analysis," 7; *Wisdom of Many*, 72.
29. Silverman-Weinreich, "Structural Analysis," 10; *Wisdom of Many*, 74.
30. Silverman-Weinreich, "Structural Analysis," 10–11; *Wisdom of Many*, 75.
31. Silverman-Weinreich, "Structural Analysis," 11; *Wisdom of Many*, 76.
32. Silverman-Weinreich, "Structural Analysis," 12; *Wisdom of Many*, 77.
33. Silverman-Weinreich, "Structural Analysis," 12; *Wisdom of Many*, 77.

Yiddish proverbs."[34] In her investigation the author discovered "not one single obligatory semantic marker for proverbs. What this analysis does show, however, is that every proverb must apparently have at least one of these semantic markers. Some kind of clever combination of words seems to be mandatory, but the actual way this is done varies."[35] Among what she terms "'phonic devices' markers" are listed rhyme, assonance, consonance, alliteration, and metric patterning, with the last of these used to emphasize the parallelism that exists in some proverbs.[36]

Silverman-Weinreich, in seeking to define the "oral quotation marks" by which the audience recognizes the proverbial status of an utterance, came closer than any of her predecessors to a useful clarification of Taylor's dilemma. Her work demonstrated that the proverbial distinction was potentially communicable yet complex, reliant in its signaling on the markers she attempted to identify but that clearly needed further study. She likewise realized that her practical examination and categorization of features in Yiddish proverbs that seemed to mark their status might need reassessment as paroemiologists sought a wider perspective on the marking process. Other languages and their cultures of communication were likely to have developed different methods of signaling the utterance of a proverb.

Shirley Arora and the Linguistic Features of Proverbiality

Taylor's oft-cited "incommunicable quality" as necessary for the recognition of a proverb gained crucial clarification, however, in the work of Shirley Arora. Arora's 1984 essay "The Perception of Proverbiality" attempted to develop a systematic, linguistically based understanding of the proverb's functional nature as first approached, albeit briefly, by Aristotle.[37] In her view, evidence for classifying an utterance as a proverb, distinct from ordinary speech, was "not so much incommunicable as manifold—a series or a set of characteristics, any one or a combination of which will serve" to signal the contrast.[38] In

---

34. Silverman-Weinreich, "Structural Analysis," 12; *Wisdom of Many*, 77.
35. Silverman-Weinreich, "Structural Analysis," 13; *Wisdom of Many*, 78.
36. Silverman-Weinreich, "Structural Analysis," 13-15; *Wisdom of Many*, 78-79.
37. Shirley Arora, "The Perception of Proverbiality," *Proverbium* 1 (1984): 1-38. Reprinted in *Wise Words: Essays on the Proverb*, ed. Wolfgang Mieder (New York: Garland, 1994), 3-29.
38. Arora, "Perception," 7; *Wise Words*, 8.

this article, she thus worked toward identifying linguistic markers, the greater density of which in a wise saying would favor its being perceived as proverbial.

Among clear markers distinguishing between conversational and nonconversational speech utterances, Arora identified, with Silverman-Weinrich, emphatic word order. Departures from ordinary word order, omissions of articles, and ellipses of the verb were also deemed distinctive. Arora showed consistent sensitivity to de Saussure's internal/external differentiation in addressing metaphor: "One of the most effective indicators of proverbiality is metaphor, the sudden shift in topic that disrupts the normal conversational flow and signals by its 'out-of-context' quality that the statement in question is to be interpreted figuratively and not literally."[39] However, this can be misleading if we are seeking internally based markers of proverbiality: "presented with an isolated statement and informed that it is a proverb, we are automatically disposed to interpret figuratively any concrete image it contains."[40] Yet in actual usage, "the perception of a statement as 'out-of-context' labels it as a metaphor, to be understood figuratively," leading in turn to its identification as a proverb.[41] "In a sense, therefore, the evidence for proverbiality that metaphor provides is not wholly internal: while some proverbs do contain metaphors, in most instances the proverb is simply a statement that becomes metaphorical only within a context that rules out a literal interpretation."[42]

Of Silverman-Weinreich's "semantic" markers, Arora considered parallelism, paradox, irony, and sharp contrasts and comparisons as additional, though not crucial, evidence of proverbiality. Lexically, rhyme and meter were seen as important factors defining nonconversational speech. "It stands to reason that the more markers a given saying possesses, the greater its chances of being perceived as a proverb at initial hearing; and conversely, a 'genuinely traditional' but unmarked saying may well fail as a proverb the first time it is heard merely because the listener does not recognize it as such."[43] She concluded her discussion of markers with this observation:

---

39. Arora, "Perception," 12.
40. Arora, "Perception," 12.
41. Arora, "Perception," 12; *Wise Words*, 11.
42. Arora, "Perception," 12–13; *Wise Words*, 11.
43. Arora, "Perception," 15; *Wise Words*, 13.

"A better understanding of the perception of proverbiality within the context of proverb performance is important therefore not only in terms of the functioning of proverbs in ordinary speech but also in terms of our understanding of the overall processes by which proverbs are created, survive, or disappear from oral tradition."[44] She determined that "it is important, nevertheless, to be aware of the criteria by which the speakers of a language judge their own proverbs, both on an abstract, generic level and at the specific level of the individual saying."[45]

Arora thus found that artificially manufactured proverbs—in other words, texts she identified as having specified proverbial features—were perceived as proverbs even when they could not be established as such by use, currency, or known traditionality in a given culture. Thus, usage by itself seems irrelevant to our perception of proverbiality, although the long-observed currency and traditionality of proverbs would be a likely result of their proven didactic value, and the familiarity of proverbial repetition could influence the hearer's judgement about the proverbial status of an utterance. Although in her theoretical discussion Arora did not pursue in further detail—beyond her critique of the proposals by Silverman-Weinreich and her own survey—the set of markers defining proverbial status, she did recognize the need for such work.[46]

From Arora's investigations, then, it became clear that Archer Taylor's "incommunicable quality" was, after all, at least potentially communicable, and, as far as we know, only in linguistic terms. The internal definition, to employ again Ferdinand de Saussure's distinction regarding the true object of linguistics as the internal approach to language, would most likely refer solely to linguistic

---

44. Arora, "Perception," 16; *Wise Words*, 13.
45. Arora, "Perception," 29; *Wise Words*, 22–23.
46. A greater appreciation of the processes involved in the hearer's perception of proverbiality may help us to arrive at an all-inclusive definition of a proverb, and why attempts to analyze the proverb on a cross-cultural or universal basis invariably meet with but limited success. And there are even broader implications as well. Archer Taylor affirms, in his chapter, "The Origins of the Proverb," that "the acceptance or rejection by tradition which follows immediately upon the creation of the proverb is a factor in its making quite as important as the first act of invention" (35). One could say more precisely "the acceptance or rejection by the hearer," for it is with the individual hearer that "tradition" begins and—with each successive performance—will be either extended or cut short. By exploring in greater detail the mechanisms underlying the perception of proverbiality, we will be enlarging our understanding of an aspect of the proverb that is indeed "quite as important as the first act of invention" (Arora, "Perception,", 29–30; cf. *Wise Words*, 23).

features that can be observed in such texts.[47] A purely functionalist approach to proverb study would inevitably base its parameters on this systematic definition of the subject.

The Contribution of Linguistically Based Approaches to Paroemiological Investigation

Studies using structuralist or generative/transformational linguistic theory have therefore helped our understanding of how a proverb comes into existence, how it is used, and the ways in which it is recognized and understood. Paroemiologists can gauge how such phrases are recognized by their audience, how they function in human communication, and how they may be interpreted in their various contexts. These paroemiologists have also become interested in the psychological reality of the proverb—that is, in how its syntax relates functionally to our linguistic competence and performance. Neal R. Norrick, in *How Proverbs Mean*, considers the semantic interpretation of structural units we recognize as containing proverbial content. While Norrick's approach—namely, that a proverb can be analyzed as a syntactic structure in a Saussurean sense, exclusive of its nonlinguistic social and cultural qualities—can feel unfamiliar from a traditionalist perspective, it empowers areas of paroemiological endeavor that had not previously come to our attention.[48]

The significance of Arora's features of markedness to our understanding of linguistically based paroemiological analysis becomes clear, especially when we approach literature in pursuit of creator-intended meaning. The wisdom formulas that the creators of literature employ may or may not have been used traditionally or in daily communication at the same time as their writing. In fact, the wisdom formulas may come from other cultures or environments,

---

47. Theoretical refinement of markers signifying that a sentence is a proverb in a linguistic sense remains a greatly desirable undertaking. At some point, as well, paroemiologists may find it convenient for comprehension, as well as for accuracy of expression, to develop terminology distinguishing between wisdom texts that are identifiable as proverbs in traditionalist terms versus those that are identifiable through a linguistic approach.

48. Neal R. Norrick, *How Proverbs Mean: Semantic Studies in English Proverbs*, Trends in Linguistics: Studies and Monographs 27 (Berlin, NY: Mouton, 1985). See also Richard P. Honeck, who in his *A Proverb in Mind: The Cognitive Science of Proverbial Wit and Wisdom* (Mahwah, NJ: Lawrence Erlbaum Associates, 1997) examines the cognitive linguistic aspects of the proverb.

the identification of which might enhance our linguistically based reading of a passage. Such considerations are at best external to our recognition of proverbial texts in their places and to our immediate analysis of the reasons for, and implications of, their existence there. Such peripheral information may incidentally inform our readings, but it is not of central importance to paroemiological investigation.

* * *

These are in brief the sorts of questions of general concern among contemporary paroemiologists who seek to restructure the discipline in theoretical, linguistic terms. In time, the applicability of their deliberations and occasional conclusions to our reading of the medieval Northern European literary corpus will, we hope, become significant and more informed by paroemiologically based literary analysis.

Recognition and Recall:
Syntactic Pattern and Lexical Kernel in an Old Icelandic Saga

From discussion above we can arrive at an understanding, at least in linguistic terms, of how an audience recognizes that an utterance is proverbial from syntactic and other markers. At the beginning of this chapter, however, we noticed how even the earliest wisdom collections demonstrated, by their inclusion of truncated forms of texts, that the paroemial identity, as well as the presumably complete form, of a proverb could be recalled by lexical allusion. In a minority of instances, the allusive process is accomplished by referring to the syntactic structure of a proverb with which the audience can be presumed to be familiar. A fairly complex example of this sort of paroemial allusion, taken from one of the *fornaldarsögur* (sagas of ancient times), *Ǫrvar-Odds saga*, follows below.

Choosing the Special Friend:
Affirmations of Social Standards in a Syntactic Pattern

The proverb "Illt er at eiga þræl at einkavin" (It's bad to have a thrall for a special friend) occurs in both *Grettis saga* and *Njáls saga*, as well as in *Konungs skuggsjá*. It also surfaces in a passage of Saxo Grammaticus's *Gesta Danorum*, where Erik the Eloquent responds to a challenge by Grep in an exchange of insults as he approaches the court of King Frodi: "Decipitur, quisquis servum sibi poscit amicum" (He is deceived who craves a servant for his friend). Saxo expands on the text of the proverb with an explanatory phrase, "Saepe solet domino verna nocere suo" (A menial often damages his master). It is obvious that aside from any particular damage slaves might do to masters, their ultimate objectives can never be the same.[49]

This proverb, which in any case clearly had currency in the medieval North, could particularly remind readers familiar with Norwegian history of Hákon jarl Sigurðarson's assassination in 995 by his thrall, Þormóðr karkr. Having lost popularity during the latter years of his reign by unrestrained greed and lechery, Hákon stayed, in his flight from Óláfr Tryggvason, with a mistress who concealed him in a hole under a pigsty. Hiding there with Hákon, Þormóðr karkr heard King Óláfr, in the yard above, make a speech in which he promised to enrich the man who would kill Hákon. Þormóðr karkr accordingly stabbed and beheaded his master, a deed for which, as a slave, he was rewarded by King Óláfr with death rather than wealth. Several other episodes in the sagas tell of similar treachery by slaves, who are often from Celtic backgrounds, are not good prospects for productive friendship as a result of their lowly status, and are generally profiled as untrustworthy by Nordic storytellers.

Another unlikely candidate for friendship is Óðinn, the treacherous god whose fickle designs in *Vǫlsunga saga* bring various members of the family of Sigmundr to power followed, suddenly and inexplicably, by their destruction. In *Ǫrvar-Odds saga*, the eponymous legendary hero, disenchanted by his dealings with the god Óðinn, uses the traditional formulaic pattern of the admonition discussed above but replaces "þræll" with "Óðinn," thus categorizing the god among the least of men: "'Eltak æsi / örhjartaða tvá, / sem fyr úlfi geitr / argar rynni; / illt er at eiga Óðin / at einkavin; / skal eigi lengr / skrattan blóta'" (I gave chase / and these gutless gods ran / like frightened goats / in front of a wolf. / It's bad to have Odin / for a bosom friend. I will no longer sacrifice to the devil).[50] The last line of this verse equates Óðinn with the shameful practice of wizardry, situating Oddr's sentiment within the category of

---

49. Saxo Grammaticus, *Gesta Danorum: The History of the Danes*, 2 vols., ed. Karsten Friis-Jensen, trans. Peter Fisher (Oxford: Oxford University Press, 2015), 1: 276-77; JGF 666; TPMA 2.255.7.

50. *Ǫrvar-Odds saga*, in *Fornaldar sögur norðurlanda*, ed. Guðni Jónsson, 4 vols. (Reykjavík: Íslendingasagnaútgáfan,1954, repr. 1959), 2:331, ch. 29; Paul Edwards and

conversion-age Christian teaching on the Norse gods. The once mighty Valfǫðr is of no better value in alliance than a slave, and has no greater power than a sorcerer.[51]

* * *

Thus the structure of a proverb, ubiquitous in pre-Christian Norse culture, can, by fairly simple lexical alteration, be used allusively to express communal consensus on a subject distant from that of its original purpose, its reworked content directing audience attention to a traditionally held truth that reinforces the negative value of associations with Óðinn.

Lexical Allusion in the Kernel of a Proverb

The allusive process is not all of one kind, however, as we noticed above. In the Old Icelandic sagas it operates far more often through *lexical* rather than *syntactic* recognition, along with sometimes significant deletion of the text, where as little as a single word recalls the proverb. Desiderius Erasmus cites such a mechanism in Latin in his introduction to the *Adages*, in the early 1500s, where he remarks that use and appreciation of proverbs in literature necessitate a comprehensive knowledge of them in their base form in order to understand more fully what one is reading:

> Even if there were no other use for proverbs, at the very least they are not only helpful but necessary for the understanding of the best authors, that is, the oldest. Most of these are textually corrupt, and in this respect they are particularly so, especially as proverbs have a touch of the enigmatic, so that they are not understood even by readers of some learning; and then they are often inserted disconnectedly, sometimes in a mutilated state . . . Occasionally they are alluded to in one word, as in Cicero in his Letters to Atticus: "Help me, I beg you; 'prevention,' you know," where he refers to the proverb "Prevention is better than cure."[52]

Hermann Pálsson, *Arrow-Odd: A Medieval Novel* (London: University of London Press, 1970), 101–2; JGF 113; *TPMA* 4, 66.

51. See my "*Odin's Old Age:* A Study of the Old Man in 'The Pardoner's Tale,'" *Southern Folklore Quarterly* 33 (1969): 24–38, especially the latter paragraphs, on his twilight years in nineteenth-century Icelandic folk stories.

52. *Desiderius Erasmus, Adages*, trans. Margaret Mann Phillips, annotated R. A. B. Mynors, Ii1 to Iv100, Collected Works of Erasmus 31 (Toronto: University of Toronto

For Erasmus, even "readers of some learning" may have difficulty identifying the proverb that is the object of the allusion. Such allusion relies on the reader's level of cultural literacy. As Wolfgang Mieder explains, "proverbs are often shortened to mere allusions owing to their general recognizability. Such truncated proverbs appear in oral speech as well as in literature of the mass media. Why should a journalist cite the entire proverb, "A bird in the hand is worth two in the bush," in a large-print headline when the remnant "A bird in the hand . . ." will bring the entire proverb to mind automatically, at least for native speakers of English?"[53] Mieder qualifies his claim for the automatic recognition of proverbial allusion to "the case of native speakers" of the language in which the paroemial process is occurring. It seems self-evident that native competence in a culture's proverbial inventory, a crucial aspect of cultural literacy, is optimal for an awareness, or understanding, of such allusions.

Our recognition of proverbial allusion might at first seem to require some revision of our assumption of the rigidity of a proverb's syntactic structure. "Earlier scholars have overstated the fixity of proverbs," observes Wolfgang Mieder. "In actual use, especially in the case of intentional speech play, proverbs are quite often manipulated."[54] However, we might ask whether our being able to recall the full text of a proverb by encountering a truncated form has to do with the syntactic structure of proverbs or with the semantic weight of words in their texts. In fact, Mieder himself refers to Neal Norrick's *How Proverbs Mean*, where—speaking of the didactic quality of proverbs—Norrick notices that "for well known proverbs, mention of one crucial recognizable phrase [i.e., part] serves to call forth the entire proverb. Let us designate this minimal recognizable unit as the kernel of the proverb. . . . Proverbs bear much greater social, philosophical and psychological significance for speakers than do other idiomatic units." From this point of view, the semantic density of proverbial material impresses such texts on our consciousness. "Consequently a speaker can call forth a particular proverb for his hearer with a brief allusion to its kernel."[55] While Mieder would minimize emphasis on the fixity of proverb texts, it might be more useful for our purposes here to observe that the

---

Press, 1982), 18.
 53. Mieder, *Proverbs*, 7.
 54. Mieder, *Proverbs*, 7.
 55. Norrick, *How Proverbs Mean*, 45.

surface structure of a proverb is more malleable than has sometimes been recognized. Perhaps a proverb's deep structure, in Chomskyan terms, remains unchanged, while its overt expression can involve potentially radically different transformations without damage to its conceptual retrievability.

Paroemiological Studies and the Literary Text in Iceland

Awareness of a culture's paroemial background as a component of accurate reading of its literature was first discussed by Erasmus, who asserted that "even if there were no other use for proverbs, at the very least they are not only helpful but necessary for the understanding of the best authors, that is, the oldest."[56] The reasons for the proverb's importance to the literary text are complex, however, and continue to be discussed by contemporary paroemiologists. Paroemiology is a critical endeavor deserving more attention than it has generally received, and this book, of course, intends to address the lacuna, particularly with regard to Old Icelandic literature.

The literary significance of the paroemial element in the sagas has been apparent to readers for over a century. In 1905, Guðbrandur Vigfússon observed the following about proverbs in his commentary on *Hrafnkels saga Freysgoða*: "These saws are to a Saga what the gnomic element is to a Greek play."[57] His friend and collaborator, F. York Powell, writing in 1896 about *Færeyinga saga*, stated that "these idioms and saws, and laconisms ... are the very life-blood of a true Saga."[58] Proverbial statements generally express the accepted communal wisdom of a culture, and usually, where a composer writes without ironic intent, he places them in the mouths of established, substantial characters: "reliable spokesmen whose pronouncements on events and persons indicate what ought to be thought of them."[59] Lars Lönnroth also notices, in his study of *Njáls saga*, that "wise community spokesmen ... tend to state their views in brief but succinct

---

56. Erasmus, *Adages*, Ii1 to Iv100, 18.

57. Guðbrandur Vigfússon, "Commentary on *Hrafnkels saga*," in *Origines Islandicae: A Collection of the More Important Sagas and Other Native Writings Relating to the Settlement and Early History of Iceland*, 2 vols. (Oxford: Clarendon Press, 1905), 2:492.

58. *The Tale of Thrond of Gate, Commonly Called Færeyinga saga*, trans. F. York Powell, Northern Library 2 (London: D. Nutt, 1896), xxxix.

59. Richard F. Allen, *Fire and Iron: Critical Approaches to* Njáls saga (Pittsburgh: University of Pittsburgh Press, 1971), 107.

speeches, where they can make use of legal quotations, proverbs, and other kinds of generalized statements often highlighted by their rhetorical form."[60] He adds, however, that "so far ... very little has been said about the function of proverbs ... in their narrative context."[61] That is still the situation today, when a volume of essays in Old Norse literature has yet to include a paroemiological study of this corpus.

This seeming neglect may largely be a reflex of the directions literary critical thinking has taken since the 1960s, when the prominence of book prose theory came to be overshadowed by attempts to restate some aspects of the earlier free prose ideas in a way that would more realistically address the formation of the extant *Íslendingasögur* in particular. While saga criticism in the latter half of the twentieth century focused on testing macrostructural approaches to the saga in order to gain access to the genre's compositional processes, the situation has now changed. A fairly chronic gap in microstructural analyses, which would include the phraseology of saga composition, makes paroemiological studies of the Old Icelandic corpus more desirable today for those who would understand the meaning of the sagas.[62]

Icelandic Paroemiography: Bibliographical Sources

Students of the sagas are not lacking in tools for such readings. The paroemiography of the Old Icelandic corpus was thoroughly addressed in the early twentieth century. Finnur Jónsson, in "Oldislandske ordsprog og talemåder," compiled an inventory of proverbs in saga literature comprising nearly one hundred pages with 494 individual word headings. Hugo Gering's "Altnordische Sprichwörter und sprichwörterliche Redensarten" soon

---

60. Lars Lönnroth, *Njáls saga: A Critical Introduction* (Berkeley: University of California Press, 1976), 88–89.

61. Lönnroth, *Njáls saga*, 89.

62. The urge to engage in a microstructural study of the sagas has been with us for some time, emerging occasionally as critical perspectives shift. Otto Springer, "The Style of the Old Icelandic Family Sagas," *Journal of English and Germanic Philology*, 38 (1939): 107–28, was cited by Paul Schach as a proponent of more precise critical attention to details of saga texts. See Paul Schach, "The Use of the Simile in the Old Icelandic Family Sagas," *Scandinavian Studies* 24 (1952): 149. Much later, W. F. Bolton justified his focus on a "single, unified, continuous passage of the saga" in this way: "The discovery of a coherent macro-structure implies that the micro-structure will be correspondingly coherent." See W. F. Bolton, "The Heart of *Hrafnkatla*," *Scandinavian Studies* 43 (1971): 35.

supplemented this compilation from Gering's own, otherwise unpublished collection. These efforts, together with a brief, additional study by Karel Vrátny, form the basis for the study of proverbs in the sagas.[63]

Other collections with Icelandic materials made before and after this period might include, but were never exclusively devoted to, the proverbs of the medieval corpus, the only exception being the online Concordance to the Proverbs and Proverbial Materials in the Old Icelandic Sagas.[64] Thus, Finnur Jónsson's 1920 *Íslenskt málsháttasafn*, a self-admitted armchair production based on previously published and unpublished collections, includes the occasional proverb from a specific saga.[65] In his helpful enumeration of predecessors, Finnur cites the fourteenth-century work of Peder Låle, which has around twelve hundred proverbs translated into Latin, and which was intended as a text for teaching students that language.[66] Finnur Jónsson also makes extensive use of a list of proverbs purportedly compiled by Hannes Þorleifsson and included by Peder Syv in the final pages of both volumes of his *Almindelige danske ordsprog* in the 1680s.[67] He is much indebted to Guðmundur Jónsson's vast *Safn af íslenzkum orðskviðum*, published in 1830, a work drawing on, among other items, a number of unpublished sources described in its introduction.[68] Finnur Jónsson uses further collections such as that

---

63. FJ; Hugo Gering, "Altnordische Sprichwörter und sprichwörtlische Redensarten," *Arkiv för nordisk filologi* 32 (1915–16): 1–31. See also Karel Vrátný, "Noch einiges zu den altisländischen Sprichwörtern," *Arkiv för nordisk filologi* 33 (1917): 58–63.

64. For data pertinent to paroemiological studies of Old Icelandic literature, see Richard Harris, "Concordance to the Proverbs and Proverbial Materials in the Old Icelandic Sagas." University of Saskatchewan, Department of English. https://researchgroups.usask.ca/icelanders/concordance.php.

65. Finnur Jónsson, *Íslenskt málsháttasafn* (Copenhagen: Gyldendal, 1920).

66. Peder Låle, *Parabolae* (Copenhagen: Gotfred af Ghemen, 1506). This was reprinted in the collection *Östnordiska och latinska Medeltidsordspråk: Peder Låles Ordspråk och en motsvarande svensk samling*, ed. Axel Kock and Carl af Petersens (Copenhagen: Berlingska boktryckeriet, 1889–94).

67. Peder Syv, *Aldmindelige danske ordsproge og korte lærdomme, med foregaaende underviisning om dennem: Samt efterfølgende tilhæng af nogle sære, som fordom have været oc endeel endnu ere brugelige i disse tre nordiske riger: Saa og et register paa titlerne og et andet paa de gamle og sielden forekommende ord* (Copenhagen: Sl. Corfitz Luftis paa C. Geertzens bekostning, 1682 and 1688; repr. 1983).

68. Guðmundur Jónsson, *Safn af íslenzkum orðskviðum, fornmælum, heilræðum, snilliyrðum, sannmælum og málsgreinum, samanlesið og í stafrófsröð* (Copenhagen: Hið íslenzka bókmenntafjelag, 1830). The collections Guðmundur Jónsson cites in his introduction might be productively examined for information about the sources of texts he himself very unfortunately neglected to include in this otherwise most exhaustive

of Hallgrímur Scheving, published in 1843 and 1847, and a series, whose compiler is unknown, which was published in the *Almanak* of the Þjóðfélag, from 1903 to 1905 and again in 1907.[69]

Until recently, the definitive, enumerative study of Icelandic proverbs was that of Bjarni Vilhjálmsson and Óskar Halldórsson, *Íslenzkir málshættir*; its second edition appeared in 1982. Although it is based on the 1920 *Málsháttasafn*, it is more comprehensive and precise than the pioneering productions of Finnur Jónsson and some of his predecessors, taking cognizance of all Finnur's sources but also going far beyond his scope to access works not yet printed in his time or in which he did not take interest.[70] In particular, Jón Jónsson Rugmann's seventeenth-century *Samling af isländska talesätt* and the sixteenth-century *Thesaurus Adagiorum* of Guðmundur Ólafsson, published by G. Kallstenius in 1927 and 1930, respectively, made available new material for the compilers.[71] Thus, many of the Old Icelandic sagas, in their various subgenres, along with editions of poetry and purely historical works, are at least selectively taken into account. References to the sagas in *Íslenzkir málshættir*, though more helpful than those of Finnur Jónsson's *Íslenzkt málsháttasafn* and even his "Oldislandske ordsprog og talemåder," are still rather sketchy, and until recently much of the paroemial material of the *Íslendingasögur* remained unnoticed by both earlier and later compilers.

The most useful collection of proverbs from Iceland today, which includes texts from saga literature, is that of Jón Geir Friðjónsson's *Orð að sönnu: Íslenskir málshættir og orðskviður*. Another encyclopedic study matching his earlier *Mergur málsins*, which was on word usages in Icelandic, this new contribution cites proverbs from saga times to recent authors, and in his introduction

---

undertaking. Moreover, Landsbókasafn Íslands and other collections in Reykjavík house compilations of proverbs from recent centuries which deserve our attention.

69. Hallgrímur Scheving, *Bodsrit til að hlýda á þá opinberu yfirheyrslu í Bessastada skóla þann maí 1843: Islendskir málshættir safnadir, útvaldir og í stafrofsrød færdir* (Reyjavík: Reykjavíkur skóli, 1843); *Almanak Hins íslenzka þjóðvinafélagsins* (Reykjavík: Ríkisprentsmiðjan Gutenberg, 1899, 1903-5, 1907, 1913).

70. Bjarni Vilhjálmsson and Óskar Halldórsson, *Málshættir*, 2nd ed. (Reykjavík: Almenna Bókafélagið, 1982).

71. Jón Jónsson Rugmann, *Jonas Rugmans samling af isländska talesätt*, Skrifter utgivna av K. Humanistiska Vetenskaps-Samfundet i Uppsala 22.8 (Upsala: Almqvist & Wiksell, 1927); Guðmundur Ólafsson, *Gudmundi Olaui Thesaurus adagiorum linguæ Septentrionalis antiquae et modernae*, Skrifter utg. av Vetenskaps-Societeten i Lund 12 (Lund: C. W. K. Gleerup, 1930).

he includes a very helpful twelve-page survey of his country's paroemiography.[72]

For readers interested in pursuing the paroemiology of medieval European literature, including that of the Old Icelandic sagas, the *Thesaurus Proverbiorum Medii Aevi* (*TPMA*) is an indispensable, if unfortunately expensive, point of departure for research. Undertaken as an expansion of Samuel Singer's *Sprichwörter des Mittelalters*, under the direction of Ricarda Liver, the project required forty years of labor by many scholars and resulted in thirteen volumes accompanied by a "Quellenverzeichnis," published 1995–2002.[73] Organized in some measure by key words and by concepts, it is available digitally (through license to subscribing institutions) as well as in hard copy. It can be rather challenging to access in the latter format, although it is useful in its comprehensive scope once the desired information is located.

Hermann Pálsson and Old Icelandic Paroemiology

Until recently, Old Icelandic paroemiology was the province of only one person, Hermann Pálsson, professor of Icelandic studies at the University of Edinburgh, who contributed much of value to the study of proverbs in medieval Icelandic literature, particularly in *Grettis saga* and in *Hrafnkels saga Freysgoða*. His primary interest was in the continental literary background of which the saga composers were aware, and in particular the extent to which their purposes were reflective of biblical ethics and medieval ecclesiastical teaching. From his point of view, for instance, the proverbial data of *Hrafnkels saga* supported its interpretation as an essay on the dangers of pride, the hero's fall and its attendant humiliation leading to a reformation of character as the denouement.

Hermann Pálsson studied in a literary critical milieu where readers of the sagas, despite their reservations regarding signaling ethical value in narration, had reached agreement that the composers wrote

---

72. Rugmann, introduction to *samling*, xii–xxxxiv; Jón Geir Friðjónsson, *Mergur málsins: Íslensk orðatiltæki: Uppruni, saga og notkun* (Reykjavík: Örn og Örlygur, 1993), 154.

73. *Thesaurus proverbiorum medii aevi: Lexikon der Sprichwörter des romansich-germanischen Mittelalters*, ed. Kuratorium Singer der Schweizerischen Akademie des Geistes- un Sozialwissenschaften, 13 vols. and "Quellenverzeichnis" (Berlin: De Gruyter, 1995–2002). Referred to hereafter as *TPMA*.

with a moral purpose that critical reading might identify. While today his work may appear to suffer from enthusiasm for exclusively continental and Christian influence on the sagas, which is difficult to justify through a careful, balanced reading, his views drew attention to the undoubted thematic significance of the paroemial presence in saga narrative.

Hermann Pálsson's work in the mid-1960s on the moral philosophy of *Hrafnkels saga*, published in 1966 as *Siðfræði Hrafnkels sögu*, in which he remarked on the continental conceptual background of proverbial expressions in the narrative, led, in 1981, to *Úr hugmyndaheimi Hrafnkels sögu og Grettlu*, where he showed how the composers of both these sagas were familiar with the continental preserves of medieval Christian proverbial wisdom.[74] In the later twentieth century, Hermann Pálsson considerably advanced the understanding of the presence and uses of proverbs in the Old Icelandic corpus. Although Hermann's work was not much engaged by his critical contemporaries, it was nevertheless absorbed by thoughtful readers of the sagas who sought to understand what that elusive literature of the medieval North was meant to be about. *Hávamál í ljósi íslenskrar menningar* and *Oral Traditon and Saga Writing*, both of which appeared in 1999, summed up much of his later and most mature thinking.[75] To the former volume he brought a lifetime of study of the relationship of *Hávamál* to Iceland's literary culture, while in the latter he adopted a usefully detailed approach to the settlement figures who would have been instrumental in maintaining the first generations of oral tradition in Iceland.

In summary, compilations of proverbs from saga literature are now extensively available, and nothing stands in the way of investigating the medieval Icelandic corpus. The present book, as well as works by other authors utilizing different theoretical approaches, is thus able to investigate more comprehensively the medieval Icelandic corpus.

* * *

---

74. Hermann Pálsson, *Siðfræði* Hrafnkels sögu (Reykjavík: Heimskringla, 1966) and *Úr hugmyndaheimi* Hrafnkels sögu *og* Grettlu (Reykjavík: Bókaútgáfa Menningarsjóðs, 1981).

75. Hermann Pálsson, Hávamál *í ljósi íslenskrar menningar* (Reykjavík: Háskólaútgáfan, 1999) and *Oral Tradition and Saga Writing*, Studia medievalia septentrionalia 3 (Vienna: Fassbaender, 1999).

From the discussion above, it will be apparent that the sentences and phrases we commonly know as proverbs are found among the earliest elements of human cultural expression. From the start, these proverbs could function effectively in allusive fragments because they adhere to syntactic structures and significant lexical items, or kernels, inherent in human language. As Shirley Arora demonstrated in the "Perception of Proverbiality," proverbs access syntactic forms universal to the human potential for expression, enabling infinitely diverse communication regarding reality and our response to it in our social behavior; in other words, making use of a structure possessing a psychological reality common to all humanity. Understood in this sense, proverbs are greatly useful in literary critical study, and against this broader background of paroemial definition, the sagas seem more susceptible to effective interpretation than might be the case otherwise.

Readers of this volume seeking a clear distinction between wisdom texts that can be defined as proverbs in traditional terms and those that cannot may be initially disappointed. Differentiating terms for these two sorts of texts are not used systematically in this volume, although it would be helpful if linguists of a paroemiological bent were to lead us toward a consensus on such terminology. Paroemiographical practice, however, has tended to neglect such distinctions.[76]

Those interested in this subject may wish to examine articles in *TPMA*, which, while including material lacking traditionalist support, similarly make no distinction. In chapter 3 of *Grettis saga*, for instance, in a verse attributed to Ǫnundr tréfótr, the speaker utters the observation, "Mart hremmir til snimma" (Much happens

---

76. Theoretical considerations of the proverb aside, see a very practical approach in F. P. Wilson's *The Proverbial Wisdom of Shakespeare*. Commenting on Morris Palmer Tilley's *Dictionary of the Proverbs in England of the Sixteenth and Seventeenth Centuries* he mentions that "in 1947 he wrote me to say how much he relied on what the sixteenth and seventeenth centuries understood as proverbial. 'Where no evidence from the collections turned up,' he went on, 'I have depended partly on the repetition of a thought and partly on "hunch." At times I have even admitted idiomatic phrases that seemed proverbial. I have erred decidedly on the side of inclusiveness.' If Tilley had excluded everything except gnomic sentences now or formerly in popular use, his dictionary would have been half as big and half as useful." Frank Percy Wilson, "The Proverbial Wisdom of Shakespeare," Presidential Address of the Modern Humanities Research Association (Cambridge: Modern Humanities Research Association, 1961), 4. The "hunch," of course, is Taylor's "incommunicable quality." And the usefulness of Tilley's work as a result of this inclusiveness is inarguable.

too early).⁷⁷ This is the only occurrence of the text recorded in Old Icelandic, and no other uses of it in medieval literature are cited. There is thus no evidence of its earlier usage or currency, and yet this authoritative compilation includes the item. This is not an isolated instance. When Grettir's father refuses to finance his trip abroad, the hero observes, "Þá er eigi þat at launa, sem eigi er gǫrt" (Then there's no need to repay that which isn't done).⁷⁸ Since this volume is devoted to reading saga literature against the broad background of the Old Icelandic proverbial inventory, it is to be hoped that readers will find, on reflection, the methods employed here satisfactory for their use.

---

77. *Grettis saga Ásmundarsonar*, ed. Guðni Jónsson, Íslenzk fornrit 7 (Reykjavík: Hið íslenzka fornritafélag, 1936), 9, ch. 3; in *The Complete Sagas of Icelanders*, ed. Viðar Hreinsson, 5 vols. (Reykjavík: Leifur Eiríksson, 1997) 2:52; not noticed by JGF; *TPMA* 4.88.

78. ÍF 7:49, ch. 17; JGF 341; *TPMA* 8.34.

CHAPTER 2

Paroemial Patterns of the Mythic and the Legendary Backgrounds

This chapter, which is made up of two major sections, will demonstrate ways in which Old Icelandic literature has, interwoven in its narratives and informing their themes, echoes of wisdom texts found in several poems of the extant corpus of the *Elder Edda*. The presence of this paroemial material in the sagas could, at least in some instances, result from literary indebtedness to this earlier poetry. For the purposes of this volume, however, it will be viewed rather as evidence that a large inventory of at least partly encoded wisdom texts existed in the culture of the preliterate Nordic world. Their common appearance in the Eddic corpus and some passages in the *Íslendingasögur* attests to their oral currency in northern cultures even after the coming of literacy to those regions, so that they remained available to saga composers and their audience as a source of reference on accepted ethical standards of behavior.

Ways of ethical thinking apparent in the thirteenth-century literature of Iceland can thus be seen as informed by this underlying cognitive patterning partly witnessed in the Eddic traditions. A study of such influence in *Hreiðars þáttr heimska* will reveal how its composer makes complex ironic use of proverbial material found in *Hávamál*, demonstrating thereby the sophisticated level of his and his readers' paroemially informed way of thinking.

The second section of this chapter is devoted to the paroemial and, more generally, to the phraseological background of the Vǫlsung-Niflung Cycle as it is witnessed in Old Icelandic literature. The image of the wolf in the proverbial inventory of the legendary

Eddic poems and accordingly also in *Vǫlsunga saga* will be studied as it is reflected in the *Íslendingasögur*.

The Witness of *Hávamál:* the Poem in the Sagas

For over a thousand years Icelanders have been accompanied in the conduct of their lives by the wisdom of *Hávamál*. Even after the Eddic poems migrated to manuscript and then to the printed page, the continuity of that oral tradition enabled and encouraged the constant and intimate presence of this ancient good advice in the communal mind.[1] In modern times, this legacy is poignantly celebrated by Halldór Laxness in *Sjálfstætt fólk*, where Bjartur, the fiercely independent farmer of Sumarhús who is symbolic of another age, comforts himself and directs his life according to the remembered dictates of this social code from the Viking era.

The 164 verses of *Hávamál*, partitioned in five or six segments and framed by vague narrative pretexts, are mostly anthological in their structuring, and any attempt to perceive a significantly coherent narrative in the poem as a whole would neglect or ignore the primary function and traditional methods of presentation of formulaically preserved knowledge, ranging from Sumerian texts of the third millennium BC to more recent times.[2] As is the case

---

1. Although this volume is not the place for a detailed discussion of the value of the *kvöldvaka*, the centuries-old custom of evening entertainmant as the socially based vehicle by which stories and poetry were shared in households on the Icelandic farmsteads up into the beginning of the twentieth century, this subject is worth careful attention as we consider the remarkable cultural continuity observable in Icelandic society. See, among others, Hermann Pálsson, *Sagnaskemmtun Íslendinga* (Reykjavík: Mál og menning, 1962); Magnús Gíslason, *Kvällsvaka: En isländsk kulturtradition belyst genom studier i bondebefolkningens vardagsliv och miljö under senare hälften av 1800-talet och början av 1900-talet*, Acta Universitatis Upsaliensis, Studia ethnologia Upsaliensis 2 (Uppsala: Almqvist & Wiksell International, 1977); Steven A. Mitchell, *Heroic Sagas and Ballads* (Ithaca, NY: Cornell University Press, 1991), 92–114; and Matthew Driscoll, *The Unwashed Children of Eve: The Production, Dissemination and Reception of Popular Literature in Post-Reformation Iceland* (Enfield Lock: Hisarlik Press, 1997), 38–46. Þórbergur Þórðarson, recalling life in the last decade of the nineteenth century at Hali í Suðursveit, on the southeast coast of Iceland, describes the *kvöldvaka* as it occurred there in the fourth volume of *Í Suðursveit* (Reykavík: Mál og menning, 1975), 403–8. Among many other witnesses to the late continuation of oral traditions in Iceland, Gísli Sigurðssson, in the first pages of his preface to *The Medieval Icelandic Saga and Oral Tradition: A Discourse on Method*, trans. Nicholas Jones (Cambridge, MA: Milman Parry Collection of Oral Literature, Harvard University, 2004), xv–xvi, engagingly describes storytelling in his youth, in the Reykjavík of the 1960s, his father and his friends gathering on Saturdays and Sundays to share remembered stories and verses.

2. Robert Alter, *The Wisdom Books. Job, Proverbs, and Ecclesiastes. A Translation with Commentary* (New York: W. W. Norton, 2010), 183, discusses the process of

generally with wisdom literature, *Hávamál* probably contains little that is novel, and its indebtedness to earlier compilations has been a matter of some study. In places, its stanzas seem to echo texts of continental wisdom, and a few passages in it are similar to some verses in the Bible, whose advice on social conduct can in turn be traced to similar sources farther to the East.[3]

However, a study of the ways, and the extent to which, the paroemial contents of *Hávamál* might be representative of particular oral traditions external to Norse culture, while undoubtedly of scholarly interest, is less likely to enhance our understanding of how the proverbs found in this poem were used by saga composers in the thirteenth century, or in most cases of how they envisioned the paroemial thrust of the texts as they placed them in their narratives. In fact, the precise quality and the means of indebtedness of the Icelandic sagas to the body of wisdom we find witnessed in *Hávamál* are matters more to the point: how are we to interpret the sense in which such texts appear and are used where composers have chosen to include them in their stories?[4]

---

anthologizing, as he observes contradictory assertions in Proverbs 26:4 and 5: "The contradiction between them stems from the anthological character of the book: the two sayings have been culled either from folk-tradition or from the verbal repertory of Wisdom schools and have been set in immediate sequence by the anthologist because of the identical wording—first in the negative and then in the positive—of the initial clause of each saying." The same process can be found in similar passages of *Hávamál*, suggesting that the same method of compilation was used there.

3. Carolyne Larrington, *A Store of Common Sense. Gnomic Theme and Style in Old Icelandic and Old English Wisdom Poetry* (Oxford: Clarendon Press, 1993), in chapter 3, "Christian Wisdom Poetry: Hugsvinnsmál," discusses such relationships between that poem, *Hávamál*, and the *Disticha Catonis*. See also her "*Hávamál* and sources outside Scandinavia," *Saga-Book of the Viking Society* 23 (1992): 141–57. For recent work, see Brittany Schorn, "'How Can His Word Be Trusted?': Speaker and Authority in Old Norse Wisdom Poetry" (PhD diss., University of Cambridge), 6: "Old Norse wisdom literature must also be viewed, like the Old English material, within the context of imported Latin learning as well as within the context of the whole body of vernacular material surviving from medieval Scandinavia and, to a lesser extent, the cognate literature of Anglo-Saxon England and other parts of medieval Europe." Dr. Schorn's interest in this subject will undoubtedly lead us to a deeper understanding of the literary expressions of early Northern wisdom. Her recent volume, based on her doctoral work, is *Speaker and Authority in Old Norse Wisdom Poetry*, Trends in Medieval Philology (Book 34) (Berlin: De Gruyter, 2017).

4. In this volume and elsewhere I have preferred to speak of those who wrote the sagas as "composers," although I realize this might be less accurate in some instances than in others. I follow here Margaret Clunies Ross, who, while discussing the nature of sagas, writes: "Unlike a large proportion of medieval Norse poetry, most sagas are anonymous, and that is another important distinction between sagas and skaldic poetry, where the tradition has preserved the names of many skalds, which probably suggests that the role of a saga author was considered less creative, more compilatory, than that of the poet." See Margaret Clunies Ross, *The Cambridge Introduction to the*

One of the purposes of this book is to address such problems, thereby enabling a deeper discussion of how proverbs are used in the sagas. To provide an example of such an internal study, and to demonstrate the usefulness of this process, we will consider an episode in *Grettis saga* where the composer has employed, in a complex and ironic way, a paroemial text found in *Hávamál*.

An Example of How a Proverb Found in *Hávamál* is Used in an Icelandic Saga

When the composer of *Grettis saga* has the hero anticipate his father's discovery of the mutilation he had inflicted on the horse, Kengála, with an observation about the unpredictable outcome of one's expectations—"Verðr þat er varir, ... ok svá hitt, er eigi varir" (The expected happens, and the unexpected too)—it is not possible to tell if he, or perhaps his hero, is deliberately alluding to what modern readers identify as the last line of stanza 40 in *Hávamál*: "margt gengr verr en varir" (much goes worse than is expected).[5] *Hávamál's* similar observation about the uncertain

---

Old Norse-Icelandic Saga (Cambridge: Cambridge University Press, 2010), 17–18. In a footnote (165n9) she continues: "The commonest verb used to express the mental effort of composing a saga is *samansetja/setja saman* 'to bring together, compile' (probably influenced by the Latin verb *componere*, 'to collect, put together'), while the verb most often used of poetic composition is *yrkja* '(literally) to work, to compose poetry'. Both verbal uses are exemplified in the quotation from 'The Saga of Þorgils and Hafliði', and it also demonstrates that composers of sagas could sometimes compose some at least of the poetry within them. *Samansetja* is also used of the compilation of historical, educational and didactic works, like Snorri Sturluson's *Edda*." I have previously discussed using this term "for the individuals who wrote the sagas, because at this stage in the progress of our literary critical understanding of the *Íslendingasögur* ... no other term seems to me so fitting. 'Author' implies an originality in the process of creativity which is not so fully present in the sagas as it is for authors of fiction in our culture, and it can thus mislead students of Old Icelandic literature. 'Author' would of course have been more appropriate in those decades when our reading was strongly influenced by the book-prose theory.... The free prose theory, revived in modified form in the beginning of the 1960s [includes] the common assumption of that 'oral family saga' to which my paper refers. It is thus now generally agreed that people "composed" narratives on the written page which they drew from various oral as well as literary sources, and the shape and content of our texts are now studied on the basis of theories with these ideas as their roots." See Richard Harris, "The Proverbs of *Vatnsdœla saga* and the Sword of Jǫkull: The Oral Backgrounds of Grettir Ásmundarson's Flawed Heroism," in *The Hero Recovered. Essays on Medieval Heroism in Honor of George Clark*, ed. Robin Waugh and James Weldon (Kalamazoo, MI: Medieval Institute Publications, 2011), 164–65. I still think, with Clunies Ross, that *composer* is the best term, both for pedagogical and literary critical purposes.

5. ÍF 7:41, ch. 14; JGF 604; TPMA 3.49; *Hávamál*, in *Eddukvæði*, ed. Jónas Kristjánsson and Vésteinn Ólason, vol. 1, *Goðakvæði*, Íslenzk fornrit 36 (Reykjavík: Hið

outcome of anticipation, used in several other Old Icelandic texts, is placed within a rather specialized verse on the insecure future of wealth saved for loved ones. The context established by the saga scene, in which this statement is found, has Grettir and his father at deadly odds—the surly and at best preheroic youth has already threatened patricide in a verse, had injured Ásmundr's back with a wool comb when he was supposed to be rubbing it, and has now flayed the skin from the back of his father's beloved horse. Normally we expect to hear proverbs from those who would embrace and project wisdom.[6] When we find them used by figures who threaten society and its status quo, we should naturally expect quite different uses to be made of them. Grettir alludes, then, to a proverb or group of proverbs suggesting the uncertain outcome of anticipated events where, however, in a moment of dramatic irony, he and the audience are fully aware of an impending tragedy for his father, who is still happily ignorant of Kengála's demise. Grettir associates himself and his purposes with goals much at odds with the world supported by the paroemial inventory from which this element is taken, and the dark humor that tinges the oddly destructive outcome is threateningly exacerbated by this wrenching juxtaposition of world views—the social norm on the one hand, and that which unrelentingly opposes it, on the other.

Here, as elsewhere, when we refer to passages in *Hávamál*, it should be kept in mind that the person writing the poem in its extant form, or some source from which he drew, often placed proverbs of general application into quite specific situations. The paroemial value of these texts is distorted and much limited if we see them only in the literary context to which they have been assigned in such compilations. While the pursuit of an allusion here to *Hávamál* in the more precise terms of literary scholarship is not productive, however, it seems likely that the composer has Grettir allude in this phrase to recognizable formulas of such oral traditional wisdom, though with an ironically subversive purpose. The composer thus

---

Íslenzka fornritafélag, 2014), 330, st. 40; *The Poetic Edda*, trans. Carolyne Larrington, rev. ed. (Oxford: Oxford University Press, 2014), 19; JGF 181; TPMA 3.49.

6. See Lönnroth, *Introduction*, 89. Commenting on a speech by Njáll where the latter employs proverbial support of his argument, the author remarks that such "reference to an acknowledged and respected principle lends credibility to the speaker's cause. At the same time, such rhetoric may help establish a moral, even though it is not directly expressed by the narrator himself." See also Lars Lönnroth, "Rhetorical Persuasion in the Sagas," *Scandinavian Studies* 42 (1970): 157–89.

encourages his audience to recall more generally a finite portion of an oral repository of communal knowledge presumably current in a preliterate Nordic Scandinavia and extending into the first centuries of Nordic literacy, an item that only incidentally finds expression in the last line of stanza 40 in *Hávamál*.

* * *

From the example used in the above exercise we can see how recognition and examination of the composer's use of proverbial material found in an Eddic wisdom text enhances our appreciation of the nuances of the scene. This effect does not imply that the composer refers, in a precise literary sense, to stanza 40 of *Hávamál* when Grettir very loosely paraphrases a passage we find there. Rather, he has Grettir call on a related, communally accepted body of wisdom, ironically implying that the outcome of anticipations can indeed be far worse than we might imagine as the subversive hero makes fun of Ásmundr's naïve admiration of Kengála. Although ultimately the nature of this repository is oral in origin and transmission, the Codex Regius itself, which contains *Hávamál* along with the main body of extant Eddic poetry, was written between 1270 and 1280. The Codex, or a copy of it or of some of its material no longer extant, could well have been available to composers at least of the later sagas; and while its contents are of oral background, the possibility of literary intertextuality is always present. Still, the preponderance of influence considered here most likely came about as a result of nonliterary processes, which becomes clear especially if we think about the continued life of these poems among Icelanders until fairly recent times.

On the Nature of the Presence of *Hávamál* Wisdom in the Sagas: the Concept of Paroemial Cognitive Patterning

It has been suggested above that when the composer of *Grettis saga* uses material found in *Hávamál*, he does so without specifically quoting from that poem in a literary sense of the sort we would find familiar for our present-day critical studies. Here we will consider how such perceived influence most likely occurs. Chapters 6, 7, and 8 of this book examine the uses of proverbial allusion at various levels of consciousness by saga composers, who in some instances inform the entire thematic agenda of their stories by subtly encouraging their audience to recall wisdom texts to which they may refer by no more than a word, or in some cases a situationally allusive scene. There, too, as with the brief instance above, we must keep in mind that the proverbs we notice in the *Íslendingasögur* might be studied more accurately if they were perceived as partly extant evidence of the early existence of a much larger and more complex oral repository of wisdom central to the ethics and mores of the preliterate culture.

Such an approach is not without precedents. In 1972 Tom Shippey considered the possibility of this sort of repository in the Anglo-Saxon world, asking how the early audience of *Beowulf* might have comprehended that poem's complex pervasive irony, never reading but only hearing it, and perhaps doing so only once. Either they "were abnormally intelligent, or . . . they had some assistance in responding which is denied to us, but which compensated for the modern reader's learned apparatus." Regarding the second possibility, he suggested that "the original audiences had some guide to response which we do not." And this, he suggested, lay in the narratives' essential conventionality, which depended on common familiarity "not only with heroic vocabulary, but also with the scenes, the characters, and the stories." "Behind them, powerfully felt, if never exactly codified, stand the controlling interests and natural ironies of the Old English heroic ethic."[7]

In 1994 Joseph Harris considered the influence of a common Germanic repository of wisdom in *Beowulf* when he adopted a nativist approach to a reading of that poem.[8] At one point, the dying hero recalls how the Geatish king Hreðel grieved without comfort for his eldest son, Herebeald, who was killed accidentally by his younger son, Hæðcyn, in a situation where there could be no question of redress for the loss. Beowulf likens the situation to that of an old man, who, lamenting the loss of a hanged son, "ōðres ne ġymeð//tō ġebīdanne burgum in innan/yrfeweardas" (cares not to wait for another heir in his hall).[9] Harris noticed a

---

7. T. A. Shippey, *Old English Verse* (London: Hutchinson, 1972), 18 and 19.
8. Joseph Harris, "A Nativist Approach to *Beowulf*: The Case of the Germanic Elegy," in *Companion to Old English Poetry*, ed. Henk Aertsen and Rolf H. Bremmer Jr. (Amsterdam: VU University Press, 1994), 45–62.
9. *Beowulf*, ll. 2451b–2453a; R. D. Fulk, Rober E. Bjork, and John D. Niles, eds., *Klaeber's* Beowulf *and the* Fight at Finnsburg, 4th ed. (Toronto: University of Toronto

"pattern of paternal grief and lament" analogous to this passage in "the genetically related sister literature in Old Norse."[10] In *Egils saga* the eponymous hero, grieving over the death of his son, Bǫðvarr, composes a lament, "Sonatorrek, a Lament for Sons," in which a passage difficult to interpret seems to suggest the traditional wisdom of producing another son to replace one who has been lost: "Þat's ok mælt, / at engi geti / sonar iðgjǫld / nema sjalfr ali / enn þann nið, / es ǫðrum sé / borinn maðr / í bróður stað" (It is also said / that no one regains / his son's worth / without bearing / another offspring / that other men / hold in esteem / as his brother's match).[11]

The first line of the stanza is used elsewhere as a formulaic introduction to proverb texts, suggesting that the composer views the replacing of one's lost son by having another as drawing on that communal body of early Germanic wisdom, of which an Anglo-Saxon as well as an Old Icelandic poet and his audience would have been aware. He considers, for evidence of such background, advice found in *Hávamál*: "Sonr er betri, / þótt sé síð of alinn, / eptir genginn guma" (A son is better, even if he is born late, / when the father is dead).[12] Speaking in conclusion of "the relationship of *Beowulf* to Germanic tradition, its position in this particular ethnic web of words," (57) Harris notices how it seems to maintain "a subterranean contact with the world of ideas, the poetic language, and the oral-literary forms of the tribes and nations that spoke the Germanic tongues."[13]

Harris's article appeared shortly after Carolyne Larrington notably adumbrated "a body of folk-wisdom, not yet in metrical form, a body which can be sensed as a living, pulsing, gnomic background to all Germanic poetry—not just verse specifically intended as didactic."[14] Her perception was shared by Susan Deskis, who

---

Press, 2008), 84; Talbot Ethelbert Donaldson, trans., *Beowulf: A New Translation* (New York: W. W. Norton, 1966), 43.

10. J. Harris, "Nativist," 53 and 51.

11. *Egils saga Skalla-Grímssonar*, ed. Sigurður Nordal, Íslenzk fornrit 2 (Reykjavík: Hið íslenzka fornritafélag, 1933), 252–53, st. 17, ch. 79; *Egil's Saga*, trans. Bernard Scudder, in *CSI* 1:154, st. 17.

12. ÍF 36, 1:336, st. 72; Larrington, *Poetic Edda*, 22; J. Harris, "Nativist," 55.

13. J. Harris, "Nativist," 57.

14. Larrington, *Sense*, 18. Intimations of a shared background orality in written texts can be found expressed in many places throughout work with the early Icelandic poetic corpus. On the subject of such interinfluence, for instance, notice the observation of David A. H. Evans, "Hugsvinnsmál" in *Medieval Scandinavia: An Encyclopedia*,

had similarly noticed how "*Beowulf* reflects an attitude towards sentential expression similar to that which must have motivated the redactor of *Hávamál*, or the Anglo-Saxon scribe who copied *Maxims II* in front of a version of the *Chronicle*. That attitude may be described in brief as a respect for and appreciation of the uses of traditional wisdom." As a concluding thought, Deskis added the following comment: "A pre-existing generic frame may absorb material from any source, and in the case of proverbial material, sources are especially nebulous."[15] It therefore seems reasonable to expand on Larrington's vision of "the gnomic background of all Germanic poetry" to include that of all Old Icelandic prose narrative as well.

In fact, it seems clear that the sagas, arising to whatever extent and by whatever means they do from oral tradition, bear compelling if uneven witness in the hands of their respective composers to that vast and in large part unexplorable paroemial inventory of shared communal wisdom to which Larrington refers, and to the fact that it was possessed by people of literate as well as those of preliterate cognitive development in thirteenth-century Iceland. In its immanent entirety it must have delineated those conceptual structures defining the behavioral expectations of the preliterate society of Iceland and indeed of its inhabitants' continental forebears. Such a repository was so deeply embedded in the consciousness and of such profound psychic impact that it informed the thinking even of the literate and in some cases highly educated thirteenth-century composers of the sagas, as well as that of the saga world characters whose utterances and undertakings they described. This paroemial cognitive patterning of the preliterate saga mind, though with as yet little clarity of form or content for us, may eventually prove most useful in our effort to understand what the sagas, written as they were on the cusp of that society's transition into literacy, were meant to be about.

---

ed. Phillip Pulsiano and Kirsten Wolf (New York: Garland, 1993), 306a: "it is more likely that all these works, *Hugsvinnsmál* included, draw on a general Norse stock of sententious phraseology." The editors of *Eddukvæði* notice similarly, in commmenting on the occurrence of the proverb, "*engi er einna hvatastr*," both in *Hávamál* 64 and in *Fáfnismál* 17, the following: "Sumir ætla að þetta sé bein lántaka frá Háv, en aðrir telja líklegra að um sé að ræða spakyrði sem verið hafi alkunnugt" (335). (Some think that this is a borrowing from *Hávamál*, but others think it is more likely to be considered an aphorism that was universally known.); ÍF 36, 1:335.

15. Susan E. Deskis, Beowulf *and the Medieval Proverb Tradition* (Tempe: Arizona Center for Medieval and Renaissance Texts and Studies, 1996), 140.

In our rather exclusively literate world it may be difficult for us to comprehend how this could be so. For us the proverb as a text has an overt and at least loosely fixed form whose iteration we anticipate in conjunction with an event or narrative of which it is illuminative.[16] Walter J. Ong observes how different are our conceptions of wisdom texts from those of people in preliterate cultures: "Fixed, often rhythmically balanced, expressions of this sort... can be found occasionally in print, indeed can be 'looked up' in books of sayings, but in oral cultures they are not occasional. They are incessant. They form the substance of thought itself. Thought in any extended form is impossible without them, for it consists in them."[17] An internalized communal inventory of behavioral codes was thus a constant in that repertoire of standards by which individual conduct was initiated, governed, and judged in preliterate culture. The sagamen of thirteenth-century Iceland wrote with a consciousness deeply informed by this code, arising through long paths of oral transmission in their preliterate ancestral background. Just as the fable and the proverb are so closely related that a fable can be seen simply as an extension of the proverb of which it is emblematic, so too episodes in sagas, or in some cases the whole narratives of sagas, are interpretable in paroemiological terms, even where the proverb, if signaled at all, is noticed by nothing more than the briefest of allusions.

The ability of Icelandic writers to employ this background of communal wisdom for their literary purposes reinforces our concept of the vigorous currency of this mnemonically preserved, ultimately cognitive, tool in the saga composer's mind as late as the thirteenth century. Persuasive evidence of this psychological reality of the proverb, not only as a building block of oral narration but also as a radical element in the origins of preliterate thought, is found in the sagas in seemingly incidental allusions to such wisdom, where there is no apparent literary thematic agenda at all.

---

16. Brief experimentation will demonstrate how frustrating a task it is to formulate a list of proverbs one knows, whereas recalling a proverb suitable to a described situation or event comes quite naturally, yielding far more abundant results. From this it seems evident that our minds do not store a discrete, independently retrievable inventory of such texts but have rather an associative competence for their usage.

17. Walter J. Ong, *Orality and Literacy: The Technologizing of the Word*, 2nd ed. (London: Routledge, 2002), 35.

"Þrínættr gestur . . ."—the Proverbial Time to Leave

An example of what is meant by the collective paroemial consciousness of early Iceland is found in chapter 78 of *Egils saga Skallgrímssonar*, just after Hákon jarl gives the court poet Einarr Helgason a shield on his returning to Iceland: "hann var skrifaðr fornsǫgum, en allt milli skriptanna váru lagðar yfir spengr af gulli, ok settr steinum" (it was adorned with legends, and between the carvings it was overlaid with gold and embossed with jewels).[18] Back in Iceland, Einarr went to visit Egill, but found him away at the time. The composer mentions that Einarr stayed for three nights, adding, "en þat var engi siðr, at sitja lengr en þrjár nætr at kynni" (it was not the custom to stay more than three nights on a visit). When he left, he went to Egill's bed closet, "ok festi þar upp skjǫldinn þann inn dýra ok sagði heimamǫnnum, at hann gaf Agli skjǫldinn" (and hung up his precious shield there, and told people of the household that it was a present for Egil).[19] Finding the gift on his return, Egill composed an ekphrastic poem celebrating the shield's artistry.

In both the Íslenzk fornrit and the Altnordische Saga-Bibliothek editions of *Egils saga*, the composer's comment on the length of Einarr's stay receives editorial attention in the form of a reference to verse 35 of *Hávamál*: "Ganga skal / skala gestr vera / ey í einum stað; / ljúfr verðr leiðr, / ef lengi sitr / annars fletjum á" (A man must go, he must not remain a guest / always in one place; / the loved man is loathed if he sits too long / in someone else's hall).[20] In Old Icelandic sources we find no explicit attestation of a proverb quoted in 1830 by Guðmundur Jónsson in his *Safn af íslenzkum orðskviðum*: "Þrínættr gestur þykir ve[r]str (þakkar stundum verst)" (A guest for three nights is thought worst [thanks worst sometimes]).[21] While there is no extant Old Icelandic paroemial source with an explicit limit on the accepted duration of a visit, Einarr's

---

18. ÍF 2:271–72, ch. 78.
19. ÍF 2:272, ch. 78; CSI 1:163.
20. ÍF 36, 1:328, st. 35; Larrington, *Poetic Edda*, 17; ÍF 2:272, ch. 78, fn 1. See also Altnordische Saga-Bibliothek 3.265n6.
21. Guðmundur Jónsson, *Safn*, 410. Guðmundur also records there a related but more expanded text: "Þrínættr gestr þykir nízkum ve[r]str, og þaðan af því leiðari, sem lengr dvelr" (The third night's guest is thought worst to the stingy, and thence the worse, as he stays longer). See JGF 191.

length of stay is remarked in the *TPMA*; and E. O. G. Turville-Petre, in his edition of *Víga-Glúms saga*, cites, in connection with a similar passage there, a Jutish proverb: "*en tredje dags gjæst stinker*" (the third day's guest stinks).²²

Whatever paroemial form the composer of *Egils saga* may have had in mind at this point, it is clear that he referred there to an item of social wisdom current in medieval Nordic thought and attested both in Germanic culture and in Europe more generally too. That the wisdom is referred to in *Egla*, but without direct, explicit reference to a formulaic memorialization of the knowledge, suggests a pattern of thinking for which a good deal of evidence can be found in the Old Icelandic corpus.

One example among many can be drawn from *Grettis saga*, where Þorkell krafla Kárnsárgoði, head of the Vatnsdœlir clan, visits Grettir's parents: "Tóku þau Ásmundr ok Ásdís við honum báðum hǫndum; var hann þar þrjár nætr, ok tǫluðu þeir mágar marga hluti milli sín." (Asmund and Asdis welcomed him with open arms. He spent three nights there, and the two kinsmen talked together about many things.)²³ Mention of the prescribed length of stay is found also when Grettir visits his maternal uncle, Jǫkull, before his fateful confrontation with Glámr: "Hann tók vel við Gretti, ok var hann þar þrjár nætr" (He welcomed Grettir, and he stayed there for three nights).²⁴ The later attested paroemial texts describe the socially ingrained custom by which people traditionally visited one another in Old Icelandic culture; such customs were encoded in the paroemial cognitive patterning of their society. There is thus a sense in which the text and the thought are one.

---

22. *TPMA* 1.446; E. O. G. Turville-Petre, *Víga-Glúms saga*, 2nd ed. (Oxford: Clarendon Press, 1960; reprint 1974), 63. The proverb that Turville-Petre cites is recorded by Svend Grundtvig. See Svend Grundtvig, *Gamle danske minder i folkemunde: folkeæventyr, folkeviser, folkesagn og andre rester af fortidens digtning og tro, som de endnu leve i det danske folks erindring / samlede og udgivne af Svend Grundtvig*. (Copenhagen: C. G. Iversen, 1854–61), 3, 214, in a list of "Ordsprog og Mundheld." See also Barend J. Sijmons and Hugo Gering, eds., *Die Lieder der Edda*, 3 vols. in 4, Germanistische Handbibliothek 7 (Halle an der Saale: Buchhandlung des Waisenhauses, 1888–1931), 1:95n to Hávamál 35: "Vgl. Plautus, Mil. glor. 741: *hospes nullus tam in amici hospitium devorti potest, / quin, ubi triduom continuom fuerit, iam odiosus siet*; ferner das jütische sprichwort (Feilberg, Ordb. I, 451ᵇ, 32): *en tredje dags gjæst stinker* (ebenso deutsch: *am ersten tag ein lieber gast, am zweiten eine last, am dritten stinkt er fast*). Vgl. Auch Weinhold, Altn. leben s. 447 und Detter-Heinzel z. St. [DA IV, 328]."

23. ÍF 7:44, ch. 16; *CSI* 2:68.

24. ÍF 7:117, ch. 34.

"þá vér fegrst mælum"—Eloquent Deception

A second and more subtle example of the use of allusion to such proverbially encoded communal wisdom is found in *Bjarnar saga Hítdœlakappa*, where Þórðr Kolbeinsson has aroused Bjǫrn Arngeirsson's permanent enmity by marrying the latter's betrothed, Oddný Þorkelsdóttir, after having falsely informed her that her fiancé had died in Russia. The two men's conflict over Þórðr's perfidy having been formally resolved by King Óláfr Haraldsson, when Bjǫrn finally returns to Iceland, Þórðr decides to invite him to spend the winter with him and Oddný on the dubious pretense of ascertaining Bjǫrn's commitment to the agreement they had reached in Norway: "'ok vil ek svá reyna skap Bjarnar ok trúlyndi við mik'" ("and in this way I want to test Bjorn's mood and his faith with me").[25] Þórðr's fair words of invitation arouse the ire of Bjǫrn's mother, Þórdís, who candidly expresses her clear insight into his character: "'Þat mun sýna, at ek mun ekki mjǫk talhlýðin. Hugðu svá at, Bjǫrn, . . . at því flára mun Þórðr hyggja, sem hann talar sléttara, ok trú þú honum eigi.'" ("It will be seen that I'm not very easily swayed by talk. Bear in mind, Bjorn, that the more fairly Thord speaks, the more falsely he thinks, so don't trust him.")[26] The Fornrit editors assume that Þórdís' perspicacity, like Einarr's social sensitivity in *Egla*, is illuminated by a passage in the primary Eddic source of traditional Norse wisdom: "Það er því líkast, sem þessi orð Þórdísar sé bergmál af Hávamálum (45. vísu), þar sem svo er að orði komizt: 'Ef þú átt annan, / þanns þú illa trúir, / vildu af hǫnum þó gótt geta, / fagrt skaltu við þann mæla, / en flátt hyggja / ok gjalda lausung við lygi.'" (It is thus most likely that this speech of Þórdís is an echo of Hávamál v. 45, where it says, "If you've another, whom you don't trust, / but from whom you want nothing but good, / speak fairly to him, but think falsely / and repay treachery with a lie.")[27] This advice, if applied to Þórðr, might well help to explain the psychology behind his motives for the invitation to Bjǫrn, and the phraseological parallels are so

---

25. *Bjarnar saga Hítdœlakappa*, in *Borgfirðinga sǫgur*, ed. Sigurður Nordal and Guðni Jónsson, Íslenzk fornrit 3 (Reykjavík: Hið íslenzka fornritafélag, 1938), 136, ch. 11; *CSI* 1:268.
26. ÍF 3:138, ch. 11; *CSI* 1:268.
27. ÍF 3:138, ch. 11, fn 1. See Larrington, *Poetic Edda*, 19, for the translation from *Hávamál*.

close as to make a convincing case for the bergmálish allusion the editors suggest.

Interestingly, readers might find similar resonance in Þórdís's warning with another passage in *Hávamál*, stanza 91, situated though it is in a passage cautioning women against trusting men: "Bert ek nú mæli, / því at ek bæði veit, / brigðr er karla hugr konum; / þá vér fegrst mælum / er vér flást hyggjum, / þat tælir horska hugi" (I can speak frankly since I have known both: / men's hearts are fickle toward women; / when we speak most fairly, / then we think most falsely, / that entraps the wise mind.).[28] Again, in studying such compilations of wisdom, it is not unreasonable to take from their ostensible narrative context passages that have broader application, since it is likely that compilers, in placing those texts, have incidentally narrowed their semantic application with their situation. However, even if we were to assume the composer's and audience's consciousness, literary or otherwise, of the entirety of stanza 91, we could then see Þórdís ironically insisting that, however deceptive Þórðr may be in his fair speech, she, though a woman, is not deceived, whereas Bjǫrn is in danger of being so.

There is no clear evidence as to which, if either, of these two extant stanzas hovered in the composer's mind as he formulated Þórdís's admonition. In any case, the resonance of the saga passage with a pattern of proverbial wisdom clearly preserved in the poem substantiates the view that thirteenth-century thinking in Iceland need not have strayed far from the ancestral, pre-Christian, Eddic standards. That the advice of *Hávamál* is often echoed, if not specifically recalled, in the wisdom that informs opinion and action in the sagas of Icelanders suggests its value as the most comprehensive extant witness to that immanent oral corpus at the roots of *paroemial cognitive patterning* in the Nordic world.

"Engi er einna hvatastr"—Some Dangers of Mannjafnaðr

A third and more complex scene in which this patterning of the cognitive process is apparent is found in *Víga-Glúms saga*, where a young Glúmr proves his maturity and gathers honor by traveling to Norway and visiting the home of his maternal grandfather, the

---

28. ÍF 36, 1:340, st. 91; Larrington, *Poetic Edda*, 24.

hersir (chieftain) Vígfúss Sigurðarson of Vǫrs. The setting of his reception is magnificent: "sá hann þar mikit fjǫlmenni ok margs konar skemmtan ok leika" (he saw a great crowd of people there, with games and amusements of all kinds), as if it were a royal court, with his grandfather "mikinn ok vegligan í ǫndvegi í skautfeldi blám, ok lék sér at spjóti gullreknu" (a big and noble-looking man in the high seat, wearing a black cloak with a hood and playing with a gold-inlaid spear).[29] He was well received until he claimed family connections with his host. He was then relegated to an unflattering place on the benches where he became "fámálugr ok ósiðblendr" (taciturn and unsociable), all in a fairly stereotypical scene of cold hesitance to accept the relationship of an Icelander visiting ancestral relatives in Norway.[30]

Glúmr gained his grandfather's acceptance only when he challenged and defeated Bjǫrn járnhauss the berserker, who with his eleven fellows was a habitual, edgy, and dangerous uninvited guest at Vígfúss's feasts. Vígfúss warned his men that Bjǫrn would be looking for a fight and ordered that they "skyldi vel stilla orðum sínum" (should be careful what they said), a restraint that would involve less disgrace than if they were to challenge him.[31] When the unpleasant intruder made his way around the hall, asking people whether they considered themselves *jafnsnjallr* (equally courageous), their replies were suitably diplomatic—until he reached Glúmr, who, reacting to his insults, "kvazk eigi vita um snilli hans,—'ok vil ek af því engu við þik jafnask, at út á Íslandi myndi sá maðr kallaðr fól, er þann veg léti sem þú lætr. En hér hefi ek vitat alla bezt orðum stilla.'" (said . . . that he did not know about his courage—"but I certainly don't want to equate myself with you, because out in Iceland a man who carried on in the way you behave would be called a fool. But here I've discovered that everyone is extremely polite.")[32] Glúmr then beat Bjǫrn mercilessly until he ran away and

---

29. *Víga-Glúms saga*, in *Eyfirðinga sǫgur*, ed. Jónas Kristjánsson, Íslenzk fornrit 9 (Reykjavík: Hið íslenzka fornritafélag, 1956), 16, ch. 6; *CSI* 2:274–75.
30. ÍF 9:17, ch. 6; *CSI* 2:275.
31. ÍF 9:18, ch. 6; *CSI* 2:275.
32. ÍF 9:19, ch. 6; *CSI* 2:276. *Mannjafnaðr* was an activity that led naturally to insults and violence. Interesting coverage of this custom is found in Karen Swenson, *Performing Definitions: Two Genres of Insult in Old Norse Literature*, Studies in Scandinavian Literature and Culture, 3 (Columbia, SC: Camden House, 1993). See also Jonathan Mark Broussard, "Waging Word Wars: A Discourse Analysis of the Patterns of Norse Masculinity Presented through Mannjafnaðr in the Icelandic Sagas," (master's

later died. While explicit formulaic wisdom is lacking in the saga and in this typically challenging scene, its inspiration is informed by awareness of a pertinent corpus and its established generic expectations on the part of the composer and his audience, as will be shown below.

In *Hrólfs saga kraka*, written down much later than *Víga-Glúms saga*, Bǫðvarr bjarki irritated the king's berserkers by refusing to admit himself less *snjallr* (valiant, courageous) than they. Rather, he boasted "at hann teldist ekki jafnsnjallr, heldr snjallari" (that he did not regard himself as equally valiant, but rather as more valiant), and proved it by nearly killing one of them. His newly valorized companion, Hjalti, did the same with another of the intruders. King Hrólfr then followed his settlement of the altercation with the observation that "þeir mætti nú sjá þat, at eigi væri neitt svá ágætt, sterkt eða stórt, at ekki mætti þvílíkt finna" (they could now see that nothing existed so famous, so strong, or so big that an equal could not be found).[33] In these remarks, the king expressed a perception that again echoes a passage in *Hávamál*: "Ríki sitt / skyli ráðsnotra / hverr í hófi hafa; / þá hann þat finnr / er með frœknum kømr / at engi er einna hvatastr" (Every man wise in counsel / should use his power in moderation; / for when he mingles with the brave he finds / that no one is boldest of all).[34]

* * *

Whatever the significance of Bjǫrn's truculent search in *Víga-Glúms saga*, the specifics of what a man willing to boast of himself that he was *jafnsnjallastr* rather than *hvatastr* might have meant for the thirteenth-century audience must await further interpretation. However, the implicitly analogous nature of the response to the formulaic patterning of the Eddic witness to this tradition is obvious when Glúmr proclaims himself unimpressed by the uninvited guest's behavior and when the king comments on the outcome of the dispute. Where this wisdom was still much encoded in formulaic

---

thesis, McNeese State University, 2003), as well as Marcel Bas and Tineke Padmos, "Two Types of Verbal Dueling in Old Icelandic: The Interactional Structure of the Senna and the Mannjafnaðr in *Hárbarðsljóð*," *Scandinavian Studies* 55 (1983): 149–74. See also Carol J. Clover, "*Hárbarðsljóð* as Generic Farce," *Scandinavian Studies* 51 (1979): 124–45.

33. FSN 1:71, ch. 37; Jesse Byock, trans., *The Saga of King Hrolf Kraki* (London: Penguin Books, 1998), 54, slightly modified.

34. ÍF 36, 1:334, st. 64; Larrington, *Poetic Edda*, 21; JGF 275; TPMA 12.326.

texts, as is most often the case with preliterate or recently literate societies, a composer of a tale could present and control the impact of scenes by appealing to that communal awareness in his audience. The composer of *Víga-Glúms saga* demonstrates, in this passage, the transition from preliterate, paroemially informed thinking to writing narrative in which he relies on the cultural literacy of his audience to convey the meaning of his story. Such examples mark the beginning of a process by which the phenomenon of *paroemial cognitive patterning* moves from a means of knowing in preliterate culture to a process of enabling the conveyance of artistic nuance by those composers who converted the Norse oral corpus into the world of the written narrative.

The Complex and Cunning Nature of Hreiðarr heimski: Reading an Old Icelandic þáttr against the Background of Paroemial Cognitive Patterning

This section presents a reading of an Old Icelandic *þáttr* in terms of the concepts that have been explained and illustrated in the immediately preceeding pages.[35] Our underlying awareness of the paroemial background of the narrative, which involves an enhanced sensitivity to medieval Iceland's cultural literacy, makes it possible to recognize certain nuances of which we might otherwise be unaware.

* * *

In a way that is typical of unintended editorial bias, the fictional character Hreiðarr Þorgrímsson's adventures are titled *Hreiðars þáttr heimska*, although manuscripts themselves set this story apart simply as "Frá Hreiðari" (About Hreiðarr). Never designated as a *fífl*, (fool, clown, boor), a term whose Anglo-Saxon cognate meant "monster," he is thus clearly different from such figures in saga literature as Helgi, the idiot son of Ingjaldr of Hergilsey in *Gísla saga*. Hreiðarr's deficiency, or perhaps mere eccentricity, is signaled with the descriptive phrase, "*var hann heima jafnan*" (he was always at home), thus placing him in the category of the *heimskr maðr* (naïve,

---

35. This section incorporates (slightly modified) text from my chapter on "The Eddic Wisdom of Hreiðarr the Fool: Paroemial Cognitive Patterning in an Old Icelandic *þáttr*," in *Literary Speech Acts of the Medieval North: Essays Inspired by the Works of Thomas A. Shippey*, ed. Eric Shane Bryan and Alexander Vaughan Ames (Tempe: Arizona Center for Medieval and Renaissance Studies, 2020), 3–27.

foolish man). As his brother tells him, discussing a projected trip abroad, "'Ekki þykki mér þér fallinn fǫrin'" ("I don't think traveling suits you").[36]

The wise treatment of the *heimskr maðr* is discussed at several points in *Hávamál*. Nordic conventional wisdom generally encouraged the isolation of individuals whose personalities and temperaments were marked by an immature impulsiveness that could give rise to scenes of derision, or even conflict, in the harshly cynical and potentially violent gatherings of warriors. At the same time, there was a recognition of the possibility that the behavior of such people was the result of insufficient experience, as adages like "því er fífl að fátt er kennt" (no wonder one is a fool, if one hasn't been taught) and "heimskt er heimalit barn" (homish (silly) is the homebred bairn) would imply.[37] Despite this proverbially remarked understanding of possible reasons for their social inadequacy, the dangers of introducing such people into society are obvious from the fact that the insecurity of social interaction in this milieu is a matter so much discussed in *Hávamál*. The requirements for social success are emphasized at the start of the poem, in stanza 6: "þá er horskr ok þǫgull / kømr heimisgarða til, / sjaldan verðr víti vǫrum / þvíat óbrigðna vin / fær maðr aldregi / en manvit mikit" (when a wise and silent man comes to a homestead / blame seldom befalls the wary; / for no more dependable friend can a man ever get / than a store of common sense).[38] One is immediately reminded of Hreiðarr's insufficiency in stanza 17, which describes the visit of a fool: "Kópir afglapi / er til kynnis kømr, / þylsk hann um eða þrumir" (The fool stares when he comes on a visit, / he mutters to himself or hovers about).[39] Silence is best: "Ósnotr maðr, / er með aldir kømr, / þat er bazt at hann þegi; / engi þat veit / at hann ekki kann, / nema hann mæli til margt" (The foolish man in company / does best if he stays

---

36. Ármann Jakobsson and Þórður Ingi Guðjónsson, eds., *Morkinskinna*. 2 vols. Íslenzk fornrit 23–4 (Reykjavík: Hið íslenzka fornritafélag, 1968), 152, ch. 26; Theodore Murdock Andersson and Kari Ellen Gade, trans., *Morkinskinna: The Earliest Icelandic Chronicle of the Norwegian Kings (1030–1157)*, Islandica 51 (Ithaca, NY: Cornell University Press, 2000), 171 (translation slightly modified here). *Hreiðars þáttr* is also edited in ÍF 10: 247–60.

37. Richard Cleasby and Gudbrand Vigfusson, *An Icelandic-English Dictionary*. 2nd ed. (Oxford: Clarendon Press, 1957), 155b and 251b. Hereafter cited as C-V. See also JGF 150 and 239.

38. ÍF 36, 1:323, st. 6; Larrington, *Poetic Edda*, 14; JGF 382.

39. ÍF 36, 1:325, st. 17; Larrington, *Poetic Edda*, 15.

silent; / no one will know that he knows nothing, / unless he talks too much).⁴⁰ The proverb, "Engi er allheimskr, ef þegja má" (No one is a total fool if he can be silent), derives from the wisdom pertinent to such situations as it is preserved in *Hávamál*.⁴¹ Thus, when the composer of this *þáttr* introduces his hero as a man who was "heima jafnan" (always at home) while his brother was abroad and a man of King Magnús's court, Hreiðarr's situation would be immediately apparent to the audience and would soon be reinforced, when he asks to go abroad, by his brother Þórðr's observation that the journey was not the right thing for him. These comments, coming as they do early on in the story, suggest to the audience that whatever the origins of his condition, Hreiðarr is homebound largely in his best interest.

Yet the reader's sympathy is engaged by Hreiðarr's insistently seeking to escape from the limited circumstances of that homely existence, which might even be regarded as a partial cause of the undeveloped state of his personality. As the narrative progresses, the surface of the good-natured bumpkin seems just that, with a somewhat more complex and cunning potential lying beneath his breathless and insistently naïve excitement over the novelty of life's experience beyond the homestead. As he argues with and manipulates people who have power over him, his surface naïvete is gradually recognized as being accompanied by a shrewd sense of strategy, which suggests a more astute character in the process of growth. When Þórðr is reluctant to take Hreiðarr along on his trip to Norway and the court because he considers him unfit for and potentially troublesome on such a journey, the latter responds with what amounts to a threat of even more trouble if he is left alone by his protective brother: "'Era þér þá betra hlut í at eiga ef ek ber á mǫnnum eða gerik aðra óvísu, þeim er um fé mitt sitja at lokka af mér . . .'" ("Your part will be no easier if I come to blows with men or am otherwise embroiled with those who are after my money and try to steal it away from me").⁴²

Having thus succeeded in getting Þórðr to take him along, in the first scene in Norway Hreiðarr heimski uses a proverb that the *þáttr*'s first audience would surely have recognized as alluding to advice represented by a couple of stanzas in *Hávamál*, and he begins

---

40. ÍF 36, 1:327, st. 27; Larrington, *Poetic Edda*, 16.
41. *Grettis saga*; ÍF 7:278, ch. 88; JGF 238; TPMA 8.373.
42. ÍF 23:152, ch. 26; Andersson and Gade, *Morkinskinna*, 171.

manipulating his brother into taking him to an assembly where he can meet the king: "'Vaki þú, bróðir! Fátt veit sá er søfr. Ek veit tíðendi, ok heyrðak áðan læti kynlig'" ("Wake up, brother. The slug-a-bed is slow to learn. I'm onto something and have just heard a strange sound").[43] Again, as in previous examples we have noticed, the allusion to the disadvantages of late rising is conceptually recognizable yet lexically imprecise, as if the composer or speaker were citing a text of which we have no clear witness: "Ár skal rísa / sá er annars vill / fé eða fjǫr hafa; / sjaldan liggjandi úlfr / lær um getr, / né sofandi maðr sigr" (He should get up early, the man who means to take / another's life or property; / seldom does the loafing wolf snatch the ham, / nor a sleeping man victory).[44] And, in the same rhetorical pattern, stanza 59 of *Hávamál* has: "Ár skal rísa / sá er á yrkjendr fá / ok ganga síns verka á vit; / margt um dvelr / þann er um morgin sefr; / hálfr er auðr und hvǫtom" (He should get up early, the man who has few workers, / and set about his work with thought; / much gets held up for the man sleeping in in the morning; / wealth is half-won by activity).[45] Hreiðarr would seem to be drawing here on a body of wisdom only partly reflected in the extant Eddic text, and yet one of which the composer could assume his audience's awareness.

In any case, his pretense, if that is what it is, of not recognizing and then of not understanding the meaning of the *hornblástr* by which a meeting with the king is called leads to the eventual realization of his previously unrevealed ambition to meet the king. Learning that the king will be there, he insists he must attend the gathering, "því at ek vilda þar koma fyrst er [ek sæja sem flesta menn] í senn" ("because I want to be the first on hand where *I can see the greatest number of men* gathered together"). When the two brothers then argue, Hreiðarr simply insists, "fara skulu vit báðir. Muna þér betra þykkja at ek fara einn, en ekki fær þú [mik lattan þessar fararar]." ("We should go together. It will not turn out better for you if I go alone, and you're not going to talk me out of this trip.")[46] He runs off to the gathering, leaving Þórðr to follow and then teasing him for running more slowly than he does.

Introduced to the king, Hreiðarr engages him in a scene

---

43. ÍF 23:153, ch. 26; Andersson and Gade, Morkinskinna, 171; JGF 637; TPMA 10.105.
44. ÍF 36, 1:333, st. 58; Larrington, *Poetic Edda*, 20; JGF 593–94 and 497; TPMA 13.176.
45. ÍF 36, 1:333, st. 59; Larrington, *Poetic Edda*, 20; JGF 29, 399 and 16.
46. ÍF 23:153, ch. 26; Andersson and Gade, *Morkinskinna*, 172. The words between asterisks are taken from manuscripts other than GKS 1009 fol. They are marked by square brackets in ÍF.

lacking courtly dignity but celebrating King Magnús's patience and compassion. Although his host welcomes Hreiðarr to stay the winter, he cautiously suggests the inadvisability of his odd visitor residing within the court itself, as "'betr þykki mér þér þar vistin felld vera er heldr er fátt manna'" ("I think you would be lodged better where there are fewer people"). But once again, Hreiðarr opts for the company of men, arguing that even in a smaller group his behavior could create problems: "'en eigi mun svá mannfátt vera at eigi komi þat þó upp er mælt verðr ... Nú kann vera at þeir reiði orð mín fyr aðra menn ok spotti mik ok drepi þat at ferligu er ek hefi at gamni eða mælik'" ("but there are never so few people that word of what is said doesn't get around ... It might happen that people are angered at my words and mock me and make too much of what I have said in jest").[47] And then he returns to the habitual argument, that he is safer with his brother, wherever his brother may be: "'Nú sýnisk mér hit vitrligra at vera heldr hjá þeim er um mik hyggr, sem Þórðr er bróðir minn, þótt þar sé heldr fjǫlmenni, en hinnig þótt menn sé fáir ok sé þar engi til umbóta'" ("It seems to me wiser to be near someone who cares for me, like my brother Þórðr, even if there are a lot of people present, rather than to be where there are few people and none to take a hand on my behalf").[48] This reasoning proves persuasive to the king, so that Hreiðarr, *heimskr* though he may in some ways seem, has succeeded in getting his way with his monarch as well as with his brother!

Hreiðars þáttr itself, though brief, is deceptively complex in its content and agenda, and it is susceptible to several different lines of interpretation that are not of immediate interest here. But by this point, a reader in possession of the most basic familiarity with the paroemial inventory of Old Icelandic culture must have felt Hreiðarr's invoking in his rhetoric the impact of the proverb "Berr er hverr á bakinu, nema sér bróður eigi" (Bare is his back who has no brother) that, though it is not in *Hávamál*, as we have that text, appears in several sagas and is used as well by Saxo Grammaticus, who for his late twelfth century *Gesta Danorum* had Icelandic

---

47. ÍF 23:153, ch. 26. Andersson and Gade, *Morkinskinna*, 172. The proverb alluded to by Hreiðarr is "Ferr orð, er (um) munn liðr" (Word travels when it leaves the mouth): JGF 427; TPMA 13.241.

48. ÍF 23:157, ch. 26; Andersson and Gade, *Morkinskinna*, 174.

informants providing narrative materials known in their country.[49] One might well recall here Carolyne Larrington's observation on the "living, pulsing, gnomic background" of which *Hávamál* provides partial witness and that lies at the cognitive core of old Nordic poetry, as well as of Nordic prose forms.[50]

Hreiðarr's repeated, near-demagogic harping on the moral responsibility of Þórðr to look after him as he draws his brother ever farther into situations where a *heimskr maðr* is proverbially unlikely to thrive, suggests a sense of irony, a tendency to cynicism, which readers might not have anticipated in the intellectual range of a man who, on the surface, appears socially inept. The composer's having his superficially foolish hero couch his arguments in the patterns of Germanic communal wisdom lends further weight to the ironic burden of the narrative.

* * *

In conclusion, we have seen how, in *Hreiðars þáttr*, a composer can use the traditional wisdom of which *Hávamál* is the primary extant encoded manifestation for various narrative purposes. On the one hand, he refers to the accepted idea that some individuals are better off at home than in public assemblies or a continental court. On the other, he lets his hero use the psychologically persuasive power of this wisdom to get his way with those whom we would prefer to have control over him.

While we might reasonably anticipate that proverbial knowledge originates, instructs, and is maintained without being subverted by the unwise or the disingenuous, or without being subjected to the third

---

49. Saxo, V. 3. 8. 280 and 281 ("Ericus itaque semifusus undum habere tergum fraternitatis inopem referebat" [Erik, leaning at an angle, remarked that a brotherless man has a bare back]). Cf. JGF 35–36; *TPMA* 2.128. For a study of Saxo's Icelandic informants, see Bjarni Guðnason, "The Icelandic sources of Saxo Grammaticus," in *Saxo Grammaticus: A Medieval Author Between Norse and Latin Culture*, ed. Karen Friis-Jensen (Copenhagen: Museum Tusculanum Press, 1981), 79–93.

50. Larrington, *Sense*, 18. Commenting in his "Foreward: Awareness of Immanence" and introducing the edited volume containing my article from which the essential content of this section on *Hreiðars þáttr* is drawn, T. A. Shippey remarks on how I have applied Carol Clover's concept of "immanent saga" to the theory of an ancient Germanic proverbial background discernible in saga narrative. "Yet again," he cautions the reader, "one has to say that this entirety can never by recovered, and no doubt was never known in full to any individual: there can be no 'set text' of it. Nevertheless, the existence of that corpus could lead not only to 'cognitive patterning'—guiding people's thoughts in real life, about which we can only surmise—but also to the kind of 'artistic nuance' which we are well able to study in particular texts, as Professor Harris does." Bryan, *Literary Speech Acts*, ix.

eye of ironic inflection, this does not prove to be the case. Although sentential strings arise from, and in their linguistic marking signal their origin in, the natural impulse to encode and to impart information about the world and the limits of productive social behavior, these formulaic admonitions can be, and are, used creatively by those composers whose purpose it was to describe the human condition in medieval Iceland with all its capacities for behavior, including those that lie far outside these normative ways. In their hands, what was initially a body of instruction in wisdom became another rhetorically based tool for defining meaning and refining nuance in their stories about the whole range of the human potential.

The Phraseological Matrix of the Vǫlsung-Niflung Cycle

In this second section of chapter 2, we will examine the phraseological and paroemial impact of the legendary Eddic poems on saga literature. First we consider how saga composers and their contemporary audience viewed with some ironic reserve the speeches, actions, and in some cases the characters, of their stories. Filtered as they were through the nostalgic veil of the Vǫlsung-Niflung legend with those pre-Christian heroic ideals it once celebrated, the robust ethical standards some saga figures seemingly embraced would not have been uncritically accepted in the postconversion Icelandic Commonwealth. We will then read passages from *Vǫlsunga saga* and the *Íslendingasögur* against the paroemial background of the Sigurd narrative as witnessed in the *Elder Edda*, seeking thereby greater literary critical objectivity in our understanding of the sagas. The chapter concludes with a brief survey of the frequently used image of the wolf, which is familiar in the stories of Sigurd, in the paroemial texts of medieval Iceland. The lupine image is well attested in the Eddic corpus, with its continental origins, and is reflected in several of the *Íslendingasögur* most closely linked with the Vǫlsung-Niflung cycle.

The Cultural Breadth of the Vǫlsung-Niflung Cycle and Its Paths of Influence on Saga Literature

The commonly acknowledged antiquity of the historical figures that the characters of the Vǫlsung-Niflungs are thought to represent reflects the immense breadth of cultural impact that the cycle could have had on the phraseology of thirteenth-century Old Icelandic and those sources from which its composers drew their versions of these heroic legends. Gunnarr, for instance, derives from the Burgundian king Gundicarius, who died in 435 AD, Atli from the Hunnish king Attila (d. 454), and Jormunrekr from Ermanaric (d. 380). In addition, there is speculation, though controversial, that Sigurd himself might owe his legendary existence to the German hero Arminius, who came from a family whose male members habitually bore names incorporating the element, *seg-* (victory), and who destroyed three of Augustus's Roman legions in the Battle of the Teutoburg Forest in 9 AD.[51] While the stories attached to historical figures in the evolution of the heroic lays commemorating the triumphs and defeats of the Germanic tribes among which they were performed often came from diverse sources and epochs, that at least one of the characters might have developed from a chieftain in antiquity makes clear how vast the possibilities have been for the accumulation and dissemination of stories through time and geography to the points when the *Nibelungenlied*, and later the *Vǫlsunga saga* and the *Íslendingasögur*, found the written page.

The Poetic Backgrounds of the Vǫlsung-Niflung Cycle in Germania

The Eddic meters, which eventually conveyed the legendary narratives in the poems familiar to us today, were also in evidence early among the Germanic peoples. As written texts from the fifth century, Eddic verses are found in runes on a Danish bracteate and on a Norwegian memorial stone. Widely embedded in Nordic culture from preliterate times, they are found also on a late twelfth-century rune stave from Bergen, in thirteenth-century scholarly works, and as versified speech of heroes in the *fornaldarsögur*. On the Continent, Saxo Grammaticus used or paraphrased heroic lays, the content of which is also in the Eddic corpus. The same poetics likely

---

51. Theodore Murdock Andersson, "The Germanic Heroic Lay," in *A Preface to the Nibelungenlied* (Stanford, CA: Stanford University Press, 1987), 3–16. A very useful coverage of the historical and legendary backgrounds of the Vǫlsung-Niflung story is provided by Jesse Byock, "History and Legend: Burgundians, Huns, Goths, and Sigurd the Dragon Slayer," in *The Saga of the Volsungs: The Norse Epic of Sigurd the Dragon Slayer*, trans. Jesse Byock (London: Penguin Books, 1999), 11–26. The best introduction to this text is still that of Kaaren Grimstad, *Vǫlsunga saga. The Saga of the Volsungs. The Icelandic Text According to MS Nks 1824 b, 40*, Bibliotheca Germanica, Series Nova, Vol. 3 (Saarbrücken: AQ-Verlag, 2000), 13–67.

Paroemial Patterns of the Mythic and the Legendary Backgrounds 55

governed those poems, which Tacitus mentions, as preserving the only record of the Germanic tribes he describes.[52]

* * *

The content and the poetic forms of the extant Eddic legacy, as is apparent from linguistic evidence, go back many centuries prior to their recording, even though the poems we have date from more recent times. The paroemial inventory we glean from this body of verse could thus reach far back toward the dawn of Germanic culture, and may well preserve cognitive patterns of wisdom from that time in northern European narrative, about which otherwise so little is known.

The Extent of Phraseological Affinities of the Legendary Eddic Corpus with the Sagas

With perhaps the partial exception of *Sigrdrífumál*, the proverbial inventory of the legendary Eddic poems resides in semi-narrative rather than primarily anthological contexts. While one portion of the former poem consists of consecutive stanzas containing proverbs, it is selective in this presentation. The proverbs of Sigrdrífa are at least vaguely pertinent to the circumstances in which Sigurd will find himself as the narrative proceeds; they are thus anticipatory in their impact. This distinction from the more generally anthological presentation of paroemial content in *Hávamál* arises from the fact that much of the legendary corpus celebrates related ideas through discrete threads of the extended narrative of Sigurd the Vǫlsung and the subsequent trials of the Gjúking dynasty on which he intrudes. The proverbs in *Sigrdrífumál* thus provide heroic commentary on character and course of action, lending dignity of stature to figures and events in the early Germanic story by linking them to the workings of the gods, and indeed of fate itself.

"But the sagamen could never keep away from the *Vǫlsunga saga* for long," Lord Raglan noticed about the influence the early

---

52. Judy Quinn, "From Orality to Literacy in Medieval Iceland," in *Old Icelandic Literature and Society*, ed. Margaret Clunies Ross, Cambridge Studies in Medieval Literature 42 (Cambridge: Cambridge University Press, 2000), 30–60. On the subject of a common Germanic poetics, see Geoffrey Russom, Beowulf *and Old Germanic Metre* (Cambridge: Cambridge University Press, 1998).

Germanic legends had on the composers of the Icelandic sagas.[53] His engagingly aristocratic predilection for robust assertions and confidently eccentric pronouncements on the patterns of heroic narrative as he saw them is well depicted here. The stories of Sigurd were indeed an essential part of the intertextual matrix of the *Íslendingasögur*. Einar Ól. Sveinsson remarked of *Njáls saga* that a person who would understand that work must be aware of the *Íslendingasögur* that preceded it because of the late, post-modern quality that pervades its pages. As one reads the lines or considers whole episodes, one recalls similar phrases and passages in other sagas with which the composer and his audience were obviously familiar, and implicit references that lent nuance to his own text.[54] A similarly complex web linking Sigurd's legendary adventures to thirteenth-century Icelandic literature drives many teachers of Old Icelandic sagas to begin their course with *Vǫlsunga saga* and its poetic antecedents, thus enabling students to grasp the integral enmeshment of these pre-Christian figures and their stories in the intertextual background of the *Íslendingasögur*.

A passage that is prophetic not only of Sigurd's life but also, in a literary sense, of the impact of his story and its associated store of wisdom about the Germanic, and especially our extant Nordic, culture, is found in stanza 15 of *Reginsmál*: "'Ek mun fœða / fólkdjarfan gram, / nú er Yngva konr / með oss kominn; / sjá mun ræsir / ríkstr und sólu, / þrymr um ǫll lǫnd / ørlǫgsímu'" ("I must nurture the battle-brave prince; / now Yngvi's offspring has come to us; / he will be the most powerful prince under the sun, / his fate-strands extend through all lands").[55] Reginn's flattery here, as he takes Sigurd further into his confidence, has resonance with the virtually mythic impact of this story on the consciousness of the medieval North in those many instances of saga narrative where one finds echoes of the ancient legend, not only in character and action but also in phraseological affinities. Here it will be seen how, particularly in those sagas whose narratives are most heavily

---

53. Fitzroy Richard Somerset (Lord Raglan), "The Norse Sagas," in *The Hero: A Study in Tradition, Myth and Drama.* (London: Methuen, 1936), 69.

54. Einar Ól. Sveinsson, *Njáls saga: A Literary Masterpiece*, trans. Paul Schach (Lincoln: University of Nebraska Press, 1971), so: 45. "Whoever undertakes a critical investigation of *Njála* must have a comprehensive knowledge of the Íslendingasögur as a whole, of their distinctive nature and artistic method ... 30. "[for] in this saga we can detect traces of all previous forms of Icelandic literature."

55. ÍF 36, 2:299, st. 15; Larrington, *Poetic Edda*, 150.

imbued with echoes of the Vǫlsung-Niflung cycle, the proverbial content inherited with this corpus enhances our understanding of what their composers meant to convey in weaving into their stories these old threads of the heroic-legendary tragedy.

Some Examples of the Phraseological Enmeshment of the Vǫlsung-Niflung Cycle in Saga Literature

The reader of Old Icelandic narratives does not have to look extensively for instances of verbal and thematic influences from stories of Sigurd the Volsung. Their heroic ethical standards provided a measure by which saga characters might be invented by composers and appreciated by their audience. Awareness of this background enhances the understanding of several passages offered here.

1. When Bergþóra declines Flosi Þórðarson's offer of reprieve from the flames at Bergþórshvóll, the saga audience cannot avoid the ironic contrast of her response: "'Ek var ung gefin Njáli, ok hefi ek því heitit honum, at eitt skyldi ganga yfir okkr bæði'" ("I was young when I was given to Njal, and I promised him that we should both share the same fate"), with Signý's determination that, not out of loyalty to her husband but because of what she has done to exact vengeance from him, the only honor left her is to die with him: "'Skal ek nú deyja með Siggeiri konungi lostig, er ek átta hann nauðig'" ("Willingly I shall now die with King Siggeir, although I married him reluctantly").[56]

2. In *Heimskringla*, when Sigurðr Búason cunningly escapes his intended execution after the Battle of Hjörungavógr, he makes himself known with the boastful comment, "'Eigi eru enn allir Jómsvíkingar dauðir'" ("Not all the Jómsvíkings are dead yet").[57] One recalls the triumphantly vengeful, twice-used exclamation, first by Sigmundr as he informs Siggeir who his burners are: "'Hér erum vit Sinfjötli, systursonr minn ... ok ætlum vit nú

---

[56]. Einar Ól. Sveinsson, ed. *Brennu-Njálssaga*, Íslenzk fornrit 12 (Reykjavík: Hið íslenzka fornritafélag, 1954), 330, ch. 129; *CSI* 3:156; *FSN* I: 128, ch. 8. Byock, *Volsungs*, 47.

[57]. Snorri Sturluson, *Ólafs saga Tryggvasonar*, in *Heimskringla*, ed. Bjarni Aðalbjarnarson, 3 vols., Íslenzk fornrit 26–28. (Reykjavík: Hið íslenzka fornritafélag, 1941–51), 285; *Ólafs saga Tryggvasonar*, ch. 41; Snorri Sturluson, *Heimskringla*, trans. Alison Finlay and Anthony Faulkes, 3 vols. (London: Viking Society for Northern Research, 2011), 1:176.

at þat skulir þú vita, at eigi eru allir Völsungar dauðir'" ("Here I am with Sinfjotli, my sister's son, ... and we now want for you to know that not all the Volsungs are dead").[58] And later, Sigurd boastingly announces his intention of visiting vengeance on King Hundingr's sons for the killing of his father: "'vilda ek, at þeir vissi, at Völsungar væri eigi allir dauðir'" ("I want them to know that the Volsungs are not all dead").[59]

3 In *Bjarnar saga Hítdœlakappa* when the *flugumenn* (assassins) return ashamed to Þórðr Kolbeinsson, having failed in their mission to kill Björn Arngeirsson, he closes the scene apophthegmatically with a brief observation: "'Þeir fara í brott, ok þykkir ill orðin ferð sín ok hneisulig, koma svá búnir á Hítarnes. Þórðr kvað sér ekki mǫnnum at nær, þótt þeir væri, ok rak þá á brott'" ("They go away, their adventure seeming to have failed disgracefully, and come in this state to Hitarnes. Thord said that he had no men nearer him though they were at hand, and drove them away").[60] This surface insult to their masculinity is given further weight as the composer of *Bjarnar saga* and his audience implicitly recall Sigmundr's disappointment in the cowardly son of his sister and King Siggeirr, whom she has sent to him as an aid in Vǫlsungr vengeance—"at hann þótti ekki manni at nær, þótt sveinninn væri hjá honum" (that he thought himself no closer to a man, even though the boy was there with him).[61] One could cite many other instances of this intertextual association of the Vǫlsung-Niflung cycle with Old Icelandic literature; a phraseological sensitivity to its narratives can provide a most persuasive basis for examining that presence.

Oath and Integrity: the Inflexible Axis of Faithfulness

Old Icelandic literature, especially in instances where it has been traditionally regarded as evincing and even valorizing the ethical culture of what is termed, so far without clear definition, the Heroic Age, often calls on allusion to events and characters of the Vǫlsung legends as a way of lending nuance to contemporary narrative. In this part of chapter 2 the preoccupation with, and brutal reinforcement

---

58. *FSN* 1:127, ch. 8; Byock, *Volsungs*, 47.
59. *FSN* 1:147, ch. 17; Byock, *Volsungs*, 61.
60. ÍF 3:176, ch. 24; *CSI* 1:287, slightly modified.
61. *FSN* 1:120, ch. 6.

of, the integrity of loyalty recommended in the Eddic corpus is seen to be ironically questioned even as its force is narrated in the later thirteenth-century *Vǫlsunga saga*. Several of the Family Sagas, in particular *Gísla saga Súrssonar*, approach the heroic patterns in the same way, and for that reason a more detailed examination of the old demands of loyalty will be helpful to our understanding of the values in play and their paroemial reinforcement in these narratives.

* * *

Pertinent to this subject, in his *Matter of the North* Torfi Tulinius studies how the composer of *Vǫlsunga saga* rendered the legendary Eddic poems in a fairly coherent prose narrative, finding that the theme of treachery or, more specifically, of trust betrayed emerges to define the meaning of the narrative.[62] He sees two categories of betrayal: that of contractual bonds and that of blood kinship. From this he derives an axis of faithfulness, to blood kinship and ancestral heritage, on the one hand, and to contractual bonds by oaths and by marriage, on the other. Signý is thus torn between the artificial kinship of herself and her family to Siggeirr by her marriage to him, and the trust she owes to her blood kin. Along this axis, she tends to the latter end in an extreme fashion, killing her children by her husband and having a child, Sinfjǫtli, with her brother, Sigmundr, as the only feasible means of providing him tangible assistance in his pursuit of vengeance against her husband for the killing of their father, Vǫlsungr. Inflexible adherence to her primary blood loyalties has led her to infanticide and incest, leaving her no choice but death with her husband:

> Ek lét drepa börn okkur, er mér þóttu of sein til föðurhefnda, ok ek fór í skóg til þín í völulíki, ok er Sinfjötli okkarr sonr. . . . Hefi ek þar til unnit alla hluti, at Siggeirr konungr skyldi bana fá. Hefi ek ok svá mikit til unnit, at fram kæmist hefndin, at mér er með engum kosti líft. Skal ek nú deyja með Siggeiri konungi lostig, er ek átta hann nauðig.

---

62. Torfi Tulinius, *The Matter of the North: The Rise of Literary Fiction in Thirteenth-Century Iceland*, trans. Randi C. Eldevik (Viborg: Odense University Press, 2002), 139–58. See also Manuel Aguirre, "Narrative Composition in *The Saga of the Volsungs*," *Saga-Book* 26 (2002): 5–37. Aguirre's argument, that the composer of *Vǫlsunga saga* wrote with greater attention to the artistic quality of his narrative in a medieval literary milieu than to the complex details of his source, does not yet seem to have found enthusiastic reception, though it is cogently executed.

(I had our children killed who seemed to me too slow in avenging their father, and I came to you in the forest in the shape of a sorceress, and Sinfjotli is our son.... In everything I have worked toward the killing of King Siggeir. I have worked so hard to bring about vengeance that I am by no means fit to live. Willingly I shall die now with King Siggeir, though I married him reluctantly.)[63]

The axis is observed generationally. Tulinius notices how an individual in the first generation is betrayed by those owing contractual loyalty, only to be avenged in each instance in the next generation by a blood relative. Tulinius identifies another axis as that of intention, where wrongdoing may be either deliberate or inadvertent.

These thematic threads clearly have their roots in the legendary poems themselves, although the saga's composer may well have brought focus to aspects of the conflicts useful to his specific purposes. Tulinius argues that he did so as a way of critically examining the ethical and moral dilemmas faced by members of warring factions in the *Sturlungaöld* (age of the Sturlungs), where "individuals must often choose between two loyalties."[64] He observes how the composer of the saga was using stories contained in "poems that thirteenth-century fighting men in Iceland must have been brought up on, for the purpose of showing the absurdity of excessive vengeance and the importance of keeping commitments."[65]

As will be developed further in chapter 3, the heroic poems of the *Elder Edda* represent a legacy of pre-Christian moral wisdom to which the Christianized and politically shifting communities of thirteenth-century Iceland must respond in seeking a way to reduce violence in conflict through compromise and reconciliation that is precluded by those old standards. As the ancient patterns of the Eddic wisdom are echoed in the *Íslendingasögur*, the process occurs in ironically situated episodes and dialogue whose dramatic impact may be critical of both contemporary behavior and of the old heroic values and ethical practices some members of thirteenth-century Icelandic society might use to justify that behavior.

---

63. *FSN* 1:127–28, ch. 8; Byock, *Volsungs*, 47, slightly modified.
64. Tulinius, *Matter*, 156. The *Sturlungaöld* extended roughly from 1220 to 1262 and was a violently chaotic period in Iceland during which powerful families vied with one another for power. The classic study of the period is that of Einar Ól. Sveinsson, *Sturlungaöld: Drög um íslenzka menningu á þrettándu Öld* (Reykjavik: Nokkrir Reykvíkingar,1940). This was translated by Jóhann S. Hannesson as *The Age of the Sturlungs: Icelandic Civilization in the Thirteenth Century*, Islandica 36 (Ithaca, NY: Cornell University Press, 1953).
65. Tulinius, *Matter*, 158.

The Eddic corpus itself is presumably free of such ironic self-criticism, voicing values and ethical standards of an earlier, less flexible, and much less conciliatory world. In surveying the paroemial inventory pertinent to Tulinius's first axis in his study of *Vǫlsunga saga*, we find Sigrdrífa's anticipatory admonition to Sigurd regarding loyalty to relatives: "Þat ræð ek þér it fyrsta / at þú við frændr þína / vammalaust verir; / síðr þú hefnir, / þótt þeir sakar gøri, / þat kveða dauðum duga" (That I advise you firstly, that towards your kin / you should be blameless; / be slow to avenge although they do harm: / that is said to benefit the dead).[66] The Valkyrie figure of Brynhildr has more to say to the hero on the subject of loyalty to oath bonds: "'Þat ræð ek þér annat / at þú eið né sverir, / nema þann er saðr sé; / grimmar limar / ganga at tryggðrofi; / armr er vára vargr'" ("That I advise you secondly, that you do not swear an oath / unless it is truly kept; / terrible fate-bonds attach to the oath-tearer; / wretched is the pledge-criminal").[67] This latter verse actually differentiates itself into three related concepts on the subject of contractual integrity: (1) That it is wise to honor one's oaths; (2) that the ways of fate can be unkind to those who do not; and (3) that an outcast, among whom are numbered the oath breakers, is wretched. As Tulinius observes of *Vǫlsunga saga*, so too the resulting conflicts of torn and betrayed loyalties are thoroughly examined in the Eddic poems from which *Vǫlsunga saga* derives. Sigurd's maternal uncle, Grípir, warns him in *Grípisspá* that he will eventually remember his oaths of loyalty to Brynhildr after he has unintentionally broken them: "Minnir þik eiða, / máttu þegja þó, / anntu Guðrúnu / góðra ráða; / en Brynhildr þykkisk / brúðr, vargefin, / snót fiðr vélar / sér at hefndum" (Though you recall your oaths you'll keep silent, / you want a good marriage for Gudrun / and Brynhild the bride will think herself disparaged, / the lady will use treachery to get her revenge).[68] Brynhildr later comes to complain of Sigurd's flaw in this regard: "'Mér hefir Sigurðr / selda eiða, / eiða selda / alla logna; / þá vélti hann mik / er hann vera skyldi / allra eiða / einn fulltrúi'" ("To me Sigurd gave oaths, / oaths he gave, and all are broken; / thus he deceived me when he should have been / completely trustworthy in every oath").[69]

---

66. ÍF 36, 2:318, st. 23; Larrington, *Poetic Edda*, 166.
67. ÍF 36, 2:318, st. 24; Larrington, *Poetic Edda*, 166; JGF 609; TPMA 2.388. See also TPMA 2.387, citing *Hugsvinnsmál*: "Fyr orðum ok eiðum Hygg ǫllum vel, Halt þín heit við fira" (Pay careful respect to all your words and oaths! Keep your promises to men!)
68. ÍF 36, 2:293–94, st. 45; Larrington, *Poetic Edda*, 145.
69. ÍF 36, 2:324, st. 2; Larrington, *Poetic Edda*, 169.

In a way that is peculiarly typical of figures caught in the narrative web of dramatically celebrated story, where apparently self-contradictory behavior and views are the result of differentiating details emphasized in various sources, she comes to accuse Gunnarr and his brothers of breaking their oaths, and she curses them for the perfidy to which she herself drove them: "'Hugða ek mér, Gunnarr, / grimmt í svefni, / svalt allt í sal, / ættak sæing kalda, / en þú, gramr, riðir / glaums andvani / fjǫtri fatlaðr, / í fjánda lið. / Svá mun ǫll yður / ætt Niflunga, / afli gengin, / eruð eiðrofa!'" ("I thought, Gunnar, that I had a grim dream, / it was chilly in the hall, and my bed was cold; / and you, lord, were riding, bereft of happiness, / with chains you were fettered among a troop of foes. / So from all of you of the Niflung line / your strength will pass away: you are oath-breakers!")[70] Her predictions echo those of Guðrún in *Guðrúnarkviða I*, who, bewailing the loss of her husband—"'sem væri geirlaukr / ór grasi vaxinn / eða væri bjartr steinn / á band dreginn, / jarknasteinn, / yfir ǫðlingum'" ("as if a leek were grown up out of the grass, / or a bright jewel threaded onto a string, / a precious gem, among the nobles")—warns her brother in the following way: "'Svá ér um lýða / landi eyðið / sem ér um unnuð / eiða svarða; / mana þú, Gunnarr, / gulls um njóta; / þeir munu þér baugar / at bana verða, / er þú Sigurði / svarðir eiða'" ("So your people and land will be laid waste, / on your account, for the oaths you swore; / Gunnar, you won't get good of the gold, / the rings will be the death of you, / for you swore oaths to Sigurd").[71]

The weight of legally enforced social judgment for such a deed is emphasized in the cunning practicality of Hǫgni's advice against killing Sigurd: "'Samir eigi okkr / slíkt at vinna, / sverði rofna / svarna eiða, / eiða svarna, / unnar tryggðir'" ("It is not fitting for us two to do this, / cutting asunder with a sword / the oaths we've sworn, the pledges made").[72] As an at least superficial remedy to

---

70. ÍF 36, 2:327, st. 16; Larrington, *Poetic Edda*, 171. For the culturally based explanation of such apparently self-contradictory behavior, see Carol Clover, "Hildigunnr's Lament," in *Structure and Meaning in Old Norse Literature: New Approaches to Textual Analysis and Literary Criticism*, ed. John Lindow, Lars Lönnroth, and Gerd Wolfgang Weber, Viking Collection 3 (Odense: Odense University Press, 1986), 141–83. This chapter was also reprinted in *Cold Counsel. Women in Old Norse Literature and Mythology*, ed. Sarah M. Anderson with Karen Swenson (New York: Routledge, 2002), 15–54.

71. ÍF 36, 2:332, sts. 18 and 21; Larrington, *Poetic Edda*, 174 and 175.

72. ÍF 36, 2:338, st. 17; Larrington, *Poetic Edda*, 179.

their contractual conflict, he advises using their younger brother, Guttormr, who is unhindered by oath ties, for the killing: "Vit skulum Guthorm / gørva at vígi, / . . . hann var fyr útan / eiða svarna, / eiða svarna, / unnar tryggðir" ("We should prepare Guthorm for the killing, / . . . he wasn't involved when the oaths were sworn, / when the oaths were sworn and the pledges made").[73] This same overriding importance of adhering to the letter as opposed to the spirit of an oath is left among the most significant features of Sigurd's conduct when, dying from Guttormr's attack, he protests to Guðrún: "'þyrmða ek sifjum, / svǫrnum eiðum, / síðr værak heitinn / hans kvánar vinr'" ("I violated neither kinship nor oaths, / so I ought not to be called his wife's lover").[74]

* * *

Tulinius's two axes of betrayal delineate with clarity the dimensions of the ethical demands of the pre-Christian world from which later medieval Icelandic society had evolved. Such is the stringent spirit of the Eddic sources of *Vǫlsunga saga*, with its harsh imposition of ideals, to which its composer, as a son of the Sturlungaöld, could not have been sympathetic. He would have felt equal distaste for the inflexible heroic integrity of Gísli Súrsson that leads to the destruction of the family whose honor he would protect, as well as for the aggressively unrelenting demands of Hildigunnr in *Njáls saga*, cold of counsel, that Flosi avenge with blood the death of her husband.[75] And if he had lived to read the version of *Grettis saga* that is extant for us, he would have disapproved of both the heroic ideals that seem satirized in Grettir Ásmundarson's exaggerated deeds and rhetoric and the hero's destructively—and proverbially—celebrated, stubborn reluctance to let go of anything, whether a grievance or a physical object representing it.[76] Those old ideals had

---

73. ÍF 36, 2:339, st. 20; Larrington, *Poetic Edda*, 180.
74. ÍF 36, 2:340, st. 28; Larrington, *Poetic Edda*, 181.
75. Vésteinn Ólason adopts a sympathetic view of Gísli's idealism in "Gísli Súrsson—A Flawless or Flawed Hero?" in *Die Aktualität der Saga. Festschrift für Hans Schottmann*, ed. Stig Toftgaard Andersen (Berlin: de Gruyter, 1999),163–75. He does this in response to Andersson's own more persuasive piece. See Theodore M. Andersson, "Some Ambiguities in *Gísli saga*: A Balance Sheet," in *Bibliography of Old Norse-Icelandic Studies 1968* (Copenhagen: Munksgaard, 1969) 7–42. For more recent coverage of the problem, see Theodore M. Andersson, *The Growth of the Medieval Icelandic Sagas (1180–1280)* (Ithaca, NY: Cornell University Press, 2006), 82–84.
76. See the discussion of Grettir's character in chapter 5, below.

served well once, but in the new age of Christian ethics and radically modernizing government, they were no longer enough.

Women and Their Paroemial Identity in the Vǫlsung-Niflung Cycle

Much has been written in recent decades about the position of women in medieval Germanic culture as well as the presentation of their character in the Old Icelandic sagas. There is little a volume such as this one could add to the discussion, but the issue of how the female figure takes its shape in the Norse Vǫlsung-Niflung complex and in the Eddic corpus is nevertheless of obvious interest to our study of proverbs and provides for a discussion of the background and significance of the place of women in *Vǫlsunga saga* and in the *Íslendingasögur*.

Skǫrungr mikill: The Woman of Unbending Character

The women of the latter narratives are admired, most notably, for their strength of character, in the first place, and for the determined imposition of their will, in the second. Njáll's wife, Bergþóra, who is surely among the most admirable women in that saga, is described as "kvenskǫrungr mikill ok drengr góðr ok nǫkkut skaphǫrð" (an outstanding woman and a fine person, but a bit tough-minded).[77] And Hildigunnr, despite her uncle's harsh words of her when she demands blood vengeance for her husband, is presented by the saga's composer with terms that are partly similar to those used for Bergþóra: "skǫrungr mikill ok kvenna fríðust sýnum . . . alla kvenna grimmust ok skaphǫrðust ok drengr mikill, þar sem vel skyldi vera" (a strong-minded woman and very beautiful . . . an unusually tough and harsh-tempered woman, but a fine woman when she had to be).[78] In *Laxdœla saga*, among the progenitors of the narrative's leading clan, we find Unnr in djúðúðga Ketilsdóttir, whose remarkable demonstrations of courage and initiative inspire the composer's observation: "má af því marka, at hon var mikit afbragð annarra kvenna" (It shows what an outstanding woman

---

77. ÍF 12:57, ch. 20; *CSI* 3:25.
78. ÍF 12:238–39, ch. 95; *CSI* 3:115.

Unn was).⁷⁹ Such brief summations of character as these, flattering the particular features of courage and determination that they do, attest to recognition in the saga world of the constant need for women's robust expression of concern where significant matters of the family are to be dealt with.

However, societal agreement regarding appropriate limits on female powers and their reputed range of abilities has, again, been the subject of much consideration, and a relatively succinct observation by Rannveig on her daughter-in-law, Hallgerðr, proves illuminating. The latter first alludes to her plans for a feud by proxy with Bergþóra as a means of gaining compensation for perceived humiliation at her hands: "Rannveig heyrði, móðir Gunnars, ok mælti: 'Þó hafa húsfreyjur verit hér góðar, þótt ekki hafi staðit í mannráðum'" (Rannveig, Gunnar's mother, overheard this and spoke: "There have been good housewives here, even though they have not taken part in manslaughter").⁸⁰

Analyses of Hallgerðr's flawed character often touch on her intrusion into areas of aggression or undue manipulation of feud processes in ways epitomized by the focus of Rannveig's disapproval. She herself comments with ironic proverbial force on her overly assertive agenda when she answers Gunnarr's suspicious query regarding the origins of some dairy products she had Melkólfr steal from Otkell of Kirkjubœr: "'Þaðan, sem þú mátt vel eta,' segir hon, 'enda er þat ekki karla at annask um matreiðu'" ("From such a place that you can well enjoy eating it," she said. "And besides, it's not for men to worry about preparing food!").⁸¹ In proclaiming, with paroemial phrasing, her adherence to women's chores lying beyond Gunnarr's responsibility, she is in fact boasting ironically of her active and persistently destructive interference in the world of men.

Readers interested in the origins of these saga-world expectations of the woman's support of her family's honor might think it useful

---

79. Einar Ól. Sveinsson, ed., *Laxdæla saga*, Íslenzk fornrit 5 (Reykjavík: Hið íslenzka fornritafélag, 1934), 7, ch. 4; *CSI* 5:3.
80. ÍF 12: 93, ch. 36; *CSI* 3:41.
81. ÍF 12:124, ch. 48; *CSI* 3:57. A note in the Fornrit edition adds that "Hér er bætt við í ÁM 163 D, fol. o.fl. pappírshdrr: '*því víða koma Hallgerði bitlingar*; er þetta alkunnar málsháttur (sjá Jonas Rugmans *Samling av isländska talesätt*, utg. av G. Kallstenius, bls. 34, 92 og tilvísanir þar)." This is an interesting, very early example of how proverbial material that is derived from saga texts makes its way into modern Icelandic culture. See chapter 9, below. See also FJ 208; JGF 52.

to review the observations of Tacitus, however accurate or well researched they were, on the support of women in men's battles:

> Close at hand, too, are their dearest, whence is heard the wailing voice of woman and the child's cry: here are the witnesses who are in each man's eyes most precious; here the praise he covets most: they take their wounds to mother and wife, who do not shrink from counting the hurts or demanding a sight of them: they minister to the combatants food and exhortation. Tradition relates that some lost or losing battles have been restored by the women, by the incessance of their prayers and by opposing their breast; for so is it brought home to the men that captivity, which they dread much more intolerably on their women's account, is close at hand.[82]

Tacitus also includes a note, which is almost too brief, on differentiated gender-based behavioral expectations for postbattle funeral rites: "Weeping and wailing they put away quickly: sorrow and sadness linger. Lamentation becomes women: men must remember."[83]

The uncompromising spirit in which heroic female figures of the sagas encourage and support family honor seems quite consonant with the responsibilities of the gender to which Tacitus presumably refers in commenting on the world of Germanic people, far from medieval Iceland in time and geographical as well as cultural distance though that world may be. The techniques of whetting developed in the narratives of the *Íslendingasögur* could well be envisaged as stemming ultimately from the female encouragement to battle that Tacitus describes. His finely noticed, near-formulaic observation, that men remember while women bewail the dead, leads us to recall Carol Clover's discussion of the twofold nature of traditional Indo-European lament patterns in which the remembrance of the former was no doubt anticipatory of eventual aggressive retributive action encouraged by the latter.[84]

---

82. Tacitus, *Germania*, trans. M. Hutton, rev. H. E. Warmington, Loeb Classical Library 35 (Cambridge, MA: Harvard University Press, 1914, rev. ed., 1970), 143.

83. Tacitus, *Germania*, 171; Margaret Alexiou, *The Ritual Lament in Greek Tradition*, rev. ed. (Cambridge: Cambridge University Press, 2002); Velma Bourgeois Richmond, *Laments for the Dead in Medieval Narrative* (Pittsburgh: Duquesne University Press, 1966).

84. Clover, "Lament." Perhaps it is only coincidental, though interesting to contemplate, that after the two young cousins, Sigmundr and Þórir, observe the killings of their respective fathers, Brestir and Beinir, in *Færeyinga saga*, the way in which Sigmundr

Hildigunnr's dramatic whetting of Flosi to take vengeance for the killing of her husband is composed of two elements native to lament traditions extending far back into cultures much earlier than hers. Lamentation for the dead, the fairly universal province of women in Western culture, consisted thematically of expressions of grief over the departed, together with demands for vengeance on the part of surviving male relatives. In performing their duty of bewailing the dead, then, women reminded men of their duty to remember and to take retributive action. So powerful was the impact of this ritualized tradition that the custom came to be actively proscribed as excessive in some continental cultures, beginning with an attempt by Solon in the sixth century BC.[85] The church found it a heathen custom and similarly discouraged its practice. Clover argues that "the laughing-crying figure that haunts Edda and saga in female form ('laughing' in revenge, 'crying' in death-grief)" derives from this lamentation pattern and that it is strikingly illustrated in *Sigurðarkviða in meiri*: "Þǫgðu allir / við því orði, / fár kunni þeim / fljóða látum, / er hon grátandi / gørðisk at segja / þat er hlæjandi / hǫlða beiddi" (All were silent at these words, / no one could understand the behaviour of women, / now she, weeping, began to speak of / that which, laughing, she'd asked the men for).[86] The results and narrative interpretations in Old Icelandic literature of what Clover terms this "organic (con)fusion" of themes are reflected in the paroemial texts pertaining to women and their nature in the Eddic corpus and its echoes in saga narrative.[87]

The stereotypically negative response of saga warriors, who are hesitant or reluctant to engage in violence, to whetting by their women has come under some scrutiny in recent critical studies.[88] Old Norse paroemial sentiment regarding the destructive influence of women's speech, where it pertains to honor and its

---

admonishes Þórir for crying. "Sveinarnir sátu á klettinum og sá upp á þessi tíðendi, ok grét Þórir, en Sigmundr mælti: 'Grátum eigi, frændi, en munum lengr'" (The boys sat on the crag and looked on at these doings and Thorir cried, but Sigmund said, "Do not cry, cousin, but remember all the longer"). *Færeyinga saga*, in *Færeyinga saga. Óláfs saga Tryggvasonar eptir Odd munk Snorrason*, ed. Ólafur Halldórsson. Íslenzk fornrit 25. (Reykjavík: Hið íslenzka fornritafélag, 2006), 17–18, ch. 7; *The Faroe Islanders' Saga*, trans. George Johnston ([Ottawa]: Oberon, 1975), 30.

85. Clover, "Lament," 164.
86. Clover, "Lament," 162, and ÍF 36, 2:327, st. 15; Larrington, *Poetic Edda*, 1/1.
87. Clover, "Lament," 180.
88. For discussion, see Jenny Jochens, "Male Reaction to Whetting," in *Old Norse Images of Women* (Philadelphia: University of Pennsylvania Press, 1996), 195–98.

maintenance, likely grows out of the whetting scene and related episodes that are descriptive or illustrative of those female social responsibilities observed so much earlier by Tacitus.

For example, in *Vǫlsunga saga*, in a conversation further pursuing the dispute of the queens in the Rhine River over the relative status of their respective husbands and Guðrún's revelation to Brynhildr regarding the conspiracy by which her marriage to Gunnarr was engineered, Brynhildr admonishes her competitor: "'Leggjum niðr ónýtt hjal'" ("Let us stop this useless chatter").[89] The reader of *Gísla saga*, one of those sagas whose conflicts and phraseology come most noticeably under the intertextual influence of the Vǫlsung-Niflung cycle, is reminded of this suggestion when Auðr halts a similarly revelatory encounter with Ásgerðr by her paroemially enforced observation: "'Opt stendr illt af kvennahjali, ok má þat vera, at hér hljótisk af í verra lagi, ok leitum okkr ráðs'" ("Women's gossip often leads to trouble, and here it may turn out to be the worst kind of trouble. We must seek counsel").[90]

Several such references to the dangers of women's talk are also found in the southern corpus of the Sigurd legend. Bewailing Kriemhild's death among the Huns—which is just one among many other tragic moments in the narrative—the author of *Div Chlage* complains, "daz leit vnd daz vngemach. / het geprvuet [v with a caret above] ir selber munt. / nv vvart ir sterben mit in chvnt. / di gerne vværen noch genesen." (The words from her own mouth had given rise to the sorrow and misery. Now it also became her lot to die along with those who would have gladly survived.)[91] Referring more directly to the original conflict, he asks, near the end of his poem, "Vvaz denne ob dvrch ir zorn. / di frovven beide vvol geborn. / gezvrnden in ir tvmpheit. / daz solde man hin han geleit. / vnde solde in han genesen lan." (So what if the two noblewomen railed at each other in such a silly, senseless way? Their quarrel should have been put aside and Siegfried allowed to live.)[92]

---

89. *FSN* 1:181, ch. 28; Byock, *Volsungs*, 84, for the masculine role in these transactions.

90. Björn K. Þórólfsson and Guðni Jónsson, eds., *Gísla saga Súrssonar*, in *Vestfirðinga sögur*, ed. Íslenzk fornrit 6 (Reykjavík: Hið íslenzka fornritafélag, 1943), 31, ch. 9; *CSI* 2:10; *JGF* 319; *TPMA* 3.373.

91. Winder McConnell, trans. *The Lament of the Nibelungen (Div Chlage)* (Columbia, SC: Camden House, 1994), 26, lines 510-13; translation on 27.

92. Ibid., 192, lines 4051-55; translation on 193.

In *The Nibelungenlied* such sentiments take a humorous turn when, after Guenther excuses Siegfried from his oath of innocence, and the latter immediately blames Kriemhild for causing the trouble: "geniuzet es mîn wîp, / daz si hât ertrüebet den Prünhilde lîp, / daz ist mir sicherlîchen âne mâze leit'" ("If my wife were to go unpunished for having distressed Brunhild I should be extremely sorry"). At this point, the two knights exchange meaningful glances. Siegfried then responds: "'Man sol sô vrouwen ziehen, . . . daz si üppeclîche sprüche lâzen under wegen. / verbiut ez dînem wîbe, der mînen tuon ich sam.'" ("Women should be trained to avoid irresponsible chatter . . . Forbid your wife to indulge in it, and I shall do the same with mine.")[93] Thus the two men blame the dispute on the quarrelsome nature of the women, avoiding altogether the real deception that brought it about.

Thesaurus Proverbiorum Medii Aevi contains more than one hundred pages of proverb citations under the category "Frau." There is a wide array of medieval wisdom on this topic, much of it of an uncomplimentary nature, but the subject dealt with here, the value of women's speech, is essential to our understanding not only of the Sigurd legend but also of its echoing passages in the *Íslendingasögur*.[94] The opinions expressed in the Middle High German sources, as well as in the Old Icelandic sagas, regarding the disruptive influence of women's conversations can be attributed, at least in part, to the traditional discussion of oral support of male responsibilities for the physical maintenance of honor, which was clearly among their duties both in early Germanic society and in preceding European cultures.

* * *

Here, as elsewhere in this volume, it will be apparent that my present interests in the proverbial inventory of the Old Icelandic cultural base extend only occasionally beyond the Scandinavian world, rarely even beyond the shores of Iceland itself. This neglect

---

93. Helmut de Boor, ed. and trans., *Das Nibelungenlied. Zweisprachig* (Cologne: Parkland Verlag, 2004), 276, Âv. 14, sts. 861, lines 1b-3 and 862, lines 1-3; Arthur Thomas Hatto, *The Nibelungenlied* (London: Penguin Books, 1969), 116.

94. *TPMA* 3.328-455. For women in Icelandic proverbs more generally, see Gisela Spiess, "Die Stellung der Frau in den Sprichwörtern isländischer Sprichwörtersammlungen und in isländischen Sagas," *Proverbium: Yearbook of International Saga Scholarship* 8 (1991): 159-78.

of the rich continental traditions of wisdom formulas, while obviously serving the economy of this present volume, is primarily the result of the directions intended for discussion here. Although a relatively learned composership and parts of its audience are by now a given in thirteenth-century Iceland, it is my assumption that much of the paroemial content used in saga narratives comes, like the stories themselves generally, from the "oral family saga" of which Theodore M. Andersson and Carol Clover have written. A survey of the paroemial inventory of the *riddarasögur* and other translated materials of Old Norse-Icelandic literature could be a welcome and illuminating addition to this discipline.[95]

In whatever ways the content of the sagas may have come to the written page, it did so with the hands of those who grew up in a contemporary Icelandic society that was largely still preliterate, and it was this legacy, not of monastic learning and its continental sources but of stories and their telling by ordinary Icelanders with good memories, that formed the absolute core of the narratives we study here. Imbued though they very likely were with patterns of biblical form and the occasional rhetoric of learned ecclesiastical style, the *Íslendingasögur* were themselves of native origin. Our concern here, too, is primarily with how the communally shared paroemial legacy was used by composers of the sagas to indicate the purposes of their narratives. Rarely would this search for proverbially enhanced textual meaning benefit from extension beyond the shores of Iceland itself, even though such undertakings would be of obvious interest and use for readers taking other paroemiological approaches to the Old Icelandic corpus.

A Proverbial Coldness of Counsel . . .

Further to this study of the paroemially reinforced character of women in the sagas, we will examine a single proverb regarding their nature and how that proverb is variously situated and used in saga narrative.

The proverb "(opt) eru kǫld kvenna ráð" ([often] the counsel of

---

95. The term *riddarasögur* applies to a group of translations of continental romances first undertaken in Norway in the thirteenth century. It also refers to indigenous Icelandic narratives composed on similar subjects. A common courtly setting distinguishes these sagas of knights from other genres.

women is cold) is not found in the extant verse or prose texts of the Vǫlsung-Niflung cycle, and yet it occurs in the two *Íslendingasögur* whose content is most clearly influenced by that background. Eddic attestation of the proverb's early existence in Norse tradition is in *Vǫlundarkviða*, which some date to the ninth century, and its inclusion in Låle's *Östnordiska och Latinska Medeltidsordspråk* indicates its continued and widespread currency in later stages of Nordic culture.[96] Its use in the *Íslendingasögur* at two crucially dramatic moments, in *Gísla saga* and in *Njáls saga* respectively, and the uncomplimentary view of women's plans or advice to which it apparently subscribes in these passages, have rendered it a popular subject among some saga critics, particularly in recent times.[97]

Gísla saga

The text of *Gísla saga* that is traditionally used and recognized as most authentic is that of AM 556 a 4to, from the later fifteenth century; it contains all three of the Old Icelandic outlaw sagas. It is generally referred to as the M-text, although the Íslenzk fornrit edition calls it E. A longer version, typically thought to have been written earlier and copied from a parchment sent to Denmark in 1662, exists in two paper copies; it has in the last decades come to

---

96. JGF 459; *TPMA* 9.198; Peter Låle, "Forndanska och latinska ordspråk: Peder Låles samling efter 1506 års upplaga med avvikande läsarter ur upplagorna av 1508 och 1515," in *Ostnordiska och Latinska Medeltidsordspråk: Peder Låles ordspråk och en motsvarande svensk samling*, ed. Axel Kock and Carl af Petersens, Samfund til udgivelse af gammel nordisk litteratur 20/⁴ (Copenhagen: Berlingska boktryckeri-och Stiljuteri-Aktiebolaget, 1889–94), 20/², 20, item 153, and "Fornsvenska och latinska ordspråk," 153, item 140.
97. Eduard Kolb, "d. Ein Sprichwort," in *Alemannisch-nordgermanisches Wortgut*, Beiträge zur schweizerdeutsche Mundartforschung, vol. 6 (Frauenfeld: Huber, 1956), 21–22, provides thorough bibliographical coverage of earlier work on this proverb. Later studies include Carol Clover, "Cold are the Counsels of Women: The Tradition Behind the Tradition," in *The Sixth International Saga Conference, 28.7–28.8 1985: Workshop papers I-II*, 1:151–75, ed. Jonna Louis-Jensen, Christopher Sanders, and Peter Springborg (Copenhagen: Det arnamagnæanske Institut, 1985); Sarah M. Anderson, "Introduction: 'og eru köld kvenna ráð,'" in *Counsel*, ed. Anderson, xii–xiii; Else Mundal, "Kǫld eru kvenna ráð," in *Kvinner og Bøker: Festskrift til Ellisiv Steen på hennes 70-årsdag 4. Februar 1978*, ed. Edvard Beyer (Oslo: Gyldendal, 1978) 183–93; Þórður Ingi Guðjónsson, "'Köld eru kvenna ráð': Um gamlan orðskvið," in *Brageyra léð Kristjáni Eiríkssyni, sextugum, 19. Nóvember 2005*, ed. Guðvarður Már Gunnlaugsson, Margrét Eggertsdóttir, and Þórunn Sigurðardóttir (Reykjavík: Menningar- og minningarsjóður Mette Magnussen, 2005), 115–19.

be regarded by some scholars as the better one.[98] The two texts are most at variance in the first eleven chapters, and the story seems more understandable in the longer version at some points, although this of course does not in itself mean it is the better text from a critical, editorial point of view.

In the passage of primary critical concern here, Þórdís the sister of Gísli the Outlaw tells her husband Bǫrkr and her other brother Þorkell how she has deciphered a verse Gísli uttered in which he cryptically boasted of killing her husband Þorgrímr: "'Ok ætla ek, . . . at þú þurfir eigi annan veg eptir at leita um víg Þorgríms, ok munu rétt búin málin honum á hendr.'" ("And I think . . . that you need not look elsewhere concerning Thorgrim's slaying. And a case would rightly be brought against him.") Bǫrkr, her new husband and the brother of the previous one, the victim in question, is enraged: "'Nú vil ek þegar aptr snúa ok drepa Gísla'" ("Now I want to turn back and kill Gísli").[99] What follows is surely the most tantalizing paroemiological conundrum in Old Icelandic literature, the passage in which three different manuscripts of the saga place the target proverb respectively in the mouths of the three different people present at the scene of revelation:

1. "'En þó veit ek eigi'" ("On the other hand, I can't be sure"), Bǫrkr continues in the shorter version, in AM 556 a 4to: "'hvat satt er í þessu, er Þórdís segir, ok þykki mér hitt eigi ólíkara, at engu gegni, ok eru opt kǫld kvenna ráð.'" ("How much truth there is in what Thordis says. And it seems to me not more unlikely that there's none. Women's counsel is often cold.")[100]
2. Now, AM 445 c 4to, containing fragmentary portions of the saga, close to the M-text, instead puts the proverb in the mouth

---

98. For earlier coverage of the different texts, see Carol J. Clover and John Lindow, eds., *Old Norse-Icelandic Literature: A Critical Guide*, Islandica 45 (Ithaca, NY: Cornell University Press, 1985), 247–49. For detailed studies, see Emily Lethbridge, "*Gísla saga Súrssonar*: Textual Variation, Editorial Constructions and Critical Interpretations," in *Creating the Medieval Saga: Versions, Variability and Editorial Interpretations of Old Norse Saga Literature*, ed. Judy Quinn and Emily Lethbridge (Odense: University Press of Southern Denmark, 2010), 123–34; Emily Lethbridge, "Dating the Sagas and *Gísla saga Súrssonar*," in *Dating the Sagas: Reviews and Revisions*, ed. Else Mundal (Copenhagen: Museum Tusculanum Press, University of Copenhagen, 2013), 77–105.

99. ÍF 6:61, ch. 19. For a very interesting and useful discussion of this passage, see Emily Lethbridge, "Who Says What in *Gísla saga Súrssonar*? Speaker Attribution in the Three Versions of the Saga," *Quaestio Insularis* 5 (2004): 42–61.

100. ÍF 6:61n3, ch. 19.

Paroemial Patterns of the Mythic and the Legendary Backgrounds 73

of Þorkell, brother of Þórdís and Gísli. A dear friend of Þórdís's first husband Þorgrímr, the man whom Gísli has killed, Þorkell is thus obviously troubled over his conflicting loyalties. Here, when Bǫrkr insists on returning for an immediate kill, Þorkell disagrees: "'ok veit ek enn ekki hvat satt er í þessu, er Þórdís segir, ok þykki mér hitt eigi ólíkara, at engu gegni'" ("On the other hand, I can't be sure how much truth there is in what Thordis says. It's just as likely that there's none"), he muses, "'ok eru opt kǫld kvenna ráð'" ("And women's counsel is often cold").[101] Immediately afterward, he adopts a pretext of needing to see a friend as a means of extricating himself from Þórdís and Bǫrkr and instead rides off to Hól and warns Gísli about his sister's revelation of his guilt. His objection and its proverbial support are thus well suited to the occasion where he forestalls the action and warns his brother of danger. Bǫrkr, on the other hand, enraged but then immediately doubting, without any logical motivation, his wife's accusation of her own brother—obviously a difficult step for her—experiences a most unlikely development in his psychology. As the editors of the Íslenzk fornrit edition notice about the reading in 445 c 4to, with Þorkell as speaker of the proverb, it is "Auðsjáanlega réttara en í" (obviously more correct than in) the primary M-text.[102]

3. The only other choice is that Þórdís says it—and it is not unheard of for women in the sagas to speak of themselves proverbially in demeaning terms, although when they do, it is with ironic implications. This variant is found in the longer version, the S-text, where, perhaps rethinking the consequences of her accusation, she counters the rage of Bǫrkr by saying she would not agree to a swift return and kill: "'Ok veit ek enn eigi hvort þetta er satt eðr ekki, ... ok eru jafnan kǫld kvenna ráð'" ("And I don't know whether that is true or not ... and the counsels of women are always cold").[103] Although there is better contextual motivation

---

101. ÍF 6:61, ch. 19.
102. ÍF 6:61n3.
103. ÍF 6:61n3. There are several passages in the Íslendingasögur where women speak disparagingly of their kind, although there they do so in ironic contexts. See *Njáls saga*, where Hallgerðr comments ironically on a woman's job, as remarked above, when Gunnarr questions the source of the cheese, which was stolen by her design: ÍF 12:124, ch. 48: "'enda er þat ekki karla at annask um matreiðu'" (*CSI* 3:57: "And besides, it's not for men to worry about preparing food"). See also Einar Ól. Sveinsson, ed., *Þorsteins þáttr stangarhöggs in Austfirðingar sǫgur*, , Íslenzk fornrit 11 (Reykjavík: Hið íslenzka

for this passage than for the version in which Bǫrkr considers the coldness of women's counsel, it could also be merely a lengthy scribal rationalization of a more difficult reading. Making the utterance Þorkell's, though, and therefore favoring the M-text, seems most plausible in light of his subsequent action in warning Gísli, and of his continued conflict over loyalties to kinship and friendship through the rest of his life in this narrative.

Regardless of who was originally meant to utter the phrase in the text of *Gísla saga*, although its specific nuances of application may vary from one speaker to another, the broader interpretation is the same: saga women plan or advise action in ways that prove destructive for those in association with them. In this they show marked similarity to the female figures of the Vǫlsung-Niflung cycle. In fact, saga composers use phraseological signals to draw the attention of the audience to that earlier Germanic background.

Njáls saga

In *Njáls saga*, which was probably composed some decades after *Gísla*, the proverb is used in a powerful episode, equal in its intensity to scenes involving Brynhildr and Guðrún in the Eddic material of the Vǫlsungs. Here Hildigunnr uses traditional rhetoric and feud ritual to put pressure on her uncle, Flosi Þórðarson, to take blood vengeance for the killing of her husband, Hǫskuldr Þráinsson the hvítanesgoði, by the sons of Njáll. She takes the cloak, a gift of Flosi, in which her husband was killed and which is covered with his dried blood, and throws it over her uncle, so the clots of blood rattle down on him: "'Skýt ek því til guðs ok góðra manna, at ek sœri þik fyrir alla krapta Krists þíns ok fyrir manndóm ok karlmennsku þína, at þú hefnir allra sára þeira, er hann hafði á sér dauðum, eða heit hvers manns níðingr ella'" ("In the name of God and all good men I charge you, by all the wonders of your Christ and by your courage and manliness, to avenge all the wounds which he received in dying—or else suffer the contempt of all men").[104] This and the

---

fornritafélag, 1950), 71: "'Satt er þat, er oss er opt sagt konum, at þar er lítit til vits at taka, sem vér erum konur'" (*CSI* 4:336: "It's true, as we're often reminded, that we women aren't very smart").

104. ÍF 12:291, ch. 116; *CSI* 3:137, slightly modified.

cloak force him into action, but not without complaint: "'Þú ert it mesta forað ok vildir, at vér tœkim þat upp, er ǫllum oss gegnir verst, ok eru kǫld kvenna ráð'" ("You are a monster and want us to take the course which will be worst for us all—cold are the counsels of women").[105]

It is not unusual for men to complain of women's whetting in the sagas, as we noticed above, and people forced on errands they know will come to no good end express similar reluctance over their assignments, sometimes in exaggerated terms, though often enough in understated ones. It is the view of Sarah M. Anderson and her colleagues that the defense of Icelandic women's right to give "cold counsel" tends to rest in saga criticism on the assumption that these saga women, who are responsible for egging men on to vengeance in the interests of maintaining family honor, "are engaging in one of the few speech acts represented by the literature as open to them, and they are speaking on behalf of the customs of their society—not in monstrous aberration from them."[106] The proverb applied by male speakers to Hildigunnr in *Njáls saga* and to Þórdís in *Gísla* has negative implications—on the one hand attempting to discredit the information provided by Þórdís Súrsdóttir about her brother's culpability for the killing of Þorgrímr goði, and on the other hand emphasizing the harshness of Hildigunnr's character in rhetorically forcing Flosi to go for blood vengeance.

It seems more productive, however, to view both these episodes in the terms discussed by Torfi Tulinius. The harsh and inflexible adherence of both women's speeches to pre-Christian standards of honor, indeed Hildigunnr's explicit challenge not only to Flosi's own manhood but also to the power of his Christ, reveals the purposes of the Christian composers. What were once obligatory traditions of maintaining family honor and the order of a society dependent on the customs of feud have now become objects of ironic commentary. The two episodes and the accompanying proverb both speak of heroic times to be admired nostalgically from a Christian distance, but not to be emulated in contemporary society. In this respect, it is interesting that at the end of the saga, Hildigunnr marries one of her husband's killers, a man who has for the last hundred pages been her uncle's archenemy.

---

105. ÍF 12:291–92, ch. 116; *CSI* 3:137.
106. Anderson, "Introduction," xii–xiii.

Readers might well question whether women's lamentation and whetting were actually a significant motivational factor in the feud conflicts of the *Sturlungaöld* and whether such scenes in the *Íslendingasögur* likewise fell under the opprobrium of the saga composer as behavioral remnants of violent, old, pre-Christian ways. Such speculation is rendered more complex by a layer of criticism that views apparently negative representations of women in the sagas as resulting from medieval Christian teaching, or, in this particular instance, from a misogynistic tendency to blame women as instigators of men's violence.

There is, furthermore, critical debate over the extent to which the *samtíðarsögur* can be regarded as accurately depicting characters and events in thirteenth-century Iceland—that is to say, the narrative shaping of historical events by the composers of these works is currently under examination.[107] David Clark, who finds several instances of female whetting or inciting in these sagas, also observes examples of women who act as mediators and try to keep the peace.[108] The *Íslendingasögur*, too, it should be noticed, have a number of pacifying female characters, and surely composers of those works were as approving of such efforts as writers of contemporary events would have been.[109] While misogynistic views may have influenced or inspired the figure of the female inciter in both genres, the impulse to violence, whatever the gender of its source,

---

107. The term *samtíðarsögur* refers to the sagas of bishops as well as the compilation known as *Sturlunga saga*. The figure of the *Hetzerin*, or female whetter, generally familiar to saga readers, was the subject of detailed study in Rolf Heller. See Rolf Heller, *Die literarische Darstellung der Frau in den Isländersagas*, SAGA: Untersuchungen zur nordischen Literatur- und Sprachgeschichte 2 (Halle an der Saale: Max Niemeyer, 1958), 98–122. The historicity of this function is considered by, among others, Jenny Jochens, "The Medieval Icelandic Heroine: Fact or Fiction?" in *Sagas of the Icelanders: A Book of Essays*, ed. John Tucker (New York: Garland, 1989), 99–126. See also Jenny Jochens, "The Female Inciter in the Kings' Sagas," *Arkiv för nordisk filologi* 102 (1987): 100–19. For a recent and very useful summarization and commentary, see David Clark, "Manslaughter and Misogyny: Women and Revenge in *Sturlunga saga*," in *Gender, Violence, and the Past in Edda and Saga* (Oxford: Oxford University Press, 2012), 142–63.

108. Clark, "Manslaughter and Misogyny," 158–61.

109. The woman of peaceful intentions, celebrated in the Old English formulaic term *freoðuwebbe* ("peace-weaver"), functions by marriage as a pacific influence between in-law nations but also as a royal adviser who urges reconciliation and resolution of conflict. An unlikely example of this ameliorating influence is seen in *Laxdœla saga*, chapter 19, where Jǫrunn, whose temper is not always restrained, persuades her husband Hǫskuldr not to attack and kill his half-brother Hrútr, with whom he has been feuding over inheritance issues.

seems from the point of view recommended by Tulinius to be an object of disapproval in the Christian setting of saga writers in the thirteenth century.

The point of such episodes as those cited above in *Gísla saga* and in *Njáls saga* is perhaps further illuminated by the audience's awareness of other instances where the proverb was used in the Old Icelandic corpus. In *Vǫlundarkviða*, the first extant text spoken by Níðuðr to his queen refers to the damage she caused by having the sinews of the talented Vǫlundr cut so he could not leave the island where he crafted treasures for the royal family. In retaliation Vǫlundr made cups and jewelry from Níðuðr's sons' heads and impregnated Bǫðvildr, the only daughter of Níðuðr and his wife. Níðuðr has reason to complain over the results of his wife's aggressive approach to labor management in that ancient legendary world of early Germania, and those who use the proverb in the *Íslendingasögur* must, like the contemporary audience, be aware of this old story—in which the queen's advice had tragically destructive results.

Meanwhile, beyond the shores of medieval Iceland, the coldness of women's counsels is attested as the subject of at least occasional comment. The mid-twelfth century *Proverbs of Alfred* mentions an unspecified Latin source for such wisdom: "For this is said in lede: 'Cold red is quene red.'"[110] And Chaucer, in "The Nonne's Priest's Tale," laments the naivety of Chaunticleer, "a cok ... that tok his conseil of his wyf, with sorwe ... Wommennes conseils been ful ofte colde; / Wommennes conseil broghte us first to wo / And made Adam fro Paradys to go, / Ther as he was ful myrie and wel at ese."[111] And then he assures his audience that it was only "in game" that he "blamed" the "conseil of women," although he does not inform us, nor is there evidence elsewhere in Middle English, about the context of proverbial tradition in which to situate his critical comment.[112] *TPMA* also notices several instances of comment in Middle High

---

110. Alois Brandl and O. Zippel, eds., "The Proverbs of Alfred," in *Mittelenglische Sprach- und Literaturproben: Ersatz für Mätzners Altenglische Sprachproben: Mit etymologischem Wörterbuch zugleich für Chaucer* (Berlin: Weidmann, 1917), 305, section 25.

111. Geoffrey Chaucer, "The Nonne's Priest's Tale," *Canterbury Tales*, line 3253, lines 3256–59. Quotations are from *The Riverside Chaucer*, ed. Larry Benson, 3rd ed. (Oxford: Oxford University Press, 1987).

112. Chaucer, *Canterbury Tales*, "Nonne's Priest's Tale," lines 3261–64.

German on the uselessness or "coldness," whatever that means in the context, of women's counsel.[113] There is also a citation from a medieval French work, so clearly the kernel of this proverb, advising caution over the "coldness"—the cruelty, the destructiveness, or perhaps originally the destructive uselessness—of women's advice, which existed elsewhere in Europe in the Middle Ages, in cultures less obsessed with the clearly defined responsibilities of men and women in a feud-based society such as that of Iceland. What such proverbial observations really meant, and whence they were derived, remain to be examined.[114]

It is tempting to try to form a conceptual progression in the occurrences of the proverb in Old Icelandic from that interpretation of "coldness" as "uselessness" that seems current also on the Continent to the perverse cruelty of Hildigunnr. Thus, the earliest attested text, in Vǫlundarkviða, has Níðuðr blame his queen for advice that is not overly cruel in itself but that leads inadvertently to brutally destructive consequences. In the case of Gísla saga, in the mouths of any of the three possible speakers, the main intent would be that Þórdís's accusation of her brother was based on her use of inadequate evidence, and thus potentially wrong and chaotically destructive. The vindictive rage and cruel demands of Hildigunnr in the somewhat later text of Njáls saga could then be viewed as representing a new and different emphasis on the value of the proverb. Unfortunately for this theory, in the Old Icelandic Hómilíubók, which dates from around 1200, in the homily on Saint John the Baptist, Herod comments, when his wife Herodias has their daughter demand the head of Saint John on a platter, "Kom það þar fram, sem mjög oft þykir verða, að köld eru kvenna ráð" (It came about, as very often seems to happen, that the counsels of women are cold).[115] Cruelty rather than destructive uselessness could certainly be seen as the drift of the proverb's meaning here, thus discouraging the temptation to find a narrowed progression of meaning in the Icelandic corpus.

*   *   *

---

113. *TPMA* 9.198, 296–99.
114. See above, chapter 1, for Neal Norrick's conception of a proverb's kernel.
115. Sigurbjörn Einarsson, Guðrún Kvaran, and Gunnlaugur Ingólfsson, eds., "Nativitas sancti Johannis baptiste," in *Íslensk Hómilíubók: Fornar stólræður* (Reykjavík: Hið íslenska bókmenntafélag, 1993), 17. Translation mine.

The proverb investigated in this section deserves more detailed and judicious attention than it has so far received in print. Its negative implications regarding the character of women seem still only vaguely explained, and our understanding, at least, of several medieval texts might be enhanced by such an undertaking.

The Alienation of the Wolves

The figure of the wolf in the phraseology of Old Icelandic literature is of course purely mythical or legendary in origin, wolves never having lived in the country and perhaps having been prohibited from import by the codes of *Grágás*.[116] The wolf is nonetheless familiar as a figurative term in several of the sagas, and especially in *Vǫlsunga saga*, where it derives from the continental legacy of the Vǫlsung-Niflung Cycle.

* * *

As a mythical threat, Fenrir, the wolf child of Loki, remains bound by Tyr's trick, awaiting freedom at Ragnarǫk, when he will swallow the sun and devour Óðinn himself. The latter feat seems to be celebrated on the eleventh-century Thorwald's Cross on the Isle of Man, and the modern proverb "Enginn gleypir sólina" (No one swallows the sun), which alludes to the hubris of undertaking a task beyond one's capabilities, may recall the former.[117] Besides an episode of shapeshifting, in which Sigurd and Sinfjǫtli take on the skins and identities of wolves, the legendary material contains only figurative,

---

116. Vilhjálmur Finsen, ed., *Grágás: Islændernes Lovbog i fristatens tid*, 2 vols. (Copenhagen: Brødrenes Berlings Bogtrykkeri, 1852), 2:189; Andrew Dennis, Peter Foote, and Richard Perkins, trans., *The Laws of Early Iceland: Grágás: The Codex Regius of Grágás with Material from other Manuscripts*, 2 vols. (Winnipeg: University of Manitoba Press, 1980), 2:204. For lupine terms designating outlawry see Mary R. Gerstein, "Germanic Warg: the Outlaw as Werewolf," in *Myth in Indo-European Antiquity*, ed. Gerald James Larson, C. Scott Littleton, and Jan Puhvel (Berkeley: University of California Press, 1974), 131–56. See also Donald Ward, "The Wolf: Proverbial Ambivalence," *Proverbium: Yearbook of International Saga Scholarship* 4 (1987): 211–24. On werewolves in Iceland, see the very interesting article by Aðalheiður Guðmundsdóttir, "The Werewolf in Medieval Icelandic Literature," *Journal of English and Germanic Philology* 106 (2007): 277–303. This article is based on a chapter in her edition of *Úlfhams saga* (Reykjavík: Stofnun Árna Magnússonar, 2001).

117. *Edda Snorra Sturlusonar: Nafnaþulur og skáldatal*, ed. Guðni Jónsson (Akureyri: Íslendingasagnaútgáfan, 1954), 1; Bjarni Vilhjálmsson, *Málshættir*, 304, from Sigfús Blöndal, *Íslenzk-dönsk orðabók* (Reykjavík: Verslun Þórarins B. Þorlákssonar, 1920–24), 773a: "ingen sluger Solen, ɔ: ingen faar det uopnaaelige"; JGF 530.

perhaps metaphorical references to these beasts: lupine, isolated humans threatening the well-being of society with destruction and especially with vengeance. Viewed as inimical to humans and human society, the image of the wolf appears in paroemial circumstances as the hostile outsider.[118]

Legendary Manifestations of the Wolf

In these limited circumstances, the wolf is a familiar figure of proverbial imagery only in the north Germanic versions of the Sigurd legend, although in the rest of medieval European literature it is fairly common and it occurs with less conceptual specialization everywhere (*TPMA* records thirty-five pages of pertinent texts, one of the longer articles in that compilation).[119] In the single instance of this usage in the Southern legendary tradition, Lord Else comments proverbially, near the end of *Div Chlage*, as the Burgundian survivors of the visit to the Huns make their way home, "'nv ist min rache an in geshæhen. /alse daz alte sprichwort sprichet. / svven der vvolf richet. / der ist errochen also vvol. / daz manz niht fürbaz rechen sol. / sprach der margrave riche'" ("Now I have had my revenge on them, just as the old saying goes: Whoever the wolf avenges has certainly been well avenged, so much so that one ought not to seek vengeance further.")[120] This is the only wolfish text from the south German tradition of the Vǫlsung-Niflung narrative. While it is similar in tone to counterparts in the North, the proverb's occurrence in several other Middle High German texts suggests that it belongs to traditions ouside the cycle itself.

Sigrdrífa advises Sigurd, in her anticipatory session with him, as follows: "'at þú trúir aldri / várum vargdropa, / hvártstu ert bróður bani / eða hafir þú felldan fǫður; / úlfr er í ungum syni, / þó hann sé gulli gladdr'" ("that you never trust / the oaths of a wrongdoer's brat, / whether you are his brother's slayer / or you felled the father; / the wolf is in the young son, / though he may be gladdened by gold").[121] "'Látum son fara / feðr í sinni'" ("Let's send the son the same way as the father"), she says in her persona

---

118. The variant term, *vargr*, is used in the Old Icelandic legal terminology of outlawry.
119. *TPMA* 13.160–95.
120. McConnell, *Chlage*, 166, lines 3516–19, translation 167; *TPMA* 9.174.
121. ÍF 36, 2:320, st. 36; Larrington, *Poetic Edda*, 167; JGF 594; *TPMA* 13.181. Although the treatment of proverbs in the sagas in this volume concentrates on the culture

as Brynhild, speaking to Gunnar of Sigurd's son in *Sigurðarkviða in skamma*; "'skalat úlf ala / ungan lengi'" ("Don't nurture for long the young wolf").[122] The imagery of the wolf and its association with treachery are used to emphasize as paramount the feud obligation of the son to take vengeance for his father's death. It is impossible to let him live, let alone trust him, and her advice is recorded also in *Vǫlsunga saga*.

There too, as in *Fafnismál*, one of the birds warns Sigurd of Reginn's intentions after the hero has killed Fáfnir—in a sense, whatever else his motives may involve, Reginn is obligated to seek vengeance for the deed he incited: "'Bróður minn hefir þú drepit'" ("You have killed my brother"), he observes, "'ok varla má ek þessa verks saklauss vera'" ("but I am hardly blameless in this deed"). Shortly afterward, he repetitiously adds, "'Þú drapt minn bróður, ok varla má ek þessa verks saklauss'" ("You have killed my brother and I can hardly be considered blameless in this deed").[123] Advising Sigurd to take the initiative and dispatch Reginn before the latter can take action himself, one of the birds calls on the same imagery as it comments: "'þar er mér úlfs vón, / er ek eyru sék.'" ("I expect a wolf when I see his ears").[124]

In *Vǫlsunga saga*, where it is Atli who plots the deaths of the Burgundians with his invitation, Guðrún tries to warn them with a cryptic message whose import, which is distorted by the messenger, is nevertheless suspected by Hogni: "'þat undrumst ek, er ek sá gersimar þær, er Atli konungr sendi okkr, at ek sá vargshári knýtt í einn gullhring'" ("When I looked at the treasures King Atli had sent us, I wondered at the wolf's hair I saw tied around a gold ring"). He goes on to say, "'ok má vera, at Guðrúnu þykki hann úlfshug við okkr hafa ok vili hún eigi, at vit farim'" ("It may be Guðrún thinks [Atli] has the thoughts of a wolf toward us, and that she does not want us to go").[125] Here the symbolic force of the wolf's hair indicates the treachery at the heart of the invitation to the land of the Huns.

---

of the Germanic North and its immediate witnesses, reminders of the much wider studies that could be made occur frequently.

122. ÍF 36, 2:337, st. 12; Larrington, *Poetic Edda*, 178; *TPMA* 13.181. The advice, not surprisingly, is not specifically Germanic. Aristotle, in the *Rhetoric*, twice quotes from the epic cycle of *Cypria*, by Stasinus: "Foolish is he who, having killed the father, suffers the children to live" (1.15 and 2. 21).

123. FSN 1:154-55, ch. 19; Byock, *Volsungs*, 65.

124. ÍF 36, 2:310, st. 35; Larrington, *Poetic Edda*, 159; JGF 594-95; *TPMA* 13.174.

125. FSN 1:200, ch. 33; Byock, *Volsungs*, 97; JGF 593; *TPMA* 13.191.

The Figurative Wolves of *Laxdœla saga*

Laxdœla saga, of all the *Íslendingasögur*, was most heavily influenced by the Sigurd legend, and it employs a proverb from *Reginsmál* where Reginn observes Sigurd's heroic potential with the comment, "'er mér fangs vón / at frekum úlfi'" ("I expect winnings from a ravening wolf").[126] Jǫrunn uses it as she persuades her husband Hǫskuldr of the inadvisability of his hostile proceedings with his brother over the latter's claim to some property: "'Nú þœtti oss hitt ráðligra, at þú byðir Hrúti, bróður þínum, sœmiliga, því at þar er fangs ván af frekum úlfi; vænti ek þess, at Hrútr taki því vel ok líkliga, því at mér er maðr sagðr vitr; mun hann þat sjá kunna, at þetta er hvárstveggja ykkar sómi.'" ("Now it seems to me it would be a better plan for you that you make your brother Hrútr an honorable offer, for a hard battle can be expected from a hungry wolf. I expect Hrútr will accept that well and gladly, for I am told he is wise. He will see that this is to the honor of you both.")[127]

When Óláfr pá (Peacock) is disappointed in his father's first attempt to arrange his marriage with Þorgerðr Egilsdóttir, he exclaims angrily, "'Nú er, sem ek sagða þér, faðir, at mér myndi illa líka, ef ek fenga nǫkkur svívirðingarorð at móti; réttu meir, er þetta var upp borit; nú skal ek ok því ráða, at eigi skal hér niðr falla; er þat ok satt, at sagt er, at úlfar eta annars ørendi; skal nú ok ganga þegar til búðar Egils.'" ("Now it is as I told you father, that I would be angry if I got dishonor from your meeting. You advised me that the matter should be raised. Now I shall manage it so that the deal doesn't fall through. And it is truly said, that wolves eat the errands of others. Now we will go immediately to Egil's booth.")[128] In the northern Sigurd stories these proverbs only occur in or are spoken by characters from the Otherworld, the place of primitive forces and unrestrained violence, rather than among the Burgundians. Whether this is so because of the respectively distinct origins of their texts or because of authorial intentions would be an interesting subject of investigation.[129]

---

126. ÍF 36, 2:299, st. 13; Larrington, *Poetic Edda*, 150; JGF 132–33; TPMA 13.165.
127. ÍF 5:47–48, ch. 19.
128. ÍF 5:64, ch. 23; JGF 594; TPMA 13.188.
129. Joyce Tally Lionarons, "The Otherworld and its Inhabitants in the *Nibelungenlied*," in *A Companion to the Nibelungenlied*, ed. Winder McConnell (Columbia, SC: Camden House, 1998), 153–71.

Paroemial Patterns of the Mythic and the Legendary Backgrounds 83

* * *

Although this chapter dealt with passages in which there are proverbs or clear allusions to communal wisdom articulated elsewhere in the *Íslendingasögur* with paroemial texts pertinent to the events and characters of the Vǫlsung-Niflung cycle, the study of proverbs in the sagas can be treated as part of a much broader field in need of careful consideration. In the literary-critical category of microstructural studies, it might be productive to consider more generally similar phraseological strings than the relatively fixed texts of proverbs themselves.

As an example, in *Vǫlsunga saga*, Hjǫrdís's unintentional revelation of her status lies in her awareness that her gold ring is cold just before daybreak: "'Faðir minn gaf mér eitt gull lítit við náttúru. Þat kólnar í óttu á fingri mér. Þat er mitt mark hér um'" ("My father gave me a small gold ring with this characteristic: Just before daybreak it becomes cold on my finger. That is how I know.").[130] In Äventiure 31 of the *Nibelungenlied*, Volker the Fiddler says, "'Mir kuolent sô die ringe, . . . , / jâ wæne diu naht uns welle nu niht wern mêr. / ich kiusez von dem lufte, / ez ist vil schiere tac.'" ("My chain-mail has grown so cool on me . . . that I fancy the night cannot last much longer. I sense from the breeze that it will soon be daylight.")[131] Without attaching any farfetched and isolated interpretive significance to this coincidence, one might nevertheless notice how interesting its existence is.

On his reluctant way to visit the Huns at the invitation of Etzel, Hagen is warned in the following way by Eckewart: "'Doch riuwet mich vil sêre zen Hiunen iuwer vart. / ir sluoget Sîfrîden: man ist iu hie gehaz. / daz ir iuch wol behüetet, in triuwen rât' ich iu daz.'" ("I much regret your visit to Hungary, for you killed Siegfried, and people hate you here. I advise you in all sincerity—be on your guard!")[132] And Dietrich warns Hagen similarly again, a few lines later: "'Sol leben diu vrouwe Kriemhilt, noch mac schade ergên . . . trôst der Nibelunge, dâ vor behúete du dich.'" ("as long as lady Kriemhild lives, harm can still be done. Be on your guard, protector of the Nibelungs!")[133] A person familiar with the

---

130. *FSN* 1:139, ch. 12; Byock, *Volsungs*, 55.
131. *Nibelungenlied*, 564, Âv. 31, st. 1849, lines 1–3; Hatto, *Nibelungenlied*, 230.
132. *Nibelungenlied*, 500, Âv. 26, st. 1635, lines 1–4; Hatto, *Nibelungenlied*, 204.
133. *Nibelungenlied*, 528, Âv. 28, st. 1724; Hatto, *Nibelungenlied*, 215.

Middle High German poem could be reminded of these scenes, however coincidentally, when, in chapter 12 of *Gísla saga*, Vésteinn, making his fateful way toward Dyrafjörðr, is warned thrice by characters, aware of the hostility awaiting him in Haukadalr, to be on his guard. First Lúta, a relative of Vésteinn's at Gemlufall, says to him, "'Vésteinn, . . . vertu varr um þik; þurfa muntu þess'" ("Vestein, . . . be on your guard. You will have good need"). And next, Þorvaldr gneisti, at Þingeyri, informs him, "'Margt hefir skipazk í Haukadal, . . . ok vertu varr um þik'" ("Much has changed in Haukadal, . . . Be on your guard").[134] And finally Geirmundr, when Vésteinn reaches Haukadalr, exclaims: "'Kom þú ekki hér á Sæból ok far til Gísla ok ver varr um þik'" ("Don't stop here at Saebol. Go on to Gisli's. And be on your guard").[135]

The extent to which the echoes of the Vǫlsung-Niflung cycle reverberate through the scenes of the *Íslendingasögur* and the mythic-heroic background of the society that created them can never be fully defined, but it is reasonable to presume that more innovative phraseological studies of texts such as these could eventually prove helpful in the attempt to do so.

---

134. ÍF 6:40, ch. 12; *CSI* 2:13.
135. Ibid.

CHAPTER 3

Paroemial Strategies, Apophthegmatic Scenes, and the Heroic Ideal in *Gísla saga*

This chapter, along with chapters 4 and 5, examines ways in which the saga composers employ proverbial material to indicate or emphasize the artistic or ideological purpose of their narratives. For paroemiological investigation, objectives and methods vary depending on assumptions about whether a proverb in a text derives fairly directly from a narrative's presumed oral background or whether it is deliberately situated by the artistry of the composer. In this and later chapters, proverbial texts are interpreted according to theories of saga composition and the narrative context of the sagas in which they occur. Thus, the following study of *Gísla saga Súrssonar* is primarily concerned with the use of proverbial sentences at the closures of dramatic scenes as a technique for signaling the point of such episodes. And in chapter 4 an examination of *Njáls saga* will demonstrate how thematic signaling is accomplished through the use of particular proverbs on more than one occasion at crucial points in the text. Finally, in chapter 5 we will consider how the composer of *Grettis saga* used proverbs to convey to the saga audience those facets of the hero's character that led to his tragic demise.

Gísla saga Súrssonar, generally thought to be among the earlier sagas, is nonetheless often regarded as the most carefully and artistically composed of its kind. This complexity suggests that it was put together in a cultural milieu where techniques of literate narrative were already familiar.[1] While noticing that such elegance "militates against a very early date" for its origin, Theodore M. Andersson

---

1. See above, chapter 2, for a discussion of the manuscript tradition of *Gísla saga*.

remarks that it shares "a focus on a single individual and a strong predilection for recording skaldic verse" with earlier sagas.[2] Its carefully controlled and symmetrically balanced scenes evoke W. P. Ker's vision of saga narrative as a "a series of pictures rising in the mind, succeeding, displacing and correcting one another."[3] This structure is most plausibly attributed to the skills of a highly literate composer. However, some features of *Gísla saga* may, purposely or not, also reflect the style of oral narrative preceding its written form.

In this saga it can be seen how themes and the significance of events are developed by means of aphoristically charged conclusions to truncated, or apophthegmatic, scenes. This narrative technique of the apophthegmatic scene is best understood in the context of critical theories arising from Andersson's neo-Freeprosaist initiative.

Critical Reception, Orality, and Literary Composition

The sagas were written soon after Iceland's preliterate age came to an end, when the oral traditions of that culture must still have been very much alive in people's social interactions. It is not surprising that various styles of narration have been observed in these works, some of a learned and ecclesiastical bent, where others offer patterns we might more readily expect from oral traditions.[4]

Critical reception of the sagas has always been linked to shifting views about (1) the extent to which the texts bear testimony to oral sagas as opposed to sagas arising from a complex and sophisticated literary movement in thirteenth-century Iceland; and (2) the manner and extent to which these narratives were drawn from that preliterate tradition to the written page. To these debates scholars have brought evidence from the most conservatively reliable sources, such as manuscript traditions, the internal witness of texts, the presence of *lausavísur* (single verses, not forming part of a longer poem) in texts, and the possible relationship of those verses to their surrounding prose. In the 1960s and 1970s some critics adopted a radical shift in the theory of saga composition with a novel restatement

---

2. Andersson, *Growth*, 78.
3. W. P. Ker, *Epic and Romance: Essay on Medieval Literature* (London: Macmillan, 1908), 237.
4. Jónas Kristjánsson, "Learned Style or Saga Style?" in *Speculum Norrœnum: Norse Studies in Memory of Gabriel Turville-Petre*, ed. Ursula Dronke (Odense: Odense University Press, 1981), 260–92.

of the free prose theory, which had fallen out of favor earlier in the century at a time when book prose theory was more popular. They based their new interpretation on more recent observations about the practice of oral traditions in contemporary cultures.

Leading this undertaking, Theodore M. Andersson reopened and restated questions left behind with the gradual literary critical submergence of the free prose theory of saga composition in mid-twentieth-century thinking.[5] In his exhaustive 1966 study, "The Textual Evidence for an Oral Family Saga," he examined and evaluated a large number of formulaic phrases drawn from the *Íslendingasögur* and sought evidence to support an oral background for the genre. He thus established the feasibility of a critical discussion of what he termed the "oral family saga."[6] Even less conservatively, critics such as Jesse Byock and William Ian Miller have used the anthropological study of distant feud cultures to understand the structuring of sagas primarily as narratives of such conflicts, presumably the stuff of preliterate entertainment in these societies, and thus likely an oral repository of legal experience and wisdom.[7] This last approach contributes immeasurably to our understanding of the *Íslendingasögur*.

Apophthegmatic Scenes and Proverbial Affirmations of the Heroic Ideal

In 1974, Carol J. Clover commented on the "return to traditionalism in saga studies" that had been effected by this strategy, and she attributed its energy in part to the recent work of folklore formalists on the nature of traditional oral narrative. These formalists produced a compositional theory that recognized several structural units in the sagas' generally

---

5. See Theodore M. Andersson, *The Problem of Icelandic Saga Origins: A Historical Survey* (New Haven: Yale University Press, 1964), which includes the most detailed study of critical traditions preceding the shift of the 1960s. For the original identification and discussion of these two points of view, see Andreas Heusler, *Die Anfänge der isländischen Saga*, Abhandlungen der königlichen preussischen Akademie der Wissenschaften, philosophische-historische Klasse, no. 9 (Berlin: Verlag der königlichen Akademie der Wissenschaften, Georg Reimer, 1914).

6. Theodore M. Andersson, "The Textual Evidence for an Oral Family Saga," *Arkiv för Nordisk Filologi* 81 (1966): 1–23.

7. Jesse Byock, *Feud in the Icelandic Saga* (Berkeley: University of California Press, 1982); William Ian Miller, *Bloodtaking and Peacemaking: Feud, Law, and Society in Saga Iceland* (Chicago: University of Chicago Press, 1990).

episodic narrative, "the most common [being] ... a kind of miniature, visual drama which most commentators call a scene."[8]

The saga scenes critically envisaged by the movement in which Clover participated are the smallest of the narrative units; they are tripartite in form, having (1) a preface, (2) a dramatic exchange or an encounter, and (3) a conclusion. The preface and conclusion are similar in that both are given to telling rather than to showing the story, to narration rather than to dramatic exchange or encounter, and to a form that is to some extent predictably patterned.[9] Thus, the preface sets the scene and conditions of the action with attendant formulas to identify persons, time, place, and situation. And the conclusion leaves the action at a point of rest, or more often of temporary rest, making way for the initiation of a succeeding but not necessarily directly related scene. Conclusions, like prefaces, are of rather fixed, standard types with generally unsurprising formulas. As Clover puts it, while "scenic narration is clearly the saga man's *modus operandi*, and the tripartite scene is clearly a normative image," variations on the anticipated structure or its execution do occur.[10] Scenes may be long or short, explosive or reflective, varying with the composer's conscious, intentional narrative flow. Such variations are part of the artistic refinement in both an oral setting and a literary one.

The Point of the Sagas

Another aspect of Andersson's reading of the sagas in this period involved his rather innovative concern with what the saga composers were writing about. As he first took up this problem, he observed that "to [his] knowledge no one has asked what the point of a saga is."[11] Although the prior consensus may have been that sagas

---

8. Carol Clover, "Scene in Saga Composition," *Arkiv för Nordisk Filologi* 89 (1974): 57-58. See also Carol Clover, *The Medieval Saga* (Ithaca, NY: Cornell University Press, 1982), 180–82.
9. Clover, "Scene," 61.
10. Clover, "Scene," 81.
11. Theodore M. Andersson, "The Displacement of the Heroic Ideal in the Family Sagas," *Speculum* 45 (1970): 576. Here Andersson cites his own previous summary of the status quo when he had observed that "there is no guiding principle laid down by the author in order to give his material a specific import. He draws no general conclusions and invites his reader to draw none. In this sense the saga is not interpretable." See Theodore M. Andersson, *The Icelandic Family Saga: An Analytic Reading* (Cambridge, MA: Harvard University Press, 1967), 32. See also Lönnroth, "Persuasion," 157–89.

did not have a point, Maarten Cornelius van den Toorn had argued fifteen years earlier that sagas were indeed written with a meaningful purpose. Pertinent to our discussion here, he had defined the "moral" as a term "we will set apart for the clearly recognizable intention which an author incorporates in his work in order to edify his readers or hearers."[12] For several decades, readers tried to answer Andersson's question from various critical perspectives. They sought help from the saga texts and from external evidence with situational value to their interpretation. In this context, Clover studied how the structuring of a scene could be used by a composer to indicate its narrative purpose.

Scenic Structure and Meaning

Of potential paroemiological interest in this regard is a structural variation producing what Clover calls the apophthegmatic scene. She borrows this term from the language of biblical formalism developed by Rudolf Bultmann in his *History of the Synoptic Tradition*.[13] In this type of scene, the conclusion is missing and the narrative ends on a spoken line of an apophthegmatic nature. Such scenes "mark a structural departure from the norm," and their closing quotations are often "the weighty and 'significant' phrases which resonate through the work."[14] Like proverbs in the sagas more generally, these concluding phrases are typically placed in the mouths of grander figures in the stories. The speakers of proverbs, and more specifically of sententious conclusions to apophthegmatic scenes, tend to be people whom the audience is inclined to trust and whose thoughts should be taken seriously. Paroemial utterances by antagonistic figures, however, typically challenge or attempt to subvert the status quo in some sense. Such material, whether spoken by admired or antagonistic characters, can thus be of essential use in our search for the meaning of a saga.

To judge by the assumptions and conclusions of Bultmann's form criticism, it seems likely that there were also scenes of an apophthegmatic

---

12. Maarten Cornelius van den Toorn, *Ethics and Moral in Icelandic Saga Literature* (Assen: Van Gorcum, 1955), 1.

13. Clover, "Scene," 64; Rudolf Bultmann, *History of the Synoptic Tradition*, trans. J. Marsh (Oxford: Basil Blackwell, 1963). See also Rudolf Bultmann, "The Study of the Synoptic Gospels," in *Form Criticism: Two Essays on New Testament Research*, trans. Frederick C. Grant (Chicago: Willet, Clark & Company, 1934; New York: Harper Torch Books, 1962), 7–76. Bultmann's critical approach was intended to discover the meaning of a biblical text through an analysis of its form.

14. Clover, "Scene," 64.

nature in the oral backgrounds of the Icelandic sagas. In these scenes, actions, speech, and the concluding pithy saying were all focused on that saying's suggestion of a narrative theme, or of dramatic import. The scene and its apophthegmatic ending could embody mutual mnemonic reinforcement.[15] In addition, the structure of such scenes would have had considerable dramatic narrative impact. A skillful composer might use them to emphasize or to clarify the point of his saga, its narrative intentions, and its moral theme—that is, what the story was really about. It will be seen below how the structure of these scenes in *Gísla saga* is artistically determined for narrative impact as well as for signaling the thematic direction of the narrative. This scenic structure may reflect methods of entertainment used prior to the coming of literacy. The apophthegmatic scene is used in this work more fully and consciously than anywhere else in saga literature.

Two Introductory Examples of the Narrative Theme of *Gísla saga*

The composer of *Gísla saga* employs a dramatic truncation of scene twice in his Norwegian prelude, where the saga's intrafamilial conflicts over honor and related themes are introduced.[16] The example concludes the unsuccessful efforts of Gísli and his father, Þorbjǫrn súrr, to halt by peaceful means the seductive visits of Bárðr of Súrnadal to his sister Þórdís. This threat to family honor is one to which they seem more sensitive than Gísli's sister and their brother Þorkell, who is on friendly terms with her suitor. When the aging Þorbjǫrn, representing the conservative heroic traditions of early Iceland, opines that if their older brother Ari were home things would go differently, Bárðr jeeringly, "kvað ómæt ómaga orð,—'ók mun ek fara sem áðr'" (said the words of weaklings were powerless— "and I shall continue as before"), using a proverb to make his point.[17] Defying

---

15. Gregori Lvovich Permyakov, *From Proverb to Folktale: Notes on the General Theory of Cliché*, Studies in Oriental Folklore and Mythology (Moscow: Nauka, 1979); Pack Carnes, ed., *Proverbia in Fabula: Essays on the Relationship of the Fable and the Proverb*, Sprichwörterforschung 10 (Bern: Peter Lang, 1988).

16. Andersson, "Ambiguities," 7–42. A continental device similar to the Norwegian prelude is discussed by William W. Ryding, *Structure in Medieval Narrative*, De Proprietatibus litterarum, series maior 12 (The Hague: Mouton, 1971). Speaking of the tendency of medieval romance writers to compose their stories in two parts, he comments: "As a matter of fact, many of the important narratives of the twelfth century show this bipartite form" (116). While the respective plots of these two parts may not be obviously related to each other, a conceptual connection between them can be observed. See also Clover, *Saga*, "Compound Structure," 42–54.

17. ÍF 6:7, ch. 2; JGF 430; TPMA 13.236.

or simply ignoring the heroic code, Bárðr asserts his determination to continue this objectionable behavior, which damages the traditionally conceived honor of Þórdís and therewith her family. In this first apophthegmatic closure of the saga, the values of the tragic hero and his father are discounted and the antagonist assumes they have no power to enforce them.

The subsequent scene in which Gísli kills Bárðr also concludes abruptly. Instead of using an apophthegmatic phrase, however, it ends with one narrative sentence. At the end of his dialogue with his brother Þorkell, who is in grief and shock over the killing of his friend, he makes what seems a terribly tactless offer of the sword he used for the deed: "ok skiptu vit sverðum, ok haf þú þat, sem betr bítr" (We'll swap swords, . . . then you'll have the one that bites better).[18] Instead of accepting the exchange of swords, Þorkell separates himself from his family for the first time and goes to stay with a close relative of Bárðr, Hólmgǫngu-Skeggi, whom he urges to take revenge. Gísli's abrupt and gratingly jocular offer of the sword cannot be seen as a serious attempt to mollify his brother but as a gloating challenge patterned in the old heroic style after he kills Þorkell's friend. Together, the endings of these two scenes emphatically mark the brutally unrestrained exercise of power that the saga later examines as a concomitant of the heroic ideal the protagonist claims to support.

The Apophthegmatic Scene and the Fate of Gísli the Outlaw

The apophthegmatic scenes in the succeeding early chapters of *Gísla saga* serve mainly to focus audience attention on the adverse influences of fate on the outlaw hero and his family. In chapter 6, the clairvoyant character Gestr Oddleifsson predicts that the proud family members Gísli—his brother Þorkell, their brother-in-law Þorgrímr goði Þorsteinsson, and Gísli's brother-in-law Vésteinn— will fall out within three years. Gísli attempts to overcome the prophetic utterance by suggesting that they take an oath of blood brotherhood. The ceremony proves a failure. At the close of the scene, Gísli tells Þorkell: "Nú fór sem mik grunaði, ok mun þetta fyrir ekki koma, sem nú er at gǫrt; get ek ok, at auðna ráði nú um þetta." (Now it went as I suspected, and this will come to nothing

---

18. ÍF 6:8, ch. 2.

which has now taken place. I expect that fate will take its course now about this.)[19] This apophthegmatic closing of the scene constitutes the first of Gísli's repeated declarations of his resignation to fate.

The covert hostility between in-laws and between Gísli and his brother obliquely referred to here comes to a head when a conversation between Gísli's wife Auðr and his brother Þorkell's wife Ásgerðr is overheard by Þorkell. It reveals Ásgerðr's vaguely defined marital infidelity with Vésteinn, Auðr's brother, and it arouses the eavesdropper's lethal anger. He announces his wrathful presence with the narrative ritual of a threatening verse. Auðr proverbially observes that "Opt stendr illt af kvennahjali" (Women's gossip often leads to trouble), and she discusses with Ásgerðr how they might avert the disaster that must otherwise result from Þorkell's furtive discoveries.

The characters of the two women are differentiated in the contrasting nature of their respective reactions. Auðr's absolute integrity of behavior leads to Gísli's further paroemial affirmation of the inevitability of fate's workings. Ásgerðr speaks confidently when Auðr asks how she will deal with her husband: "Leggja upp hendr um háls Þorkatli, er vit komum í rekkju, ok mun hann þetta fyrirgefa mér, ok segja þá lygi" (I'll put my arms around Thorkel's neck when we go to bed and say it's a lie. Then he'll forgive me).[20] But confronted subsequently in a bedroom scene by Þorkell over his discovery that she is unfaithful emotionally, if not necessarily physically, she is forced by his initial hostility into offering him one of two choices:

> Sá er annarr, at þú tak við mér ok lát sem ekki sé í orðit. Ella mun ek nefna mér vátta nú þegar ok segja skilit við þik, ok mun ek láta fǫður minn heimta mund minn ok heiman fylgu, ok mun sá kostr, at þú hafir aldri hvíluþrǫng af mér síðan."

> (One is that you take me in and act as if nothing has happened. Otherwise I will call witnesses at once and say I divorce you, and I will have my father reclaim my bride-price and my dowry. Then in that case, you will never have my bed company again.)[21]

---

19. ÍF 6:24, ch. 6; JGF 14: "Auðna ræðr lífi," cited in *Orkneyinga saga* and *Hrólfs saga kraka*. Not found in *TPMA*.
20. ÍF 6:31, ch. 9; *CSI* 2:10, slightly modified; JGF 319; *TPMA* 3.373.
21. ÍF 6:33, ch. 9.

Auðr's solution, however, is put into effect: "Segja Gísla bónda mínum allt þat, er ek á vant at rœða eða af at ráða" (Tell my husband, Gisli, everything I have left unsaid as well as all that to which I cannot find a solution).[22] When she accordingly tells Gísli what has happened, he concludes the scene using two proverbs linked to the inevitability of what is fated:

> Eigi sé ek hér ráð til," sagði hann, "þat sem duga mun. En þó mun ek ekki kunna þik um þetta, því at mæla verðr einnhverrr skapanna málum, ok þat mun fram koma, sem auðit verðr.

("I see no plan that will work," he said, "but I shall not be angry with you for this, for Fate must find someone to speak through. Whatever is meant to happen will happen.")[23]

Fate figures large in the succeeding pages as the composer moves his narrative toward the first violent results of *kvennahjal* (women's chatter). As tensions build, Þorkell, who has done little in the meantime but brood on his wife's affair with Vésteinn, moves with Ásgerðr to his friend Þorgrímr's neighboring farm at Sæból, just as he had previously left his family for the enemy's camp when Gísli killed Barðr. Gísli, anticipating and attempting to avert the polarization of feeling between his household and Þorgrímr's that will result from Þorkell's move, tries to dissuade him from leaving. "Saman er brœðra eign bezt at líta ok at sjá" (What brothers own jointly is best seen together), he observes proverbially, but his efforts are fruitless.[24] The immediate effects of Þorkell's departure are minimized, further devaluing his character. Never having been helpful anyway, and by now clearly a negative presence at Hóll, Þorkell does not damage his brother Gísli's interests by leaving. The composer abruptly concludes this scene with the terse observation that Gísli felt the farm "saknar engis í, at nú sé búit verra en áðr" (had lost nothing that made the situation worse than before).[25] Þorkell's presence had become at least passively hostile, and his departure, practically speaking, brought about no damage to the labor force.

---

22. ÍF 6:32, ch. 9; *CSI* 2:10.
23. ÍF 6:33–34, ch. 9; *CSI* 2:10, slightly modified; JGF 387; *TPMA* 4.401. The second proverb is not in *TPMA*, but see JGF 14 for close variants.
24. ÍF 6:34, ch. 10; *CSI* 2:11; JGF 111; *TPMA* 2.130.
25. ÍF 6:36, ch. 10.

Soon afterward, at the Winter Nights' festival, Auðr tells Gísli her one desire—namely, that her brother Vésteinn, who they think is abroad, should also be there to celebrate with them: "Annan veg er mér þetta gefit, því at ek vilda gjarna gefa til, at hann kœmi hér nú eigi.' Ok fellr þetta þeira tal þar niðr." ("That's not how I feel," ... "I would gladly pay a great deal for him not to come here now." And this ended their conversation.)[26] The composer uses Gísli's words at the closing of this scene to imply that the presence of Vésteinn at Hóll would lead to his drastic harm, as indeed proves to be the case.

When news arrives that his friend is nevertheless coming to Haukadalr, Gísli immediately takes action and sends messengers to warn him not to proceed, but to no avail. Their meeting with him is fatefully delayed, and the composer contrives a typically heroic passage for Vésteinn's response to their efforts when they belatedly reach him with Gísli's warning: "nú falla vǫtn ǫll til Dýrafjarðar, ok mun ek þangat ríða, enda em ek þess fúss." (now all waters flow towards Dyrafjord and that is where I shall ride. Besides, I want to.) When Gísli learns of this, he concludes the scene apophthegmatically with a another proverbially phrased reference to fate's inexorable power: "Svá verðr nú at vera" (Then this is the way it has to be).[27]

Vésteinn, characterized by the composer as the type of the naïve returnee to Iceland, arrives, despite Gísli's desperately urgent efforts to halt his journey and thereby avert the workings of fate. Unaware of the hostilities that have grown between the two households, he immediately persuades Gísli to give some tapestries he acquired abroad to Þorkell, who understandably if ungraciously refuses them at the end of this first scene of homecoming: "Þó værir þú makligr, þó at þú eignaðisk alla, ok vil ek eigi þiggja gripina; eigi eru launin sýnni en svá." (It would be better if you took them all. I don't want to accept these gifts—any return of them doesn't seem likely.) The composer concludes by apophthegmatically using a phrase that alludes to fate's inexorable workings: "Nú ferr Gísli heim, ok þykkir honum um allt einn veg á horfask" (Gisli goes home and it seems to him that everything is pointing in one direction).[28]

Apophthegmatic scenes are more numerous and of greater dramatic impact in this earlier part of *Gísla saga*. The scenes that

---

26. ÍF 6:37, ch. 10.
27. ÍF 6:40, ch. 12; *CSI* 2:13; not in *TPMA*, but see JGF 614–15.
28. ÍF 6:42, ch. 12. Similarly ill-fated, *naïve returnees* to the Icelandic saga world are Eyvindr Bjarnason in *Hrafnkels saga* and Þorvaldr Tungu-Oddsson in *Hœnsa-Þóris saga*. I am grateful to Jeffrey Turco for pointing out this character type to me.

precede the killing of Gísli's brother-in-law Vésteinn focus attention on this first violent step in working out the family conflict that is brought to the surface of the story by the women's chatter. They serve to impose a dramatic emphasis on the tension that is building in the narrative and the inevitability of its denouement. They are almost entirely informed by the fate Gísli and to some extent the composer of the saga see as primary in the hero's world.

Fate and Gísli's Character

Studies of Gísli's character must at some point account for the composer's concluding assessment at his death: "at hann hefir inn mesti hreystimaðr verit, þó at hann væri eigi í ǫllum hlutum gæfumaðr" (although he had been a valiant man, he was not in all respects a lucky man).[29] Lars Lönnroth, in a note to his 1969 paper on "The Noble Heathen," remarked on the likelihood that "the use of such terms as *gæfa* and *hamingja* in the sagas partly reflects the use of *fortuna* and (especially) *felicitas* in Latin historiography. While *fortuna* is primarily to be considered as blind chance, governing the destinies of men from without, *felicitas* (like *gæfa*) is often considered as an innate quality, found in noble characters."[30] It has been the custom to contrast an external fate that destroys Gísli despite his nobility of character and behavior with that internal fate seen in Grettir's undoing, which is perhaps best explained as a matter of fated character made worse by his confrontation with Glámr and the latter's curse. However, a closer reading of *Gísla saga* might challenge this assessment of Gísli.

Fate and the Heroic Ideal

Theodore M. Andersson contended that the Old Icelandic sagas, written as they were in the thirteenth century and later, reflect an awareness resulting from social progress that renders the heroic mode obsolete: "The heroic frame of reference is significant not as a sign of continuity but because it shows so clearly how values have changed."[31] As he puts it, "what gives a consistency to the

---
29. ÍF 6:115, ch. 36.
30. Lars Lönnroth, "The Noble Heathen: A Theme in the Sagas," *Scandinavian Studies* 41 (1969), 28–29n67. See the passage on *ógæfa* by Einar Ól. Sveinsson, below, in chapter 5, the section titled "Order and the Triumph of Chaos: 'Eigi má við ǫllu sjá.'"
31. Andersson, "Ambiguities," 41.

ethical temper of these sagas is precisely a sense of proportion and moderation. They are written against excess."[32]

Gísli is represented as inflexibly and thus excessively embracing pagan heroic values in his own conduct as well as in his expectations of others. This mindset is reinforced by the conservative stance of his father, Þorbjǫrn súrr, who demands that his sons maintain family honor, even, if necessary, by violent means. This approach to the conduct of life is, in the composer's view, not altogether wholesome. In fact, this severe adherence to the old heroic value of family honor and to a perceived necessity of its violent maintenance sets the hero at odds with his siblings. It impels him to kill several of his sister's suitors and, eventually, even her husband, at the same time as he bereaves his brother, Þorkell, of his friends. And it is such harshness of behavior that leads to the hero's outlawry and death. Gísli finds his only encouragement of this rigid and violent ethic in his father, whose goading leads to his first killings to protect Þórdís's and their family's honor. As an outlaw, he invokes his father's spirit at the end of his last verse, when he is dying. Ironically, Gísli's protection of his family's honor destroys that family—his brother helps him only minimally, and his sister betrays him into outlawry. Instead of a victim of external fate, Gísli might in some respects be more accurately viewed as bringing about his own harm, as well as that of others, by his naturally, internally fated preference for the ethics of the traditional heroic ideal.

When Gísli asks his brother, Þorkell, what he will do to help him in his outlawry, the latter offers only the following words:

"At gera þik varan við, ef menn vilja drepa þik, en bjargir veiti ek þér engar, þær er mér megi sakar á gefa. Þykki mér mikit af gǫrt við mik, at drepinn er Þorgrímr, mágr minn ok félagi ok virðavinr."

(I can give you warning if men want to kill you, but I can afford you no help that might lead to my being accused. I feel I have been greatly wronged by Thorgrim being slain, my brother-in-law, my partner and my good friend.)

Here again, Gísli objects: "Var eigi þess ván um slíkan mann sem Vésteinn var, at eigi myndi mannhefndalaust vera . . ." (It was

---

32. Andersson, "Displacement," 588.

unthinkable that a man such as Vestein should not be avenged). He emphatically closes this truncated scene when he complains of his brother's disregard for family loyalty: "mynda ek eigi þér svá svara sem þú svarar mér nú ok eigi heldr gera" ("I would not answer you as you now answer me, nor would I act as you do").[33]

Although a modern reader might perceive Gísli as lamenting in self-pity, he is in fact expressing his disappointment with his siblings' refusal to keep the terms of that earlier, heroic mode of behavior to which he and their father are devoted. The composer of this saga consistently delineates Gísli as the unwavering, stringent proponent of those pre-Christian heroic ideals of Eddic legendary poetry for which his siblings, with their values realistically situated in the milieu of Commonwealth Iceland, have little regard. From Andersson's point of view, Gísli's tragedy lies in his being a hero in whom there is no sense of that displacement of the heroic ideal exhibited in the saga world, and who is thus alienated by his siblings' new version of social reality.

Fate and the Generation Gap

One might also consider whether the tragically isolated figure of this outlaw, who alienates even his own relatives, is better understood in light of Paul Schach's "Some Observations on the Generation-Gap Theme in the Icelandic Sagas," where he examines "a basic theme in saga literature, the theme of the unbridgeable gap between representatives of two generations who embody two antagonistic, diametrically opposed, irreconcilably conflicting cultures."[34] Typically, a father and his son are at odds over methods of dealing with conflict between their family and members of their community. Such stories, symbolic of the "transition from the savage culture of the Viking Age to the farming community of the Icelandic Commonwealth," make father and son adversaries with sometimes tragic consequences, especially when the father's conservative, Heroic Age values overcome his son's reluctance to pursue aggressive action in the interests of family honor.[35]

---

33. ÍF 6:63, ch. 19.
34. Paul Schach, "Some Observations on the Generation-Gap Theme in the Icelandic Sagas," in *The Epic in Medieval Society: Aesthetic and Moral Values*, ed. Harold Scholler (Tübingen: Max Niemeyer, 1977), 367.
35. Schach, "Some Observations," 373.

In *Gísla saga*, the relationship between father and son cannot be said to be adversarial in any sense. However, owing to Þorbjǫrn's harshly conservative ideological influence on his son and Gísli's resultant adherence to the heroic mode, both father and son place themselves in conflict with the interests of Þorkell and Þórdís and present themselves as adversaries of Icelandic society in the Saga Age. This conflict leads to Gísli's death and the destruction of his family. Schach sees the theme of the generation gap as even more meaningful "when understood within the cultural milieu in which the sagas were composed: the almost incredibly savage, creative Age of the Sturlungs."[36] The tragedy of *Gísla saga*, and perhaps, by extension, that of Icelandic society itself in the bloody Sturlung Age—if that is indeed the allusion the composer intended—arises from the persistent resolution of conflict through violent interactions, interactions that are not dissimilar from those recommended in the legendary heroic Eddic texts of the Viking Age. This resolution contrasts with the adjustment of objectives and methods to the humane and socially responsive mores of which Icelanders were capable by the thirteenth century, and to which they were by then vigorously encouraged by the teachers of their church. Thus the destruction of Gísli, like that of Icelandic society itself in the Sturlung Age, might be regarded as the result of an internal fate or an element of character rather than of some impersonal, external influence.

Gísla saga and the Pagan-Christian conflict

If Schach's conception of the generation gap in the sagas can be accurately described as the conflict "between representatives of two generations who embody two antagonistic, diametrically opposed, conflicting cultures," then conflicts over the cultural transitions attendant on the conversion from paganism to Christianity would run parallel to it.[37] The prose of *Gísla saga*, however, contains no evidence of its composer's concern with these latter conflicts. In fact, very little in Gísli's behavior or in his overt character can be taken to indicate his representation as a Christian figure. The composer might be implying that Gísli and Vésteinn were primesigned while

---

36. Schach, "Some Observations," 381.
37. Schach, "Some Observations," 367.

they traveled together or that they had at least come in contact with Christian teachings because Gísli "lét af blótum, siðan hann var í Vébjǫrgum í Danmǫrku" (no longer sacrificed after he had been in Viborg).[38] The discontinuation of this custom is set in contrast with Þorgrímr's holding a sacrifice to Freyr at such at a Winter Nights' feast.[39]

As Lars Lönnroth suggests, however, not sacrificing to the gods did not necessarily mean that one was a Christian—the noble heathens consciously eschewed "sorcery and pagan idolatry"—and it is quite clear that Þorkell and Þorgrímr did not engage in such sacrifices; indeed, the contrast between them and Gísli, which is emphasized by their differences in behavior, is a matter most usefully explained by Lönnroth's distinctions.[40] And Vésteinn, whose character is otherwise little developed, may well show his pagan nobility of spirit rather than any Christian leanings when he stops on his journey to Haukadalr to settle a quarrel between two farmhands, who are fighting with their scythes.[41] This scene, which is contrastively analogous with Snorri's account of Óðinn as Bǫlverkr maliciously causing slaves to kill one another while fighting over possession of his whetting stone, suggests Vésteinn holds ideals based on sensitivity to social balance rather than on the models of the ancient god of treachery and battle reflected in the Eddic legendary poems of the Vǫlsungs.[42]

It should further be noticed, with regard to ideologically based conflict in the saga, that Gísli's siblings are not Christian and in no way appear to be motivated by the Christian amelioration of the pagan heroic virtues that readers may find, for instance, in the latter part of *Njáls saga*. Þorkell and Þórdís are in Þorgrímr's household during the sacrifices, and neither has anything Christian associated with their departure from the narrative. Þórdís simply goes off to Eyri to live at Þórdísarstaðr after she divorces Bǫrkr. Nothing more is mentioned of her, although at the end of *Eyrbyggja saga* a detail about her exhumation might allude to a common assumption

---

38. ÍF 6:36, ch. 10.
39. ÍF 6:50, ch. 15; *CSI* 2:17.
40. Lönnroth, "Heathen," 16.
41. ÍF 6:39, ch. 12; *CSI* 2:12. For an interesting study of this episode and other mythical parallels in saga narrative, see Haraldur Bessason, "Mythological Overlays," in *Sjötíu ritgerðir helgaðar Jakobi Benediktssyni, 20. Júli 1977*, ed. Einar G. Pétursson and Jónas Kristjánsson, 2 vols. (Reykjavík: Stofnun Árna Magnússonar, 1977), 1:273–92.
42. Andersson, "Displacement," 593.

regarding evidence of her not having attained salvation: "Þá váru ok upp tekin bein Þórdísar kerlingar, dóttur Þorbjarnar súrs, móður Snorra goða, ok sagði Guðný þau vera lítil kvenmannsbein ok svá svǫrt, sem sviðin væri" (The bones of the old woman, Thordis, the daughter of Thorbjorn Sur and the mother of Snorri Godi, were also exhumed, and Gudny said they were small female bones, and as black as if they had been singed).[43] The absence of explicitly Christian behavior among the saga's characters finds contrast only with the journey of Auðr and Gunnhildr to Hedeby at the end of *Gísla saga*, where they "tóku . . . við trú ok gengu suðr ok kómu eigi aptr." (took the Christian faith and then went south and came to Rome. They never returned.)[44]

However, the verses attributed by the composer to Gísli—and critical opinion is in agreement that this attribution is false, indeed that these verses were composed much later than the hero's own time, probably in the twelfth century, if not in the thirteenth century, and by the saga composer himself—we do find expressions of a conflict between paganism and Christianity, especially in verses pertaining to two dream women, one of them good, the other evil.[45] Here the psyche of the speaker in these poems is presented as torn between the two belief systems. If we consider the verses as a corpus distinct from the saga itself, one used by the composer to augment his story, then the disparity between the verses' ideological concerns and those represented in such detail in the thirteenth-century prose becomes understandable. The composer emphasizes the significance of these dream women's verses by introducing the first verse in chapter 22 in a passage that starts with an obvious authorial aside: "Gísli var vitr maðr ok draumamaðr mikill ok berdreymr. Þat kemr saman með ǫllum vitrum mǫnnum, at Gísli hafi lengst allra manna í sekð gengit annarr en Grettir Ásmundarson." (Gisli was a wise man who dreamt a great deal and whose dreams were prophetic. All knowledgeable men agree that Gísli survived as an outlaw longer than any other man, except Grettir Asmundarson.)[46] The latter

---

43. Einar Ól. Sveinsson and Matthías Þórðarson, eds., *Eyrbyggja saga*, Íslenzk fornrit 4 (Reykjavík: Hið íslenzka fornritafélag, 1935), 184, ch. 65; *CSI* 5:218, slightly modified.
44. ÍF 6:118, ch. 38; *CSI* 2:48, slightly modified.
45. E. O. G. Turville-Petre, "Gísli Súrsson and his Poetry: Traditions and Influences," *Modern Language Review* 39 (1944): 374–91, repr. E.O.G. Turville-Petre, *Nine Norse Studies* (London: Viking Society for Northern Research, 1972), 118–53. See also Peter Foote, "An Essay on the Saga of Gisli and its Icelandic Background," in *The Saga of Gisli*, trans. George Johnston, 112–23 (Toronto: J. M. Dent, 1971).
46. ÍF 6:70, ch. 22; *CSI* 2:27.

sentence is immaterial to the narrative at this point, and the former one seems redundant because Gísli has already had dreams that were prophetic or interpretive of events. The relatively unusual clumsiness of this interpolation probably results from the composer's intention of marking the significance of the dream verses that follow while at the same time introducing this new source material into the saga.

A few lines later, Gísli describes the good dream woman in a prose passage that ends with her warning him against pagan practices: "'ok hon réð mér þat, meðan ek lifða, at láta leiðask forna sið ok nema enga galdra né fornesku ok vera vel við daufan ok haltan ok fátœka ok fáráða.'" ("And she advised me, while I lived, to stop following the old faith, and to study no charms or ancient lore. And she told me to be kind to the deaf and the lame and the poor and the helpless.")[47] His succeeding verses quoting her lessons end the episode and chapter in the fashion of a truncated scene with an emphasis on her Christian advice, which is paraphrased by the prose that introduces it: "Baugskyndir, hjalp blindum, / Baldr, hygg at því, skjaldar, / illt kveða háð ok hǫfum, / handlausum tý, granda" (Take care to help the blind, / ring-giver, shield of Balder. / men say that mockery and hurting the lame is evil. Help those who are handless.)[48]

Again, this is advice that the composer is at no great pains to have the hero follow in the prose narrative. In fact Gísli, in the role of trickster-outlaw, had earlier given his cloak to the stupid thrall, Þórðr inn huglausi, knowing that this act of generosity would lead to the recipient's death. On later occasions when he does give to the poor, it is only because they have helped save his life. A response moved by gratitude is a noble but not an exclusively Christian gesture.

Among the lessons of the good dream woman, in verse 19, are pacific admonitions: "Vald eigi þú vígi, / ves þú ótyrrinn, fyrri, / morðs við mœti-Njǫrðu, / mér heitið því, sleitu" (Don't be the first to cause a fight, / be peaceful to the proud gods of slaughter. / Promise me that).[49] While Gísli cannot be said to have been the first to start a fight, he does not, as has already been noticed, show tendencies to turn the other cheek. He utters some bloodthirsty verses after learning that he has not been saved from outlawry by Vésteinn's uncles with their feeble support at the assembly. They

---

47. ÍF 6:70, ch. 22; CSI 2:27, slightly modified.
48. ÍF 6:73, st. 19, ch. 22.
49. ÍF 6:72, st. 19, ch. 22.

attended "ok koma engu áleiðis um sættina, ok kalla men, at þeir hafi illa borit sik, svá at þeim hafi næsta í allt skap komit." (But they made no headway with a settlement. Indeed, it was said that they handled matters so badly that they were close to tears before it was over.)[50] Pondering this outcome, he promises vengeance for the outlawry against Bǫrk and Steinn: "Þat á bláserkjar Berki, / bǫ́ru hreins, ok Steini, / veitir dags ens vegna, / valdr hermila at gjalda" (Giver of pure gold, / this blue-armoured warrior / shall cruelly repay / both Bork and Stein).[51] And he repeats this threat in another verse, following the first dire revelations of the evil dream woman: "Verr hafa vápna snerru / vekjendr, þeirs mik sekðu, / brynju hatrs ens bitra / beiðendr, ef nú reiðumk" (They will surely feel / my weapons bite their armour / if rage comes upon me now).[52] The scene is then abruptly closed, the composer simply remarking, "eru nú kyrr tíðendi" (things were quiet for a while).[53]

Later in the narrative, after he has been warned against violence by the good dream woman, Gísli's first response, after learning about the proximity of Vésteinn's sons, derives from his ingrained and violent heroic reflex: "'Ekki má ek þat standask, at sjá bróður-bana mína ok vera ásamt við þá'" ("I could not bear to see my brother's killers or to be with them").[54] The tension of the scene is broken only at its conclusion, when Gísli learns Auðr has already sent them away—"Gísli sagði, at þann veg var ok allra bezt, at þeir hittisk eigi. Ok sefask hann brátt, ok eru nú kyrr ein tíðendi." (Gisli said it was better that they did not meet. Then he soon calmed down and things were quiet for a while.)[55]

Although he is not receptive to the most basic Christian teachings about personal forgiveness and the accompanying divine redemption, the good dream woman attempts to show him the potential for his salvation: "Heim bauð með mér sínum / saum-Hlǫkk grǫ́um blakki, / þá vas brúðr við beiði / blíð, lofskreyti ríða." (The thread-goddess invited / the praise-maker to ride / on a grey steed to her home. / The lady was gentle with the invitation.)[56] She promises to heal

---

50. ÍF 6:67, ch. 21; CSI 2:25.
51. ÍF 6:68, st. 15, ch. 21; CSI 2:26, st. 14.
52. ÍF 6:77, st. 22, ch. 24; CSI 2:30, st. 21.
53. ÍF 6:77, ch. 24; CSI 2:30.
54. ÍF 6:93, ch. 30; CSI 2:38.
55. ÍF 6:94, ch. 30; CSI 2:38.
56. ÍF 6:94–95, st. 25, ch. 30; CSI 2:38, st. 24, modified.

him, and she offers him a soft place to rest and the ultimate wealth of spiritual redemption.

The evil dream woman returns, however, claiming that nothing her competitor promised will be realized: "'Nú skal ek því ǫllu bregða, er in betri draumkona mælti við þik, ok skal ek þess ráðandi, at þér skal þess ekki at gagni verða, er hon hefir mælt'" ("Now I shall destroy everything that the good dream-woman has said to you and I will make certain that nothing come of what she has promised").[57] His following verses describe, as did previous ones, her anointing him with blood, and she now places a bloody cap on his head. The woman seems to curse him with perdition when she exclaims "Allvaldr hefir aldar / erlendis þik sendan / einn ór yðru ranni / annan heim at kunna" (He who rules all has sent you / alone from your house / to explore the other world).[58] He will never be together in the afterlife with the better dream woman, she proclaims: "Skuluða it . . . / saman verja, / svá hefr ykkr till ekka / eitr góðmunnr leitat" (You two will never / embrace together, / thus will your great love turn to grief).[59] This vision of his spiritual alienation, not unlike some passages in the Old English elegies, describes suffering far beyond that of the ephemeral situation he experiences in his earthly life as an outlaw.

If Gísli's conflict with contemporary society over its lack of support for the heroic mode is tragic in an earthly sense, the reader must wonder what the composer intended to suggest as the outcome of his relationship with the good dream woman of Christian persuasion, and thus with his own spiritual welfare: "'sekr emk við her nekkvat'" ("I am an outlaw to most men"), he complains to Auðr; "'bíðum brodda hriðar'" ("only arrow-storms await me").[60] There is no longer a chance of peace for him in this life and, as he anticipates his end, he sees his good dream woman weeping for him, "grátandi, brá váta, / ok eld-Njǫrun ǫldu / allskyndila hyndi, / hvat hyggr mér, en mæra, / mín sár, und því váru" (Her brow was wet, the eyes / of that bonnet-goddess were weeping. / And that wave of gold-fire / soon bound up my wounds. / What message, think you, / has this dream for me?)[61] His own question, which is

57. ÍF 6:102, ch. 33; CSI 2:41.
58. ÍF 6:102, st. 29, ch. 33; CSI 2:42, st. 28.
59. ÍF 6:102, st. 29, ch. 33.
60. ÍF 6:107, st. 35, ch. 33; CSI 2:43, st. 34.
61. ÍF 6:109, st. 38, ch. 33; CSI 2:44, st. 37.

emphasized by its conclusion of this scene, extends to a time after his death and seems difficult to answer. Later that summer, as his enemies prepare to kill Gísli at his hiding place under the cliffs, he asks them to pause and he speaks his final verse. It ends not with a pious sentiment that might have found the approval of the good dream-woman but with the proud assertion of his commitment to the pre-Christian heroic mode of conduct, and he attributes his adherence to this portion of his heritage to his father's influence: "Vel hygg ek, þótt eggjar / ítrslegnar mik bíti; / þá gaf sínum sveini / sverðs minn faðir herðu" (I greet the sword's honed edge / that bites into my flesh, / knowing that this courage / was given me by my father).[62] A sense of finality in this statement is conveyed by the composer's next statement: "Sjá er in síðasta vísa Gísla" (This was Gisli's last verse).[63] The saga suggests an association between his father's influence and the twofold tragedy of Gísli's demise: heroic in this world, and spiritual in the next.

* * *

The composer of *Gísla saga* conveys the point of the story in unmistakable terms by closing truncated scenes with significant comments by notable, or in some cases subversively hostile, characters. Further, these scenes end apophthegmatically in many cases. The hero sides conservatively with his father against the new, socially oriented mores of Commonwealth Iceland, explicitly citing indebtedness to his father for this aggressive heritage at the very conclusion of his tragedy. In the earlier chapters of the saga, as the narrative moves toward Gísli's outlawry, most of the paroemial texts he utters attribute to fate the depressing cascade of his misadventures. What the composer himself may have meant by this choric set of laconic observations is another matter, and the text provides no help to our understanding.

From the hero's point of view, external fate has arranged enmities and injuries that will lead to his demise, and his proverbial utterance could be taken merely as part of a not unfamiliar ritual of a saga hero on his way to death. The point of the saga, however, may have more to do with his internal sense of fate, according to the distinction between *fortuna* and *felicitas* set out by Lars

---

62. ÍF 6:114, st. 40, ch. 36; *CSI* 2:47, st. 39
63. ÍF 6:115; *CSI* 2:47.

Lönnroth's observation cited above.[64] And this point lies in how his character predisposes him to adhere to the ethics of those heroic ideals preached by his father. Meanwhile, the composer's placement of the verses as summaries of conversational scenes with the admonitions and predictions of Gísli's dream women is meant to clarify the more subjective aspects of the hero's quest for honor, adding Christian spiritual nuance to what would otherwise have been only an examination of the negative value of the heroic ideal in Commonwealth Iceland.

---

64. Lönnroth, "Heathen," 28–29n67.

CHAPTER 4

Paroemial Thematic Signaling in *Njáls saga*

The composers of the sagas showed varying levels of skill and education, along with widely varying degrees of ecclesiastical influence. And they used proverbs in respectively different ways, especially in the most accomplished narratives. *Njáls saga* occupies a special place in the genre and an examination of its origin and literary qualities will facilitate study of its composer's highly skilled uses of proverbs to illuminate the narrative.[1]

While it is impossible to establish a firm date for most *Íslendingasögur*—estimates vary widely for some of them—the origin of *Njáls saga* is an exception because the proposed dates are within a period of about thirty years. Its use of the Old Norse laws of *Járnsíða* places it after 1271. The existence of its earliest known manuscript fragment, in AM 162 b, fol., and its occurrence in *Reykjabók*, AM 468, 4to, suggest it must have been written before 1300.[2] Albert Ulrik Bååth emphasized the composer's careful artistry by claiming that he conceived the saga's last word "då han nedskrifvit den första linjen" (when he had written down the first lines).[3] By the time of *Njáls saga*'s composition the genre of the *Íslendingasögur* had been long been established, and its composer drew on many of its predecessors, recalling characters and phrases

---

1. This section is based on and uses some material from my article, "'The Hand's Pleasure in the Blow is Brief': Proverbs Escalating Danger in the Revenge Pattern of *Njálssaga*," *Proverbium* 18 (2000): 149–65
2. ÍF 12, lxxv–lxxxiv.
3. Albert Ulrik Bååth, *Studier öfver kompositionen i några isländska ättsagor* (Lund: Fr. Berling, 1885), 159.

from these forerunners in the thirteenth-century tradition. Einar Ól. Sveinsson's statement, which has at times been disheartening to students of Old Icelandic literature, that whoever "undertakes a critical investigation of *Njála* must have a comprehensive knowledge of the *Íslendingasögur* as a whole, of their distinctive nature and artistic method," takes into account the work's late appearance in the genre as well as the broad literary sweep of its individual composition.[4]

A paroemiological approach to *Njáls saga* is thus best conducted with reference to its origins primarily within a literate environment. While its author may have created passages alluding in style to oral techniques of narration, and while some content likely came from oral sources, the great body of the work speaks of a remarkably clever and perspicacious mind writing in a literary context. Some passages are copied from written sources, including legal texts. Scholars have studied how at several points the composer used materials originally of continental and ecclesiastical background. There are even claims that its author had an ideological agenda.[5]

Ideological Agendas

Craig Davis sees the saga describing a world relatively new to its audience, one in which the traditional postconversion "tension between Church and chieftaincies in the old commonwealth, between secular and clerical culture" had been made obsolete as Iceland came under control of the Norwegian crown: "*Njál's saga* thus implicitly confirms the new institutional *status quo* in Iceland; it works to reconcile its audience to the new coalition of ecclesiastical and royal authority."[6] Views of this sort are not new, but their usefulness in approaching the saga's thematic structure is limited. "I consider it more likely that this work of narrative art is the creation of a much more complex mentality than that of a propagandist,"

---

4. Einar Ól. Sveinsson, *Masterpiece*, 45.

5. Besides Einar Ól. Sveinsson's meditation, cited above, several other full-length works have been written in English on the various aspects of *Njáls saga* criticism alluded to in the preceding paragraphs. These include Allen, *Fire*, Lönnroth, *Introduction*, and William Ian Miller, *Why is Your Axe Bloody? A Reading of* Njáls saga (Oxford: Oxford University Press, 2014). See also Andrew Hamer, *Njals Saga and its Christian Background: A Study of Narrative Method*, Germania Latina 8, Mediaevalia Groningana New Series 20 (Leuven: Peeters, 2014).

6. Craig Davis, "Cultural Assimilation in *Njáls saga*," *Oral Tradition* 13 (1998): 453.

Einar Ól. Sveinsson wrote, "a mentality which endeavors to fathom the mystery of reality, and we shall have to seek to comprehend this mentality if we hope to approach an understanding of its creation."[7]

Fate

Early and still persistent attempts to define the author's purpose exclusively in terms of the working of fate sometimes also limit the interpretation of the saga. Bååth, true to his vision of the sagas generally as celebrating a fatalistic worldview, concluded his thoughts on the *þættir* he saw underlying this long narrative with the observation that its author

> (is able to adhere firmly to a precisely thought out plan, based on belief in Fate, which finds throughout expression in prophecies and innuendos about the future. He allows the historical as well as the lovingly handled legal material to subordinate itself generally to this plan.)[8]

Again, Einar Ól. envisaged an author of a more humane intellectual bent, one seeking "to find purpose and direction in the seemingly chaotic flow of events, and it is well to keep in mind that he thought less in terms of logic and doctrine than in pictures of human life, events, and people."[9] References to fate and illustrations of its inexorable workings thread their way through the entire story, but it is a story about much more than the realization of this external urge in matters of human affairs.

Paroemial Density and Usage

There are more than fifty proverbs and proverbial phrases in *Njáls saga*, constituting a relatively high density of occurrence for its genre. Peter Hallberg observed that about 41 percent of *Njáls saga*'s 97,000

---

7. Einar Ól. Sveinsson, *Masterpiece*, 182.
8. Bååth, *Studier*, 160. Translation mine. The original Swedish reads as follows: "Förmått hålla fast vid en noga genomtänkt plan, bygd på ödestron, som altigenom får si uttryck i förutsägelser och antydningar om det vardande. Såväl det historiska som det med förkärlek begagnade juridiska materialet låter han i allmänhet underordna sig denna plan."
9. Einar Ól. Sveinsson, *Masterpiece*, 182.

words make up dialogue, and this is probably the main reason for its impressive paroemial inventory.[10] Proverbs, like similes, metaphors, and the other devices with which we almost unconsciously strengthen and adorn our conversations, are often found in sagas in proportion to the amount of direct speech they contain, and it is in direct speech that they nearly always occur. Their continued greater frequency of conversational use in some cultures today, especially those with recent preliterate backgrounds, is well attested.[11]

* * *

In a narrative as complex as *Njáls saga*, readers might expect various uses of paroemial content: to express the author's own views or views held by people of significance in the story, views that are possibly representative of their society's wisdom. It is reasonable to survey this inventory as a way of exploring the intentions with which this work was written. This study will examine how the proverbs in *Njáls saga* are used by its composer to help his audience understand his artistically unified vision of a world where others might see neither unity, nor pattern, nor meaning.

Twice-Used Proverbs and the Repetitive Style of *Njáls saga*

Proverbs that occur twice, or in one case thrice, are of primary concern in this approach because they illustrate how the composer uses repetition as part of a complex strategy of composition. Einar Ól. Sveinsson observed how a reader "is startled when he is shown for the first time the numerous and varied ways in which the individual scenes of *Njáls saga* are connected with each other . . . these reveal a far greater degree of planning and deliberation than one

---

10. Peter Hallberg, "Några anteckningar om replik och dialog i *Njals saga*," in *Festschrift Walter Baetke, dargebracht zu seinem 80. Geburtstag am 28 März 1964*, ed. K. Rudolph, R. Heller, and E. Walter (Weimar: Böhlau, 1966), 130. See also Irmgard Netter, *Die direkte Rede in den Isländersagas*, Form und Geist: Arbeiten zur germanischen Philologie 36 (Leipzig: Hermann Eichblatt, 1935). Netter presents a table of direct speech statistics for the *Íslendingasögur*, on pages 17 and 18. A more comprehensive study of the density of proverb occurrence in the sagas in relation to the amount of direct speech found in them might be helpful to our further understanding their presence in these texts.

11. Arabic conversation cannot exist without a remarkably heavy paroemial component; Slavic language speakers use proverbs more than English speakers; and in many African cultures the proverb is essential to communication and valued in affairs of law and government. See, for example, John Messenger, "The Role of the Proverb in a Nigerian Judicial System," *Southwestern Journal of Anthropology* 15 (1959): 64–73.

would expect to find in our ancient literature."[12] Of special interest for this study, he refers to "repetitions of words or details, sometimes in the form of a direct reference to what has already happened (recapitulations, quotations, allusions); sometimes the connection is tacitly understood."[13] This method is subtle and it requires that the reader carefully consider minutely planned intentions and agendas.

At the Narrative Core of the Conflict . . .

The tragedy of *Njáls saga* stems from an argument in chapter 35 between Hallgerðr and Bergþóra, the respective wives of the story's heroes, Gunnarr and Njáll. Hallgerðr, as a guest in Bergþóra's house, is angered at not being given the seat of honor at a feast: "Hvergi mun ek þoka, því at engi hornkerling vil ek vera" (I'll not move aside, and I won't sit in the corner like a cast-off hag), she declares.[14] Reacting to this perceived insult to her dignity, Hallgerðr instigates a series of homicidal episodes that are reciprocated by Bergþóra in an oddly conducted feminine feud by proxy. The tragic denouement of *Njáls saga* can be traced to moments of violence, lines of loyalty, and long-remembered injuries originating in this initial conflict between the two women. This narrative situation is defined by Ian Maxwell in his well-known observation: "A seemingly small cause, the grudge of a socially slighted woman, is transmitted and transformed and combined in a complex pattern of causes until it has at last attained its end and disrupted a whole society in the process. It is a process that one can follow with unfaltering interest and contemplate with a sense of completeness."[15] The composer of *Njáls saga* used proverbs and proverbial phrases in diverse ways to effect the realization of the centralizing process Maxwell here describes in outline.

A Fly in the Mouth

The entire tragic devastation of *Njáls saga* is brought about by a mere handful of evil individuals who impose their designs on the

---

12. Sveinsson, *Masterpiece*, 46.
13. Sveinsson, *Masterpiece*, 47.
14. ÍF 12:91, ch. 35; *CSI* 3:40.
15. Ian Maxwell, "Pattern in *Njáls saga*," *Saga-Book* 15 (1957–59): 36.

workings of a society whose members are, at best, unaware of their plotting or, at worst, indifferent to it. The composer shows how unwitting people can become victims of these designs, working their own demise as they are manipulated into seeking that of others. Here we will examine how a repeated proverbial phrase about flies, one that metaphorically describes the manipulative techniques by which evil may be perpetrated, is used by the composer to assess the distance in intelligence between an instigator and the person who is the object of influence. The phrase whose implications are under discussion here, "at koma flugu í munn einhverjum" (to put a fly in someone's mouth), most likely derives from the predatory activity of fly fishing, the fly being the metaphorically figured lure by which a victim is brought to his or her demise.

Hallgerðr and Sigmundr

As Hallgerðr and Bergþóra run through members of their households in their exchange of killings resulting from the contested seating arrangement, the destruction escalates as they choose victims of gradually elevated status. The financial value of compensation increases as the victims progress from servants to distant and then nearer relatives of the feuding parties. Emotions sharpen as the odds rise. The penultimate loss comes when Bergþóra delegates the task of killing Hallgerðr's kinsman, Brynjólfr, to Þórðr leysingjason, the much-loved foster father of Njáll's sons. This task is also inevitably lethal to Þórðr. His resulting death, at the hands of Gunnarr's kinsman Sigmundr Lambason, is never forgiven by the sons of Njáll, and Skarpheðinn's quest for vengeance has far-reaching consequences. The composer introduces Sigmundr in terms that are both superlative and ultimately unflattering: "Hann var metnaðarmaðr mikill ok skáld gott ok at flestum íþróttum vel búinn, hávaðamaðr mikill, spottsamr ok ódæll" (He was full of ambition and a good poet and skilled in most sports; he was boisterous, sarcastic and overbearing). Sigmundr's uneven portrait is further colored by the poor quality of the company he keeps in his friend Skjǫldr, "sœnskr maðr ok illr viðreignar" (a Swede and a vicious man to deal with).[16]

---

16. ÍF 12:105, ch. 41; *CSI* 3:48.

In chapter 42, Sigmundr returns to Hlíðarendi to report the killing of Þórðr leysingjason to Hallgerðr. Rannveig, Gunnarr's mother and a figure of stature in the story, attacks him verbally. William Sayers has noted the importance of her influence on the reader's point of view: "The counsel and criticism of [Gunnarr's] mother Rannveig offer a corrective to his actions that one might call the authorial or community perspective." He appends a pertinent note to this observation:

> Rannveig is a far more skillful creation than might be first noticed. In line with the above comments on possibly representing an authorial voice, she appears to speak in common sense, for the moral code and from a knowledge of human nature . . . This combination allows her to foresee likely outcomes to events, although her foresight is less uncanny than Njál's second sight. Rannveig's statements, some in indirect speech but the most telling in direct, typically come toward the end of chapters, as clinching, concise, often proverbial (under) statements from the community perspective.[17]

The audience must then take into serious account her response to the news of Þórðr's killing. Although she reassures Sigmundr that Gunnarr will extricate him from this predicament, she adds a warning with an interesting proverbial phrase that seems to have piscatorial reference: "En ef Hallgerðr kemr annarri flugu í munn þér, þá verðr þat þinn bani" (But if Hallgerd puts another fly in your mouth it will be your death).[18]

The image of putting a fly in someone's mouth, with deadly result, is subject to different interpretations. Although it is most commonly thought to be derived from the ancient art of fly-fishing, Guðbrandur Vigfússon associated it with assassination by sorcery: "Wizards were said to bewitch flies and send them to kill their enemies (vide *galdra-fluga*, *gand-fluga*), hence the phrase *gína við flugu*, or *taka flugu*, to swallow the fly or to carry the fly, i.e. *to be the fool of another man*, esp. in a wicked and fatal business." And

---

17. William Sayers, "Gunnarr, His Irish Wolfhound Sámr, and the Passing of the Old Heroic Order in *Njáls saga*," *Arkiv för nordisk filologi* 112 (1997): 58n39. Sayers also considers Rannveig's pronouncement in a manner similar to my discussion of apothegmatic scene endings in chapter 3, in the section "Apophthegmatic Scenes, and Proverbial Affirmations of the Heroic Ideal."

18. ÍF 12:109, ch. 42; *CSI* 3:50.

he cites the definition "*flugu-maðr, m. 'a man of flies,' a wizard,"* which he notices "occurs in this sense in the old Swed. Law (Verel.): hence metaph. *a hired bandit, an assassin.*"[19]

While it may be useful to keep the implications of this view in mind as we study the pertinent texts of *Njáls saga*, editors of the saga and most readers prefer an interpretation that plays Hallgerðr not as a sorceress but, by metaphorical implication, as a fisherman with Sigmundr as her prey. In the first edition of *Mergur málsins*, Jón Geir Friðjónsson notices the allusion to sorcery in other contexts but sees the passages in *Njáls saga* as using the implied metaphor of the fly-fisherman's bait.[20] Thus, when Gunnarr returns from the Alþingi the composer has him caution his kinsman in chapter 44: "Meiri ertú ógiptumaðr en ek ætlaða, ok hefir þú til ills þína mennt. En þó hefi ek nú gǫrvan þik sáttan, ok skyldir þú nú eigi annarri flugu láta koma í munn þér." (You're a man of more bad luck than I thought, and you make evil use of your gifts. But I've made a settlement for you, and you must not let Hallgerd put another fly in your mouth.)[21] Twice, then, while being warned, Sigmundr is compared to a fish that is a victim of its own mindless temptations, rising stupidly to Hallgerðr's deadly bait. In fact, he does so a second time, despite this sage advice.

The metaphorical image of these two passages is underscored a few pages later as Njáll's sons ready themselves to kill Sigmundr, who failed to follow good counsel. He devised verses disparaging their manhood, thus leaving himself open to legal slaying despite Gunnarr's recent settlement for the killing of Þórðr. In a ritualized dialogue that anticipates violence and death, Njáll, who is alerted at night by the sound of an axe clanging, asks his sons where they are going with their weapons. "Leita sauða þinna" (To look for your sheep), Skarpheðinn answers. "Ekki mundu þér þá vera vápnaðir, ef þér ætlaðið þat, ok mun annat vera ørendit" ("You wouldn't be armed if you planned that, so it must be something else"), Njáll objects, to which Skarpheðinn replies, "Laxa skulu vér veiða, faðir, ef vér rǫtum eigi sauðina" (We're going salmon fishing, father, if we don't find the sheep). And Njáll, with strategic cunning as well as clairvoyant vision, responds, "Vel væri þat, þó at svá væri, at þá

---

19. C-V 162a.
20. JGF 154.
21. ÍF 12:111, ch. 44; *CSI* 3:51.

veiði bæri eigi undan" (If that's so, then it would be a good thing if the prey didn't slip away).²²

Þorvaldr inn veili and Úlfr Uggason

Thematic signaling through repetition of the fly image occurs in a much later episode in chapter 102, where Úlfr Uggason the *skáld* resists baiting by heathens, led by Þorvaldr inn veili, who wants to taunt him into killing King Óláfr Tryggvason's aggressively enthusiastic Christian missionary, Þangbrandr. Refusing to rise to this lure, Úlfr responds with a verse:

> Tekka ek, sunds þótt sendi
> sannreynir boð, tanna
> hvarfs við hleypiskarfi,
> Hárbarðs véa fjarðar;
> erat ráfáka rœkis,
> rǫng eru mál á gangi,
> sé ek við mínu meini,
> mínligt flugu at gína.
>
> (Though the dear friend
> of the drink of Odin's hall
> orders me, I am not
> accepting the offered bait;
> I won't fall for the fly
> from the sea-faring fellow;
> bad things are brewing —
> I'd better watch out.)²³

"'Ok ætla ek ekki,' segir hann, 'at vera ginningarfífl hans, en gæti hann, at honum vefisk eigi tungan um hǫfuð'" ("I don't intend to be one who runs his fool's errand," he said, "and he'd better take care that his tongue doesn't twist itself around his head").²⁴ A few pages later, as predicted, Þorvaldr is killed—ironically—by the violent missionary Þangbrandr.

---

22. ÍF 12:115, ch. 44; *CSI* 3:53.
23. ÍF 12:263–64, st. 8, ch. 102; *CSI* 3:124.
24. ÍF 12:263–64, st. 8, ch. 102; *CSI* 3:124, modified; *TPMA* 13.444.

This passage occurs near the center of *Njáls saga,* five chapters before the composer presents a series of sketches of Iceland's conversion to Christianity. He describes a process that is eventually conducted according to lawful procedures. However, it occurs in a society beset by disruptive influences that can have potentially disastrous effects during any significant conflict. At one moment Christians and pagans have made for themselves two sets of laws, respectively, creating a situation that threatens to become chaotic:

ok sǫgðusk hvárir ór lǫgum annarra, ok varð þá svá mikit óhljóð at lǫgbergi, at engi nam annars mál. Síðan gengu menn í braut, ok þótti ǫllum horfa til inna mestu óefna.

(and declared themselves no longer bound by law to the other. Then there was such an uproar at the Law Rock that no one could hear anyone else. After this men went away, and everyone thought that things looked dangerous.)[25]

Through the decisions of a pagan arbitrator, order is restored in the form of a legal, if not spiritually based, conversion of the country to Christianity. Thus, the threat of chaos is thwarted and the Icelandic Commonwealth survives this crisis.

It is in the midst of this Christianizing episode and the threat the conversion process poses to community order that a pagan, Þorvaldr veili, tries to entice Úlfr Uggason into killing Þangbrandr. The composer works his refusal into the narrative in the metaphorical terms of a *lausavísa* (single stanza), expressing the same prudent restraint that would have saved Sigmundr's life, had the latter chosen to exercise it rather than allowing Hallgerðr to lure him further into her feud. The figures of Sigmundr and Úlfr in this saga differ in stature and gravitas, as do the respective contexts in which the composer employs images of lures and fishes. Contrastive situations and characters juxtaposed by phraseological echoes, especially those with paroemial associations, are sometimes employed by this author with ironic intent. Such is the case here.

On one hand there is the trivial gullibility of the doomed

---

25. ÍF 12:271, ch. 105; *CSI* 3:127.

Sigmundr, a brave and in some ways talented but arrogant warrior flawed also by lack of good judgement. In his superficial existence, he carries out the most tragically destructive of all the killings in *Njáls saga*. On the other hand, there is Úlfr Uggason, little discussed in *Njáls saga* but obviously known from what Carol Clover has identified as Iceland's "immanent saga."[26] He is featured in *Laxdœla saga* as the composer of the ekphrastic and decidedly pagan *Húsdrápa* (ca. 985), which honors the mythologically descriptive carvings on the walls of Óláfr pái's magnificent hall at Hjarðarholt. Úlfr is a most respectable person of substance who uses the same metaphorical terms as Rannveig did in admonishing Sigmundr to express his contemptuous rejection of Þorvaldr veili's invitation to pagan treachery. If, among the threads of *Njáls saga*, we see reflections of a cosmic conflict between order and chaos, then these two men are contrastively linked by phraseological echoes as representatives of the two sides of this conflict. Similar, ironically induced linkage is used by the composer elsewhere and indicated by the repeated occurrence of proverbial texts in his saga. Subtle and complex repetitions of paroemial texts offer metaphorically marked paths toward the meaning of the narrative.

Bad Plans and Evil Seed: the Antagonistic Mechanism of *Njáls saga* in Proverbial Terms

As was observed earlier, the conflicts of *Njáls saga* are instigated by a very few individuals who evince different manifestations of ill nature and ill will. Their motivations are described in varying detail with equally varying clarity for a modern reader trying to understand the composer's purposes. The two major antagonists, Hallgerðr Hǫskuldsdóttir and Mǫrðr Valgarðsson, are presented quite differently with reference to their respective urges to destruction. The evil brought about by Hallgerðr is attributed to *bad plans*. In the case of Mǫrðr, however, the composer uses the imagery of plants—of *seeds* and of *roots*—in paroemial references to the depth and spreading influences of the evil scheming in his story.

---

26. See Carol Clover, "Long Prose Form," *Arkiv för nordisk filologi* 101 (1986): "that a whole saga existed at the preliterary stage not as a performed but as an immanent or potential entity, a collectively envisaged 'whole' . . . " (34).

Hallgerðr: ill ráð

The composer does not for the most part describe in useful detail Hallgerðr's emotions or motives.[27] A fundamental problem with her character is immediately evident in the well-known second scene of the saga, where her uncle Hrútr, responding to her father's questioning him about her beauty, replies, only after a second urging, "Œrit fǫgr er mær sjá, ok munu margir þess gjalda; en hitt veit ek eigi, hvaðan þjófsaugu eru komin í ættir várar." (The girl is very beautiful, and many will pay for that. But what I don't know is how thief's eyes have come into our family).[28] Whether the pejorative term *þjófsaugu* (thief's eyes) anticipates specifically her later instigation of theft from the farmer Otkell, or whether it refers more generally to a flawed character, it casts a doubtful shadow on her beauty.[29] The comment falls into the same category as another made by Hrútr when Gunnarr comes to the brothers at the Alþingi to ask for her in marriage: "hon er blandin mjǫk ..." (she has a mixed character).[30] Both observations are difficult to interpret and indicate a problem in her personality that is never clearly defined.

Her insecure and rather easily hurt pride, perhaps meant by the author to be derived from her uncertain sense of her own value, seems to be at the core of this problem. When she was married by her father's arrangement and without her consultation to Þorvaldr Ósvífrsson, a man she considered beneath her, she reacted by having him killed. This disastrous conclusion of her first marriage is referred to by her second suitor, Glúmr Óleifsson, as "bad luck": "Má, at hana hendi eigi slík ógipta í annat sinn ..." (It may be that she will not have such bad luck the second time).[31] Her insecure pride was also the source of irritation when she felt insulted by Bergþóra's

---

27. An interesting exception to this rule is found in her quarrel with her second husband, Glúmr Óleifsson, after he has struck her: "Hon unni honum mikit ok mátti eigi stilla sik ok grét hástǫfum" (She loved him greatly and was not able to calm herself, and wept loudly). ÍF 12:48, ch. 16; CSI 3:22.
28. ÍF 12:7, ch. 1; CSI 3:2.
29. Other physical features suggestive of less fortunate aspects of her character are discussed by Ari Cornelius Bouman in *Patterns in Old English and Old Icelandic Literature*, Leidse germanistische en anglistische reeks van de Rijksuniversiteit te Leiden 1 (Leiden: Universitaire Pers Leiden, 1962). See especially the chapter "Literature and Myth, the Picture of Hallgerðr Hǫskuld's Daughter," 1–13, for her long hair and her nickname, *langbrók*.
30. ÍF 12:86, ch. 33; CSI 3:38.
31. ÍF 12:42, ch. 13. Hallgerðr's associations with *ógæfa*, the misfortune that can come to pervade one's character and life, would be an interesting subject of study.

imposition on her of an inferior seating assignment at the feast. Denied the right to make decisions for herself, and feeling slighted by the decisions others made for her, she became destructive. That urge to destroy, trivially motivated though it is, runs pervasively and with powerful effect through the tragedy.

Like a few other great writers preceding the development of psychiatric theory, the *Njáls saga* author, with his deep understanding of human nature, performs a plausible analysis of his own. He describes through her actions and speech Hallgerðr's *ógipta* in her desperate need to prove her value through complex manipulation with seductive and ostensibly amicable behavior. Such challenges are epitomized, for instance, in the language she uses with her father after discovering her engagement to Þorvaldr: "Nú em ek at raun komin um þat, er mik hefir lengi grunat, at þú mundir eigi unna mér svá mikit sem þú sagðir jafnan . . ." (Now I have proof of what I have long suspected, that you do not love me as much as you have always said).[32] A few critics, from Hans E. Kinck and some nineteenth-century Icelandic poets to recent feminist interpreters of the saga, have found her reactions and motives justified and would claim for her a sympathetic reading. The quality of the company she keeps and numerous comments made about her and to her by figures whom the reader is inclined to trust argue strongly against such generous views.[33]

Hrútr's blunt, earliest signal that Hallgerðr's character was somehow flawed and potentially dangerous was initially realized in the bloody conclusion of her first marriage, to Þorvaldr Ósvífrsson. Having goaded her unwanted husband to commit an injury to her in the form of a slap on the face that drew blood, she then arranged for his assassination in an episode that in itself is brief and without long-term effects on the overall narrative. Ósvífr, who had been dubious about his son's marriage to her anyway, comments bitterly, "Illa gefask ills ráðs leifar; ok sé ek nú allt eptir, hversu farit hefir" (Bad things come from bad plans, and now I see how it has gone).[34]

---

32. ÍF 12:31, ch. 10; *CSI* 3:13.

33. Hans Ernst Kinck, "Et par ting om ættesagen, skikkelser den ikke forstod," in *Til Gerhard Gran: 9. december 1916, fra venner og elever*, ed. Anders Krogvig (Kristiania: Aschehoug, 1916), 32–58. Einar Ól. Sveinsson, *Masterpiece*, 118–21.

34. ÍF 12:37, ch. 12; see fn 5: "Leifar táknar hér: það sem eftir lifir af ráðununum; afleiðingar" (Leifar here means that which remains of the plans; leavings [remnants]); *CSI* 3:16; JGF 459; *TPMA* 9.187.

When Skarpheðinn and his brothers kill the reckless and foolish Sigmundr Lambason, Gunnarr rebuffs Hallgerðr's complaint over Skarpeðinn's killing of Sigmundr: "Slíks var honum ván, . . . því at illa gefask ill ráð, ok hefir hvárttveggja ykkat opt gráliga gǫrt til annars" ("This was to be expected for Sigmund . . . for bad things come from bad plans, and you and Skarphedin have often behaved spitefully to each other").[35] Gunnarr thus further defines her role in the world of evil plans, reinforcing the value of Ósvífr's judgement about her. His laconic comments on the killing of his own relative are clearly meant by the composer to identify beyond all doubt the source of those bad plans from which these deaths have come, as well as to anticipate the growth thence of nearly all the tragedy of *Njáls saga*.

Mǫrðr: illar rœtr and illt korn

The narrative's second primary antagonist, Mǫrðr Valgarðsson, is less ambiguous, both in his association with evil and in our awareness of his motivations. The composer introduces this complex and cunning villain immediately after telling the story of how Gunnarr retrieves Unnr's marriage dowry from her first husband, Hrútr Herjólfsson, which he had kept when she left him. With her marketability thus renewed, she enters the marriage that produces her son Mǫrðr. Valgarðr inn grái then came

> at biðja Unnar, ok giptisk hon Valgarði án ráði allra frænda sinna, en þat þótti Gunnari illa ok Njáli ok mǫrgum ǫðrum, því at hann var maðr grályndr ok óvinsæll. Þau gátu sér son, er Mǫrðr hét, ok er sá lengi við þessa sǫgu. Þá er hann var fullkominn at aldri, var hann illa til frænda sinna ok einna verst til Gunnars; hann var slœgr maðr í skapferðum ok illgjarn í ráðum.

> (to seek the hand of Unn, and she married Valgard without the advice of her kinsmen. Gunnar and Njal and many others thought badly of this, because Valgard was a mean-spirited and unpopular man. They had a son, who was named Mord, and he will play a long role in this saga. When he was fully grown he was bad to his

---

35. ÍF 12:117, ch. 45; CSI 3:54.

kinsmen, and to Gunnar worst of all. He was devious by nature and malicious in his counsels.)[36]

And in chapter 46, just prior to the story of his helping Otkell and Skamkell bring charges against Gunnarr for his wife's thievery, the composer comments in the following way about Mǫrðr: "hann var slœgr ok illgjarn. Þá var Valgarðr útan, faðir hans, en móðir hans ǫnduð. Hann ǫfundaði mjǫk Gunnar frá Hlíðarenda." (He was devious and malicious. His father Valgard was abroad at the time, and his mother had died. He was very envious of Gunnarr of Hlidarendi.).[37] Resentful indebtedness to Gunnarr for his very life and jealousy of Gunnarr's success and stature seem the earlier motives for Mǫrðr's evil urge, although after Gunnarr's death, he turns this same hostility elsewhere.

His later mischief, however, which is directed against the sons of Njáll, is undertaken only at the insistence of Valgarðr, who returns to Iceland and finds it Christianized. In addition, the status of his *goðorð* (chieftancy), which had been left in Mǫrðr's hands, has been much eclipsed by the power of Njáll's family and especially by Hǫskuldr Hvítanesgoði's charismatic popularity. "Illa hefir þú launat mér goðorðit, er ek fekk þér í hendr, at fara svá ómannliga með" (You've repaid me poorly, with your unmanly handling of the godord I turned over to you), the father growls at his son. He continues:

> Vil ek nú, at þú launir þeim því, at þeim dragi ǫllum til bana. En þat er til þess, at þú rœgir þá saman ok drepi synir Njáls Hǫskuld. En þar eru margir til eptirmáls um hann, ok munu þá Njálssynir af þeim sǫkum drepnir verða.
>
> (Now I want you to repay them in a way that will drag them all to their deaths. The way to do this is to turn them against each other with slander, so that the Njalssons kill Hoskuld. Many men will take action for this slaying, and the Njalssons will be killed because of this.)[38]

---

36. ÍF 12:70, ch. 25; *CSI* 3:30.
37. ÍF 12:119, ch. 46; *CSI* 3:55.
38. ÍF 12:275, ch. 107; *CSI* 3:129.

The depth of Mǫrðr's evil, which is exacerbated by his utter lack of character under threat of his father's malevolent influence, constitutes a deadly parody of the sagas' generation gap theme, as Paul Schach observed that paradigm.[39]

His malevolence is manifest in chapter 109 as he tries to stir Hǫskuldr to anger with Njáll's sons by lying about them. Hǫskuldr, the paragon of noble behavior, responds with disgust:

> Er hér svá skótt at segja . . . um mik, at þú segir aldri svá illt frá Njálssonum, at ek muna því trúa. En þó at því sé at skipta ok segir þú satt, at annat hvárt sé, at þeir drepi mik eða ek þá, þá vil ek hálfu heldr þola dauða af þeim en ek gera þeim nǫkkut mein. En þú ert maðr at verri, er þú hefir þetta mælt.

> (Let it be said here and now that no matter what evil you speak of the Njalssons I will never believe it. And even if it happened that you told the truth and it came down to their killing me or my killing them, I would much rather suffer death from them than do them any harm. And you are all the worse for having spoken these things.)[40]

Analyses of Mǫrðr that compare him to the nebulously evil Iago neglect the concise moments in the composer's subjective analysis of his psyche. The writer defines the motives of Mǫrðr, and makes clear his father's influence on them.

When Mǫrðr, who, in the second part of the saga, has recently converted to Christianity, succeeds at his father's insistence in manipulating the sons of Njáll into killing their foster-brother Hǫskuldr Hvítanesgoði, the ramifications are far-reaching. For Hǫskuldr had married, by Njáll's arrangement, Hildigunnr Starkaðardóttir, "allra kvenna grimmust ok skaphǫrðust ok drengr mikill, þar sem vel skyldi vera" (an unusually tough and harsh-tempered woman, but a fine woman when she had to be).[41] And she in turn was the niece of Flosi Þórðarson, "hǫfðingi mikill; hann var mikill vexti ok styrkr, manna kappsamastr" (a great chieftain. He was big and strong and very forceful).[42]

---

39. Schach, "Generation-Gap." See chapter 3, the section "Fate and the Generation-Gap," for a fuller discussion of this concept.
40. ÍF 12:278, ch. 109; CSI 3:131.
41. ÍF 12:238–39, ch. 95; CSI 3:115.
42. ÍF 12:238, ch. 95; CSI 3:114.

When Flosi hears of Hǫskuldr's killing, he laments, "Þat hefir nú víst at hǫndum borit, at ek mynda gefa til mína eigu, at þetta hefði eigi fram komit; er ok illu korni sáit orðit, enda mun illt af gróa" (It's true that I would give everything I own if this matter which has come into my hands had never come to pass. But when evil seed has been sown, evil will grow).[43] Flosi is aware in advance of Mǫrðr's designs and tries unsuccessfully to persuade Hǫskuldr to relocate his household to a less hostile neighborhood. As a Christian he deplores the coming tragedy that is born of pagan ethical assumptions and eventually unfolds in the retaliatory burning of Njáll and his family, a project in which he himself must take the leading role. Egged on with remarkable frenzy by Hildigunnr in her recent widowhood, Flosi thus eventually finds himself prohibited by honor from financial settlement for the killing. The remembered power of her rhetoric and her husband's bloodied cloak force him to seek the blood vengeance that he would naturally prefer to avoid, there now being a compelling spiritual reason to do so.

Flosi's utterance about evil seed may have several references. Mǫrðr, who owes his existence to Gunnarr from a union the latter and Njáll both deplored, twice urges the burning of the hero in his home during the attack at Hlíðarendi. Leon Podles's doctoral dissertation, "Njáls saga: Pagan Myth and Christian History," studies in part the character of Hǫskuldr Hvítanessgoði in a chapter on "Martyrdom and the Dying God," which examines him as "the first sacrifice in the saga."[44] Recalling that Hǫskuldr is cut down when he is out planting seeds, he notices how Gunnarr was once injured by Otkell while sowing in his field. Both assaults were instigated or at least facilitated by Mǫrðr Valgarðsson: "The event itself is a seed planted in the ground of time, and can grow to a size out of proportion to its original dimensions, throwing out branches in unexpected directions."[45] The image of the good farmer Hǫskuldr, planting before he perished through Mǫrðr's machinations, has a starkly contrastive association with the imagery of Flosi's proverb when he hears of Hǫskuldr's killing.

In the negotiations for compensation, Njáll appeals to Flosi at the Alþingi for a peaceful settlement, speaking of his love for his

---

43. ÍF 12:288, ch. 115; CSI 3:135; JGF 488; TPMA 9.422.
44. Leon J. Podles, "Martyrdom and the Dying God, in "*Njals saga*: Pagan Myth and Christian History" (PhD diss., University of Virginia, 1975), 119.
45. Podles, "Pagan Myth and Christian History," 112–13.

deceased foster son: "Ek vil yðr kunnigt gera, at ek unna meira Hǫskuldi en sonum mínum, ok er ek spurða, at hann var veginn, þótti mér sløkkt it sœtasta ljós augna minna, ok heldr vilda ek misst hafa allra sona minna ok lifði hann" (I want you to know that I loved Hoskuld more than my own sons, and when I heard that he had been slain I felt that the sweetest light of my eyes had been put out, and I would rather have lost all my sons to have him live). Asking for a hearing, he observes: "Svá sýnisk mér sem þetta mál sé komit í ónýtt efni, ok er þat at líkendum, því at af illum rótum hefir upp runnit" (It appears that this case has come to nothing, which is as it should be since it sprang from evil roots).[46] And the most immediate, most obvious evil source to which he refers in this proverbial phrase, as members of the assembly well know, is the skulduggery of Mǫrðr Valgarðsson. Mǫrðr's overzealous pursuit of Hǫskuldr's destruction, to which his pagan and maliciously jealous father had goaded him, was followed by further manipulations, which led to this legal stalemate.

Here, though, one must recall that Hǫskuldr's killing by Skarpheðinn and his brothers had been preceded some years earlier by the death of Hǫskuldr's father, Þráinn Sigfússon, at their hands—and that his death had resulted from hostilities partly instigated and partly exacerbated by Hallgerðr. Þráinn was present, after all, at the killing of Þórðr leysingjason mainly because of Hallgerðr, his mother-in-law: "Mágr þœtti mér þú vera ... ef þú dræpir Þórð leysingjason" (I would consider you a true son-in-law ... if you killed Thord Freed-man's son), she declared, maliciously testing the power of her influence on him.[47]

The proponents of feud theory have shown in their critical readings how old injuries lie dormant and are recalled in more heated moments of the feud process, in real life as well as in saga literature. William Ian Miller, in his study "Justifying Skarpheðinn," discerns two operational patterns in explaining feud conflict in the sagas: the "balance-sheet model," with its adherence to retributive justice within a social system more or less sustained by law; and the underlying, politically motivated pattern according to which feuding families and clans remained in a state of potential conflict

---

46. ÍF 12:309, ch. 122; CSI 3:146.
47. ÍF 12:107, ch. 41; CSI 3:49.

so long as their respective interests were in mutual competition.⁴⁸ It was in fact the latter impulse that drove the continued interest in maintaining the score where injury and redress were concerned, and in *Njáls saga* we sometimes find clear reference to this real, underlying motivational source of overt conflicts.

For instance, Skarpheðinn makes explicit these lingering resentments arising from underlying competition in an exchange with Kári as they go off to kill Þráinn at the Battle of Markarfljót. Having heard Skarpheðinn's conversation with Njáll in which he says he is going to look for sheep, and in which Njáll recalls that the last time he said this, he was hunting men, Kári asks, "'Hvé nær mæltuð þér þetta fyrri?' . . . 'Þá vá ek Sigmund hvíta, frænda Gunnars,' segir Skarpheðinn. 'Fyrir hvat?' segir Kári. 'Hann hafði drepit Þórð leysingjason, fóstra minn,' segir Skarpheðinn" ("When was the other time you said this?" . . . "When I killed Sigmund the White, Gunnar's kinsman," said Skarphedin. "Why?" said Kari. "He had killed Thord Freed-man's son, my foster-father," said Skarphedin).⁴⁹ And thus, in this exchange, some early retributive actions initiating the overt level of motivations behind the feud are made clear. Those motivations, in turn, spring from the destructive plans and evil seed of Hallgerðr and of Mǫrðr, respectively. The connections are illuminated by repeated proverbs on the begetting of evil by evil, and also by suggestions that the evil of Mǫrðr is of a darker, more insidious, and more pervasive nature than that of Hallgerðr.

The *illt korn* and its *illar rœtr* with which the evil of Mǫrðr is associated by proverbs and proverbial phrases are alluded to on a number of occasions as men of good will negotiate with one another in attempts to extricate their respective parties from the chaotic conflicts resulting from his schemes. Hǫskuldr Hvítanesgoði, a man whose already refined moral sensibilities are swiftly enlightened by the teachings of early Christianity in Iceland, spurns with disgust Mǫrðr's attempts to draw him into enmity with the Njálssons: "þú ert maðr verri, er þú hefir þetta mælt" (And you are all the worse for having spoken these things).⁵⁰ Skarpheðinn and his brothers, who are less susceptible than their foster-brother to conversion, are,

---

48. William Ian Miller, "Justifying Skarpheðinn: of Pretext and Politics in the Icelandic Bloodfeud," *Scandinavian Studies* 55 (1983): 317.
49. ÍF 12:232, ch. 92; CSI 3:111–12.
50. ÍF 12:278, ch. 109; CSI 3:131.

although perhaps for ulterior reasons, less discerning of Mǫrðr's true destructive intentions and eventually give in to his manipulation.[51] Yet the saga composer has Skarpheðinn identify the plot as theirs, not his own, the latter refusing to acknowledge any independent wish on his own part to kill Hǫskuldr: "Gera skal þér kost á þessu . . . ef þú vill fara með oss ok gera at nǫkkut" (You shall have what you want . . . provided that you go along with us and take part).[52]

Although men see Mǫrðr's evil, his eloquence, like that of Milton's Satan, easily overcomes their reservations, and they eventually fall in with his designs. First, when Þorgerðr, the widow of Þráinn Sigfússon, asks Ketill of Mǫrk if he wants Mǫrðr to give notice of the slaying of her son Hǫskuldr, whom Ketill had taken to foster and whom he had promised protection, Ketill is initially reluctant: "því at fleirum þykki mér sem illt leiði af honum en gott" (for it seems to me that evil comes from him more often than good).[53] But Mǫrðr reassures him, and we are told that "þá fór honum sem ǫðrum, at svá þótti sem Mǫrðr mundi honum trúr, ok varð þat ráð þeira, at Mǫrðr skyldi lýsa víginu ok búa málit at ǫllu til alþingis" (Ketill was the same as other men—he believed that Mord could be trusted—and they agreed that Mord should give notice of the slaying and prepare the case for action at the Althing).[54]

Later, when Flosi tells his father-in-law, Hallr of Síða, of Mǫrðr's support in his suit against the Njálssons, the latter observed that "allt illt við Mǫrðr at eiga, — 'ok muntú þat reyna, áðr þessu þingi er lokit'" (it was bad to have dealings with Mord—"and you'll have proof of this before the Thing is over").[55] Men are taken in by him, yet they have an underlying awareness that the trouble they are in is linked to his machinations, even as he claims to help. After the burning at Bergþórshváll, Gizurr hvíti is insistent that Mǫrðr should prosecute the case. Ásgrímr reports him saying "at Mǫrðr skyldi sœkja, þótt honum þœtti illt, — 'skal hann því þungast at hafa, at honum hafa ǫll málin verst fari'" (that Mord should prosecute, even

---

51. Miller, "Justifying," 327, and especially 331. The peacemaker cannot escape responsibility for his peacemaking.
52. ÍF 12:280, ch. 110; CSI 3:132.
53. ÍF 12:283, ch. 112; CSI 3:133.
54. ÍF 12:283, ch. 112; CSI 3:133. Notice the authorial comment here.
55. ÍF 12:297, ch. 119; CSI 3:140.

if he didn't like it—"he should have the heaviest burden because his part in all these matters has been the worst").[56]

The evil referred to by these paroemial segments prevails in *Njáls saga* precisely because of the imperceptive nature of the innocents, or the indifference of the many. In such a society, the feud mentality, of which Hallgerðr and Mǫrðr take advantage and which they pervert to their own ends, provides fertile ground in which bad plans may flourish in the company of evil born of evil seed and fed from evil roots.

The Proverbial Wisdom of Feud Conflict in *Njáls saga*

The *Íslendingasögur* examine feuds between families; *Njáls saga*, in its extended narration of strife between the Sigfússons and the Njálssons, does so too. Interfamilial conflict in Iceland is not always their subject, however. In some instances a feud occurs primarily within a family, as in the case of *Laxdœla saga*; and *Egils saga* describes competition between the Icelandic family of Kveld-Úlfr and the royal family of Norway. As was observed earlier, in chapter 2, the figures and conflicts of the Vǫlsung-Niflung legends provide resonant background for characters and events of the *Íslendingasögur*. It is clear that the saga authors of the thirteenth century used this old mythic pattern to illuminate the more immediate feuds they attempted to describe, and at some level to censure, in the stories of their ancestors.

The prelude in the first chapter of *Vǫlsunga saga* begins, as we noted earlier in chapter 2, with an interfamilial feud between two men, Sigi, son of Óðinn, and Skaði, stemming from Sigi's blood revenge against Skaði's slave Breði for his loss of face in a hunting expedition. It ends with an intrafamilial strife in which Sigi is plotted against by his in-laws and succumbs to their homicidal machinations. As the descendants of Óðinn make their way in this prehistoric saga world, intermarriage between clans results in intrafamilial competition and tragedy. The most interesting conflicts become those between loyalty to relationships of birth, of blood, on the one hand, and of marriage, of contract, on the other. In the *Íslendingasögur*, narrative interest is fed by such conflicts in loyalty

---

56. ÍF 12:345, ch. 132; *CSI* 3:164.

resulting from a highly developed awareness of relational lines of responsibility for the maintenance of family honor. The composer of *Njál saga*, our focus here, repetitively employs several proverbs that describe the subtleties of the feud process.

"Náit er nef augum"

The enmeshment of family relationships in medieval Iceland made difficult the maintenance of integrity in fulfilling one's obligations of loyalty. In *Njáls saga*, Ingjaldr of Keldur and Ketill of Mǫrk, two of Njáll's relatives by nonconjugal alliance and by marriage, are caught in the final stages of hostility with the Sigfússons as they plan retribution for the killing of Hǫskuldr Þráinsson. Ingjaldr of Keldur, uncle of Njáll's bastard son Hǫskuldr, is married to Þraslaug Egilsdóttir, the niece of Flosi Þórðarson. When she demands Ingjaldr's support in the action over the killing of Hǫskuldr Hvítanesgoði, she reminds him of this marital association, which brings him into conflict with his family loyalty to the Njálssons: "Þat ætlaða ek, þá er ek gipta þér bróðurdóttur mína, at þú hétir mér því at veita mér at hverju máli" (I thought, when I married you to my brother's daughter, that you promised to support me in all things).[57] Ingjaldr remains uncommitted as this interview closes, and in the end he reneges on his obligations by marrying into Flosi's camp, a breach of duty for which the latter attempts to kill him following the burning. His disloyalty, in particular, could be regarded as more reprehensible since he had taken an oath of participation in the attack on Bergþórshváll following the breakdown of reconciliation at the Alþingi. Wounded by Flosi's spear in their meeting on opposite sides of the Rangár, Ingjaldr sends it back, killing Flosi's nephew Þorsteinn Kolbeinsson. Ingjaldr's dilemma is no isolated situation in the saga, however, and in episodes below we find paroemial commentary on this frequently recurring problem. This difficulty is in fact observed paroemially in the proverb "náit er nef augum" (the nose is close to the eyes), which the composer of *Njáls saga* uses strategically on two occasions.

First, Ketill Sigfússon of Mǫrk is married to Þorgerðr Njálsdóttir. With his father-in-law, he fosters Hǫskuldr Þráinsson after Þráinn is killed. When he convinces Hǫskuldr's mother, Þorgerðr

---

57. ÍF 12:293, ch. 116; *CSI* 3:138.

Glúmsdóttir, to agree to the transaction, he promises vengeance if her son is killed. She reminds him of this commitment after the killing: "Nú er Hǫskuldr dauðr, sem vit vitum. Ok mun þú nú, hverju þú hézt, þá er þú tókt hann til fóstrs." (Now Hoskuld is dead, as we know. Keep in mind now what you promised when you took him as your foster-son.) Ketill, however, cites his conflicting loyalties: "Þat má vera . . . at ek hafa þá nógu mǫrgu heitit, því at ek ætlaða ekki, at þessir dagar mundu verða" (It may well be . . . that I made many promises then, because I never expected that days like these would ever come). He goes on to observe, proverbially, "enda em ek við vant um kominn, því at náit er nef augum, þar er ek á dóttur Njáls" (In fact, I'm in a difficult position, since I'm married to Njal's daughter, for the nose is near to the eyes).[58]

Second, when commenting on the interconnectedness of his position in the network of feud obligations, Ketill Sigfússon echoes proverbially the cautionary advice of Hrútr Herjólfsson to his half-brother Hǫskuldr Dala-Kólsson when the latter hesitates to compensate Ósvífr for Hallgerðr's arrangement of the killing of his son Þorvaldr as a means of ending her first marriage. Hǫskuldr had objected to Ósvífr's demand as follows: "Eigi drap ek son þinn, ok eigi réð ek honum banaráð" (I didn't kill your son, and I didn't plan his death). He had done so, however, with some appreciation of the complainant's situation: "en þó heldr þik várkunn til at leita á nǫkkur" (but it's understandable that you should turn somewhere). Hrútr, proverbially wise in this saga, suggests the complex ramifications of Ósvífr's injury and the need for its extrajudicial redress:

> Náit er, bróðir, nef augum, ok er nauðsyn at drepa niðr illu orði ok bœta honum son sinn ok rífka svá ráð fyrir dóttur þinni, því at sá einn er til, at þetta falli niðr, því at þá er betr, at fátt sé um talat.

> (The nose is near to the eyes, dear brother. We must forestall evil rumours and compensate him for his son and in this way restore your daughter's standing; our only choice is to have this case dropped, for it will be better if it is not much talked about.)[59]

---

58. ÍF 12:282, ch. 112; CSI 3:133; JGF 414; TPMA 13.463.
59. ÍF 12:39, ch. 12; CSI 3:17: "Hǫskuldr mælti: 'Þat mun mér sízt í tauma ganga, er Hrútr segir mér, at hér mundi til mikillar ógiptu draga um kaup þessi'" (Hoskuld said, "It never happens that Hrut's predictions go wrong, and he said that great misfortune

Whether or not one accepts the validity of the more specific parallels in *Njáls saga* to current events of thirteenth-century Iceland, the atmosphere created by the severe retributive action of the saga, together with its depiction of the dysfunctionality of legal processes in addressing such action, has a compelling resonance generally with the circumstances of the Sturlung Age. The politically incestuous nature of the lines of loyalty and of competitive hostility in the power struggles the composer had seen during his own time is also reflected here. The proximity of the nose to the eyes must have been part of the consciousness of every participant in, or observer of, the widely extended feuds by which a handful of families sought to build and consolidate power over large portions of the country in the years leading to Norway's takeover of Iceland.

"Jafnan orkar tvímælis"

Concomitant with this wisdom was the anxiety-inducing awareness that whatever steps one took to maintain honor, nothing could ever lay to rest permanently the upheavals of the retributive process, emanating as they did from those long, slow, but massive tectonic collisions of clans competing for territorial dominance. Any hostile act, any move to regain honor lost in a previous injury, was bound to have eventual negative repercussions after temporary victory. Thus, in chapter 44, Bergþóra eggs her sons on to violent retaliation for the malicious verses of Sigmundr, which are inspired by Hallgerðr's venom. Using the language of Miller's balance sheet model, she announces, "Gjafir eru yðr gefnar feðgum, ok verðið þér litlir drengir af, nema þér launið" (Gifts have been given to you all, father and sons, and you will come off as little boys if you don't repay them).[60] When Skarpheðinn objects to her fuming—"Ekki hǫfu vér kvenna skap . . . at vér reiðimsk við ǫllu" (We're not like women, that we become furious over everything)—she goads him with Gunnarr's reaction: "Reiddisk Gunnarr þó fyrir yðra hǫnd . . . ok þykkir hann skapgóðr; ok ef þér rekið eigi þess réttar, þá munuð þér engrar skammar reka." (But Gunnar became furious,

---

would come from this marriage"). ÍF 12.36, ch. 12; *CSI* 3:16: "Þórarinn mælti: 'Nú er sem jafnan, at þat mun bezt gegna, at þín ráð sé hǫfð.'" (Thorarin said [to Hrútr], "Now, as always, it's best that your advice be followed") ÍF 12.43, ch. 13; *CSI* 3:19.

60. ÍF 12:114, ch. 44; *CSI* 3:52.

on your behalf, . . . and he is said to be gentle. If you don't set this to rights you will never avenge any shame.)

At her continuing remonstrations Njáll intervenes, proverbially admonishing patience and restraint: "Kemsk, þó at seint fari, húsfreyja. Ok ferr svá um mǫrg mál, þó at menn hafi skapraun af, at jafnan orkar tvímælis, þó at hefnt sé." (Everything works out, woman, though it may take time. It happens in many cases where men's tempers have been tried that the effect is double-edged, even after vengeance has been taken.)[61] His closing proverbial recognition of reciprocity in feud takes into account the impossibility of truly conclusive reconciliation in a feud-based society. Although a settlement has been reached for Sigmundr's killing of Þórðr leysingjason and Njáll's sons have promised to stand by it, the competitively fueled resentment lingers unabated, and Skarpheðinn's qualified reservation in his promise to his father was explicit: "ef til verðr nǫkkut með oss, þá munu vér minnask á inn forna fjandskap" (if anything comes up between us, we will have this old enmity in mind).[62] Similarly, even after Sigmundr is dead as a result of the *laxveiði* (salmon fishing) expedition and is finally compensated for, the same lingering resentment between his relatives and the sons of Njáll will be alive.

In chapter 91, when Skarpheðinn and his brothers continue to use the humiliation that Grímr and Helgi claim to have suffered at the hands of Hákon jarl during the Atlantic interlude as a pretext for hostilities with Þráinn, Njáll offers them advice that echoes his words to Bergþóra. Rather than immediately killing Þráinn and his men, they must be patient: "Þat mun þykkja um sakleysi, ef þeir eru drepnir, ok er þat mitt ráð at skjóta at sem flestum um at tala við þá, at sem flestum verði heyrinkunnigt, ef þeir svara illa" (It would seem unjustified if they were killed now, and my advice is that you send as many people as possible to talk to them, so that if they make ugly remarks many will hear them). Although initially people may accuse them of cowardice for their restraint, self-control will pay off: "skuluð þér þat þola um stund, því at allt orkar tvímælis" (you must put up with that for a while, for whatever is done has a

---

61. ÍF 12:114, ch. 44; *CSI* 3:53. William Ian Miller. "The Central Feud in *Njáls Saga*," in *Sagas*, ed. Tucker, 292-322. This chapter is a revised version of "Justifying." See also JGF 317; *TPMA* 7.271; JGF 583; *TPMA* 13.463.

62. ÍF 12:111, ch. 43; *CSI* 3:51.

double-edged effect), he advises them proverbially. The sharp edge of the abuse will also sharpen support for their taking retribution for the slander. He adds that if they had sought his advice, "þá munduð þér aldri hafa orði á komit, ok myndi yðr þá engi svíviðing í vera" (you would never have spoken about this matter at all, and there would be no disgrace in that). As it is, the political reality they have created is harsh, and its results are inescapable: "nú hafið þér af ina mestu raun, ok mun þat þó svá aukanda fara um yðra svíviðing, at þér munuð ekki fá at gǫrt, fyrr en þér leggið vandræði á yðr ok vegið með vápnum, ok er því langa nót at draga." (Now you face a very hard trial: your disgrace will grow to the point where you have no other choice than to deal with the difficulty and wield weapons to kill. That is why we must lay out our net so carefully.)[63] He concludes thus, having emphasized the fact that the killings will not end their hostilities and that they must proceed with the utmost care, so as to inflict the greatest possible damage while leaving the least vulnerability to further retribution.

The primary consideration for the ethical basis of behavior as suggested by the proverbs of feud conflict discussed above lies quite simply in the anticipated result. One's actions must be measured according to the desired degree of damage they will inflict and the likely repercussion the damage will provoke. The fact that such wisdom, originating in a pre-Christian Norse society, appears to be celebrated by a late thirteenth-century saga composer writing for a society that has been Christian for nearly three centuries affirms what we already know from *Sturlunga saga* and related sources: the ethical standards actually in force had not changed much with the new faith. In fact, the nostalgic element of *Njáls saga* and others of its genre easily suggests a shared sense of a Golden Age, when people had behaved in better ways than could be said of them when the composer wrote, or when at least they could have been excused on the grounds of lacking Christian awareness. Concomitant with this ironic criticism of thirteenth-century mores, we find a sense of nostalgia for a time that may never have been except in the mind of those who created and appreciated the saga world.

Magnanimity of spirit and nobility of behavior could be, and were, attributed to pagan heroes of the *Íslendingasögur*, as well as

---

63. ÍF 12:226, ch. 91; *CSI* 3:108; *TPMA* 8.470.

to Christians.⁶⁴ And while feud wisdom dealt in the harsh terms of injury and revenge, it was tempered by the awareness of a need for abiding patience and even prudent restraint. It was an acknowledged fact, as observed proverbially in *Vatnsdœla saga*, that "blóðnætr eru bráðastar" (blood nights are the most furious) in the saga world as in the Sturlungaöld.⁶⁵ It is in recognition of this primitive and often excessively destructive urge to vengeance that Óláfr pái Hǫskuldsson can tell his son Kjartan in *Laxdœla saga* to delay retaliation when it emerges that Guðrún's brothers have stolen from his wife Hrefna the headdress Ingibjǫrg had given him in Norway:

> Enn vilda ek sem fyrr, at þú létir vera ok hjá þér líða þetta vandræði; mun ek leita eptir þessu í hljóði; því at þar til vilda ek allt vinna, at ykkr Bolla skildi eigi á; er um heilt bezt at binda, frændi.

> (As before, I should still like you to ignore this incident and let it pass. I shall make discreet inquiries about it myself, for I would do anything to prevent a breach between you and Bolli. Whole flesh is easier to dress than wounds, my son.)⁶⁶

This same spirit of prudence is also inherent in Skalla-Grímr's advice to his son Þórólfr, when the latter wants to return to Norway and pursue further his friendship with Eiríkr blóðøx Haraldsson, despite their two families being in a feud with each other. "Skalla-Grímr latti hann, sagði, at þá var gott heilum vagni heim at aka; 'hefir þú,' sagði hann, 'farit fremðarfǫr mikla, en þat er mælt, er ýmsar verðr, ef margar ferr.'" (Skallagrim tried to discourage him, reminding him that "it is better to ride a whole wagon home." "Certainly you have made an illustrious journey," he said, "but there's a saying, "the more journeys you make, the more directions they take.")⁶⁷ Þórólfr's father refers to this same economy of hostility, but with reference to long-range political competition rather than immediate retribution, which the composer of *Egils saga* presents as central to the underlying

---

64. Lönnroth, "Heathen," 1–29.
65. Einar Ól. Sveinsson, ed., *Vatnsdæla saga*, Íslenzk fornrit 8 (Reykjavík: Hið íslenzka fornritafélag, 1939), 64, ch. 24; *CSI* 4:31; *JGF* 58; *TPMA* 2.50.
66. ÍF 5:143, ch. 46; Magnus Magnusson and Hermann Pálsson, trans., *Laxdæla saga* (London: Penguin, 1969), 166; *JGF* 234; *TPMA* 4.444.
67. ÍF 2:96, ch. 38; *CSI* 1:76; *JGF* 597; *TPMA* 12.311.

enmity between Þórólfr's relatives and the most powerful family in Norway.

The implications of the political awareness represented in the proverb "(Jafnan/allt) orkar tvímælis" ((Always/Everything) whatever is done has a double-edged effect) are far-reaching in the saga world; accordingly, the ethics of retribution are much more limiting than might at first seem credible to a reader unfamiliar with the conditions of feud established in the *Islendingasögur*. The inevitable reciprocity of injury in feud is celebrated paroemially in other ways aside from those discussed above.

The composer of *Njáls saga* has shown how the evil of a very few can violently disrupt the relatively benign complacency of the majority despite the well-intentioned efforts of good people in society. Gunnarr and Njáll in the late pre-Christian era keep the peace at all costs, frustrating the intentions of Hallgerðr and the responses of Bergþóra by sacrificing the potentially more stringent maintenance of their respective reputations for the sake of their friendship. As Njáll once predicted would be the case, their friendship is maintained but at great expense.[68] Such restraint among heathens as practiced by these two men is augmented, if not replaced, following the conversion by varying sensitivity to violence and killing among adherents of the new faith, where their wavering reluctance to pursue blood vengeance may now be seen as a factor in the degree to which they have assimilated Christian ethics.

Njáll himself, whom the composer represents as having experienced a partial revelation of divine love and who became an early convert to Christianity, nevertheless retains much of the pagan ethic, with its heroic restraint, in his position as leader of his family in its competition with the Sigfússon clan. Of all the saga's preconversion characters, he applies this pagan ethic to his dealings with the utmost care, counseling against and avoiding violent confrontation wherever possible. Until his sons kill Hǫskuldr Hvítanesgoði, Njáll never wavers in seeking survival for himself and his family in the disheartening light of his clairvoyant awareness of their inevitable doom. Despite his ingenuity, the darkness, which is personified as well as spread by Hallgerðr and Mǫrðr, prevails. Njáll struggles against its chaotic and destructive force

---

68. ÍF 12: 87, ch. 33; *CSI* 3:38.

until nearly all members of the opposing parties, none of whom are particularly evil in themselves, are dead. The theme of *Njáls saga* is somehow embedded in this tragic pattern, and it seems likely that the composer has used the structure of his work to illuminate and emphasize his purposes.

"At skamma stund verðr hǫnd hǫggvi fegin": Seeking the Point of *Njáls saga*

When Rannveig, who is aware of the consequences, learns that Sigmundr has killed Þórðr leysingjason, she observes, in warning him, "Þat er mælt, at skamma stund verðr hǫnd hǫggvi fegin, enda mun svá hér" (There's a saying, ... that the hand's joy in the blow is brief, and so it will be here).[69] She thus recalls the communal wisdom of retaliatory conflict discussed above, and she uses a formula that combines the transitory celebration of a moment of victory with an awareness of inevitable revenge for the blow. As noticed above, Njáll twice observes that "allt orkar tvímælis" (whatever is done has a double-edged effect), referring to the tragically circular process of retributive justice in feud. The composer places this comment, which is marked by its proverbial status, with the crucial killing of Þórðr leysingjason, from which, as we have observed above, the remainder of *Njáls saga*'s narrative thread can be seen to grow.[70] This proverb is used three times in *Njáls saga* but it is found nowhere else in the *Íslendingasögur*.

Early in the second part of the saga—in chapter 99, when Lýtingr reports to Hǫskuldr Þráinsson Hvítanesgoði his slaying of Njáll's bastard son Hǫskuldr—the leader of the Sigfússon clan echoes Rannveig's proverbial assertion: "Mun hér sannask þat, sem mælt er, at skamma stund verðr hǫnd hǫggvi fegin, enda þykki mér nú sem þér þykki ísjávert, hvárt þú munt fá haldit þik eða cigi" (Here is the proof of the saying that "the hand's joy in the blow is brief," and now it seems to me that you must be in some doubt as to whether you'll be able to save your life).[71]

Even though Lýtingr's fear for his life is justified, the narrative

---

69. ÍF 12:109, ch. 42; CSI 3:50; JGF 283; TPMA 10.120. A form of this proverb is found also used by Saxo, book 5, in the story of Eric Disertus: Saxo, 284-85.
70. JGF 583; TPMA 13.463.
71. ÍF 12:253, ch. 99; CSI 3:120.

result of the killing lies first in its resolution between Hǫskuldr and Njáll without his sons' presence at their meeting. Waking to learn of their reconciliation, Grímr exclaims, "Þat var illa" (That's bad). Njáll does not disagree, but he excuses his unilateral action: "Ekki myndi Hǫskuldr ... hafa skotit skildi fyrir hann, ef þú hefðir drepit hann, er þér var þat ætlat" (Hoskuld wouldn't have been able to shield Lyting ... if you had killed him, as you were meant to). Their smoldering resentment of the position and power of their *fóstbróðir* again rekindled, Skarpheðinn tells Grímr, "Telju vér ekki á fǫður várn" (Let's not blame our father).[72] The vengeance he will soon take for the manufactured grievances supplied by Mǫrðr is clearly fed both by the killing of his half-brother and by its resolution. The thread of the saga's feud is crucially renewed by this incident, which is as important to the plot in its consequences as the killing of Þórðr leysingjason is.

There is thus a second result of the episode. Lýtingr's suddenly conceived and seemingly gratuitous killing of Hǫskuldr Njálsson and its aftermath have again moved the political competition of the two clans into an active retributive phase, even though the composer ends this particular episode with the comment, "Nú er at segja frá því, at þessi sætt helzk með þeim" (It has to be said that this settlement between them was kept).[73] It is this chance renewal of hostility that will lead to the killing of Hǫskuldr Hvítanesgoði and then to the burning of Njáll and his family.

The proverb appears in the text a third time in the last part of the saga when Flosi Þórðarson, leader of the burners, goes about Iceland seeking support in arranging a settlement for the atrocity. His father-in-law Hallr of Síða, one of the earliest converts to Christianity, comments on his now vulnerable situation: "Nú er svá orðit, sem mælt er, at skamma stund verðr hǫnd hǫggvi fegin. Ok er sá nú allr einn í þínu fǫruneyti, er nú hefr eigi hǫfuðs, ok hinn, er þá fýsti ins verra." ("It's turned out just as the saying goes, that the hand's pleasure in the blow is brief. Now the same men in your following who were eager to do wrong are afraid to hold their heads high.")[74] This scene precedes the concluding chapters of *Njáls saga*, in which Njáll's son-in-law, Kári Sǫlmundarson—who had

---

72. ÍF 12:254–55, ch. 99; *CSI* 3:121.
73. ÍF 12:255, ch. 99; *CSI* 3:121.
74. ÍF 12:349, ch. 134; *CSI* 3:165.

been introduced into Iceland and his family by means of a chance interaction with Grímr and Helgi during the Atlantic interlude—having escaped from the burning at Bergþórshváll, ranges over Iceland and the North Atlantic, taking blood vengeance on nearly all the burners.

Thus, in each of the three parts of the saga, a character whose dignity and wisdom are commonly respected uses this same proverb to comment on a killing the results of which will have far-reaching implications for the plot. No one knows how the composer of *Njáls saga* perceived its macrostucture; nor can we even be sure that he did so in any conscious way. Views on the subject abound, however, several of them having in recent decades been generated by the application of various theories of saga composition. Paul Schach lays out the old, generally accepted tripartite division, composed of (1) the story of Gunnarr, (2) the burning of Njáll, and (3) "the relentless quest of Njál's son-in-law Kári for vengeance."[75] Stefán Einarsson, in his *History of Icelandic Literature*, suggests that the rest of the narrative depends on this tripartite structure: "This three-domed architecture is supported and thrown in relief by many secondary pinnacles and niches, all blending into one harmonious whole."[76] His observations are similar to those of Einar Ól. Sveinsson, who details the division in his 1954 edition and who, in his *Njáls Saga: A Literary Masterpiece*, remarks that "each of these three parts, which are clearly separated from each other, again falls into distinct acts, which are again subdivided into scenes (to use somewhat loosely the terminology of drama), and the division between the acts and sometimes also between the individual scenes of an act is likewise usually quite clear."[77]

This view is most coherently justified by W. P. Ker, whose reading is based on a sensitive observation:

> It falls into three divisions, each of these a story by itself, with all three combining to form one story, apart from which they are incomplete. The first, the story of Gunnar, which is a tragedy by itself, is a necessary part of the whole composition; for it is also the story

---

75. Paul Schach, *Icelandic Sagas*, Twayne's World Authors Series, Scandinavian Literature (Boston: Twayne, 1984), 117.
76. Stefán Einarsson, *A History of Icelandic Literature* (Baltimore: Johns Hopkins Press, 1957), 146–47.
77. Einar Ól. Sveinsson, *Masterpiece*, 53.

of the wisdom of Njal and the dignity of Bergthora, without which the second part would be insipid, and the great act of the burning of Njal's house would lose its depth and significance. The third part is the payment of a debt to Njal, Bergthora, and Skarphedinn, for whom vengeance is required; but it is also due even more to Flosi their adversary. The essence of the tragic situation lies in this, that the good man is in the wrong, and his adversary in the right. The third part is required to restore the balance, in order that the original wrong, Skarpedinn's slaughter of the priest of Whiteness, should not be thought to be avoided in the death of its author.[78]

Teaching and reference texts up to the middle of the twentieth century concur with this view. In E. V. Gordon's introduction to reading passages from *Njáls saga* he provides simply a survey of the saga's three parts.[79] Interestingly, even Denton Fox, who for some reason claimed to hold a different view of the structure itself, was nonetheless able to perceive that the saga's three heroes were Gunnarr, Njáll, and Kári.[80]

A single proverb, even when repeated three times in *Njáls saga*, whose composer uses repetition of phrase for the establishment and reinforcement of meaning, does not of course define the structure of a whole saga, if indeed there is any structure to be defined in terms of which we are presently aware. The repetition of this proverb, however, at a crucial point in each of these three generally agreed-on sections, given what we have seen of the subtle use of repetition in other cited instances, certainly lends phraseological evidence supporting such a division of the narrative. At the same time, the composer's use of this proverb to signal these divisions of the saga suggests that he attached paradigmatic significance to

---

78. Ker, *Epic and Romance*, 190–91. Guðbrandur Vigfússon may have been the first critic to describe thus the structure of *Njáls saga* in his study of the major Icelandic sagas, in the Prolegomena to his 1878 edition of *Sturlunga saga*. See Guðbrandur Vigfússon, *Sturlunga Saga including the Islendinga Saga of Lawman Sturla Thordsson and Other Works*, 2 vols. (Oxford: Clarendon Press, 1878), 1:xlii–xliii.

79. E. V. Gordon, *An Introduction to Old Norse*, 2nd ed., rev. A. R. Taylor (Oxford: Oxford University Press, 1957), 87.

80. Denton Fox, "*Njál's Saga* and the Western Literary Tradition," *Comparative Literature* 15.4 (1963): 289–310. Imaginatively, on 293: "Although the saga breaks very obviously into two main parts, it can also be divided more precisely into five sections." And rather fancifully, on 309: "We see Kari as the final hero, uniting in himself the figures of the heroic individual, Gunnar, and the man of justice and Christianity, Njal, but finding for himself a new solution, and one which involves life, not death."

its wisdom. The concept of the brief joy of blows rendered in feud conflict summarizes the innate instability of order in a feud-based society, where "allt orkar tvímælis" (whatever is done has a double-edged effect); at the same time. it emphasizes the tragic vulnerability of such a society's members to the incidental blows of retributive justice.

Primal Chaos and the Urge to Order: Proverbial Commentary on lǫg í landi, the Felling of Trees, and the Social Order

Hallgerðr's evil plans bring about the immediate deaths of a few men and plant seeds of enmity that eventually flourish in the central tragedy of the saga. Mǫrðr Valgarðsson is much more dynamically involved in those later processes of destruction, challenging the social urge to order by inciting distrust and hatred among men who would otherwise have, at most, only passive urges to be at odds with one another. Mǫrðr's destructive character is defined as evil in *Njáls saga*, which is situated within the early Christian community of Iceland's saga world, where he is a reluctant and easily discouraged convert to the new religion. However, he can also be viewed in a pre-Christian ethical perspective as contributing to that chaos from which the world's ephemerally established order evolved and to which it must inevitably return at Ragnarǫk.

The Mythological Overlay of Chaos

As Einar Ól. Sveinsson observed while describing how the characters in *Njáls saga* display "distinct family traits, which can be traced from ancient lines," the eponymous hero himself "bears the family mark of Óðinn, but this family line is difficult to trace; and Njáll has many characteristics which can be derived from elsewhere."[81] Similarly, Mǫrðr Valgarðsson, identified at one point by Lars Lönnroth as Njáll's "evil counterpart" in that he instigates and provides plans for the antagonistic element of the narrative, might well be viewed as a figure of Loki. While Richard North identifies him as envy in Christian emblematic terms, his personality and attitudes, including his envious nature, clearly also mark him as the trickster proponent of destructive

---

81. Einar Ól. Sveinsson, *Masterpiece*, 33.

ends in the North Germanic pantheon, where the Christian conflict of good and evil was preceded by the eventually tragic struggle of order against the eternal and all-encompassing power of chaos.[82]

As Ian Maxwell has observed, the feud between the two women is realized in the disruption of all Icelandic society. So too that disruption, contrary to Richard Allen's view, seems to find clear epic expansion at the conceptual level in its resonance with the cataclysmic *Vǫluspá*, "where the world of gods and men falls apart into the blaze and extinction of *ragnarǫk* only to emerge into a new light."[83] While Loki lives among and seems to be one of the Æsir, his jealousy of Baldr's invulnerability makes him plot his destruction by Hǫrðr, and at *Ragnarǫk* he leads the forces of Hel and fights Heimdallr until they kill each other. As Gangleri says, commenting on the god's deviousness to Hárr, "Allmiklu kom Loki á leið, er hann olli fyrst því, er Baldr var veginn, ok svá því, er hann varð eigi leystr frá helju" (It was quite an achievement of Loki's when he brought it about first of all that Baldr was killed, and also that he was not redeemed from Hel).[84]

In *Njáls saga* Mǫrðr is seen to be similarly cunning in bringing about his kinsman Gunnarr's death. Taking advantage of the power of law and the quirks of fate, he helps the poorly sighted Otkell prove that Hallgerðr's slave Melkólfr stole the cheese at Kirkjubær, but he does this secretly. Later, once Otkell and Skamkell are killed, he instructs Þorgeirr Starkaðarson in how Njáll has predicted that if Gunnarr kills twice in the same family bloodline it will be his death. He tells Þorgeirr to involve his namesake Þorgeirr Otkelsson:

> Ok ef þit eruð á einum fundi, þá skalt þú hlífa þér, en hann mun ganga fram vel, ok mun Gunnarr vega hann. Hefir hann þá vegit tysvar í inn sama knérunn, en þú skalt flýja af fundinum. En ef honum vill þetta til dauða draga, þá mun hann rjúfa sættina. Er þat til at sitja.
>
> (If the two of you are together in a fight, you must protect yourself and let him go ahead, and Gunnar will slay him. Then he will have

---

82. Lönnroth, *Introduction*, 27; Richard North, *Pagan Words and Christian Meanings*, Costerus new series 81 (Amsterdam: Rodopi, 1991), 172–75.
83. Maxwell, "Pattern," 33–34; Allen, *Approaches*, 131.
84. Guðni Jónsson, ed., *Edda*, 84, ch. 50; Snorri Sturluson, *Edda*, trans. Anthony Faulkes (London: J. M. Dent and Charles E. Tuttle, 1998), 51.

killed twice within the same bloodline, and you must flee the fight. If this is to lead to his death, he will have to break the settlement made for his slaying. For that we will just sit and wait.)[85]

Thus, patient inaction will bring about the destruction Mǫrðr seeks to cause, and he has no compunction about making a sacrifice of Þorgeirr Otkellsson for these ends. His utter lack of regard for humanity at points such as this contributes to the view of his character's participation in the figure of Loki.

Njáll, Beleagured Proponent of lǫg í landi

In the context of a society whose order is thus threatened by such chaotic forces with mythic resonance, several comments by Njáll, "lǫgmaðr svá mikill, at engi fannsk hans jafningi" (so well versed in the law that he had no equal), on the necessity of law for the maintenance of order are surely to be viewed in a serious light.[86] These comments can be interpreted or applied to our critical understanding of what the saga is about.

After he prevents Þorgeirr Starkaðarson and Þorgeirr Otkelsson from attacking Gunnarr, Mǫrðr having provided false information about the illegality of Gunnarr's actions, Njáll leads discussion at the Alþingi over what legal course is needed for dealing with these peacebreakers. When Mǫrðr claims Gunnarr had himself broken the settlement made after he was attacked at Knafahólar by Starkaðr and his men, Njáll responds, showing how Gunnarr had in fact acted within the law and offering the famous proverbial comment, "Eigi er þat sættarrof . . . at hverr hafi lǫg við annan, því at með lǫgum skal land várt byggja, en með ólǫgum eyða" (It's not breaking a settlement . . . if a man deals lawfully with another—with law our land shall rise, but it will perish with lawlessness).[87] The composer adds that the two Þorgeirrs, learning how they had been misled by Mǫrðr, "tǫlðu á hann mjǫk ok kváðusk af honum hljóta þetta fégjald" (rebuked him strongly and said that the fine would be his fault).[88]

Robert Cook has described in detail ways in which *Njáls saga*,

---

85. ÍF 12:168, ch. 67; *CSI* 3:79.
86. ÍF 12:57, ch. 20; *CSI* 3:25.
87. ÍF 12:172, ch. 70; *CSI* 3:82; JGF 375; *TPMA* 4.428.
88. ÍF 12:173, ch. 70; *CSI* 3:82.

"more than any other family saga," is about law: "The first person mentioned—though he initiates only one case and is a minor figure in the saga—is described in terms of his ability at law."[89] And yet oddly, as many have remarked, the law does not prove effective for maintaining order in long range terms in society: "That no conflict is settled in court . . . is part of a larger irony, and no doubt a deliberate irony, since it is so obvious in the saga: law, even the elaborate law code of medieval Iceland, is incapable of controlling violence. As the saga progresses, there is increasing emphasis on blood vengeance. . . ."[90]

Nevertheless, the extent to which Njáll will rely on law for the resolution of conflict is demonstrated when, to secure peace with the Sigfússon clan, he seeks to have Hǫskuldr Þráinsson elevated to a *goðorð*, thus making him acceptable in marriage to Flosi's niece Hildigunnr Starkaðardóttir. With all the existing *goðorðs* taken, he has used flawed advice to sabotage legal proceedings at the Alþingi, succeeding so well thereby in the delay of justice that by the next year's meeting, people are extremely frustrated. When Njáll calls for men to give their lawsuits, they complain "at lítils þœtti þat koma, því at engi kœmi sínu máli fram, þótt til þinga væri stefnt,—'ok vilju vér heldr . . . heimta með oddi ok eggju'" (that it was hardly worth it, for even cases brought to the Thing were getting nowhere—"and we would rather . . . press our claims with point and edge"). Feigning dismay at the anger to which his own muddling of legal processes has purposely brought them, Njáll urgently disputes the course of violence to which they would resort:

Svá má eigi, . . . ok hlýðir þat hvergi at hafa eigi lǫg í landi. En þó hafið þér mikit til yðvars máls um þat, ok kemr þat til vár er kunnum lǫgin ok þeim skulum stjórna. Þykki mér þat ráð, at vér kallimsk saman allir hǫfðingjar ok talim um.

(That you must not do, . . . for it would never do to be without law in the land. But there is much truth in what you say, and those of us who know the law should shape it. The best step, it seems to me, is for us to call a meeting of all the chieftains to talk about it.)[91]

---

89. Robert Cook, introduction to *Njals Saga*, trans. Robert Cook, rev. ed. (London: Penguin, 2002), xxiii.
90. Cook, introduction, xxv.
91. ÍF 12:242, ch. 97; *CSI* 3:116.

Alluding here to the proverbial statement he cited in discussion with Mǫrðr, which is well known in other contexts and which is referred to later by Þorgeirr ljósvetningagoði as he proceeds to lay down the first laws of the conversion, he suggests in solution a fifth court, and *goðorðs* with it, as a court of appeals from the decisions of the quarter courts. And thus for his own reasons Njáll reshapes the country's constitution, in this pseudohistorical episode, for the marriage of his foster son, even recommending him to the assembly as one of the new *goðar*. His intentions in this gross manipulation of his countrymen and their law appear benign; indeed, he openly explains to them the background of his need to establish Hǫskuldr in a *goðorð*, to obtain a good marriage for him, as part of a prolongation of attempted settlement over his sons' killing of Þráinn Sigfússon. This interestingly complex approach to the improvement of his own family's political situation seems in some ways to place him in the family of Óðinn, to call to mind Einar Ól. Sveinsson's thinking, but its purpose was a benign continuation of efforts he had made ever since the killing of Þráinn in order to head off an eventual confrontation between his own sons and Þráinn's heir and most likely avenger.

The Fostering of Hǫskuldr Þráinsson: "Oft er úlfr í ungum syni"

It cannot be denied that Njáll had undertaken the fostering of Hǫskuldr Þráinsson with great care, however unfortunate its consequences proved to be. Although immediate hostilities over the killing of Þráinn Sigfússon had been alleviated in the settlement arranged between Njáll and his son-in-law Ketill Sigfússon of Mǫrk, the underlying competitive conflict between the Njálssons and the Sigfússons over political dominance in their neighborhood would continue, with Hǫskuldr likely to become the next leader of his father's family, and this could make him a valuable ally if he proved to be of suitable character. It was for such reasons that Njáll himself had undertaken the fostering in the first place only with great circumspection. He had arranged first for Ketill of Mǫrk to take him from Þorgerðr by an agreement in which—ironically, as it turned out—Ketill promised her he would avenge Hǫskuldr if he were killed by weapons. Second, in a carefully worded interview with the boy, he had established that Hǫskuldr bore no apparent ill will over his father's killing by the Njálssons and he had assessed positively the magnanimity of his character. Hǫskuldr accepted a gold ring that Njáll offered him, and when the latter then asked if the boy knew how his father died, he answered, "Veit ek, at Skarpheðinn vá hann, ok þurfu vit ekki á þat at minnask, er sætzk hefir á verit ok fullar bœtr hafa fyrir komit" (I know that Skarphedin killed him, but we don't have to remind ourselves of that, since the matter was settled and full compensation was paid).[92] From this ideal pre-Christian response Njáll determined Hǫskuldr was not in himself a threat to the welfare of his family. "Betr er svarat... en ek spurða, ok munt þú verða góðr maðr" (Your answer is better... than my question... you will be a good man), he observed, alluding to his fears over the potential threats for which he had probed in their brief interchange: "Nú vil ek bjóða þér fóstr, ef þú vill þiggja" (I want to make you my foster-son, if you will accept the offer).[93] In the years following, as Hǫskuldr and his foster-brothers matured, he seemed from the composer's account to be a much loved member of their household.

To the audience of *Njáls saga*, the inadvisability of taking Hǫskuldr into Njáll's own home would have been immediately obvious, since he was the member of his family on whom further responsibility for vengeance for his father's death would eventually fall, despite the settlement that had already been arranged. At this point, the audience of the saga must have been acutely conscious of the sort of political wisdom expressed in Brynhildr's proverbially reinforced advice to Sigurd in *Vǫlsunga saga*, as we noticed above: "Ok trú ekki þeim, er þá hefir felldan fyrir föður eða bróður eða annan náfrænda, þótt ungr sé. Oft er úlfr í ungum syni" (And do not trust any man, even though he is young, whose father or brother or close kinsman has been killed by you; often a wolf lies in a young son).[94] Based by that saga's composer on a passage found in *Sigurðarkviða in skamma*—"Látum son fara / feðr í sinni, / skal-a úlf ala / ungan lengi" (Let's send the son the same way as his father!

---

92. ÍF 12:236–37, ch. 94; CSI 3:114. Here the young Hǫskuldr displays an admirable precocity of understanding and a forbearance in using already the language of feud lamentation and vengeance to deny any necessity for the continuation of the process in the instance of his father's killing by the sons of Njáll. See footnote in chapter 2, section "*Skǫrungr mikill*: The Woman of Unbending Character," for the pertinent conversation of Sigmundr and Þórir following the killing of their fathers, Brestir and Beinir, in *Færeyinga saga*.
93. ÍF 12:237, ch. 94; CSI 3:114.
94. FSN 1:163, ch. 21; Byock, *Volsungs*, 71; JGF 583; TPMA 13.181.

/ Don't nurture for long the young wolf)—it captures the essence of long-range political necessity as it impinges on Njáll's agenda in his complex pursuit of alliance with the enemy through the fostering of Hǫskuldr.⁹⁵

However his character or disposition might develop as he matured, his responsibilities to his own family's interests were likely to lead eventually to conflict with the sons of Njáll. It is to this danger that Flosi alludes when Njáll first attempts to arrange a marriage between Hǫskuldr and Flosi's niece Hildigunnr: "Vel er slíkt stofnat ... en þó hafið þér hættumikit hvárir við aðra, eða hvat segir þú frá Hǫskuldi?" (That's a good plan ... but the relationship between you and Hoskuld is very precarious. What can you say about Hoskuld?)⁹⁶ Miller discusses Njáll's complex motives in bringing this proverbial wolf cub into his home. He had recognized the boy as a peacemaker, like himself, and therefore a future leader of his clan to be cultivated through the close ties that resulted from his inclusion in this way. Also, by fostering Hǫskuldr he gave compensation beyond the formal settlement itself, "ritually humbling himself before the Sigfússons, who undoubtedly feel humbled themselves by having accepted compensation for their brother rather than having pursued vengeance."⁹⁷

Readers have explored various interpretations of Njáll's character and motives to comprehend how, with his inimitable legal expertise and unfailing clairvoyance, he could prove unable to save himself and his family from that destruction, the inevitability of which he was aware for such a long time. The tragedy is alluded to so frequently in the narrative that a complete summary of those instances, some more explicit than others, would necessitate recounting much of the book. From the second page, where Hrútr observes of Hallgerðr and her *þjófsaugu*, "Œrit fǫgr er mær sjá, ok munu margir þess gjalda" (The girl is very beautiful, and many will pay for that), one is conscious of inevitable doom.⁹⁸ It is Njáll himself who wishes Gunnarr would not go to the Alþingi, where he will meet and become betrothed to Hallgerðr, and Njáll's reaction to the engagement is emphatically clear: "Af henni mun standa allt it

---

95. ÍF 36, 2:337, st. 12; Larrington, *Poetic Edda*, 178; see *TPMA* 13.181.
96. ÍF 12:241, ch. 97; *CSI* 3:116.
97. Miller, "Justifying," 326. See *JGF* 161 and *TPMA* 7.42 for the proverbial demarcation of status in the fostering contract.
98. ÍF 12:7, ch. 1; *CSI* 3:2.

illa, er hon kemr austr hingat" (All kinds of trouble will arise from her if she comes east).⁹⁹ Repeatedly, his pronouncements anticipate the destruction of his family, and one is lulled into acceptance by the time he tells Skarpheðinn, after learning of the killing of Hǫskuldr, that he sees what will follow: "'Hvat mun eptir koma?' segir Skarpheðinn. 'Dauði minn,' segir Njáll, 'ok allra sona minna'" ("What will follow?" says Skarphedin. "My death," says Njal, "and those of my wife and all my sons").¹⁰⁰ Just as the processes of law prove dysfunctional for staving off the chaotic forces at work in the world of *Njáls saga*, so does the clairvoyant hero's gift seem ultimately useless in protecting his family from those influences. Readers in fact argue most persuasively that after the killing of Hǫskuldr Hvítanesgóði, Njáll quits trying to save his family, either out of recognition of the hopelessness of the situation, or out of a conviction that his sons deserve to die for this killing. References to law in its relation to the conversion and the Christian faith may well be helpful to our understanding of Njáll and his apparent shift toward self-destruction.

The Conversion to Christianity

When Þangbrandr, the robust emissary of King Óláfr's Christian mission to Iceland, contemplates his relative lack of success in attempting to bring its people into the fold, he is comforted by the early convert Gestr Oddleifsson, the other clairvoyant of note in *Njáls saga* and a mostly benign prophetic figure in several other sagas: "Þú hefir þó mest at gǫrt ... þó at ǫðrum verði auðit í lǫg at leiða" (You've done most of the work ... even though others may be destined to make the faith law).¹⁰¹ The composer thus links Þangbrandr's clumsy conversion methods, which are energetic to the point of homicide, to the legally arbitrated resolution of the potentially devastating religious conflict between pagans and Christians at the Alþingi.

Only two chapters later, in a scene that, in its intensity, anticipates the Alþingi meeting where settlement is reached for the burning, Christians and pagans move to form two autonomous political

---
99. ÍF 12:87, ch. 33; *CSI* 3:38.
100. ÍF 12:281, ch. 111; *CSI* 3:133, slightly modified.
101. ÍF 12:268–69, ch. 103; *CSI* 3:126.

groups: "gengu hvárirtveggju til lǫgbergs, ok nefndu hvárir vátta, kristnir menn ok heiðnir, ok sǫgðusk hvárir ór lǫgum annarra, ok varð þá svá mikit óhljóð at lǫgbergi, at engi nam annars mál" (both sides went to the Law Rock and both, Christians and heathens, named witnesses and declared themselves no longer bound to the other. Then there was such an uproar at the Law Rock that no one could hear anything).[102] As arbitrator of the situation, the pagan Þorgeirr goði, who is chosen by the *lǫgsǫgumaðr* and early Christian convert Hallr af Síðu, emerges from a day spent under his cloak to observe proverbially, in a passage bearing conceptual associations with Njáll's earlier response to Mǫrðr Valgarðsson when they argued over Gunnarr's culpability: "Svá lízk mér sem málum várum sé komit í ónýtt efni, ef eigi hafa ein lǫg allir, en ef sundr skipt er lǫgunum, þá mun ok sundr skipt friðinum, ok mun eigi við þat mega búa" (It appears to me that our affairs will be hopeless if we don't all have the same law, for if the law is split then peace will be split, and we can't live with that).[103]

When everyone assents to his asking pagans and Christians to abide by the one law he will lay down, Þorgeirr proceeds to institute the first basic statutes of Christian law in Iceland. The composer follows the text of *Kristnisaga* for these details. Although pagans consider themselves deceived, he writes, the law takes effect. But just as the law of *Njáls saga* in pre-Christian Iceland proved inadequate in its purpose, failing to control the competitive activities of powerful clans, so too would it fail in the postconversion era, if not owing to Icelanders' early confusion over its Christian implications then surely owing to the cynical misapplication of its force.

The Case of Ámundi inn blindi: "svá nær hjarta"

The composer makes it clear at the beginning of chapter 106, on the first page of his new, Christian, saga that new ideological conflicts, while they do not replace those based on the old ties of loyalty, nevertheless become part of the current political reality that has resulted from the change in faith. In chapter 106, which occurs immediately after the account about Þorgeirr's decision—which is designated in saga time as "þrim vetrum síðar" (three

---

102. ÍF 12:271, ch. 105; *CSI* 3:127.
103. ÍF 12:271–72, ch. 105; *CSI* 3:127; JGF 374; *TPMA* 4.428.

years later) and which in Finnur Jónsson's view was intended to be relative to the events of chapters 98–99 rather than dating from the conversion itself—another fateful figure suddenly emerges at this time at the Þingskálaþing.[104] Ámundi the blind is introduced as seeking compensation from Lýtingr of Sámstaðir for killing his father, Hǫskuldr Njálsson. When Lýtingr, who also appeared suddenly and with weak narrative motivation in the story, committed this rather spontaneous killing in chapter 98, he justified himself as follows: "Þat vitu allir, at ek hefi ekki við bótum tekit eptir Þráin, mág minn; skal ek ok aldri una því, at engi komi mannhefnd eptir hann" (Everyone knows that I have not received any compensation for my brother-in-law Thrain, and I'll never be content until there is blood revenge).[105]

In fact, he had no pressing legal right to any compensation, given that he was married to a sister of Þráinn. Because, like his father, Ámundi was *laungetinn* (born out of wedlock), he had no more right to compensation by existing law than had Lýtingr, although their respective legal situations as well as their underlying motivations were quite different. Nevertheless, in a subsequent speech he seems to appeal to another law, one recognizing a new and unusually sensitive basis for compensatory rights:

> Eigi skil ek, . . . at þat muni rétt fyrir guði, svá nær hjarta sem þú hefir mér hǫggvit; enda kann ek at segja þér, ef ek væra heileygr báðum augum, at hafa skylda ek annathvárt fyrir fǫður minn fébœtr eða mannhefndir, enda skipti guð með okkr!

> (I don't find that to be just before God, . . . seeing that you struck so close to my heart, and I can say this: if I were sound in both my eyes, I would either have some compensation for my father or take blood revenge. And now may God settle matters between us.)

When Ámundi suddenly gains his sight, he praises God: "Lofaðr sé guð, dróttinn minn! Sé nú, hvat hann vill" (Praise be to God, my Lord. Now I see what He wants), he declares, and immediately sinks his axe into Lýtingr's head.[106] He thus takes the vengeance

---

104. ÍF 12:272, ch. 106; *CSI* 3:128; Finnur Jónsson, ed., *Brennu-Njálssaga (Njála)*, Altnordische Saga-Bibliothek 13 (Halle an der Saale: Max Niemeyer, 1908), 247n.
105. ÍF 12:249–50, ch. 98; *CSI* 3:119.
106. ÍF 12:273, ch. 106; *CSI* 3:128.

he had conditionally vowed in his peculiarly Christian version of a *heitstrenging*, and after this his blindness returns.

Einar Ól. Sveinsson, carefully restricting himself to a physiological discussion of the scene, noticed that such temporary gifts of sight have actually occurred naturally. He cites a 1799 biography of Björn prófastr Halldórsson, who "hafi þrívegis fengið sjónina allra snöggvast, eftir að hann var orðinn blindur" (had on three occasions momentarily regained his sight after he became blind).[107] He assumed the event in *Njáls saga* was based on similar instances known from its composer's own time. Finnur Jónsson reacted to the passage with some religious aversion, observing that Ámundi's triumphant cry praising God "ist nach unserem Gefühl eine Blasphemie; die ganze (selbstverständlich erdichtete) Geschichte sieht aus wie eine misslungene Nachbildung einer Legende." (is according to our sense blasphemy. The whole obviously invented episode appears to be an unsuccessful imitation of a miracle story.)[108] While Einar Ól. Sveinsson's remarks could well account for such an event if it occurred, the composer hardly had the intention of presenting it as an inexplicable quirk of nature. One immediate reaction could be that this is a false miracle, its fruits being destructive of human life and therefore devoid of goodness, one produced not by God but by Satan, however sympathetically figures in the story may view the situation.

However the composer of *Njáls saga* intended the miracle of Ámundi's empowering gift of temporary vision to be interpreted in the context of the new religion, its narrative purpose can be seen as twofold: In local terms it provides another scene in which Njáll forms an agreement with Hǫskuldr, reinforcing again the latter's position as head of the Sigfússon clan and thus the target of its enemies. Far more importantly, it acts as a prelude, heralding the ideological conflicts that will be interwoven with the pagan ethicality of traditional feud patterns as they are pursued among Iceland's early Christians. Where the concept of forgiveness could not be wholly assimilated, the weight of feud responsibilities remained primary, as future events make clear. It is in anticipation of these uncertainties that Njáll reassures Ámundi of his justification in seeking compensation for his father's killing. This is the only

---

107. ÍF 12:273n3, ch. 106.
108. Finnur Jónsson, ed., *Brennu-Njálssaga (Njála)*, 248.

instance in the *Íslendingasögur* when a person speaks of an injury incurred *nær hjarta* (close to my heart). And, whatever the relative date of the event intended by the composer, this is understandably the first time in *Njáls saga* that anyone has brought up the subject of God with references to the justice of actions and how closely they affect the heart.[109]

The Gradual Process of Conversion: "eigi fellr tré við it fyrsta hǫgg"

In chapter 103, when Gestr Oddleifsson is consoling Þangbrandr over the rather incomplete state of his Christianizing efforts, he assures him about a resolution of this ideological conflict through law—a notoriously inadequate means of resolving anything in this story, as we have noticed—and he comments proverbially, "En þat er sem mælt er, at eigi fellr tré við it fyrsta hǫgg" (As they say, a tree doesn't fall at the first blow).[110] Although the two men are speaking of the formal public conversion, which is indeed accomplished by law a couple of chapters later, the composer meant for Gestr's observation to have a wider and more subjective application. In part, he addresses the slow process of conversion, which applies not only to the whole of society and its public acceptance of Christianity but also to its individuals, for whom spiritual conversion, with the attendant recognition of the significance and the ethical implications of Christian teaching, is a much slower and more difficult task.

The unwillingness, or failure, of men and of some women in this story to honor the principles of arbitrated settlement, with the concomitant demand of adherence to its spirit beyond specific points of agreement, can be reformed only if people are both desirous and capable of observing a moral force that encourages faithfulness to an imposed resolution, without recourse to further occasions of violence. Only such an adherence can halt the cyclical continuation of the political competition that traditionally drives feud in society. Judith Jesch views Hǫskuldr Þráinsson as the only person in the saga who saw how "secular ideas of conflict resolution and religious [by which she of course means 'Christian']

---

109. The phrase is used, however, in *Hávamál* 95: "Hugr einn þat veit / er býr hjarta nær, . . ." (The mind alone knows what lies near the heart . . .) ÍF 36, 1:341, st. 95; Larrington, *Poetic Edda*, 25.

110. ÍF 12:269, ch. 103; *CSI* 3:126; JGF 575; *TPMA* 10.111.

ideas of appropriate behaviour come together," and who "knew even in his childhood that a settlement should be adhered to. Hǫskuldr's insight is not recognised by the other characters and it dies with him when he is killed."[111] Other readers have noticed the various levels of spiritual awareness achieved by different figures in this story following the introduction of Christianity into its world in chapters 100 to 105.

Hǫskuldr's less socially and spiritually sensitive contemporaries are seen to err in their assessment of him. George Clark interprets Skarpheðinn's erroneous anticipation of Hǫskuldr's hostile intentions toward his family in terms of the goodness of the Hvítanesgoði's character and his failure to understand what it means in a Christian moral climate: "The tragic irony of the situation lies in Skarpheðinn's awareness that Hǫskuldr is a good man, and therefore a man who would inevitably avenge his father's death. Skarpheðinn does not realize that Hǫskuldr's ethics are unlike his own, that Hǫskuldr's goodness moves in the direction of saintliness."[112] Like other readers, Clark and Jesch see in Hǫskuldr the composer's ideal of goodness—a moral excellence to which in his youthful, pre-Christian state he was already sensitive and which with his postconversion awareness even found fruition in the saintlike acceptance of his death at Skarpheðinn's hands: "Guð hjálpi mér, ok fyrirgefi yðr!" (May God help me and forgive you).[113]

Judith Jesch, commenting on how most resolutions in *Njáls saga* are reached by arbitrated and thus private settlement, notices that among the *Íslendingasögur* the term *góðir menn* is used repeatedly by the composer of *Njáls saga*, and only by him, to refer to arbitrators in such proceedings, where in law texts such figures were termed *sáttarmenn*.[114] As conflicts in this work tend to move ever more strenuously toward blood revenge, they do so, she observes, because individuals do not keep to the agreements laid down in settlements by arbitration. In Miller's interpretation of feud

---

111. Judith Jesch, "'Good Men' and Peace in *Njáls saga*," in *Introductory Essays on Egils saga and Njáls saga*, ed. John Hines and Desmond Slay (London: Viking Society for Northern Research, 1992), 79.
112. George Clark, "*Beowulf* and *Njálssaga*," *Proceedings of the First International Saga Conference, University of Edinburgh, 1971*, ed. Peter Foote, Hermann Pálsson, and Desmond Slay (London: Viking Society for Northern Research, 1973), 86.
113. ÍF 12:281, ch. 111; *CSI* 3:132.
114. Jesch, "'Good Men,'" 64–82.

theory, this is because the long-range political competition between entities in conflict is in no way resolved by such agreements, which are temporary at best and focused only on immediate sources of irritation or injury. Jesch sees the phrase *góðir menn* in *Njáls saga* as having three objects of reference: "(1) the morally exemplary individual, ... (2) the pool of honourable men who will strive to achieve peaceful resolution of conflicts by arbitration and ... (3) the righteous and law-abiding members of the community who stand beside God in judgement on an individual who breaks the rules."[115] Taking the prominent use of *góðir menn* in this narrative as a clue to its interpretation, she observes how the usual arbitrators of settlements are among the most eager to accept Christianity and thus, presumably, the most sensitive to the ethical burden entailed in its accompanying spiritual recognition. "There is no doubt that alongside the depiction of conflict between men, whether as individuals or in groups, the other major theme of *Njáls saga* is the acceptance of Christianity in Iceland."[116]

Among Jesch's arbitrators of particular good will is Hallr of Síða, Þangbrandr's first host and convert in Iceland, and a man who is especially sensitive to the Christian understanding of forgiveness and the necessity of its moral implications in effecting lasting peace. Hallr exercises a newfound humility while trying to bring the two sides together at the Alþingi following the burning. Having proclaimed his willingness "at sýna þat, at ek em lítilmenni" (show now that I'm no great hero), he offers to forego traditional compensation for his recently killed son, Ljótr, in the interests of achieving a settlement:

Allir menn vitu, hvern harm ek hefi fingit, at Ljótr, son minn, er látinn. Munu þat margir ætla, at hann muni dýrstr gǫrr af þeim mǫnnum, er hér hafa látizk. En ek vil vinna þat til sætta at leggja son minn ógildan ok ganga þó til at veita þeim bæði tryggðir ok grið, er mínir mótstǫðumenn eru.

(All men know what sorrow I have been dealt in the death of my son Ljot. Many will expect that payment for his life would be higher

---

115. Jesch, "'Good men,'" 68.
116. Jesch, "'Good men,'" 77. Bernadine McCreesh writes persuasively on the composers' representation of the influential Christian element in some *Íslendingasögur* in "How Pagan Are the Icelandic Family Sagas?" *Journal of English and Germanic Philology* 79 (1980): 58–66, and "Structural Patterns in *Eyrbyggja saga* and Other Sagas of the Conversion," *Medieval Scandinavia* 11 (1978/9): 271–80.

than for the others who have died here. But for the sake of a settlement I'm willing to let my son lie without compensation, and what's more, offer both pledges and peace to my adversaries.)[117]

Such magnanimous humility, which goes beyond anything imaginable in the pre-Christian ethic, sets an example of what is required if the retributive cycle of violence is to be broken.

As the saga composer emphasizes repeatedly, the pressure of Christian moral responsibility is felt also by Flosi, as the leader in gaining justice for the killing of Hǫskuldr Þráinsson. His initial impulse is to seek nonviolent legal redress, as he tells the wrathfully grieving Hildigunnr after her husband's death when she asks what action he will take. "Sœkja mun ek mál þitt til fullra laga eða veita til þeira sætta, er góðir menn sjá, at vér sém vel sœmðir af í alla staði" (I will prosecute the case to the full extent of the law, or else make a settlement that good men regard as honourable to us in all respects). Hildigunnr makes clear her opposition to his noble restraint, which is reinforced by Christian sensibility, when she throws Hǫskuldr's cloak with his clotted blood on it over her uncle so that "dunði þá blóðit um hann allan" (the dried blood poured down all over him). She exclaims,

> Þessa skikkju gaft þú, Flosi, Hǫskuldi, ok gef ek þér nú aptr. Var hann ok í þessi veginn. Skýt ek því til guðs ok góðra manna, at ek sœri þik fyrir alla krapta Krists þíns ok fyrir manndóm ok karlmennsku þína, at þú hefnir allra sára þeira, er hann hafði á sér dauðum, eða heit hvers manns níðungr ella.

> (This cloak, Flosi, was your gift to Hoskuld, and now I give it back to you. He was slain in it. In the name of God and all good men I charge you, by all the wonders of your Christ and by your courage and manliness, to avenge all the wounds which he received in dying—or else suffer the contempt of all men.)

It is explicitly, and ironically, by his Christ and not hers, nor by the Christ of those who seek blood vengeance, that Hildigunnr challenges her uncle with these most urgent words. When he answers, "Þú ert it mesta forað ok vildir, at vér tœkim þat upp,

---

117. ÍF 12:408 and 411–2, ch. 145; CSI 3:194 and 195.

er ǫllum oss gegnir verst" (You are a monster and want us to take the course which will be worst for us all), he voices the Christian response to pagan retributive ethics as well as the pragmatic political understanding that no peace can come from such a worldview.[118] His subsequent actions reinforce our interpretation of the spiritual depth at which he abhors Hildigunnr's perverse whetting.

Flosi's awareness of the spiritual peril in which he places himself and his followers as they set out for the onerous task of blood vengeance on a Sunday morning is implicit as the composer has him prepare for the adventure by attendance at church: "Flosi lét snimma veita sér tíðir dróttinsdaginn; síðan gekk hann til borðs" (Early on the Lord's Day Flosi had lauds sung for himself and then went to table).[119] And his most poignant statement recognizing their spiritual predicament comes a short while later with the acknowledgement that the only way to end the standoff at Bergþórshváll is with fire:

> Nú er þat sét, at vér getum þá eigi með vápnum unnit. Er sá nú margr, at eigi gengr jafnskarpliga at sem ætluðu. En þó munu vér nú verða at gera annat ráð fyrir oss. Eru nú tveir kostir, ok er hvárrgi góðr: sá annarr at hverfa frá, ok er þat várr bani, en hinn annarr at bera at eld ok brenna þá inni, ok er þat þó stór ábyrgð fyrir guði, er vér erum kristnir sjálfir. En þó munu vér þat bragðs taka.
>
> (It's clear now that we cannot defeat them with weapons—there are many here who are not attacking as sharply as they said they would. Now we'll have to try something else. There are two choices, and neither of them is good: one is to turn back, but that would lead to our death; the other is to bring fire and burn them inside, and that's a great responsibility before God, for we're Christian men. Still, that is the course we must take.)[120]

It is noticeable that burning their adversaries is now treated as "stór ábyrgð" (a great responsibility) or action for which they will be answerable before God, reminding the reader that this would not have been so before they adopted Christianity.

The composer uses the proverb of the felled tree again to

---

118. ÍF 12:291, ch. 116; CSI 3:137.
119. ÍF 12:322, ch. 126; CSI 3:152.
120. ÍF 12:327–28, ch. 128; CSI 3:154.

underscore the significance of its previous use by Gestr when at the Alþingi, Flosi's men attempt to bribe Eyjólfr Bǫlverksson to undertake their legal defense for the burning. The project is a difficult one, since lawyers who defend unpopular cases run the risk of themselves becoming victims of the feud process. During the tense course of this persuasion there is bitter irony as the composer has Hallbjǫrn inn sterki unwittingly repeat, albeit in this drastically different context, the comforting words earlier addressed to Þangbrandr by Gestr Oddleifsson: "Eigi fellr tré við it fyrsta hǫgg, vinr . . . ok sit hér fyrst hjá oss" (A tree doesn't fall at the first blow, friend. Just sit here with us for a while).[121] In agreeing to the defense of the burners, Eyjólfr also takes on himself, in such a society, his own death, as Snorri goði warns him when he spies the arm ring he accepted as payment in advance "skyldi þessi hringr eigi verða þér at hǫfuðbana" (may this bracelet not be the cause of your death).[122] At this point so many opportunities for forgiveness and the halting of the retributive process have been passed by without action that there can be no hope of resolution within the traditional system of addressing such feud-based conflicts. In this scene there is no room for an awareness of the new Christian spiritual reality. Many strokes remain before the tree of which Gestr spoke to the disheartened Þangbrandr will be felled, and the composer of *Njáls saga* must have felt, even as he wrote, that its roots remained in the internecine conflicts of his time. Njáll himself, the central figure of the main part of the saga, supernaturally wise and preeminently a good man, provides, with what seems to be his self-destructive behavior, a paradigm of the ideological conflict between paganism and Christianity about which the composer writes.

Old Law and New Law: Christian Ethics and Pagan Values

The introduction of Christianity into Iceland, which is pretty much at the center of *Njáls saga*, in fact also constitutes the introduction of a new sort of conflict into the feud-ridden community. As the country anticipates its conversion to the new faith in the opening lines of chapter 100, and just before the composer introduces Þangbrandr as the first notable herald of salvation there, many

---

121. ÍF 12:367, ch. 138; *CSI* 3:174.
122. ÍF 12:369, ch. 138; *CSI* 3:175.

people are saying "at slíkt væri mikil firn at hafna fornum átrúnaði" (that it was a great scandal to reject the old faith). But Njáll in his wisdom muses for the audience on the change that is to come, wistfully sketching a world he will never see, and the composer uses his vision as an ironic commentary on the world in which he himself has lived: "Svá lízk mér sem inn nýi átrúnaðr muni vera miklu betri, ok sá mun sæll, er þann fær heldr" (It seems to me that this new faith is much better, and that he who accepts it will be happy).[123] Considering the pattern of this conflict, Lönnroth whimsically compares the stories of Gunnarr and of Njáll in the composer's clerical mind to the Old and New Testaments.[124] Thus, the Old Law under which the tragedy of Gunnarr occurred is replaced by the New Law with its concepts of forgiveness and redemption and the much-increased sense of moral responsibility that accompanies them. Whether or not this typological comparison was consciously intended by the saga's composer, the clerical discipline of his mind could easily have imbued his vision with such a pattern.

Njáll, who proverbially never lies and who needs no advice from others, might be reasonably taken for a reliable source of wisdom in this saga, to some extent at least the composer's own voice, the choric commentary on the action. Readers might trust that his vision will be the most enlightened of any in the story. Under the Old Law he always first counsels restraint; he wants Gunnarr to avoid meeting the wife from whose disturbed character the cataclysmic events of the saga will eventually proceed. Where there is conflict, his advice is practical, useful for friends and lethal for their adversaries. His last comment prior to the conversion episode, answering his sons' objections to his taking a settlement for Lýtingr's killing of their half-brother, is "Ekki myndi Hǫskuldr ... hafa skotit skildi fyrir hann, ef þú hefðir drepit hann, er þér var þat ætlat" (Hoskuld wouldn't have been able to shield Lyting, . . . if you had killed him, as you were meant to).[125]

In the initially confusing early light of Christianity and the complex moral challenges it brings to Iceland's society, however, Njáll's interpretations of what is right become difficult for readers to comprehend. He does not rebuke Ámundi for killing Lýtingr

---

123. ÍF 12:255, ch. 100; CSI 3:121.
124. Lönnroth, Introduction, 148.
125. ÍF 12:254–55, ch. 99; CSI 3:121.

when his sight was mysteriously granted to him; rather, he takes the incident as a sign, "því at slíkt er mjǫk á kveðit, en viðvǫrunarvert, ef slíkir atburðir verða, at stinga eigi af stokki við þá, er svá nær standa" (for such things are preordained, and when they occur they are a warning not to spurn the claims of close kin).[126]

When his sons plan to kill Hǫskuldr Þráinsson, and Bergþóra asks Njáll what they are discussing, he answers, "Ekki em ek í ráðagerð með þeim" (I am not in on their planning), and he adds his assumed disapproval: "sjáldan var ek þá frá kvaddr, er in góðu váru ráðin" (I was seldom left out when their plans were good), indicating that Njáll is no longer in control of, or even influential on, his sons' activities.[127] "Hǫrmuleg tíðendi" (Tragic news), he exclaims when told of the killing, "ok er slíkt illt at vita, því at þat er sannligt at segja, at svá fellr mér nær um trega, at mér þœtti betra at hafa látit tvá sonu mína ok væri Hǫskuldr á lífi" (and terrible to hear, for it is fair to say that I am so overcome with grief that I would rather have lost two of my sons, as long as Hoskuld were still alive).[128] Njáll is not alone in bearing the challenges of the new moral conflict. Flosi, primesigned on his way to the Alþingi meeting of pagans and Christians and, as we have seen above, clearly as conscious of Christian moral responsibility as his adversary, remarks about Hǫskuldr's killing to Þorgrímr skauti:

> Þat hefir nú víst at hǫndum borit, at ek mynda gefa til mína eigu, at þetta hefði eigi fram komit; er ok illu korni sáit orðit, enda mun illt af gróa.

> (Now it has turned out so that I would give everything I own if this matter had never come to pass. But when evil seed has been sown, evil will grow.)[129]

It is in the narrative about the outcome of the Hvítanesgoði's killing that the extent of Christian moral impact on the newly converted community is tried; Njáll and Flosi are the most complex and interesting subjects of this influence.

---

126. ÍF 12:274, ch. 106; CSI 3:129.
127. ÍF 12:280, ch. 110; CSI 3:132.
128. ÍF 12:281, ch. 111; CSI 3:133.
129. ÍF 12:288, ch. 115; CSI 3:135, slightly modified.

The Judgement of Njáll

In pagan terms, Njáll would rather have lost two of his own sons "ok væri Hǫskuldr á lífi" (as long as Hoskuld were still alive) at this point, and his clairvoyance in any case encompasses the death of himself and all his family. When he places the silk robe and the pair of boots on the wergild pile for Flosi at the Alþingi, readers might wonder if Flosi's explosive reaction, which is nearly inexplicable to us, was not, after all, precisely what he had intended to elicit instead of reconciliation. Although the boots included in the gift are difficult to understand, the robe must have reminded Flosi of Hildigunnr's dramatically symbolic challenge to his honor.

One could argue against such motivation for this fateful generosity, given the various distinctive terms denoting such garments. The *silkislœður*, or trailing gown, which Njáll places on the pile, apparently as a gratuitous act of generosity, is in fact a different garment from the *skikkja*, or mantle. The latter is Flosi's gift to Hǫskuldr, a gift Hildigunnr returned with the clotted blood (although in English translations of the saga "cloak" is the term normally used for both).[130] Suggestions that there was something particularly feminine or even effeminate about the *slœður* are not supported by use of the term elsewhere in the *Íslendingasögur*. And Egill Skallagrímsson, about whom there is nothing effeminate, celebrates in a *lausavísa* in his saga the gift of a *silkislœður* from his friend, Arinbjǫrn.[131] Later, in chapter 79, the composer of the saga attributes to Egill a *vísa* in which he blames his son Þorsteinn for some unspecified treachery after he borrows and ruins the gown on his expedition to the Alþingi.[132] In *Vatnsdœla saga*, Bergr inn raki returns from Norway with a *slœður* of good cloth, the lower portion of which he cuts off because it is soiled from riding.[133] Both garments, which are of continental origin, are worn by men and, as frequently happens with treasures brought from abroad, are damaged with their use in Iceland. When Hallfreðr vandræðaskáld

---

130. For a discussion of the Old Norse terms translatable in English as "cloak" and their possible distinctions, see Hjalmar Falk, *Altwestnordische Kleiderkunde mit besonderer Berücksichtigung der Terminologie* (Kristiania: Jacob Dybwad, 1919), 160–61 and 178–85.
131. ÍF 2:213, ch. 67.
132. ÍF 2:274, ch. 79.
133. ÍF 8:84, ch. 31.

uses the term in a kenning of stanza 22, calling Kolfinna "Sif karms slœðu" (the goddess of the gown-chest), he does not imply that the *slœður* is necessarily a woman's garment.[134] In any case, Njáll's apparent act of generosity, the gift on top of the payment, normally a moment that would increase face for both parties, is what provides the pretext for Flosi's withdrawal from the reconciliation to which he had previously agreed. His exchanges with Skarpheðinn now degenerate into insults of a legally actionable quality, where blood vengeance becomes the only option. Njáll's keen awareness of the future surely precludes his having left the cloak and boots for Flosi in error over the anticipated reaction.

The likelihood of Njáll's gifts to Flosi being in some way intentionally self-destructive could be viewed as a trend that continues when, in chapter 128, as the attackers approach Bergþórshváll, he orders his family to go indoors. Outside, it would have been difficult if not impossible to kill them all, whereas once they are inside they can be killed by being burned alive. When his sons are reluctant to comply, Njáll complains that they were previously more obedient to his wishes, reminding them implicitly that their killing of Hǫskuldr is the reason they are in this predicament: "Nú mun sem optar, at þér munuð bera mik ráðum, synir mínir, ok virða mik engis. En þá er þér váruð yngri, þá gerðuð þér ekki svá, ok fór yðr þá betr." (Now it will be, as often before, my sons, that you'll ignore my advice and show me no respect. When you were younger you didn't do so, and you were better off.) Countering Helgi's acquiescence to this admonition—"Geru vér sem faðir várr vill; þat mun oss bezt gegna" (Let's do as our father wishes—that will be best for us)—Skarpheðinn expresses his scepticism, saying "Eigi veit ek þat víst . . . því at hann er nú feigr" (I'm not so sure about that . . . for now he is a doomed man), but then he relents, accepting their imminent doom, and the family enters the house.[135]

The as yet unresolved conflict of Old and New Law is seen in Njáll's last pronouncements, first in his Christian reassurance as the women start suffering from the flames: "Verðið vel við ok mælið eigi æðru, því at él eitt mun vera, en þó skyldi langt til annars slíks. Trúið þér ok því, at guð er miskunnsamr, ok mun hann oss eigi bæði

---
134. ÍF 8:184, ch. 9. Translation mine.
135. ÍF 12:326, ch.128; *CSI* 3:154.

láta brenna þessa heims ok annars." (Bear this bravely and don't express fear, for it's only a brief storm, and it will be a long time before we have another like it. Have faith that God is merciful, and that he will not let us burn both in this world and in the next.)[136] Thomas D. Hill uses a contemporary theological discussion to clarify the actions of Njáll. Citing medieval writers who assert that God does not judge or punish us twice for a sin, he assumes that Njáll's comforting words to his household mean the suffering they experience in the conflagration will be sufficient to make expiation for, among other sins, the crime of killing Hǫskuldr Hvítanesgoði. He also argues that Njáll's decision to allow the destruction of his family is motivated further by a very practical hope that their absence will lead to a more peaceful state of society.[137]

The composer recalls again Njáll's sensitivity to the pagan ethic of the unforgiving Old Law, however, when Flosi offers him and Bergþóra an exit from the burning farmhouse: "Eigi vil ek út ganga, því at ek em maðr gamall ok lítt til búinn at hefna sona minna, en ek vil eigi lifa við skǫmm" (I will not leave, for I'm an old man and hardly fit to avenge my sons, and I do not want to live in shame).[138] The inability of this early Christian to live injured without vengeance, his choice being death rather than that unheroic option, is clearly intended by the composer as a last reference to the difficulty with which the tree of the Old Law is made to fall. While Njáll can envisage a time when men will be fortunate enough to live under the New Law, that time has not come yet, and his death is preferable, even though Christian teaching would require him to remain alive if he can.

To its last page, the saga continues with the revenge of Kári, who escaped the burning, on Flosi's followers in Iceland and abroad until at last, in a scene contrastively parallel to Flosi's unfriendly visit to Ásgrímr Ellida-Grímsson at Bræðratunga in chapter 136 he returns to Iceland, wrecking his ship at Ingólfshǫfði. As it snows thickly, he plans "at fara til Svínafells ok reyna þegnskap Flosa" (to go to Svinafell and test Flosi's magnanimity).[139] It is a friendly test, however, and it follows the penitent visits to Rome

---

136. ÍF 12:328–29, ch.129; *CSI* 3:155.
137. Thomas D. Hill, "Njáll's Comforting Words: *Brennu-Njáls saga*, Chapter 129," *Saga-Book of the Viking Society for Northern Research* 41 (2017): 71–78.
138. ÍF 12:330, ch.129; *CSI* 3:156.
139. ÍF 12:463, ch. 159.

for absolution made voluntarily by both these leaders. Freed of the sins stemming from adherence to the unforgiving ethics of the Old Law, they find reconciliation in submitting to the moral demands of the New Law, and Kári marries Hildigunnr, widow of the man Skarpheðinn tragically killed. We do not learn about her reaction to this seemingly unlikely union.

* * *

The careful construction of *Njáls saga* was noticed by such disparate readers as Albert Ulrik Bååth and Einar Ól. Sveinsson, as it still is by any who read it today. It displays more than any other member of its genre the sophistication of uses that can be made of proverbial material in saga telling, both for thematic signaling and also for the suggestion and adjustment of nuance in implication and interpretation. The effects of temptation on such different characters as Sigmundr and Úlfr Uggason, for instance, are drawn with the image of the fly, the lure on the line, seeking its prey. Essential differences between the respective evils of Mǫrðr and Hallgerðr are drawn by the distinctions in paroemial imagery discussed above. And the breadth and agonizing depth of a culture's religious conversion are epitomized by the figurative felling of trees, slowly and with an enormous impact. Throughout the whole narrative we are reminded of the inevitability of retaliation for violence, the hand's brief joy in the stroke, in the pagan ethic that might have been ameliorated by Christian teaching. The author of *Njáls saga* was as much a master of the paroemial inventory of his culture and its literary uses as he was of everything else in the artistry of his narrative.

CHAPTER 4

Grettis saga and the Paroemial Delineation of Character

The frequency of proverbs and related texts in *Grettis saga* is among the highest of any of the sagas in the Old Icelandic corpus, with *Njáls saga* ranking a rather distant second. Perhaps the inclusion of wisdom texts was regarded as more fashionable by the end of the thirteenth century, or perhaps their use may simply have reflected the needs of composers writing at that time.[1] It might be pertinent to notice that these two works, among the latest to reach their respective extant forms, were also both seriously devoted to the examination of character. The types of proverbs that were placed in the mouths of saga figures help to define them as surely as we reveal ourselves through our choices of words and formulaic texts in ordinary speech. Saga composers, where they were not simply relying on the record of oral tradition, could use such texts in significant ways in their delineation and reinforcement of character.

Grettir, the Man and the Legend

So many of the recorded adventures of Grettir the Strong are of a fantastic nature that it is difficult to conceive of him as a historical figure. Yet exist he did, though his real existence must be somewhat diminished in stature when we compare him with the hero of *Grettis saga*. Guðni Jónsson, in the introduction to his

---

1. For another explanation, consider the correlation of paroemial frequency in saga narrative with the density of reported conversation, see a footnote in chapter 4, the section "Paroemial Density and Usage."

edition of this work, demonstrated the outlaw's renown among his countrymen as it is witnessed both in historical sources and in thirteenth-century Icelandic literature. An unattributed note in *Gottskálksannáll* places his birth in 1005, which is probably wrong, and *Landnámabók* includes his family's genealogy, referring to him there as "inn sterki" (the strong).[2] There we also find a record of his killing Þorbjǫrn øxnamegin Arnórsson as well as Ormr, one of the sons of Þórir of Garðr.[3] In addition, various sagas whose composition took place previous to the one we have about Grettir mention his exploits, so that, as Guðni Jónsson observes, "er meira en nóg til þess að sýna, að Grettir hefir verið frægur í sögum og nafn hans alkunnugt, ok í annan stað, að höfuðdrættirnir í ævi hans, eins og frá þeim er sagt í Grettis sögu, hafi við söguleg rök að styðjast" (there is more than enough to show that Grettir was famous in stories and his name was universally known, and besides, that the main episodes in his life as they are related in *Grettis saga*, were based on historical evidence).[4] Much thought has been expended on what the composer of the extant version of *Grettis saga* intended his audience to learn from the way in which he chose to describe this life with the materials available to him and the narrative shaping that he imposed on those materials.

The Structural Core of *Grettis saga*

We cannot, as we might with *Njáls saga*, conduct a structural analysis of the text with the assumption that its composer had in mind its last lines when he composed its first. Rather, Grettir's life forms the saga, with several episodically generated subdivisions in its text, which is of two main parts: his activities and accomplishments up to the curse of the revenant Glámr, in chapter 35; and the resultant

---

2. Guðni Jónsson, ed., *Grettis saga Ásmundarsonar: Bandamanna saga. Odds þáttr Ófeigssonar*, Íslenzk fornrit 7 (Reykjavík: Hið íslenzka fornritafélag, 1936), xxxi (Formáli, §2: "*Grettis saga og ritaðar heimildir*"); Jakob Benediktsson, ed., *Landnámabók*, in *Íslendingabók: Landnámabók*, ed. Jakob Benediktsson, 2 vols., Íslenzk fornrit 1 (Reykjavík: Hið íslenzka fornritafélag, 1968), 1:198–99 (*Sturlubók*, 161; *Hauksbók*, 130). Regrettably, I have not seen Örnólfur Thorsson, "Orð af orði: Hefð og nýmæli í *Grettlu*" (Master's thesis, Háskóli Íslands, 1993).

3. *Grettis saga*, xxxi (Formáli); ÍF 1:211, 213 (*Sturlubók*, 173; *Hauksbók*, 139); ÍF 1:281 (*Hauksbók*, 214).

4. *Grettis saga*, xxxi (Formáli).

decline in his powers and fortunes, which leads to his eventual death on Drangey in chapter 82. The progress of his demise is studied in this second part.

The beginning and end of the saga are no longer problematic for us. Its Norwegian prelude has been commonly recognized as thematically anticipatory of the main conflicts in Grettir's life, and the concluding episode in Constantinople, *Spesar þáttr*, has come to be seen as providing, in the adventures of his brother Þorsteinn, a positive resolution to some aspects of the hero's conflicted, restless existence on the spiritual as well as the physical edge of Christian society.[5] The extent to which the composer envisaged this last section as a positive version of a heroic life well lived might be debated, depending on how readers interpret what seems in this work to be a nostalgic admiration for the more robust undertakings of Grettir's Viking warrior ancestors as well as his heroic feats, utterances, and posturings.

The proverbs of *Grettis saga* are not used to describe a sharply demarcated thematic structure, as they seem to be in *Njáls saga*; nor are they placed or repeated in such a way as to define clearly those topics that the composer would discuss. However, some phraseological recurrence in the text appears to signal or accentuate the composer's conceptual agenda—for some readers, indeed, to a very great extent.[6]

Heroic Age and Heroic Nostalgia

Grettir inn sterki Ásmundarson was born last of all the heroes of the classical *Íslendingasögur*, and his saga, one of a small number of sagas devoted to the biographical study of an individual rather than to chronicling the partial history of a family or a clan, is among the latest compositions of that genre, probably dating from somewhere in the early decades of the fourteenth century. Perhaps it is not all that surprising, given such great historical and cultural distance

---

5. Guðni Jónsson, ÍF 7. xiv-xvi; Andrew J. Hamer, "*Grettis saga* and the *iudicium dei*," in *Northern Voices: Essays on Old Germanic and Related Topics Offered to Professor Tette Hofstra*, ed. Kees Dekker, Alasdair MacDonald, and Hermann Niebaum, Mediaevalia Groningana, n.s. 11 / Germania Latina 6. (Leuven: Peeters, 2008), 19–40.
6. Laurence de Looze, "The Outlaw Poet, The Poetic Outlaw: Self-Consciousness in *Grettis saga Ásmundarsonar*," Arkiv för nordisk filologi 106 (1991): 85–103. Örnólfur Thorsson, "Farið á hriflingabjörgum í Grettlu," in Strengleikar slegnir Robert Cook, 25. Nóvember 1994, ed. Margrét Eggertsdóttir et al. (Reykjavík: Menningar og minningsjóður Mette Magnussen, 1994), 79–83; Russell Poole, "Myth, Psychology, and Society in *Grettis saga*," *Álvíssmál* 11 (2004): 3–16.

from its beginnings, that the story is permeated with a sense of nostalgia for a near-legendary Nordic past, a nostalgia that has yet to be analyzed with any sense of completion. The first word of its thirteen-chapter Norwegian prelude, however, is "Ǫnundr," the name of the Viking adventurer who was Grettir's great-grandfather. This preliminary section focuses unusually its attention on development of character in the outlaw hero's aristocratic warrior background, which is situated in the context of a pre-Christian saga world version of the Heroic Age, long before the outlaw hero's birth.[7] The composer meant for his audience to see his hero with reference to the talents and traits of his wellborn forebears, who were generally successful in their gratuitously violent pursuits, as is emphasized in this introductory section of the story.

Kathryn Hume captured with comprehensive clarity the sense that Grettir's pre-Christian aristocratic-heroic aspirations bring him into fatal conflict with the saga world of eleventh-century postconversion Iceland. This world's norms are well established and challenged or subverted by only a few individuals other than himself, individuals who occupy the sometimes supernatural fringes of an otherwise static and homogeneous community.[8] In fact, although Hume's analysis is useful and consistently illuminates Grettir's character, it describes only part of the saga's meaning. The story, which is episodic in nature, is deceptively simple. Like *Beowulf*, with which it has been studied for nearly two centuries because of the two works' seemingly analogous situations and events, its story is so simple that it is easily rendered into a book for children. Yet, like *Beowulf*, the narrative has been studied in detailed and complex terms, including an interesting and useful psychoanalytic approach.[9] Such endeavors have not yielded much consensus beyond Hume, however, and there may be reasons for this difficulty that are not yet clear to us.

---

7. The Heroic Age, whether as a cultural historical or a literary critical construct, needs to receive further and more up-to-date analysis than it has at present, especially concerning its uses in medieval Germanic literature.

8. Kathryn Hume, "The Thematic Design of *Grettis Saga*," *Journal of English and Germanic Philology* 73 (1974): 469–86. The idea was not, at that time, hers exclusively. See the introduction to Denton Fox and Hermann Pálsson, trans., *Grettir's saga* (Toronto: University of Toronto Press, 1974), viii–ix: "Grettir's character is like a larger version of Onund's, but he is born too late, and into a Christian and civilized world, where the heroic virtues are no longer sufficient."

9. Poole, "Myth," 3–16.

Order and the Triumph of Chaos: "Eigi má við ǫllu sjá"

Thomas Bredsdorff, in *Chaos and Love*, has discussed ways in which a "second pattern"—second, that is, to the urge to power that primarily governs saga literature—can be discerned in some representatives of the genre. This second pattern "testifies to the erotic drive as a dangerous force that breaks down order and causes events to unfold blindly."[10] Psychoanalytic views aside, the erotic drive cannot be said to exist in any urgently overt way with the character of Grettir. His few dalliances are sparsely and unromantically described, and his male member seems, at least in a state of repose, oddly and significantly diminished in proportion to the otherwise impressively masculine frame of the hero. However, Bredsdorff blames this second pattern, used by saga composers to "tell of how dangerous it is to follow the impulse that goes with the emotions," for the social chaos to which such behavior leads in these narratives.[11] In *Grettis saga* the hero's impulsive though nonerotic actions lead him on a path from ordered environment into the chaotic world whose denizens he fights, ironically protecting society—which rejects and eventually destroys him—from those forces that are inimical to its stability. The triumph of chaos in Grettir's world is evident in several respects in the paroemial matrix of the narrative, as we will notice below.

With only a slight variation of wording on each occasion, the proverb "Eigi má við ǫllu sjá" (No one can provide for everything) is used three times in *Grettis saga* by three different speakers.[12] These speakers have each found themselves in conflicted situations, the urgency and complexity of which have led them beyond their ability to make satisfactory decisions from their own or others' points of view. For two of the speakers, this dilemma is caused by Grettir, who is himself the speaker on the other occasion.

Barði Guðmundarson speaks the proverb first when Þórarinn spaki, his foster-father, objects to his having invited Grettir along to the Battle of the Heath, which is also described in *Heiðarvíga saga*. Concerned over the makeup of Barði's projected company, Þórarinn touches on the hero's annoyingly inconsistent value:

---

10. Thomas Bredsdorff, *Chaos and Love. The Philosophy of the Icelandic Family Sagas,* trans. John Tucker (Copenhagen: Museum Tusculanum Press, 2001), 22.
11. Bredsdorff, *Chaos,* 23.
12. JGF 501; *TPMA* 10.373.

"mikit afbragð er Grettir annarra manna, þeira er nú er kostr á váru landi" (It is true that Grettir is the greatest of all men now living in our country), he observes, but Þórarinn is troubled over his "mikill ofsi" (unbridled temper) and is hopeful "at eigi sé allir ógæfumenn í þinni ferð" (that not everyone on your expedition is a man of ill-fortune).[13] Barði, dismayed that Þórarinn would "fyrirmuna mér ins vaskasta manns, hvat sem í gerisk; má eigi fyrir ǫllu sjá" (grudge me the bravest man, whatever happens, ... No one in my straits can provide for everything), nevertheless acquiesces and refrains from taking Grettir with him to Borgarfjǫrðr.[14] Grettir confronts Barði as he is returning from the battle and challenges him over having been omitted from the adventure. Barði refuses to fight him: "Legit hafa mér andvirki nær garði en at berjask við þik fyrir sakleysi" (I have business more urgent than having a pointless fight with you), he says, ignoring his parting insults. "Ok varð ekki af kveðjum með þeim at skilnaði" (They did not bother to wish each other farewell) is the litotic close to this scene.[15] The composer wrote this scene primarily to offset the physical advantage of Grettir's company in battle with the greater liability of his presence there as an *ógæfumaðr*, which is what Þórarinn called him.

Einar Ól. Sveinsson, in his literary study of *Njáls saga*, described the quality of *ógæfa* with great understanding:

> We come closest to the essence of *ógæfa* if we call it *mein* (hurt, harm, damage, disease, sore), a word which encompasses every aspect of this complex of ideas, including the connotation of sin in the Christian sense of the word, although, of course, its basic sense is originally different. *Ógæfa* is like an infectious disease, which is carried from one individual to another. It lives in men and in their deeds, spreading poison and infection in all directions. It is a natural phenomenon, and natural phenomena are oblivious to justice, guilt or innocence. *Ógæfa* infects and corrupts everyone who crosses its path and does not possess a sufficient power of resistance to it.[16]

---

13. ÍF 7:104, ch. 31; *CSI* 2:98.
14. ÍF 7:105, ch. 31; *CSI* 2:98.
15. ÍF 7:106, ch. 31; *CSI* 2:99.
16. Einar Ól. Sveinsson, *Masterpiece*, 192. The *gæfa/ógæfa* dichotomy in the definition of character in the *Íslendingasögur* is an unresolved matter of continuing and indeed renewed interest: See Peter Hallberg, "The Concept of *gipta-gæfa-hamingja* in Old Norse Literature" in *Proceedings of the First International Saga Conference* (Edinburgh August

Already his *ógæfa* prohibits Grettir from inclusion in the affairs of men where Iceland's greatest fighter would otherwise be of strategic use. Denied the challenges offered within normal society, he is driven elsewhere by his aggressive nature to try his heroic gifts, taking monsters and demons for his adversaries. In fact, only a few lines later, at the end of chapter 31, the narrator explicitly signals Grettir's frustration in this regard: "Þá þótti Gretti mikit mein, er hann mátti hvergi reyna afl sitt, ok fréttisk fyrir, ef nǫkkut væri þat, er hann mætti við fásk" (He sorely regretted not having anything to test his strength against, and asked around for a challenge to take up).[17] Significantly, this episode occurs immediately before those chapters in which he approaches his ultimate nemesis, Glámr, at Þórhallsstaðir, Forsœludalr, which is inland from the Vatnsdalr area of his maternal ancestors. Here, though, even before the curse of Glámr, which makes Grettir's condition hopeless and his relationship with his world disintegrate to the brink of destruction, Barði's frustrating inability to include him in a battle where he would most wish to do so anticipates the tragedy of his unfortunate life in showing his undesirability in affairs where his great strength could otherwise be of use.

The proverb is employed a second time by Grettir himself in the much debated chapter 52, which is found also as the first chapter of *Fóstbrœðra saga*, as a prelude to that narrative's long moral examination of how individuals choose to make use of the powers God has given them. The episode is thought to be derived by the composer of *Grettis saga* from the former work.[18] By this point in the story, the outlaw's fortunes have dwindled considerably. Cursed by Glámr, and accused unfairly, as even his most reliable relative King Óláfr Haraldsson supposes, of intentionally killing the sons of Þórir of Garðr, he has recently returned to Iceland. There he has learned all at once of his father's death, of his brother Atli's slaying,

---

21–29, 1971), ed. Peter G. Foote, Herman Pálsson, and Desmond Slay (London: Viking Society for Northern Research, 1973); Hermann Pálsson, "Um gæfumenn og ógæfu í íslenzkum fornsögum," in *Afmælisrit Björns Sigfússonar*, ed. Björn Þorsteinsson and Sverrir Tómasson (Reykjavík: Sögufélag, 1975), 135–53. More recently, see Bettina Sejbjerg Sommer, "The *Norse Concept of Luck*," Scandinavian Studies 79 (2007): 275–94; Kirsi Kanerva, "*Ógæfa* (misfortune) as an Emotion in Thirteenth-Century Iceland," Scandinavian Studies 84 (2012): 1–26.

17. ÍF 7:107, ch. 31; CSI 2:100.

18. See Jónas Kristjánsson, *Um Fóstbrœðrasögu* (Reykjavík: Stofnun Árna Magnússonar, 1972) for this and other matters concerning the composition of *Fóstbrœðrasöga*.

and finally of his being declared an outlaw at the Alþingi—in absentia and with no opportunity to defend himself—as a result of importunate pressure applied by Þórir in revenge for his sons. When Snorri goði fails to have him cleared of outlawry the following year, the composer describes how Grettir goes ranging in predatory fashion through the Westfjords district, in Langadalr, south of Vatnsfjǫrðr, taking whatever he wants or needs from the local farmers and making a destructive nuisance of himself. Although he is not here, as he is in the corresponding episode in *Fóstbrœðra saga*, described figuratively as a "troll fyrir durum" (a troll on their doorstep), the humorous treatment of his rampage—"gengu þeir allmisjafnt af, en allir sǫgðusk nauðgir láta, þegar hann var á brottu" (Some were more reluctant than others, but after he had gone they all said they had had no choice)—continues when a group of shepherds catch him off guard, sleeping in the woods, and then report to the local farmers "at sá dólgr væri kominn í byggðina, at þeim þótti ekki dæll viðfangs" (that a great brute had arrived in the district whom they did not think would be easy to deal with).[19]

He is then ignominiously captured, but the farmers, who are of humble status, cannot agree how to keep such an imposing figure until the return of their *goði* (chieftain), Vermundr inn mjóvi, from the Alþingi. Meanwhile Vermundr's wife, Þórbjǫrg in digra, who conducts her husband's administrative work in his absence, comes suddenly across them as they are preparing to hang the outlaw for the damage he has inflicted on their property. A "skǫrungr mikill ok stórvitr" (woman of firm character and foresight), as she is described by the composer, she halts the execution, making Grettir promise to cease his depredations in the district and not to take vengeance on her men for the humiliation he has suffered.[20] She asks Grettir what brought him "at þú vildir gera hér óspekðir þingmǫnnum mínum" (to want to come here and cause trouble to my thingmen)? "Eigi má við ǫllu sjá" (You can't provide for everything), he complains proverbially, adding in the same strain, "vera varð ek nǫkkur" (I had to be somewhere). Her comment on the luckless nature of his situation—namely, that "vesalmenni þessi skyldi taka þik" (these wretches capture you)—poignantly accentuates the aristocratic aspect of Grettir's background. Because of

---

19. ÍF 6:122, ch. 1; *CSI* 2:330; ÍF 7:166-67, ch. 52; *CSI* 2:129.
20. ÍF 7:169, ch. 52; *CSI* 2:130.

his status and the respected status of his family, she orders her farmers to let him go, as the composer presents his version of the scene in this saga: "ofráð mun þat verða yðr Ísfirðingum, at taka Gretti af lífi, því at hann er maðr frægr ok stórættaðr, þó at hann sé eigi gæfumaðr" (executing Grettir will be more than you men of Isafjord can handle, because he is a man of renown and great family, even though fortune does not favour him).[21] Grettir's proverbial response to Þorbjǫrg's question summarizes his awareness of the desperate point to which his career has brought him. He has by this time no other way of staying alive than by foraging in the manner to which his outlawry has reduced him.

The proverb is used a third time in chapter 81. Grettir is depicted as a most extreme version of such an abjectly alienated figure, swollen and blackened from the infection caused by the sorcery of his adversary Þorbjǫrn ǫngull's elderly foster-mother, Þúríðr. He lies incapacitated on Drangey while Þorbjǫrn seeks passage there from Halldórr Þorgeirsson á Hofi. The inadvisability of this journey is made clear when Þorbjǫrn tells him he has been encouraged to go by the old crone, and Halldórr objects that the results of such an expedition cannot be good: "því at hon er fjǫlkunnig, en þat er nú fyrirboðit" (she is a sorceress and that is forbidden now).[22] Þorbjǫrn, however, "mikill... ok sterkr ok harðfengr ok ódæll" (a big, strong man, tough to deal with and ruthless), has been driven to such measures by a series of humiliations suffered in his previous attempts to rid the island, the care of which lies in his legal possession, of the outlaw's presence.[23] The social pressures of honor attendant on these setbacks have forced him to extremes that will lead to his own destruction. "Ekki má fyrir ǫllu sjá um þat" (I can't provide for everything), he tells Halldórr, heedless by now of the legal and spiritual dangers in which he has placed himself by resorting to sorcery: "Um skal nú lúka á einnhvern hátt, ef ek má ráða" (I shall put an end to this somehow if I have my say). And ignoring Halldórr's warning that "at eigi mun allt kristiligt í þessum ráðum" (some of this plan is not completely Christian), he proceeds to Grettir's lair and thus eventually to his own destruction, borrowing a boat for the journey to Drangey.[24]

---

21. ÍF 7:169, ch. 52; *CSI* 2:131.
22. ÍF 7:257, ch. 81; *CSI* 2:174.
23. ÍF 7:226, ch. 70; *CSI* 2:159.
24. ÍF 7:257, ch. 81; *CSI* 2:174.

One may observe that in each instance the character uttering the proverb under discussion speaks *in limine*, as he moves with understandable anxiety into a less predictable world, one that is more dangerous and edged with the threat of chaos and perhaps of annihilation. Barði would grasp at the doubtful security of having with him Iceland's most powerful warrior on his way to the Battle of the Heath and its obviously uncertain outcome. Grettir speaks as he envisages himself moving into a chaotic state of outlawry that can only end with his death. And Þorbjǫrn ǫngull, as is made clear in dialogue several times in the chapters preceding his shameful killing of the disabled Grettir, is at some level aware that he has transgressed the legal and moral boundaries of society. His campaign to cleanse Drangey of its occupants is misconceived and pursued with obsessive urgency; and more importantly—to this untidy and disintegrative progress of the narrative—it is done to salvage his fragile honor, which is damaged so much by previous failures to rid the island of the outlaw. The thrice-shared paroemial observation reminds the audience of the desperation with which an individual faces dangers lying beyond the world of peaceful predictability in situations where feud, outlawry, or the dangers of the supernatural threaten the stability of his community, or indeed of his very psyche.

As critics began to undertake an examination of the thematic content of the sagas in the 1970s, the question, articulated by T. M Andersson, arose that if indeed the sagas impose values on action, then, "is the chief value really honor?"[25] The sagas, he felt, in their "ethical temper," exhibit "a sense of proportion and moderation. They are written against excess."[26] Thus, in our view of the implications of the composer's use of the proverb, "Eigi má við ǫllu sjá" (no one can provide for everything), we must take into account how members of society who deal with Grettir in matters pertinent to his outlawry, as well as to the outcast figure himself, are led astray by a lack of moderation—Grettir's, in his adherence to outmoded heroic ideals of behavior and style; and his acquaintances', in their desire and attempts to gain control over his violently eccentric presence in their midst. The composer of *Grettis saga* has selected and arranged his material keeping in mind ways in which

---

25. Andersson, "Displacement," 577.
26. Andersson, "Displacement," 588.

the outlandishly distorted heroic figure of Grettir, both in himself and in his relationships with society, presents a set of challenges to society's stability by giving way to such impulsive excess.

Proverbs from the Infancy of the Hero: Precocious Saboteur

While the proverb may well originate as a set of syntactic structures used to formulate and transmit orally based wisdom in a preliterate age, its texts and the patterns informing them came to function in other ways and for other purposes in the process of communication. In sagas, it is true, proverbs have served as signals of value when uttered by respected figures, thus representing the communal wisdom on a subject and at the same time presumably establishing the composer's own view of an incident or of a character's behavior in the narrative. In the later sagas, however, the traditional values of Iceland's settlers and early society are questioned if not challenged, and there wisdom texts are recruited as tools of this subversion. Placed in the mouths of less respected or even untrustworthy people and expressing negative views that criticize society's traditional values, they come to represent the interests of the disenfranchised. They give voice to critical social commentary, in some cases even on the part of the composers themselves.

What we might term this "subversive mode" of proverb use is found first in *Grettis saga* in the infant stories of the hero. Recalling the Infancy Gospel of Thomas in the Greek form, where the young Jesus uses his divine powers in very human immature ways, these stories are intended to reveal in Grettir's behavior the innate impulses of his early character.[27] Leading to those frequently expressed assessments of his lucklessness as he makes his way through life, these negative traits are painfully clear and still unmodified by those adult constraints that he to some extent developed and sometimes imposed on himself in later years. In a reader response-based study of Grettir's character Robert Cook remarked that by the end of this passage on the hero's childhood "the reader is not certain whether

---

27. Maria Bonner, "Grettir's First Escapades: How To Challenge Your Father And Get Away With It: A Case Study In Historical Dialogue Analysis," in *Frederic Amory in Memoriam. Old Norse-Icelandic Studies*, ed. John Lindow and George Clarke (Berkeley, CA: North Pinewood Press 2015), 184–212. See also Ronald F. Hock, ed., *The Infancy Gospels of James and Thomas: With Introduction, Notes, and Original Text featuring the New Scholars Version Translation (Scholars Bible)* (Sonoma, CA: Polebridge Press, 1996).

he has met a tyrannous and unreasonable father, an incorrigible and sadistic ten-year-old, or a budding hero not content with menial tasks"; indeed, readers themselves have not reached a consensus in this matter so far.[28] It is interesting to observe the proverbs Grettir uses in this series of confrontations with his father over his assignment of what the youth considers undesirable and demeaning chores.

Having killed the goslings put into his care because he found them boring—the composer remarks of his limited emotional range that "hann var lítill skapdeildarmaðr" (he had a fairly short temper)—he grins at his father's fury and celebrates this atrocity with half a *lausavísa* (single stanza), concluding, "enn þótt ellri finnisk, / einn berk af sérhverri" (and if older ones are there as well / I can deal with them single-handed).[29] Readers might see a threat of patricide in these lines, although in doing so they might paint Grettir in too dark a shade. When Ásmundr proclaims that he won't be dealing with geese anymore, his son responds, "Vinr er sá annars, er ills varnar" (A true friend spares others from evil).[30] This proverb is found in *Hugsvinnsmál*, the Icelandic rendering of the *Distichs of Cato*, and it falls into a category that describes the obligations of friendship.[31] The use of this type of proverb here might be viewed as mock-heroic because it ironically places Ásmundr's geese within his circle of friends. Grettir's utter lack of sympathy with his father's efforts is underscored in the next lines when he is told he will be given another job. "Fleira veit sá, er fleira reynir" (The more you try, the more you learn), he quips, employing a wholesome, if self-righteous, sentiment, but obviously without the slightest intention either of trying or of learning anything at all.[32]

Turned now to the task of massaging his father's back by the fire of an evening, he is again chided: "Nú muntu verða af þér at draga slenit, manskræfan" (You ought to shake off that laziness of yours for once, you layabout). "Illt er at eggja óbilgjarnan" (It's a bad thing to goad the obstinate), says Grettir, who, undertaking this new chore, then scratches his father's back with a wool comb.[33] Here,

---

28. Robert Cook, "The Reader in *Grettis saga*," *Saga-Book* 21.3–4 (1984–85): 137.
29. ÍF 7:37, ch. 14; *CSI* 2:64 and 65.
30. ÍF 7:38, ch. 14; *CSI* 2:65; JGF 633; TPMA 4.47.
31. See Birgita Tuvestrand, ed., *Hugsvinnsmál: Handskrifter och kritisk text* (Lund: Carl Bloms Boktryckeri, 1977), 84. See also Halldór Hermannsson, ed., *The Hólar Cato: An Icelandic Schoolbook of the Seventeenth Century*, Islandica 39 (Ithaca, NY: Cornell University Press, 1958).
32. ÍF 7:38, ch. 14; *CSI* 2:65; JGF 468; TPMA 9.163; FJ Proverb word 461, 201.
33. ÍF 7:38, ch. 14; *CSI* 2:65; JGF 109; TPMA 9.276.

Grettir again draws ironically on the language of heroes as he pursues a conflict with his father, attacking him physically, undoubtedly inflicting some degree of injury.

The story now escalates, in feud fashion, to Grettir's destruction of Ásmundr's favorite horse Kengála, for whom his master has an unusually affectionate admiration, one oddly reminiscent of Hrafnkell's for Freyfaxi. The horse, whose abilities in Ásmundr's eyes include weather prediction, refuses to go out after Grettir has flayed her back, and Ásmundr mistakes this for a sign of snow coming. "Skyzk þeim morgum vísdómrinn, er betri ván er at" (Wisdom falls short where it is most expected), comments Grettir—again, with a two-sided thrust—seemingly on the wisdom of both horse and master![34] When Ásmundr approaches Kengála, concerned that she has not fed well that season, he is nevertheless confident in her health: "þú munt sízt bregðask at bakinu, Bleikála" (your back will be as firm as ever, Kengala), Grettir says, "Verðr þat, er varir, ... ok svá hitt, er eigi varir" (The foreseeable happens, and also the unforeseeable, too); and when the hide comes away from her back in Ásmundr's hand, Grettir grins.[35] The latter segment of this quadripartite type proverb is common in the Old Norse paroemial inventory, but the former seems the composer's own. One wonders what could have been foreseeable in this situation, other than Grettir's lethal sabotage of his horse-keeping job, especially in light of the damage he attempted to do to his father's back during the massaging incident.

While Grettir's relations with his parents and the extent and cause of his proclivity for ill-natured behavior and conflict are left unresolved by the composer, his sense of himself seems initially clear. In nearly simultaneous publications, the translators of the 1974 *Grettir's saga* and Katheryn Hume first treated him as an anachronistic hero, one possessing the aristocratic warrior traits of his great-grandfather Ǫnundr Tré-fótr, but caught in a Christian land, a settled society of farmers and merchants. At one point, "þótti Gretti mikit mein, er hann mátti hvergi reyna afl sitt, ok fréttisk fyrir, ef nǫkkut væri þat, er hann mætti við fásk" (Grettir sorely regretted not having anything to test his strength against, and asked around [if there was anything of the sort that he might

---

34. ÍF 7:40–41, ch. 14; *CSI* 2:66; JGF 642; FJ Proverb word 459, 200.
35. ÍF 7:41, ch. 14; *CSI* 2:66; JGF 604; TPMA 3.49.

undertake]).³⁶ When, at the age of fourteen, he is restrained by adults from killing Auðunn, a slightly older relative and playmate who he feels has humiliated him, he insists there's no need to hold him like a mad dog: "Þræll einn þegar hefnisk, en argr aldri" (Only a slave takes vengeance at once, and a coward never).³⁷ The coldly murderous intent of this utterance, which is obviously related conceptually to the now clichéd Sicilian proverb about revenge being a dish best served cold, calls on rigid codes of vengeance that are out of place in the context of Grettir's youth, his surrounding family, and the Christian setting. The present critical view of Grettir as the aristocratic warrior hero born too late is so clearly and productively traceable throughout the entire narrative of his life that one must conclude it was also close to the point of this saga in the composer's mind, even though that point itself may still elude us. And the proverbs the composer imputes to him in scenes from his early life sketch rough lines of the adult Grettir's character, which is at such odds in value and behavior with the society in which he must live.

The Composer's Vision of Iceland's Heroic Settlement

The narrative as well as familial background for this destructively idealistic character is established by the composer in those early chapters of the saga discussed above, where his ancestor Ǫnundr seeks heroic adventures for the sheer excitement they offer. Unlike most Norwegians of the *Íslendingasögur* who took up the cause against King Haraldr hárfagri for ideological reasons, he and his friends joined forces with Þórir haklangr and Kjǫtvi konungr at Hafrsfjǫrðr because "þeim var mikil forvitni á at reyna sik, ok sǫgðusk þeir vildu þar vera, sem strǫngust væri orrostan" (they were eager to put their strength to the test, and said they wanted to be put in the thick of the battle). An epic level of significance in this conflict is remarked by the composer: "Þessi orrosta hefir einhver verit mest í Nóregi; koma hér ok flestar sǫgur við, því at frá þeim er jafnan flest sagt, er sagan er helzt frá gǫr." (The battle was one of the greatest ever fought in Norway. Most sagas refer to it, because it is such matters that sagas usually relate.")³⁸

---

36. ÍF 7:107, ch. 31; Fox, introduction to *Grettir's Saga*, viii–ix; Hume, "Design," in *Grettir's Saga*, 469–86.
37. ÍF 7:44, ch. 15; CSI 2:68; JGF 667; TPMA 9.177.
38. ÍF 7:5, ch. 2; CSI 2:50.

Even after the loss of his leg in this greatest of battles, Ǫnundr tréfótr remains a vigorous heroic warrior, challenging with Þrándr the Vikings Vígbjóðr and Vestmarr, the raiders of the Hebrides, who laugh when they learn who has come for them: "Troll hafi Tréfót allan, / trollin steypi þeim ǫllum. Ok er oss þat fásét, at þeir menn fari till orrustu, er ekki megu sér." (May the trolls swallow you whole, Tree-leg, / may the trolls topple you all. . . .It's not often we see men go into battle who can't even stand up for themselves.) The proverbially based response of Ǫnundr will be echoed in later chapters by his outlaw descendant, both literally and figuratively: "Ǫnundr kvað þat eigi vita mega, fyrr en reynt væri" (Onund said that there was no telling until it was put to the test).[39] Later, when Vígbjóðr, whose arm is hacked off by Ǫnundr, is dying and Vestmarr has fled, the victor responds with equal cruelty to the Viking's earlier insults, also in verse: "Séðu, hvárt sǫr þín blœða; / sǫttu nǫkkut mik hrøkkva; / auðslǫngvir fekk enga / einfœttr af þér skeinu; / meir es mǫrgum, snerru, / málskalp lagit, Gjalpar / brjótr esat þegn í þrautir / þrekvanðr, en hyggjandi." (See if your wounds bleed. / Did you see me flinch? / You did not deal a scratch to me, / the one-legged slinger of riches. / Many breakers of battle-axes / are more brag than brains. / That man was not generous / with his strength when challenged.)[40]

When Þrándr has decided to go to Iceland, he asks his friend if he will come along, but Ǫnundr, speaking in litotic terms, says, "Kvezk áðr vilja finna frændr sína ok vini suðr í landi" ([that he wants] to go and see his kinsmen and friends in the south of Norway first).[41] His true intentions, which he carries out, are to head south and slaughter Hárekr, *ármaðr konungs* (the king's agent), whom Haraldr has placed in control of Ǫnundr's ancestral holdings.[42] This heroically subdued way of speaking is not alien to the rhetoric of Grettir when he finds himself in situations of violence.

Honoring Þrándr's parting request that he look after those relatives whom he is leaving behind in Norway, Ǫnundr takes energetic vengeance for the killing of Ǫndóttr kráka by Harald's

---

39. ÍF 7:11, st. 2, ch. 4; *CSI* 2:53, st. 2; JGF 467; *TPMA* 9.163; FJ Proverb word 333, 181.
40. ÍF 7:12–13, st. 3, ch. 4; *CSI* 2:54, st. 3.
41. ÍF 7:16, ch. 6.
42. ÍF 7:17, ch. 7.

man, Grímr hersir. Ǫnundr and his companions burn Grímr in his home as he is preparing a feast for Auðunn jarl, and Ásgrímr Ǫndóttsson humiliates the jarl, giving him the feminine nickname *geit* (nanny goat).[43] Although Ǫnundr would have preferred they kill him—"væri þat Haraldi konungi hefnd nǫkkur fyrir þat, er vér hǫfum misst fyrir honum fé ok frændr vára" (That would be some sort of revenge upon King Harald for the losses we suffered on his account)—Ásgrímr avers that their humiliation of the jarl, leaving him alive to endure it, was greater vengeance.[44] From the entertaining chaos of this violently heroic world, Ǫnundr descends, with reluctance, upon Iceland, seeking a place of refuge in which to settle. His accompanying verse with its sentiments has about it an anticlimactic quality, as if anything about real life is over for him: "nú verðr á skæ skorðu, / skaldi sígr, at stíga / út með einum fœti / Íslands á vit, þvísa." (Now with one leg I must mount / my steed of the waves, / bound for Iceland's shores. / This poet is past his prime.)[45] When he is generously given land by Eiríkr snara, he seems ungrateful as he complains of his losses in Norway and what is being substituted for them: "hefk lǫnd ok fjǫlð frænda / flýt, en hitt es nýjast, / krǫpp eru kaup, ef hreppik / Kaldbak, en ek læt akra" (I have left behind many kinsmen / and lands to reach this pass: / I have struck a harsh bargain, swapped / my fields for the cold-backed mountain).[46] Answering what one might interpret as heroic resentment at the loss of power and wealth—and in the process depicting moods not altogether different from those found in the later verses of Egill Skalla-Grímsson—his friend Eiríkr admonishes him as follows: "Margr hefir svá mikils misst í Nóregi, at menn fá þess ekki bœtr; hygg ek ok, at numin sé flest ǫll lǫnd í meginheruðum; kenn ek því eigi at fýsa þik heðan í brott; mun ek þat halda, at þú hafir af mínum jǫrðum, þat er þér hentar." (Many people have lost so much in Norway, ... that will never be made good. I think almost all the land has been settled in the main districts, so I would not encourage you to leave this place. I shall keep my word and you can have whatever of my land that you like.)[47]

---

43. ÍF 7:18, ch. 7.
44. ÍF 7:19, ch. 7; *CSI* 2:56.
45. ÍF 7:20, st. 4, ch. 8; *CSI* 2:57, st. 4.
46. ÍF 7:22, st. 5, ch. 9; *CSI* 2:58.
47. ÍF 7:22–23, ch. 9; *CSI* 2:58.

The Decadence of Heroism in Early Icelandic Society

A more generally diffuse descent in *Grettis saga* from a once brilliant and proudly heroic world to a mundane society given to petty squabbles is exemplified in Iceland's second-generation territorially based disputes, which form the groundwork of feud generally in the sagas: "Engi varð áskilnaðr með mǫnnum þar, meðan inir ellri menn lifðu; en þá er Eiríkr var látinn, þótti Flosa Kaldbeklingar eigi hafa lǫgligar heimildir á jǫrðum þeim, er Eiríkr hafði gefit Ǫnundi" (No quarrels occurred while the older men lived, but after Eirik died, Flosi claimed that the people from Kaldbak had no legal right to the lands that Eirik had given to Onund).[48] As in other *Íslendingasögur*, *Grettis saga* notices that the heroic magnanimity of spirit of Iceland's settling generation is lost in the competition that accompanies a rising population and its urge to flourish. Eiríkr's son Flosi initiates an assassination attempt against Þorgeirr Ǫnundarson, but this attempt is foiled by a leather bottle strapped on the victim's back. Mistaking the squishing noise of the bottle, which is penetrated by the axe, for the sound of mortal wounding, Þorgeirr's would-be killer flees, and Þorgeirr obtains from the incident the humorous nickname *flǫskubakr* (bottle-back). This adventure inspires a droll poem: "Fyrr lauguðu frægir / fránhvítinga rítar / rausnar menn í ranni / ræfrhvǫssu bensævar; / nú rauð, sás vas víða, / vámr, frá tekinn sóma / benja skóðs af bleyði / bæði hlýr í sýru." (In the old days, heroes would bathe / shield-biters like shimmering fish / in a sea of blood flowing from wounds / deep as sharp-pointed roofs. / Now the weakling who never won / renown far and wide has smeared, / from sheer cowardice, both sides / of his axe with curdled whey.)[49] Such a nickname provides a jarring contrast with the heroic associations found among those of the previous generations and casts the event itself not only as disgraceful but as the work of people who have sunk below the moral level of their progenitors.

The next conflict between the two feuding groups occurs over the carcass of a whale, which is stranded on a portion of the shore that the people of Kaldbakr feel lies in their scavenging territory: "Fáir menn hǫfðu þar vápn, nema øxar þær, er þeir skáru með hvalinn, ok skálmir" (Hardly anyone had any weapons apart from the axes and

---

48. ÍF 7:26, ch. 11; *CSI* 2:59.
49. ÍF 7:27, st. 6, ch. 11; *CSI* 2:60, st. 6.

knives they were using to cut up the whale).⁵⁰ With these decidedly unheroic tools of battle, the men attack one another, even resorting to the use of whale bones: "Leifr, bróðir Ívars, laust félaga Steins í hel með hvalrifi. Þá var með ǫllu barizk, því er till fekksk, ok fellu þar menn af hvárumtveggjum." (Ivar's brother Leif clubbed one of Stein's companions to death with a whale rib. They fought with everything they could lay their hands on, and men were killed on both sides.)⁵¹

This altercation intentionally depicts a society discouragingly inferior to that of Grettir's adventurous ancestors who sought violence to try their strength where the battle was fiercest, and the situation is made even less admirable in the paltry weapons chosen, or at their disposal, for the battle. The degeneracy painted in the scene is celebrated in these verses: "Hǫrð frák heldr at yrði / hervǫpn at Rifskerjum, / mest því margir lustu / menn slyppir hvalklyppum; / en malm-Gautar móti / mjǫk fast hafa kastat, / oss lízk ímun þessi / óknyttin, þvestlyttum." (I heard they were rather hard, / the weapons wielded at Rifsker; / many men struck out, armed / only with strips of whalemeat. / The metal-Goths gave / as good as they got: / they lobbed lumps of blubber. / That was a brawl, not a battle.)⁵² Having grown up among men whose defense of their honor was so diminished in style that they resorted to combat using whale bones, Grettir can be seen striving for more traditionally heroic ways of establishing and maintaining his reputation. His two swords, both of which have names, are a far cry from the battle equipment his relatives use in this dismal scene. But it remains to consider in what further ways the outlaw hero is to be viewed as alienated from his own society by his peculiar, sometimes usefully heroic, aspiration.

The Hero in an Age of Decadence

Grettir exhibits difficulty in relating productively to men and especially to figures of authority, beginning with his father. Þorfinnr, for instance, with whom he stays in Norway, does not inspire his amicability. In fact, while first staying with him, Grettir seeks instead

---

50. ÍF 7:30, ch. 12; *CSI* 2:61.
51. ÍF 7:30, ch. 12; *CSI* 2:61–62.
52. ÍF 7:31, st. 7, ch. 12; *CSI* 2:62, st. 7.

another male friend, Auðunn, a neighboring farmer, who is himself presumably not on the best terms with Grettir's host. Only when he has performed the heroic feat of killing the berserkr Þórir and his followers is he finally accorded an honorable welcome, which, as he notices with formulaic comment, he would have accepted earlier: "mynda ek þegit hafa, þó at þú hefðir fyrr boðit" (I would have accepted your offer earlier too).[53] This comment makes clear the reason for Grettir's initial unfriendliness with his host, who had not made him welcome in a manner suitable to heroic warriors.

With Hafliði, however, who takes him to Norway in his ship when he first leaves Iceland as an outlaw, Grettir becomes a respectful and cooperative friend, despite the inauspicious beginnings of this, his first ocean voyage. Heather O'Donohugue explains this inconsistency of relationship in terms of the ability of the men he meets to interact with him on a poetic level. Her purpose is to present Grettir as a poet-hero, where his verses "give expression to his inner life." Taciturn in youth, he disdains "ordinary conversational discourse with those around him in favour of cryptic, stylized skaldic verse," which marks "his separate nature." "Grettir," she says, "only has relaxed, friendly relations with other poets—or at least, with characters who are willing to respond in kind to Grettir's poetic discourse."[54] While Ásmundr never communicates with his son at this level, Hafliði is able to arouse him to labor with verses. Admitting that it would be "simplistic to suggest that Grettir obeys Hafliði's injunction because it is expressed in skaldic verse," Heather O'Donohugue claims, "this stylized poetic exchange reflects in its symmetry the close, and exclusive, relationship between Hafliði and Grettir, and their natural affinity is reflected in it."[55] O'Donohugue's interesting observation about Grettir's selective friendliness and the oddly limited social environment of poetic communication that it suggests may well identify a method the composer employs to describe the condition according to which he consents to interaction with others.

Grettir responds, then, even in his earliest days, to those who are willing to treat him as one would treat a Viking hero of literary tradition. In fact, it is through reference to that literary tradition

---

53. ÍF 7:72. ch. 20; CSI 2:82.
54. Heather O'Donoghue, *Skaldic Verse and the Poetics of Saga Narrative* (Oxford: Oxford University Press, 2005), 183.
55. O'Donoghue, *Skaldic Verse*, 195–96.

that he may be most clearly defined. To begin with, we are told that although he eschews the farm chores, "Eigi lagðisk hann í eldaskála ok var fátalðr lengstum" (He did not lounge around in the fire-hall, and he was taciturn most of the time). He does not, therefore, fall in with the literary tradition of the coal-biter hero spending his time by the fire. Nor does he engage in feats of strength at this point, demonstrating as some heroes do their precocity: "eigi vissu menn gǫrla afl hans, því at hann var óglíminn" (no one knew how strong he was, because he was not a wrestler). He does show high verbal aptitude, however, as might be expected of a hero who will celebrate his own feats: "Orti hann jafnan vísur ok kviðlinga ok þótti heldr níðskældinn" (He often made verses and ditties that tended to be scornful).[56] "Aldri er dugr í þér" (You're good for nothing), exclaims Ásmundr, whose insult results in Grettir's attack with the woolcomb—and yet it is not quite accurate to accuse him of real laziness.[57] Rather, he refuses to do jobs that he despises and he remains inert unless he feels sufficiently challenged by person and circumstance to perform at a level worthy of a hero, or at least of a literary hero.

Perhaps it is not so much the poetry Haflíði uses that persuades Grettir to help save the ship when it is taking in water but the heroic spirit of the captain's poetry and of the noble challenge it represents. Haflíði addresses Grettir with his request for help by appealing to his sense of how his inaction will seem to a woman on board to whom he has taken a liking: "Stattu upp ór grǫf, Grettir, / grefr knǫrr hola vǫrru; / minnsktu á mǫl við svanna / meginkátr enn glaðláta; / fast hefir hrund at hǫndum, / hǫr-Nauma, þér saumat; / skorð vill, at vel verðir / viðr, meðan lǫnd eru niðri." (Stand up from where you're buried, Grettir, / the ship is furrowing the waves deep / while you chatter cheerfully / with that glad-hearted woman. / She has rolled up your sleeves, sewn them / tight around your arms, that woman, / she wants you to respect / your companions who are working below.)[58] Faced with this nobly worded challenge, which uses the formulas and concepts of honor that are typical of the heroic tradition, Grettir responds in kind: "Stǫndum upp, þó at undir / alltíðum skip ríði; / veitk, at víf mun láta / verr, ef ek ligg á

---
56. ÍF 7:42, ch. 14; CSI 2:67.
57. ÍF 7:38, ch. 14; CSI 2:65.
58. ÍF 7:54, st. 15, ch. 17; CSI 2:73.

knerri; / því mun ǫllungis illa / aldygg kona hyggja / hvít, ef hér skal láta / hvert sinn fyr mik vinna." (I stand up, how much beneath me / the ship is heaving and pitching, / I know the woman will frown / on me for slouching on board. / That maid of fair spirit and face / is sure to disapprove / if I let others here / always do my work for me.)[59] And only then does he undertake the chore of emptying the bilge, not being content with approaching the task as a menial or demeaning one but treating it heroically, using so much energy that eight men are required to keep up with the buckets he fills.

What would seem in other circumstances an unpleasant and boring task is thus recommended instead as a heroic feat, and he gains from that the admiration due to heroes, even if in this case it is only the admiration of merchants: "Þaðan af skiptisk mjǫk un orðalag kaupmanna við Gretti, því at þeir sá, hvat hann átti undir sér fyrir afls sakar; var hann ok þaðan frá inn frœknasti til liðs, hvers sem við þurfti." (After this, the merchants spoke very differently about Grettir, because they saw what he could accomplish on account of his great strength. He also turned out to be very energetic in helping them afterwards with whatever was needed.)[60] As a hero he has become a more useful member of the ship's company—that is, of his immediate society—having derived from his feat the status within it that he finds appropriate to his background and capabilities.

The Flawed Hero ("Engi maðr skapar sik sjálfr")

Grettir is imbued at his birth with this brittle persona, with its fatal inflexibility of response, and it is essential to that *ógæfa* that haunts his life and that he is never able to escape. Capable only of action situated in the heroic setting, but denied that setting by the mundane and diminished world of postconversion Iceland with its ploddingly industrious farmers and pragmatically ambitious merchants, he is eventually limited to conflict with denizens of the Otherworld. His heroic stature is enabled only by a class of adversary that, on the one hand, qualifies him as a truly epic hero, pursuing monsters where ordinary humans cannot go, with his strength enabling him to defeat forces beyond the power of ordinary human strength. And

---
59. ÍF 7:54, st. 16, ch. 17; *CSI* 2:73.
60. ÍF 7:55, ch. 17; *CSI* 2:73–74.

yet, on the other, these remarkable qualities and abilities, though useful to society, are inextricably bound up with that inflexible element of his character that leads to his demise.

Opposed to this tragically idealistic self-image is the gradually dawning awareness of himself simply as an outlaw, a wolf among men, his hopes of legal redemption at the mercy of his cousin Saint Óláfr dashed by a botched ordeal ritual and the king's observation that it happened through his impetuousness: "hlýtr jafnan illt af athugaleysinu; ok ef nǫkkurum manni hefir verit fyrirmælt, þá mun þér hóti helzt." (Rashness always breeds trouble. If any man has ever been accursed, it must surely be you.)[61]

Later, as they lie in their beds one morning, his brother Þorsteinn Drómundr speaks to Grettir about his arms: "einskis manns handleggi hefi ek slíka sét" (I have never seen any man with such arms). "Ek mynda ekki slíku til leiðar koma, sem ek hefi unnit, ef ek væra eigi allknár" (I would never have accomplished the deeds I have done if I weren't stoutly built), he answers. "Betr þœtti mér, . . . þó at væri mjórri ok nǫkkuru gæfusamligri" (I would have preferred less muscle and more good fortune), says Þorsteinn, to which Grettir comments, "engi maðr skapar sik sjálfr" (no man is his own creator).[62] Here his keen awareness of himself as the ógæfumaðr of the Norse heroic world is made tragically apparent.

Intimations of Alienation: "vera varð ek nǫkkur"

Perhaps the climax of his proverbial expression of this growing perception of himself as an outlaw rather than as an aspiring hero of the saga world can be found at that moment after Þorbjǫrg in digra saves Grettir from being hanged, when she asks him how he came to be in the area, troubling her farmers. He answers, "Eigi má nú við ǫllum sjá; vera varð ek nǫkkur." (You can't provide for everything. I had to be somewhere.) Guðni Jónsson, in his *Íslenzk fornrit* edition of the saga, noticed the allusion in the second part of Grettir's reply to the proverb, "Einhvers staðar verða vondir að vera" (Bad people have to be somewhere"), the only extant attestation of which is found in a *þjóðsaga* from the *Álfarit Ólafs Sveinsson í Purkey*.[63] This tale concerns Gúðmundur

---

61. ÍF 7:134, ch. 39; CSI 2:113; JGF 15; TPMA 8.353.
62. ÍF 7:137, ch. 41; CSI 2:114; JGF 508; TPMA 3.42.
63. ÍF 7:169, ch. 52; CSI 2:131; JGF 646.

biskup Árason (1161–1237), who went about Iceland consecrating sources of drinking water, as well as mountains and hills. When he consecrated Látrabjarg, a promontory in the Westfjords district, a voice asked him to cease this practice for this reason: "því undan þínum bænum og aðgjörðum verðum vær að flýja, en einhvörstaðar verða vondir að vera" (because we must flee from your prayers and actions, and bad creatures have to be somewhere).[64]

Guðni Jónsson's inclusion of this proverb in his note to the text in his edition of the saga attests to its appositeness here, and the context of its utterance is certainly appropriate to Grettir's own situation. Thus, as he responds to Þórbjǫrg's remonstrations, Grettir tacitly accepts his status among the *vondir* (bad) creatures of Iceland. The once proudly independent, aristocratic warrior hero has become aware of a new self-image, as an outcast, self-isolated by temperament, seeking his home in the desert, followed in the moonlight only by his shadow, like the pitiable iconic figure of Sigurður Sigurðsson's "Útilegumaðurinn":

> Ég sé þig elta heim í hreysið
> við hraunið—máni að baki skín,
> þinn eigin skugga, auðnuleysið,—
> sem eitt hélt tryggð við sporin þín.

> (I see you hunt a place in the desert among the lava—
> moon shines at your back
> your own shadow, luckless
> which alone follows in your tracks.)[65]

The Moral and Spiritual Implications of Grettir's Heroic Grasp: "Ekki læt ek laust þat, sem ek hefi hǫndum á komit"

The fatal intransigency of Grettir's character is proverbially emphasized by the composer in commenting on his violently retentive nature. This unyielding grasp, physically demonstrated in his refusal to let go of his treasured sword from Kárr's howe, even after his

---

64. Jón Árnason, *Íslenzkar Þjóðsögur og Æuintýri*, 6 vols. (Reykjavík: Bókaútgáfan þjóðsaga Prentsmiðjan Hólar, 1954–61), 6, 11. Taken from the anecdote, "Álfarit Ólafs Sveinssonar í Purkey." I am grateful to Oren Falk for pointing out to me the potential value of this information.

65. Sigurður Sigurðsson frá Arnarholti, "Útilegumaðurinn," in *Tvístirnið*, ed. Jónas Guðlaugsson (Reykavík: Prentsmiðjan Gutenberg, 1906), 52. Translation mine.

own death, might also suggest the composer's conclusion regarding this alienated figure's spiritual condition at the close of his life.

Although Grettir differs from his fellow legendary outlaw Gísli Súrsson in attempting to follow a heroically violent approximation of the pre-Christian Nordic warrior rather than in rigidly adhering to the constraints of an earlier ethic that place him at odds with contemporary society, the two are alike in the insistent inflexibility of their behavior. And in both instances, it is partly this lack of complaisance that leads to their undoing. For Grettir this emotionally based conservative tendency is reflected in his stubborn and retentive nature. When, in chapter 71, farmers first discover his presence on Drangey as they approach the island to fetch their sheep in the middle of winter, they offer to let him keep the sheep he had slaughtered while they take the rest. Grettir responds by saying, "Vel er þat boðit, en þó munu nú hvárir hafa þat, sem fengit hafa" (That's a fine offer, . . . but now each of us shall keep what we already have), the hostility of his sardonic response grounded in the proverbial wisdom of conflict. He then claims that he will never leave Drangey until he is taken away dead, adding "ekki læt ek laust þat, sem ek hefi hǫndum á komit" (I'm not letting go of what I've got my hands on).[66] His final remark contains an allusion to a paroemial text, cited by *TPMA*, which had been used of Grettir by the narrator earlier, in chapter 60, where he was under attack by farmers of Mýrar who were angry about his having acquired their livestock. When he sees them approaching at Hítará he drives the animals out on to a narrow point of land in the river to save them for after the battle: "því at hann vildi aldri laust láta þat, sem hann fekk hǫndum á komit" (because whenever he got his hands on anything he never wanted to let go of it again).[67]

This unwillingness, or perhaps even inability, to let go is first depicted in chapter 16 as Grettir contends with Skeggi over a bag of food both of them claim to own. Seizing it and pulling on it, they are unable to resolve the dispute when Skeggi suddenly alludes to Grettir's superior background, attributing to that alone Grettir's apparent sense of entitlement to the food: "Undarliga ætli þér, . . . þó at menn sé eigi jafnstórauðgir allir sem þér Miðfirðingar, at menn muni eigi þora at halda á sínu fyrir yðr" (It's strange of

---

66. ÍF 7:228, ch. 71; *CSI* 2:160; *TPMA* 7.276.
67. ÍF 7:195, ch. 60; *CSI* 2:144.

you to suppose, ... that just because not all the people in Vatnsdal are as rich as you, they wouldn't dare to keep hold of what's theirs against you). Grettir, perhaps with proverbial allusion, "kvað þetta eigi eptir mannvirðingu ganga, þótt hverr hefði þat, er ætti" (said people should have what was theirs, whatever their status).[68] When Skeggi strikes at Grettir with his axe, Grettir, still grasping the bag with his right hand, grabs the axe with his left, wrenches it free, and drives it through Skeggi's skull. Although it was clear previously that Grettir had been eager to do such a thing, this is his first killing of a man, and the details of the event would suggest for a thirteenth-century audience, as well as for us, an egregious overreaction on the aspiring young warrior's part. While he had a right to respond defensively to being threatened with Skeggi's axe, there was no need for the argument to have reached the point of hostility it did, and the composer uses the passage to delineate Grettir's violently impulsive nature in keeping so aggressively for himself what he regards as his property.

Although his ability to defend himself against all human adversaries seems consistently affirmed throughout the story, there is one clear exception. Chapter 54 contains an anecdote about Grettir's contest with "Loptr," a man whose wide brimmed hat conceals his face in Odinic manner but who is later identified as Hallmundr, who inhabits a cave at Balljǫkull with his hefty daughter. When Grettir asks him to "leggja nǫkkut plagg af því, sem þú ferr með" (hand over some of your belongings to me), he responds in a manner that is eerily reflective of Grettir's own possessiveness: "ekki vil ek svá láta þat, er ek á, ok fari hvárir sinn veg." (I won't hand over what's mine. Let's be going our separate ways.) They then proceed to have a tug of war with the reins of "Loptr's" horse.[69] This is the one instance in the saga where an apparently human character proves stronger than the adult hero. A verse attributed to Grettir comments on this unique moment thus: "staddr vildak svá sjaldan, ... þás ófælinn álar / endr dró mér ór hendi" (Seldom I would seek such a meeting, / ... as when that man, undaunted, / drew the reins from my hands"). And when the two become further acquainted it emerges that Hallmundr is more than human, presumably also having a giant background, which explains Grettir's inability to get the better of

---

68. ÍF 7:46, ch. 16; CSI 2:69; JGF 110: "Best er að hver eigi það hann á."
69. ÍF 7:175 and 175–76, ch. 54; CSI 2:134.

him.⁷⁰ Only in this instance are his physically unequalled grasp and his determination to apply it possessively met with frustration.

The Significance of Swords of the Dead

The composer's purpose in emphasizing proverbially this feature of Grettir's stubborn character may gain some clarity in the final episode of his life when he dies defending himself with Kársnautr, the weapon he had extracted from the grave of Kárr inn gamli, the mound dweller of Háramársey, in chapter 18.

In that episode, some details of which have reminded readers of Beowulf's descent into Grendel's Mere, the young Grettir, newly arrived in Norway on his first journey in outlawry, stays with Þorfinnr Kársson, whose undead father ravages the neighborhood, forcing land owners to vacate, and thus leaving his son in possession of the whole island. This collusive relationship between Þorfinnr and his dead father does not present an optimal situation for Grettir's heroic intrusion, but he nevertheless invades Kárr's underground dwelling, slays the revenant by beheading him with his maternal ancestral sword, Jǫkulsnautr, and returns with much treasure from the mound. Although readers might expect Þorfinnr to be angry with Grettir for plundering his father's grave, his host comments questioningly on his resulting lateness for supper and, when he learns the story, remarks as follows:

> Ekki mun þér allt í augu blœða, ok engan hefir þessa fýst fyrr, at brjóta hauginn; en fyrir því at ek veit, at þat fé er illa komit, er fólgit er í jǫrðu eða í hauga borit, þá mun ek ekki gefa þér hér skuld fyrir, með því at þú fœrðir mér; eða hvar náðir þú saxinu góða?
>
> (You are not a man of faint heart. No one until now has ever been keen to break into that mound. I know that it is a waste of treasure to bury it in the ground or a mound, so I cannot say you have done wrong, because after all you brought it to me. And where did you find that fine short-sword?)⁷¹

This scene, where Grettir has laid to rest the protective revenant of his host's father, thus depriving him of the supernatural source

---

70. ÍF 7:177, st. 45, ch. 54; CSI 2:135, st. 45. ls 3, 5–6.
71. ÍF 7:60, ch. 18; CSI 2:76.

of his dominant power, could have ended in a retributive or punitive response from Þorfinnr, if the composer had intended to tell a different story. Instead, his host congratulates the hero, finding no fault in his adventure, as he says, since Grettir brought to him the treasure, which he clearly acknowledges would be useless if left in the ground. In accompanying his approval with this supportive citation of an element of wisdom regarding treasure, Þorfinnr incidentally paraphrases aphoristically expressed sentiments regarding the uselessness to men of such hidden riches observed in *Beowulf*, where Beowulf's retainers leave with him in his barrow the treasure he had gained by killing the dragon: "forlēton eorla ġestrēon eorðan healdan, / gold on grēote, þǣr hit nū ġēn lifað, / eldum swā unnyt swā hit (ǣro)r wæs" (They let the earth hold the wealth of earls, gold in the ground, where now it still dwells, as useless to men as it was before).[72]

The traditional story pattern in which the composer has placed Grettir tells of a hero who dispatches his supernatural adversary—often a giant, but in this case a revenant—usually with his victim's own sword, and who then departs, taking the weapon with him from the Otherworld back to human society, where he himself then possesses it and its attendant powers. The formula of this traditional narrative is partly fulfilled here in *Grettis saga*, since the hero uses Jǫkulsnautr for the killing but also brings back the revenant's own sword on his return from the grave mound. When Grettir, who is hopeful that his host may reward him with it for retrieving the treasure—as might well happen in such episodes—expresses an interest in Kárr's sword, Þorfinnr replies, "sýna skaltu nǫkkut áðr, þat er frægð þykki í vera, en ek gefa þér saxit, því at þat fekk ek aldri af feðr mínum, meðan hann lifði" (you must prove your prowess before I give you the sword, because my father never gave it to me while he was alive).[73]

From this readers may anticipate Grettir's need to fulfill the narrative equivalent of a *forsending* (testing feat), of the sort that is typical in the *fornaldarsögur* or *þjóðsögur* (folktales), from traditions written down later than most of the Íslendingasögur, in order to win the weapon.[74] And that, of course, proves the case

---

72. *Beowulf*, ll. 3166–68; *Klaeber's Beowulf*, 108; Donaldson, trans., *Beowulf*, 55.
73. ÍF 7:60, ch. 18; CSI 2:76.
74. Einar Ól. Sveinsson, *Verzeichnis isländischer Märchenvarianten: Mit einer einleitenden Untersuchung*, FFC 28, no. 83 (Helsinki: Helsinki Suomalainen

when he, by trickery, deceit, and strength, slaughters the marauding Þórir and his berserks when they come to Háramársey at Jól in Þorfinnr's absence. After Grettir's departure, Þorfinnr expresses his gratitude by giving him "saxit góða; þat bar Grettir, meðan hann lifði, ok var in mesta gersemi" (the fine short-sword which Grettir carried for the rest of his life and was a precious piece of work).[75] Grettir's adventures on Háramarsey, then, mark the beginning of his career as an exorcist but they also leave him with a gift from the exclusive world of the un/dead, the Otherworld visited only by heroes—for example, Grendel's Mere or the Hades to which Aeneas goes to find Anchises. The fate that this treasure bears with it proves to be of a double-edged nature.

At two points in this episode it can be seen that the composer drew selectively, with his own narrative purposes, from traditions and generic possibilities inherent in its type.[76] First, the quelling of the revenant could have been treated with hostility by Þorfinnr, as Grettir's friend Auðunn had in fact warned him: "Let ek þik, ... at fásk þar við, því at ek veit, at Þorfinnr mun fjándskap á þik leggja" (I advise you not to get involved in this, ... because I know Thorfinn will hate you for it).[77] Instead, that quelling met with Þorfinnr's at least qualified approval. Second, when Þorfinnr, according to generic expectation, might have given his ancestral sword to Grettir as a reward for this feat, he instead made him wait until he had performed a deed of fame. Usually in such stories the ruler assigns a specific deed to the hero, but here the deed comes to Grettir by chance in the form of Þórir and his marauding band. Whatever the composer's intentions may have been for developing Grettir's character and career in the reworked details of this episode, his purposes for the narrative thread had to do with Grettir obtaining from the grave mound the weapon—namely, Kárr's short sword— that he would soon come to use for the rest of his life. The sword is the property of a *haugbúi* (mound-dweller), and it therefore has the unfortunate burdens associated with such a provenance, yet it

---

Tiedeakatemia Academia Scientiarum Fennica, 1929), xxxii–xxxiii; Einar Ól. Sveinsson, *Um íslenzkar þjóðsögur* (Reykjavík: Sjóður Margrétar Lehmann-Filhés, 1940) 247–48. The motif seems to be Celtic in origin. See Einar Ól. Sveinsson, "Celtic Elements in Icelandic Tradition," *Béaloideas* 16 (1957): 3–24.

75. ÍF 7:73, ch. 20; *CSI* 2:82.

76. See the very interesting article by Oren Falk, "The Vanishing Volcanoes: Fragments of Fourteenth-Century Icelandic Folklore," *Folklore* 118 (April 2007): 1–22, on features of hidden treasure stories.

77. ÍF 7:57, ch. 18; *CSI* 2:75.

is also a *minjagripr* (heirloom), which Þorfinnr remarks had never before left the family.⁷⁸ This weapon, then, is imbued with those two aspects we have noticed in Grettir's own character: on the one hand, the aristocratic nature of its origins; on the other hand, its monstrous associations—in this case, associations with the dead.

Later, in chapter 43, we learn that Grettir gave his maternal family's ancestral sword Jǫkulsnautr to Atli, who has it with him when he is killed by Þórbjǫrn Øx, but who lacks the opportunity to use it. Grettir himself keeps Kársnautr as his weapon of choice until his death on Drangey. Heather O'Donohugue has noticed that Grettir is "one of a company of legendary figures who brings the past into the present—like Beowulf—by unearthing the treasure buried with the dead."⁷⁹ We should observe, in addition, that the unearthing of such unnatural wealth traditionally brings with it a sense of the power of its origin. When, later in the narrative, Grettir dispatches his supernatural foes with the sword from Kárr's mound, he can be seen as using on them a weapon from their own world, with its equivalence to their unearthly power in their undead, and unredeemed, state. What the composer wishes to suggest about Grettir's own character on the basis of his attachment to such a weapon is a question worth considering.

Grettir's Last Grasp

When Grettir is in his last struggles with Þorbjǫrn ǫngull on Drangey, he is so weak he cannot rise from his knees: "greip hann þá saxit Kársnaut" ([He] grabbed his short-sword Kar's Gift), the composer tells us.⁸⁰ And this is a grip that, like Grettir's hold elsewhere in his story, does not yield—here, even at his death. When Þorbjǫrn and his companions think he is no longer alive, Þorbjǫrn tries to take the sword from his grasp, saying he has carried it long enough: "En Grettir hafði fast kneppt fingr at meðalkaflanum, ok varð ekki laust" (But Grettir clenched his fingers so tightly around the hilt that it would not come free). Again, the composer notices Grettir's stubborn retention of what he owns. When all attempts fail, Þorbjǫrn chops off his hand, so that "réttusk fingrnir ok losnuðu af meðalkaflanum" (the fingers straightened out and released their

---

78. ÍF 7:59, ch. 18; *CSI* 2:75.
79. O'Donohugue, *Poetics*, 208.
80. ÍF 7:260, ch. 82; *CSI* 2:175.

grip on the hilt).[81] And it is then with this sword, retrieved from the undead and used by its owner in laying to rest supernatural beings, that his killer decapitates Grettir, treating his victim much as he himself had treated the monstrous creatures with whom he contended in his career as an exorcist.

Grettir's two named swords are clearly of great qualitative significance to his warrior stature. The composer has specified in brief detail, but sufficiently for his audience, the origins of each, in addition to suggesting the implications of those origins for the powers and fortune with which they may imbue their owner. I have discussed the symbolic ambiguity of Ásdís's gift of her ancestors' sword to Grettir when he leaves Iceland in his first outlawry elsewhere. She presents it in chapter 17 with an abbreviated history: "Sverð þetta átti Jǫkull, fǫðurfaðir minn, ok inir fyrri Vatnsdœlar, ok var þeim sigrsælt; vil ek nú gefa þér sverðit, ok njót vel." (This sword belonged to my grandfather Jokul and the most prominent people of the Vatnsdal clan, and it brought them many triumphs. I want to give to you this sword. Make good use of it.")[82]

The literary context for this speech is in *Vatnsdœla saga*, which purports to tell the history of Ásdís's aristocratic family in the north of Iceland. From the early, fabulously recounted chapters of that saga, we learn of the legendary Norwegian nobility from which she is indeed descended, although by an odd circumstance. Her maternal ancestor, Þorsteinn Ketilsson, married Þórdís Ingimundardóttir jarls after killing her outlaw brother, Jǫkull. As he was dying, Jǫkull had made his vanquisher promise to marry his sister and see that the family offspring were named after him. From their union is born Ingimundr, Ásdís's great-great-grandfather, the settler and first chieftain of Vatnsdalr. The *hamingja* of this family, dictated by *forlǫg*, informs the narrative theme of *Vatnsdœla saga*, and the audience of *Grettis saga* were surely just as aware of the oral backgrounds of the literary work as they were of the text itself. They would also have known of Þorsteinn's maternal ancestry, his mother having been a daughter of Án bogsveigir, whose saga is among the four *Hrafnistumannasögur*, stories about the quasi-legendary, giant-loving inhabitants of Hrafnista, in the far north of Norway. The presence of giants in Ásdís's familial background creates a generally sublimated thread of impulsiveness and violence, and thus

---

81. ÍF 7:261, ch. 82; *CSI* 2:176.
82. ÍF 7:49–50, ch. 17; *CSI* 2:71. Harris, "Backgrounds," *Hero*.

of *ógæfa*, in *Vatnsdœla saga*, with several men named Jǫkull in this family ending up in a bad way—beginning, of course, with Þórdís's outlaw brother. The sword Ásdís gives Grettir, which she claims was *sigrsælt* (victorious) for her ancestors, thus retains other less fortunate associations, as does Grettir's own aristocratic yet irritable, impulsively violent giantlike character. His eventual disposal of Jǫkulsnautr as a gift to Atli does not seem to have left it imbued with unalloyed good luck. It is worth considering what luck might thus have been expected by the audience to attend Kársnautr, which can be interpreted as "Kárr's gift," but which more accurately could have meant "an object used, or whose use was enjoyed, by Kárr."[83]

Objects retrieved from the Otherworld or from Otherworld figures of Icelandic saga do not convey to their new owners consistently reliable success. Perhaps Gramr, the sword that, according to *Vǫlsunga saga*, Sigmundr pulls from the tree, Barnstokkr, where it was placed by a disguised Óðinn, constitutes an archetypal example here. It brings with it Óðinn's protection, but the advantage of that protection is qualified by the ephemeral nature of his favors. As Sigmundr wields it for the last time in battle with King Lyngvi it breaks when he strikes it against a spear held by Óðinn, who is again in disguise. Repaired for his son, Sigurd, by Reginn, it is used by Sigmundr on several adventures; it is finally used at his death to cut in half his assailant, the young Guttormr. The sword represents the gift of Óðinn's power and protection, but its value is mixed, as is the reliability of its first owner.

Kársnautr is thus likely to have represented more than a mere physical object, a treasured weapon, unearthed from a grave, when the composer of *Grettis saga* and his audience saw it in the hands of his hero. It would also have carried with it the presence of its original owner, as well as the ethos of Kárr's world, that of the undead, the plane of the unredeemed. For members of the composer's Christian milieu Grettir's short sword would have come from a place inhabited only by those who would never gain salvation. Readers have found it notable that this hero is peculiarly fixed on such creatures, apparently since he found no humans worthy of his aggressive attentions, and that his heroism is in fact inextricably bound up with the task of exorcising beings in a state that was

---

83. Harris, "Backgrounds," *Hero*, 162–63, for discussion of such sword names using *-nautr*.

itself inimical to those who were alive and who sought a Christian salvation.

There is some division in views about what this preoccupation tells us, about what we may reasonably conclude on other grounds, and about Grettir's own spiritual condition at the end of his life. Andrew Hamer places great weight on the hero's spiritual corruption resulting from his dealing with unclean spirits, attributing to this association his inability, as a sinner, to undertake the hot iron ordeal to prove his innocence of intentionally killing the sons of Þórir Skeggjason í Garði. From this point of view, "Grettir, a Christian, fails to make a new start, . . . is outlawed, . . . and dies as an outcast from God and society."[84]

On a more positive note, Denton Fox and Hermann Pálsson, in the introduction to their translation of the saga, remark how "by the end, Grettir's trials seem to have purified him; he still never gives way, but he seems motivated more by bravery and intelligence, and less by pride."[85] Readers of the Old Icelandic sagas have in some instances noticed evidence of moral change or spiritual progression in some of the characters with which the sagas are peopled; indeed, with Grettir inn sterki, there could be arguments in favor of such growth. A composer would likely anticipate the influence on his character of so many years in isolation, of the struggle simply to maintain his bare existence. Grettir has treated Glámr, "the despicable buffoon, with great tolerance."[86] And he declares explicitly his familial dependence and thus, at last, his human vulnerability, when, wounded by Þorbjǫrn, he addresses Illugi as follows: "Berr her hverr á bakinu, nema sér bróður eigi" (Bare is the back of a brotherless man).[87] It seems reasonable to suppose that at his death Grettir has progressed from the prickly son of a harsh father, imbued with the irritable impetuosity of his giant kin, to an adult who is aware of relational value. Although it may be the case, as I tried to show several decades ago, that the composer of the extant *Grettis saga* ironically situates his tragic hero in the narrative

---

84. Hamer, "iudicium," 17 and 20. See also Bernadine McCreesh, "Grettir and Glámr—Sinful Man Versus the Fiend: An Allegorical Interpretation of a Fourteenth-Century Icelandic Saga," *Revue de l'Université Ottawa/University of Ottawa Quarterly* 51 (1981): 180–88.
85. Fox and Pálsson, *Grettir's Saga*, xiii.
86. Fox and Pálsson, *Grettir's Saga*, xiii.
87. ÍF 7:260, ch. 82; CSI 2:176; JGF 35–36; TPMA 2.128.

pattern of a physical monster in his last scene on Drangey, he seems internally changed in a way that makes him a more sympathetic figure by the time of his death.[88] The misplaced aristocratic warrior, the self-idealized literary hero caught in a world that has no need for such heroism, in constant search of a worthy challenge, is much reduced, crippled personally by the curses of Glámr and Þúríðr, and physically by the latter's sorcery. His appearance is distorted by the gangrenous wound when he is confronted by his slayer in his eyrie refuge, and the saga's composer employs the ultimate irony in having Þorbjǫrn ǫngull attribute to Christ his success in overcoming Grettir. "Kristr vísaði oss leið" (Christ showed us the way), he says, as though proclaiming his victim's sympathy with, or indeed membership in, the monstrous tribe of Cain. This bluff is in turn called by Grettir: "En ek get, . . . at in arma kerlingin, fóstra þín, hafi vísat þér, því at hennar ráðum muntu treyst hafa" (I would guess, . . . that wretched old crone, your foster-mother, showed you the way, because you have surely trusted in her advice).[89] This interchange in itself, with the outlaw's explicit distinction between the powers of good and evil, would seem to clarify the spiritual condition in which Grettir meets his death.

* * *

More than any other narrative among the *Íslendingasögur*, *Grettis saga* makes obvious use of proverbs to delineate the character of the hero, as well as to clarify the composer's purposes in telling his story. The paroemial material used by the young hero in the infancy episodes leaves imprinted on the reader's mind the cynically aggressive nature of his temperament, just as proverbs that he uses later in life indicate his maturing awareness of his unfortunate and alienated situation. We are struck, finally, at the end of his life, by his tragically belated recognition of his dependence on familial relationship for his very survival.

---

88. Richard L. Harris, "The Deaths of Grettir and Grendel: A New Parallel," *Scripta Islandica* 24 (1973): 25–53.
89. ÍF 7:260–61, ch. 82; *CSI* 2:176.

CHAPTER 6

Various Uses and Variant Forms of Proverbs in the Sagas
The Proverbial Foolishness of Hrafnkels saga Freysgoða

Chapters 3, 4, and 5 explored how reading some sagas against the proverbial background of their content helps us understand and appreciate more fully the meaning their composers attached to their stories. The use and placement of proverbial texts can be seen to signal the themes of these sagas. This analysis shows that such witnesses of traditional wisdom might direct or illuminate these stories but also that they could be used for ironic or even subversive purposes in cases where the values and priorities of the saga world and, by extension, those of thirteenth-century Icelandic society, came under question.

At least some of the later sagas, however, exhibit a more sophisticated level of paroemial involvement in a narrative, implying ethical value by alluding to proverbial wisdom rather than making a direct statement. These composers clarified the point of their stories by allusive reference to a proverbial wisdom that is never explicitly formulated in the narratives. This chapter, as well as chapters 7 and 8, will consider some examples of how this was accomplished. In *Hrafnkels saga Freysgoða*, a single phrase uttered by one character alludes to a proverb whose force will be apparent throughout the narrative, a proverb that therefore communicates the point of the saga. In *Hœnsa-Þóris saga* a paroemially allusive phrase that is syntactically identical to the one noticed in *Hrafnkels saga* is used similarly to identify a proverb by which the meaning of this work can also be interpreted. This strategy produces a paroemial impact at least as strong as, if not stronger than, the sort of explicit proverbial comment examined previously. What we study here should not, of course, be confused with the phenomenon of paroemial cognitive patterning, a subject of chapter 2, where the communal proverbial background of a culture can be observed influencing the patterns of ethical thought displayed in a narrative. Rather, the processes of allusion discussed below are in the first place conscious on the part of a composer, intentional in their initiation, and undertaken with a literary purpose.

The Sagas of Wealth and Power

This chapter and chapter 7 are devoted to two rather short sagas, *Hrafnkels saga Freysgoða* and *Hœnsa-Þóris saga*. Both of these works have been classed among a larger group now thought to have been inspired by conflicts over power between the traditional leaders of the Commonwealth of Iceland and those who succeeded them as Iceland came under Norwegian rule. Events recounted in stories such as these were of course meant to have taken place some centuries earlier than their composition, yet it is recognized that their narratives are particularly reflective of that radically changing society in which the composers and their audience found themselves—in the Iceland of roughly the 1280s.

Farmers and merchants with newly acquired wealth, presumably the result of energetic husbandry and shrewd trading practices rather than of those unscrupulous political strategies that led some *goðar* to economic dominance over increasingly larger geographic areas of twelfth- and thirteenth-century Iceland, assume greater importance in several such narratives. *Bandamanna saga* and *Hœnsa-Þóris saga* are among those of obvious sympathetic interest to this newly developing middle class. In both these sagas the aristocratic *goðar* have become greedily corrupt, eagerly selling their power even in situations where doing so will work to the detriment of a just society. And in both sagas they are thwarted in their irresponsibly self-centered ambitions.

In this context, *Hrafnkels saga* could be seen as sympathetic to the old rulers and their rather exclusive skills in aristocratic leadership, its hero's cunning and his executive skills rendering him capable and deserving of the authority that Sámr, his adversary, proved

Various Uses and Variant Forms of Proverbs in the Sagas 199

unable to manage. Readers can also, and more reasonably, find themselves ultimately critical of the brutality with which *goðar* like this saga's dangerous hero have come to conduct themselves. The new social and political realities are no less formidable than before, but they demand a subtler hand in the imposition of power, with more acute sensitivity to communal approval of leaders' actions and characters than might once have been necessary for the maintenance of their privileged status. In this sense, then, *Hrafnkels saga* can be seen as falling in with *Bandamanna saga* and *Hœnsa-Þóris saga* in condemning the ways of the traditional but now decadent leadership of Iceland.

It is no doubt in recognition of such considerations of political practice that *The Complete Sagas of Icelanders* groups together in volume 5, under the heading "Wealth and Power," *Eyrbyggja saga, Hrafnkels saga Freysgoða, Hœnsa-Þóris saga, Bandamanna saga,* and *Hávarðar saga Ísfirðings,* along with a few thematically related *þættir.*[1] Theodore M. Andersson, in his *Growth of the Medieval Icelandic Sagas,* in a chapter entitled "Pondering Justice," treats *Hœnsa-Þóris saga, Hrafnkels saga,* and *Bandamanna* as works that "share a new skepticism about governance, specifically the reliability of chieftains, since all three focus on the demise of chieftains."[2] The two sagas chosen from this group for examination here share interesting similarities in their respective narrative forms and their proverbially informed thematic significance that make their consecutive treatments mutually beneficial to our literary critical understanding of them both.

---

1. For an earlier consideration of sagas that were thought to be inspired by these conflicts, see Vésteinn Ólason, "Concentration of Power in Thirteenth-Century Iceland and Its Reflection in Some Íslendingasögur" (paper presented at the Alþjóðlegt fornsagnaþing, Reykjavik, Iceland, August 2–8, 1973), http://www.sagaconference.org/SC02/SC02.html. Vésteinn Ólason's attention to these matters is found in his *Dialogues with the Viking Age. Narration and Representation in the Sagas of the Icelanders,* trans. Andrew Wawn (Reykjavík: Heimskringla, 1998), 180–90. Concise coverage of the process is in Helgi Þorláksson, "Historical Background: Iceland 870–1400," in *A Companion to Old Norse-Icelandic Literature and Culture,* ed. Rory McTurk (Oxford: Blackwell, 2005), 148–52. An extensive study of the power shift and its representation in the subject of this chapter is found in Uwe Ebel, *Der Untergang des isländischen Freistaats als historischer Kontext der Verschriftlichung der Isländersaga: Zugleich ein Beitrag zum Verständnis der "Hœnsa-Þóris saga,"* Wissenschaftliche Reihe 2 (Metelen: Dagmar Ebel, 1989). A useful appendix with excerpts from texts of historical pertinence to these issues is found in Uwe Ebel, ed., *Hœnsa-Þóris saga: Mit Anhang, Skizzen und Nachwort* (Metelen: Dagmar Ebel, 1989), 63–78.
2. Andersson, *Growth,* 162.

The Composition and Structure of *Hrafnkels saga Freysgoða*

Hrafnkels saga, one of the shortest narratives among the *Islendingasögur*, is also remarkable for having a significant body of literary criticism as its focus, a body that in its various published forms has become much larger than the length of the text itself might lead readers to anticipate. There are several reasons for this. First, the story has been the subject of much literary critical debate since 1939. It was indeed a primary text in the argument waged between those who advocated the essentially literary nature of the genre, the book prose theory, and adherents of the free prose theory, who wanted to emphasize its oral origins and historical reliability. Thus, both E. V. Gordon in 1939 and Sigurður Nordal in 1940, though on slightly different grounds, found much in the saga that could not be true, arguing that it is primarily a literary production that should be read and appreciated as an artistically composed work of fiction, rather than as an orally distorted history.[3] Second, in the 1970s, other than Hermann Pálsson, who emphasized the continental and Christian influences, much of the interest in *Hrafnkels saga* turned from doubts over its historicity and a focus on its author's literary skills to a reading of the saga against the background of a tradition termed the oral family saga, which emphasized the survival of historically reliable material though acknowledging literary influences. Finally, it should be said that students of Old Icelandic often first encounter this work as the edition included by E. V. Gordon in his *Introduction to Old Norse*, and indeed in its complete form in the grammar's second edition, which is from 1957. This ready availability of *Hrafnkels saga* for classroom translation and discussion over many decades thus encouraged a close attention never paid to other members of its genre.

There is now general agreement that *Hrafnkels saga*, like other members of this subgenre, was composed fairly late in the thirteenth century. Its manuscript tradition is discussed above, in chapter 2. As I have argued elsewhere, it seems to me highly likely that we can reach a subtler understanding of the point of this story through an

---

3. E. V. Gordon, "On *Hrafnkels saga Freysgoða*," *Medium Ævum* 8 (1939): 1–32. Sigurður Nordal, "*Hrafnkatla*," Studia Islandica 7 (Reykjavík: Ísafoldarprentsmiðja, 1940); Sigurður Nordal, Hrafnkels Saga Freysgoða: *A Study*, trans. R. G. Thomas (Cardiff: University of Wales Press, 1958).

explicit allusion, which occurs at its outset, to a traditional Icelandic proverb, "Illt er heimskum lið at veita" (It's bad to give help to the foolish).[4] This proverb, which has in any case an undoubtedly universal application, is attested in the paroemial marginalia of the sixteenth-century MS AM. 604, 4to, in the hand of Tómas Arason of Mosvellir, Önundarfjörður. There, at the bottom of I.74.D.7., it completes a set of three proverbs on the dangers of association with fools. The other two are "Fátt er verra en vara heimskan" (Little is worse than being foolish) and "Seint er heimskan at snotra" (A foolish person is slow to become wise), and they occur at the bottom of pages 5 and 6, respectively. First published by Kristian Kålund in *Småstykker 6*, the collection of paroemes and other sentential texts has remained relatively unnoticed until recently, and Kålund's method, while accurate enough, did not represent the occasional conceptual continuity of the items in situ.[5] As Christine Schott points out in her immensely interesting Háskóli Íslands master's thesis on marginalia in some Icelandic manuscripts, "the cynicism of the marginalia [in AM 604, 4to] is easily missed in referring only to Kålund's edition, in which he breaks up paired items in order to classify each part by subject."[6] For whatever reason, Tómas's mind was clearly devoted to just one topic where the marginalia of these pages are concerned. All these texts are found in Guðmundur Jónsson's compilation, and they remind the reader of passages in *Hávamál* on the disadvantages of dealings with a *heimskr* person—that is, etymologically, one who is better off staying home than going out in the world.[7]

The Key Proverbial Allusion in *Hrafnkels saga*

Clearly, it is to an internalized corpus of just such admonitions that the composer of *Hrafnkels saga* has Sámr Bjarnason refer when he gives in to the urgings of his uncle Þorbjǫrn to take up the case

---

4. JGF 240; TPMA 8.380. This section is a reworking of my article, "The Proverbial Heart of *Hrafnkels saga Freysgoða*: 'Mér þykkir þar heimskum manni at duga, sem þú ert,'" *Scandinavian-Canadian Studies* 16 (2006): 28–54.
5. JGF 239 and 240; Kristian Kålund, "1886. 7. En islandsk ordsprogsamling fra 15de århundrede," in *Småstykker 1–16*, Samfund til udgivelse af gammel nordisk litteratur (Copenhagen: S. L. Møllers bogtrykkeri [1884–91]), 131–84.
6. Christine Schott, "Footnotes on Life: Marginalia in Three Medieval Icelandic Manuscripts" (master's thesis, Háskóli Íslands, 2010), 30.
7. See above, chapter 2, for discussion of proverbs about fools, in the section on *Hreiðars þáttr*.

against Hrafnkell Freysgoði Hallfreðarson for the killing of Þorbjǫrn's son, Einarr: "Ófúss geng ek at þessu. Meir geri ek þat fyrir frændsemi sakar við þik. En vita skaltu, at mér þykkir þar heimskum manni at duga, sem þú ert." (I go into conflict with Hrafnkel unwillingly. I do this mainly for the sake of my relationship with you. But you ought to know that I think in helping you I'm helping a fool.)[8] He has several reasons for his reluctance.

First, Hrafnkell is an aggressively difficult man, dangerous to contend with, "linr ok blíðr við sína menn, en stríðr ok stirðlyndr við Jǫkulsdalsmenn, ok fengu af honum engan jafnað. Hrafnkell stóð mjǫk í einvígjum ok bœtti engan mann fé, því at engi fekk af honum neinar bœtr, hvat sem hann gerði." (Mild and gentle with his own people, but stiff and stubborn with the people of Jokulsdal who never received any justice from him. Hrafnkel was often involved in single combats and never paid anyone reparation. No one received any compensation from him, whatever he did.)[9]

Second, aside from the inadvisability of taking action against an *ójafnaðarmaðr* who never paid compensation for any killing, Sámr is slowed in his response to Þorbjǫrn's importunities by the fact that, for once in his life, Hrafnkell had indeed offered a most generous compensation for Einarr. Since "mér þykki þetta verk mitt í verra lagi víga þeira, er ek hefi unnit" (I regard this deed as one of the worst acts I have committed), he promised Þorbjǫrn a lifetime supply of food, provision for his many sons and daughters to start them off in life, anything the farmer wants from his possessions, and a good deal else![10] Incredibly, with a mixture of perversity and the foolishness of false pride, Þorbjǫrn declined this virtually unique offer, a better deal than can be found for a similar killing anywhere else in the *Íslendingasögur*: "Ek vil eigi þenna kost" (I don't want that offer), he responded, insisting rather "at vit takim menn til gørðar með okkr" (choose others to arbitrate a settlement between us).[11] Since this demand was based

---

8. Jón Jóhannesson, ed., *Hrafnkels saga Freysgoða*, in *Austfirðinga sǫgur*, Íslenzk fornrit 11 (Reykjavík: Hið íslenzka fornritafélag. 1950), 108, ch. 3; *CSI* 5:267. See below, chapter 6, for analogous syntactic construction in *Hœnsa-Þóris saga*. See ÍF 3:17, ch. 6; *CSI* 5:245.
9. ÍF 11:99, ch. 2; *CSI* 5:262.
10. ÍF 11:105, ch. 3; *CSI* 5:265.
11. ÍF 11:106, ch. 3; *CSI* 5:266. This impetuous, laconic rejection of a reasonable resolution of Hrafnkel's outrageous act is remarkably similar to Hœnsa-Þórir's ultimate

on Þorbjǫrn's presumptuous assertion of social equality between the two men, Hrafnkell declined.

Þorbjǫrn's wealthy brother, Bjarni, whom he had approached first for litigational help, refused outright, noting that the adversary had "marga málaferlum vafit, er meira bein hafa í hendi haft en vér" (complicated many law cases with stronger men than ourselves), and bluntly observing, "Sýnisk mér þú vitlítill við hafa orðit, er þú hefir svá góðum kostum neitat" (I think you're stupid to have turned down such a good deal).[12] Justifying his decision, and by extension criticizing his brother proverbially as he did so, he commented, "sá er svinnr, er sik kann" (it's a wise man who knows himself).[13] The foolishness of Þorbjǫrn's prideful behavior with Hrafnkell colors the atmosphere of his conversations with his relatives as he seeks help from them to undertake aggressive legal redress for the unlawful killing of his son.

* * *

From the point of view of the composer of this saga, however, the foolishness seems not to be Þorbjǫrn's alone. Sámr, in his justifiably reluctant undertaking of the case, is bluntly critical of his uncle's absurd rejection of Hrafnkell's offer and makes explicit the flaw of this motivating figure in the story's conflict as he foolishly undertakes to help the cause of a foolish man. His doing so directs our attention, in turn, to the ill-advised behavior of most other members of the drama. In fact, nearly all the significant characters of this story display some failure of wisdom in their dealings at some point in the narrative. In the interests of approaching the composer's intentions as they are suggested by the proverbially allusive passage presented above, which seems to me to be of central importance to the theme of the saga, it may be helpful to examine in some detail the steps by which Þorbjǫrn arrived at his unsupportable situation, and then how, in the denouement of the narrative, we can observe further examples of foolish behavior and decisions among the cast of characters.

---

refusal to let Blund-Ketill buy his hay: "enda vil ek eigi selja" (besides, I don't want to sell). See ÍF 3:15, ch. 5; CSI 5:243.

12. ÍF 11:106–7, ch. 3; CSI 5:266.
13. ÍF 11:106, ch. 3; CSI 5:266; JGF 552–53; TPMA 3.28.

The Origins of Foolishness: Þorbjǫrn and Hrafnkell Freysgoði

The description of Þorbjǫrn at the start, of a man possessing "fé lítit, en ómegð mikla" (few livestock, but many dependents), is not a promising indication of wise husbandry.[14] He has, furthermore, delayed until too late in the season when he tells Einarr, his oldest son, that he will have to leave home and find a job: "því at ek þarf eigi meira forvirki en þetta lið orkar, er hér er, en þér mun verða gott til vista, því at þú ert mannaðr vel" (because I need no more labor than the rest of the household can provide, and you will have a good chance of getting service because you are well accomplished). His son's own reaction indicates Þorbjǫrn's lack of good judgement in waiting too long with this news: "Of síð hefir þú sagt mér til þessa, því at nú hafa allir ráðit sér vistir, þær er beztar eru, en mér þykkir þó illt at hafa órval af." (You've told me about this too late, because now all of the best positions are taken. I don't like having to choose from what's left.)[15] And at his interview with Hrafnkell, the most likely landowner to have a job for him in the district, Þorbjǫrn's improvidence is further underscored when the goði asks, "Hví leitaðir þú þessa svá síð, því at ek munda við þér fyrstum teki hafa?" (Why are you asking for this so late? I would have taken you on first?) So it is, then, in the first place, because of his father's poor or at least slow judgement that Einarr enters service in the position and household where he will find his death.

His death, in turn, will come about as a result of Hrafnkell's foolishly enthusiastic attachment to his horse Freyfaxi, with regard to whom he has taken what the composer seems to view as an unnecessary and perhaps even prideful oath, affirming that he would "þeim manni at bana verða, sem honum riði án hans vilja" (bring about the death of any man who rode it without his permission).[16] The sagas do contain other characters who display irritability with those who ride their horses without permission, but in this case Hrafnkell is sharing his horse with Freyr, a fact that interestingly seems to justify the stringency with which the goði enforces this prohibition.[17] Readers who defend his later actions point to his proverbial

---

14. ÍF 11:100, ch. 3; CSI 5:263.
15. ÍF 11:101, ch. 3; CSI 5:263.
16. ÍF 11:100, ch. 3; CSI 5:263.
17. See below, chapter 8, the section Þorgeirr and Þormóðr, for an episode in

justification of himself when he warns his new shepherd about the horse: "Ger nú sem ek mæli, því at þat er forn orðskviðr, at eigi veldr sá, er varar annan" (Now do as I say, because there is an old saying that he who gives warning is not at fault). Such readers also point to Einarr's prompt and unquestioning willingness to comply with this stricture as Hrafnkell and Einarr make their oral contract.[18]

This commitment is neglected, however, when Einarr, who is worried about thirty sheep that have strayed off and who needs a horse to cover a wide search area, proves unable to find one willing to be ridden, and he "hyggr, at Hrafnkell mundi eigi vita, þótt hann ríði hestinum" (thinks that Hrafnkel would not find out if he rode the stallion). The sacred horse, which is standing close by, as if asking for the experience, carries him for the whole day, becoming "vátr allr af sveita, svá at draup ór hverju hári hans, var mjǫk leikstokkinn ok móðr mjǫk ákafliga" (so soaked in sweat that it was dripping off every hair. He was splattered with mud and terribly exhausted).[19] Being thus soiled at the end of his strenuous workout, his untidy condition being humorously described in order to form a contrast with his exalted status with his foolishly doting master, Freyfaxi, who is suddenly less tired from his day's work, unexpectedly "tekr ... á mikilli rás ofan eptir gǫtunum" (set off down the track at great speed) to report to his master.[20]

The stereotypical love of the Icelandic farmer for his horse makes for entertaining material elsewhere in the sagas. Some aspects of this passage must remind readers of Ásmundr Þorgrímsson's love for Kengála and his conviction, for instance, that the beast could predict the weather. As Grettir observes, "illt þykki mér at trausta merinni, því at þat veit ek engan fyrr gǫrt hafa" (I'm wary of trusting the mare, because I've never heard about anyone who has until now).[21] The honing of modern sensitivities to what is conceived of as the dignity of animals has perhaps dulled our recognition of the obvious humor with which saga narratives treat relationships between beasts and doting masters.

Fóstbrœðra saga where Hávarr Kleppsson is killed by Jǫðurr of Skeljabrekka when he objects to the latter's having ridden his horse further than he had allowed.

18. ÍF 11:102, ch. 3; CSI 5:263; JGF 603; TPMA 12.355. Translation slightly modified.
19. ÍF 11:103, ch. 3; CSI 5:264.
20. ÍF 11:104, ch. 3; CSI 5:264.
21. ÍF 7:40, ch. 14; CSI 2:66.

Thus, Hrafnkell is represented as possessed of a more than judicious fondness for his horse, a fondness rationalized by its sacred association with his friend Freyr in such a way as to make its desecration by Einarr even more ludicrous to the thirteenth-century audience. "Hvat mun garprinn vilja, er hann er heim kominn?" (What should the champion want that he should have come back home?) he asks indulgently, rising from his table on Freyfaxi's arrival at the door. "Illa þykki mér, at þú ert þann veg til gǫrr, fóstri minn, en heima hafðir þú vit þitt, er þú sagðir mér til, ok skal þessa hefnt verða. Far þú til liðs þíns." (I don't like the way you've been treated, my foster-son. But you had your wits about you when you told me of this. It shall be avenged. Go to your herd.) At this command, Freyfaxi, with his remarkable understanding of Old Icelandic, goes obediently, "þegar upp eptir dalnum til stóðs síns" (straight up the valley to his horses).[22] Hrafnkell's rigid adherence to his oath when he kills Einarr, while being justified in an extreme ideological context of pre-Christian heroic value, is thus rendered questionable with this humor—how seriously are we meant to take the motives and values of a man who loves his horse beyond moderation? How foolish was his formalized commitment to the defense of Freyfaxi's honor? We move, then, through a rather darkly humorous passage in which Einarr progresses inexorably, seemingly oblivious of the threat to his safety, toward his demise as he chooses to ride the only forbidden horse of his employer, and designated by an engagingly mischievous fate as the only one readily available to him.

Hrafnkell's Foolish Oath and Foolish Pride

When he confronts Einarr over the unforgivable infraction, Hrafnkell discounts the value of the thirty sheep that were lost and found in comparison to the loss of his horse's purity: "Hann kvazk ekki at slíku telja. 'Eða hefir ekki verr at farit? . . . hefir þú ekki nǫkkut riðit Freyfaxa mínum hinn inn fyrra dag?'" (He said that that was of no real importance. "Hasn't something worse happened? . . . But did you ride Freyfaxi yesterday?") Readers have remarked on Hrafnkell's verbal reluctance here and regret later,

---

22. ÍF 11:104, ch. 3.

at the killing of Einarr: "En við þann átrúnað, at ekki verði at þeim mǫnnum, er heitstrengingar fella á sik, þá hljóp hann af baki til hans ok hjó hann banahǫgg" (But with that belief that nothing goes well for men who bring on themselves the curse of a broken oath, he leapt from his horse to him and struck him a deathblow).[23] To the thirteenth-century Christian audience of the saga, surely, Hrafnkell's affirmation of the sanctity of Freyfaxi in the inflexible yet rhetorically regretful adherence to his oath must have appeared at least as unsympathetic. Some critics have seen in it signs of pride, and perhaps one should add to that the foolishness of overweening pride, the proverbial outcome of which is never good, particularly in medieval Germanic literature. Even Hrafnkell admits the foolishness of this act in the very next scene, where he laments the perceived necessity of killing Einarr as he seeks to console the aggrieved father, Þorbjǫrn: "En vit munum opt þess iðrask, er vit erum of málgir, ok sjaldnar mundum við þessa iðrask, þó at vit mæltim færa en fleira" (But we often have cause to regret having said too much, and we would more seldom have cause for regret it we spoke less rather than more).[24]

The improvidence of Þorbjǫrn, the fecklessness of Einarr, and Hrafnkell's foolishly proud adherence to arbitrary rule lead, then, to the scene presented above, in which Þorbjǫrn, with an astounding lack of wisdom and overcome by misplaced pride, flatly refuses an offer of the best life he might ever have had. The unflattering observation with which Sámr accompanies his reluctant and inadvisable assent to help his foolish old uncle, Þorbjǫrn á Hóli, and to seek redress from Hrafnkell Freysgoði for the slaying of his son may seem to a casual reader of sagas nothing more than the fatalistic pessimism with which a man sometimes announces his undertaking to help an unpromising relative or to carry out some obviously ill-fated errand. The proverbial allusion contained in his comment, however, suggests the possibility of thematic signaling, especially when we notice nearly all the characters in this narrative displaying foolishness of various sorts that make them difficult to help.

In his pride Hrafnkell was foolishly oblivious of the danger in which he placed himself when he ignored Sámr's proceedings: "ok

23. ÍF 11:105, ch. 3; JGF 242; TPMA 2.388.
24. ÍF 11:106, ch. 3; CSI 5:265.

þótti hlœgiligt, er Sámr hefir tekit mál á hendr honum" (and found it ridiculous that Sam had taken on a case against him).²⁵ Arriving at the Alþingi to learn of Sámr's presence there and determination to continue his suit, "Honum þótti þat hlœgiligt" (he found it ludicrous).²⁶ His sophisticated appraisal of Sámr's disadvantages might well be tempered by his consciousness of the proverbial danger of underestimating one's enemy, and the composer seems repeatedly to emphasize his negligence of the potentially adverse outcome of the proceedings.

Þorbjǫrn's Awakening: the Communal Response to Foolishness

The foolishness of Þorbjǫrn and of Sámr taking legal action against Hrafnkell becomes obvious at the Alþingi, when the chieftains universally refuse to help them: "einn veg svǫruðu allir, at engi kvazk eiga svá gott Sámi upp at gjalda, at ganga vildi í deild við Hrafnkel goða ok hætta svá sinni virðingu." (They all gave the same reply. None of them felt that they owed Sam anything to make it worth their while entering into a dispute with Hrafnkel, and risking their honour.) This is the case particularly because of his flawless success rate in litigation: "hann hafi alla menn hrakit af málaferlum þeim, er við hann hafa haft" (he had routed everyone in legal cases they had taken up with him).²⁷ Þorbjǫrn's original foolishness, which has led them to this impasse, is reiterated by Sámr when Þorbjǫrn's courage fails and he wants to flee for home: "þat er vel, af því at þú vildir ekki annat en deila við Hrafnkel ok vildir eigi þá kosti þiggja, er margr mundi gjarna þegit hafa, sá er eptir sinn náunga átti at sjá." (That's very good. All you wanted to do was have a dispute with Hrafnkel. You didn't want to take the other alternative which many others would have gladly accepted if they had to seek redress for a close relation.)²⁸ When Þorbjǫrn weeps tears of hopeless frustration, the modern reader may feel sympathy with him, but there is also a sense that a *heimskr maðr* has thrust himself into public dealings where he has no place and from which he cannot profit.

---

25. ÍF 11:108, ch. 3; *CSI* 5:267.
26. ÍF 11:109, ch. 3; *CSI* 5:268.
27. ÍF 11:110, ch. 3; *CSI* 5:268.
28. ÍF 11:110, ch. 4; *CSI* 5:268.

The Þjóstarsynir and the Instability of Intervention Where the Foolish Are Concerned

The deus ex machina device by which the composer affords a near magical solution to the hopelessness of this situation materializes in the form of the Þjóstarsynir, men of power from a distant place. These men live about as far from the conflicts of Laugardalr as it would be possible to live on Iceland, and they turn up at the Alþingi with a suddenness that catches the reader's breath and strains the boundaries of realistic narrative. Þorkell Þjóstarson, the irresponsible traveler, agrees to inveigle his generally more judicious brother, Þorgeirr goði, into undertaking support for the case of Þorbjǫrn and Sámr. Although Þorkell is sympathetic to the plight of these underdogs, he is not fully cognizant of the details concerning local conflicts, as is often the case with the newly returned in Old Icelandic stories.[29]

The Sophistry of Persuasion

W. F. Bolton brought to readers' attention the lack of integrity in the actions and arguments of Þorkell in the process of manipulating his brother, Þorgeirr: "Er honum þetta nauðsyn, en eigi seiling, þó at hann mælir eptir son sinn" (For him it is not greed, but necessity that makes him bring a suit for the killing of his son), Þorkell insists, striving to ennoble Þorbjǫrn's case by omitting to report the unique offer of settlement Hrafnkell had made and that Þorbjǫrn, with his foolish vanity, had rejected. And his claim that all the other chieftains' refusal to help "sýna í því mikin ódrengskap" (shows how ignoble they are) neglects the executive wisdom with which they recognize the inadvisability of tangling with Hrafnkell for no compelling reason of their own.[30] When Þorgeirr succumbs to his brother's urgings, it is not because of such specious arguments but

---

29. See, for instance, Sámr's brother, Eyvindr Bjarnason, also in *Hrafnkels saga*; the newly returned Vésteinn, the friend and brother-in-law of Gísli Súrsson, in *Gísla saga*; and Þorvaldr Tungu-Oddsson in *Hœnsa-Þóris saga*. All these characters are in various ways associated with misfortune through an insufficient intimacy with community tensions and conflicts. See chapter 3, the section Fate and Gísli's Character for a discussion of the naïve returnee.

30. ÍF 11:114, ch. 4; CSI 5:270; Bolton, "Heart," 41. See below, the vacuous argumentation of Hœnsa-Þórir, resisting Blund-Ketill's attempts to acquire hay from him without incurring legal difficulties.

because he resorts to an irrational appeal to their kinship, as Þorbjǫrn had done with Sámr before him: "Kann vera, at Þorkell leppr komi þar, at hans orð verði meir metin" (It may be that Thorkel Streak will find a place where his words are more appreciated).[31] Wisely pessimistic about their success, Þorgeirr cautions, "'Munu þit þá hafa annat hvárt fyrir ykkart þrá, nǫkkura huggan eða læging enn meir en áðr ok hrelling ok skapraun'" ("Your persistence will then reward you with consolation, or disgrace, or yet more anguish and torment"). Þorgeirr then foolishly gives in to his brother, and for the wrong reasons, as he clearly sees the folly of the cause itself.[32]

Sámr's Ascendant: the Rule in a Fool's Kingdom

The force of the related proverb, "Illt er að setja heimskan hátt" (It is bad to raise a foolish person to a high station), must be felt by the audience of *Hrafnkels saga* as Sámr, from the very moment of judicial success, demonstrates an absence of executive ability, a constitutional inadequacy of leadership, which will eventually prove his undoing.[33] With Hrafnkell now outlawed, Sámr becomes immoderately ostentatious in his prematurely assumed victory: "En Sámr var á þingi ok gekk mjǫk uppstertr" (Sam stayed at the Thing and strode about very haughtily).[34] His ignorance about the next steps of prosecution is surely more helpful to the literary intent of the composer than it is an accurate reflection of legal knowledge typical for his time, especially for one who has been described as "lǫgkœnn" (versed in law)—unless, of course that description was also humorous. Þorgeirr asks, "Þykkisk þú nú nǫkkuru nær en áðr" (Do you think you're any better off now than before)? and Sámr seems content with their immediate victory, being peculiarly unaware of the necessity for the *féransdómr* (court of confiscation) by which Hrafnkell is to be deprived legally of home and property, maybe even of his life, and certainly to be made a full outlaw.[35]

Sámr's most devastating act of foolishness, though, occurs when

---

31. ÍF 11:115, ch. 4; *CSI* 5:271.
32. ÍF 11:115–16, ch. 4; *CSI* 5:271.
33. JGF 240. GJ 181.
34. ÍF 11:117, ch. 4; *CSI* 5:272.
35. ÍF 11:118, ch. 4; *CSI* 5:272. Sámr's naïveté is matched by that of Oddr Ófeigsson in *Bandamanna saga*, when he assumes that remaining litigation poses no threat to him.

he spares the life of his adversary because he has so many dependents. Hrafnkell, pleading for his men's lives, has admitted, "þat er mér engi ósœmð, þótt þér drepið mik. Mun ek ekki undan því mælask." (It is no dishonor to me if you kill me. I will make no protest against that.)[36] And one of the Þjóstarsynir comments on the foolishness of Sámr's leniency as follows: "Muntu þessa mest iðrask sjálfr, er þú gefr honum líf" (You yourself will most regret having given Hrafnkel his life).[37] But the wisdom of chieftains far outstrips the judgment of this well-to-do novice in the world of power, whose motives, whatever they actually are, lead him to this misplaced and crucially self-destructive act of mercy. Sámr's weakness of character or, as Edward Condren describes it, his lack of "excellence" is hinted at when he invites Hrafnkell's old supporters to a meeting and offers "at vera yfirmaðr þeira í stað Hrafnkels. Menn játuðusk undir þat ok hugða þó enn misjafnt til." (To be their leader in place of Hrafnkell. People accepted this, but there were mixed feelings about it.)[38] There is in Sámr's offer of support an element that does not elicit confidence from this group of farmers, who sense that he is, in his character, unequal to the role. When Hrafnkell eventually kills Eyvindr, Sámr's most powerful relative, and proceeds to regain his position in the community, the turn of events is not surprising.

Critical Views of Hrafnkell's Rehabilitation

Since readers first ventured to contemplate what *Hrafnkels saga* is about, they have divided generally into two respectively opposing camps when it comes to the character of the hero and whether that character changes in any way as a result of the hero's defeat by Sámr and the Þjóstarsynir.

Guðbrandur Vigfússon, who was uninfluenced by any of this array of opinions, all of which came long after him, considered the saga to be about how "Hrafnkel, in his great devotion to his god Frey, who had prospered all his undertakings, makes a reckless oath, the keeping of which leads him into manslaying against his

---

36. ÍF 11:120, ch. 5.
37. ÍF 11:121, ch. 5; *CSI* 5:274.
38. ÍF 11:123, ch. 6; *CSI* 5:275; Edward I. Condren, "On Civilizing Hrafnkell," *Modern Language Notes* 88 (1973): 532 of 517–34.

will, whence trouble and disaster come upon him." The trouble "comes of a presumptuous devotion springing rather from pride than love," and in the outcome "the character of its hero, whose dross is burnt out of him by the fire of sudden affliction, ... is restored, like Job or Prospero, to such higher position as he is now worthy of."[39] Guðbrandur, the first to allude to Hrafnkell's pride and its redress as the subject of the saga, thus leads a long line of critics who might be termed "redemptivists," in viewing the work as a study of how pride can be corrected through its resultant fall. In later years, however, readers have been concerned about the way in and the extent to which that pride or overweening arrogance of behavior may have changed in the process of Hrafnkell's adverse experiences. These "behaviorists" see the change, if there is any, in his more careful conduct not the correction of pride but of overweening and overt arrogance, the foolish abrasiveness of his character being softened, his assertion of power becoming more subtle where possible.

Arguments in both camps must take into account a passage in the saga that continues the description of the effects of his fall on the harshly aggressive *goði*:

Hann fekk brátt miklar virðingar í heraðinu. Vildi svá hverr sitja ok standa sem hann vildi. Í þenna tíma kómu sem mest skip af Nóregi til Íslands. Námu menn þá sem mest land í heraðinu um Hrafnkels daga. Engi náði með frjálsu at sitja, nema Hrafnkel bæði orlofs. Þá urðu ok allir honum at heita sínu liðsinni. Hann hét ok sínu trausti. Lagði hann land undir sik allt fyrir austan Lagarfljót. Þessi þinghá varð brátt miklu meiri ok fjǫlmennari en sú, er hann hafði áðr haft. Hon gekk upp um Skriðudal ok upp allt með Lagarfljóti. Var nú skipan á komin á *lund* hans. Maðrinn var miklu vinsælli en áðr. Hafði hann ina sǫmu skapsmuni um gagnsemð ok risnu, en miklu var maðrinn nú vinsælli ok gæfari ok hœgri en fyrr at ǫllu.

(He soon won great respect in the district. Everybody was glad to stand or sit, just as he wished. At that time, the traffic of ships from Norway to Iceland was at its height. Most of the land in the district was settled during Hrafnkel's day. Nobody was allowed the freedom

---

39. Guðbrandur Vigfússon, *Sturlunga* I, Prolegomena, lviiin; II, 492.

to stay there unless Hrafnkel granted them permission. Everyone had to promise him their support. He promised them his help and support in return, and took control of all the land east of Lagarfljot. This assembly district soon became much greater and more populous than the one he had had before, stretching out to Selfljot, all the way up Skridudal, and all the way along Lagarfljot. A great change had suddenly taken place in that the man was much more popular than before. He had the same temperament as regards his helpfulness and generosity, but was now a more gentle man than before, more restrained in all ways.)⁴⁰

The crux of interpretation of this passage lies in the word *lund*, the result of a silent emendation from *land*, on the latter of which all manuscripts agree. Made by most editors since it was introduced by Peder Goth Thorsen and Konráð Gíslason, this emendation places the significance of the sentence in which it occurs with the material following rather than with what immediately precedes it.⁴¹ In the next edition of the saga, Jakob Jakobsen leaves *land* without comment on the emendation other than noticing the variant *lǫnd* in C. He also adds, among others, the variant from ÁM551c, 4to, "*á-hans*] *brátt mikil, at* D," which, if adopted, would connect the "*skipan*" (*change*) to the next sentence.⁴² We can see from this variant that a copyist in the occasionally diverging tradition represented by this manuscript did not think that the subject of change was Hrafnkell's real estate holdings or political control but rather the swift growth of his relative popularity.

Pierre Halleux was the first to question the redemptivist line of interpretation, remarking on Konráð Gíslason's silent emendation, which "unfortunately and wrongly replaced the *land* (territory) by the word *lund* (state of mind) in spite of the fact that all manuscripts had *land*."⁴³ Rather than observing him exhibiting a change in his pride, Halleux sees him learning to hide the harsher sides of his character that inspired his insecure popularity with his neighbors,

---

40. ÍF 11:124–25, ch. 7.
41. Peder Goth Thorsen and Konráð Gíslason, eds., *Sagan af Hrafnkeli Freysgoða* (Copenhagen: Trykt hos B. Luno, 1839), 35.
42. Jakob Jakobsen, *Austfirðingar sǫgur* (Copenhagen: Samfund til udgivelse af gammel nordisk litteratur, 1902–3), 126.
43. Pierre Halleux, "Hrafnkel's Character Reinterpreted," *Scandinavian Studies* 38 (1966): 43.

and led to his downfall. There was then no significant moral change; instead, as Halleux puts it in his translation, "The man was still keen on acting in his own interest and kept his inclination to munificence." He relinquishes paganism not through spiritual disillusionment or enlightenment, which one might be inclined to see if one were to seek a Christian interest at work in the narrative, but because it is unprofitable. He has realized the importance of obtaining local support "through his behavior, just because this may serve his own interest." Halleux concludes thus: "The main features of this pagan chief are self-interest and pride, somewhat tempered after his downfall, yet through selfish motives. The author of the saga does not feel sympathy for such people."[44] After Halleux, and then Bolton, who sees a dark world in which Sámr wins "by force, not by legal process, . . . [there being] no principle of stability in the victory," the lists of the redemptivists dwindle, and readers move toward subtler approaches to the passage in question and the light it throws on the nature of the hero.[45]

F. J. Heinemann sees Sámr's sparing of Hrafnkell's life as "foolish and motivated by vanity"; and when Eyvindr, who has returned from abroad, chooses to ride past Hrafnkell's dwelling in his newly acquired continental splendor, he is "foolish to expose himself to Hrafnkel's might for the sake of delivering an insult."[46] Heinemann assumes the composer approves when Hrafnkell kills Eyvindr because it is an act of legitimate retribution: "the author suggests that judgment and strength are also requisites for the successful Icelandic chieftain."[47]

With the evolution of behaviorist principles in *Hrafnkels saga* criticism, sympathy for the hero builds, to the point where Peter Hallberg sees no moral judgment at all. Hrafnkell, he claims, has "outwitted Sámr, he has turned out to be too clever for him."[48] And Sámr's innate inferiority to a man of the *goði* class bcomes a fashionable topic. Klaus von See, though admitting he makes a good chieftain, also notices his shortcomings:

---

44. Halleux, "Hrafknel's Character," 44.
45. Bolton, "Heart", 46.
46. Frederik J. Heinemann, "*Hrafnkels saga Freysgoða* and Type-Scene Analysis," *Scandinavian Studies* 46 (1974): 114.
47. Heinemann, "Type-Scene Analysis," 115.
48. Peter Hallberg, "Hunting for the Heart of *Hrafnkels saga*," *Scandinavian Studies* 47 (1975): 464.

Es fehlt ihm das Zeug zum Häuptling, die selbstgewisse Art, Macht zu üben. So rechtfertigt die Saga schliesslich den politisch-sozialen status quo, die Zweiteilung der Gesellschaft in die Schicht der Häuptlinge und die Schicht derer, die von den Häuptlingen die smámenn genannt werden.

(He is lacking the stuff of a chieftain, the innate skill in exercising power. Thus, in the end the saga justifies the sociopolitical status quo, the division of society into the class of chieftains and the class of those who were called by the chieftains the smámenn [people of no consequence]).[49]

Henry Kratz agrees that the saga's composer is also aware of "the untenable position of the little man who has come into power beyond his capabilities," although he contends that "pride, haughtiness and arbitrary exercise of power are berated and the rights of the weaker subject are championed."[50] In attempting to approach an ethical system in the saga that is potentially illuminative of Hrafnkell's presumed change, R. D. Fulk identifies two groups of characters. On the one hand, there are the "ideologues," who are single-minded in the "prosecution of their honour" where "the old Germanic code of honour and vengeance is naturally the proving ground for the moral opposition explored in the saga."[51] On the other hand, there are the "pragmatists," who "also live by the Germanic ethics of honour and vengeance, but who regard them as good only insofar as they accomplish practical, social ends."[52] Given these two poles of behavior, Hrafnkell may be studied as shifting along the spectrum from a rigid ideological worldview to a more realistically functional one. As a pragmatist he kills Eyvindr, "not for the sake of any supercilious sense of honour, but rather for the sake of retaining the confidence of servants and supporters, and maintaining peace in his home."[53] Here we find echoes of Condren

---

49. Klaus von See, "Die *Hrafnkels saga* als Kunstdichtung," *Skandinavistik* 9 (1979): 56. Translation mine.
50. Henry Kratz, "*Hrafnkels saga*: Thirteenth-Century Fiction?" *Scandinavian Studies* 53 (1981): 443.
51. R. D. Fulk, "The Moral System of *Hrafnkels saga Freysgoða*," *Saga-Book* 22 (1986): 3.
52. Fulk, "Moral System," 4.
53. Fulk, "Moral System," 20.

and those "primitive traits" he identifies that are clearly related to the rigid ideology that Fulk says Hrafnkell overcomes as he seeks more effective methods of leadership.[54] Jan Geir Johansen, who also discounts the silent emendation of *land* to *lund*, sees no development of Hrafnkell's character in this story. Rather, the saga "demonstrates that men of quality, such as Hrafnkell, cannot be suppressed by those of lesser mettle, like Sámr. Conversely men like Sámr will not triumph long over men of quality, inherent defects in character make it impossible."[55]

Theodore M. Andersson was very much among the redemptivists in 1967 when he called this "the most obviously moralistic of the sagas." Speaking of "the history and reform of [Hrafnkell's] personality," he claimed that Hrafnkell "is purged by the action." "The phenomenon of the defective chieftain is familiar," Andersson wrote, "but nowhere else is he remade into an effective chieftain."[56] He revisited the discussion in 2006, however, with a very different vision of the work: "The debate is in effect between those who construe the story morally and those who construe it politically. The problem of the moralists is that Hrafnkel kills Eyvindr *after* his apparent change of heart."[57] Seeing no justification for this act, he contends, "It is not only a modern readership that would find Hrafnkel's killing of Eyvind repugnant." But that act in itself is not what the saga is about: "*Hrafnkels saga* is about two chieftains, both of them unfinished, each defective in his own way." Other sagas may be "positive blueprints" for the good chieftain, but this saga is not: "Whether we look at it through a moral lens or a political lens, it appears to offer only an array of the deficiencies that afflict the Icelandic chieftaincy."[58]

Hrafnkell Sheds His Foolishness

As for Hrafnkell himself, much of the point of this saga may be discerned in the composer's humorous account of his reactions to defeat and the steps he takes to reestablish himself. The *goði*

---

54. Edward I. Condren, "Civilizing," 531.
55. Jan Geir Johansen, "The Hero of *Hrafnkels saga Freysgoða*," *Scandinavian Studies* 67 (1995): 283 of 265–84.
56. Andersson, *Saga*, 282.
57. Andersson, *Growth*, 181.
58. Andersson, *Growth*, 182.

who killed a man for riding his and Freyr's horse now becomes a pagan atheist: "Ek hygg þat hégóma at trúa á goð" (I think it is vanity to believe in gods), he declared when he heard of the destruction of his temple and its idols and Freyfaxi; "sagðisk hann þaðan af aldri skyldu á goð trúa, ok þat efndi hann síðan, at hann blótaði aldri" (and said that from that time onwards he would never believe in them. He kept his word, and after this never made any more sacrifices).[59] Having become more astute from his trials, he has come to realize that whatever power is to be achieved in this world will be obtained to the extent that he helps himself to it, and that it will be acquired from his moderated transactions in society rather than being simply imposed by arbitrary force or by the threat of force.

However one chooses to view the opinions voiced in the long and unfinished discussion concerning the point of *Hrafnkels saga*, it is certain that Hrafnkell, by the time of his reinstatement, is a man who would never again allow himself to be trapped by the foolish rigidity of character that led to the killing of Einarr. In this respect, his story differs radically from the tragedies of Gísli Súrsson and Grettir, where the former is defeated by his innate unfailing sympathy with that inflexible view Johansen describes, and where the latter's fall occurs within the context of his adherence by temperament to customs and values echoing the more violent behavior of the heroic Viking age. Hrafnkell sees the foolishness of his original stance regarding modes of aristocratic behavior in a world where the psychological realities of a gradually changing Icelandic society have become too complex for the old ideologies to have effective applicability in contemporary situations.

Sámr's Demise and the Point of the Saga

The point of this reassessment is driven home at the end of the saga when Sámr goes to plead with the Þjóstarsynir to come back and restore him to the position of power he lacked the ability to hold for himself. Kindly rebuffed by Þorgeirr, he is reminded, "Fýstum vit þik, at þú skyldir Hrafnkel af lífi taka, en þú vildir ráða" (We urged you to execute Hrafnkel; we thought that most advisable for

---

59. ÍF 11:124, ch. 7; *CSI* 5:276, modified.

you, but you wanted to have your own way).⁶⁰ Sámr had insisted on making an executive decision for which he was not, as an ordinary farmer, sufficiently equipped. His misplaced exercise of what he seems to have supposed was magnanimity led to his unfortunate plight for which he now seeks additional help from the brothers. "Megum vit ekki hafa at þessu gæfuleysi þitt. Er okkr ok ekki svá mikil fýst at deila við Hrafnkel, at vit nennim at leggja þar við virðing okkra optar." (We can't have anything to do with this lucklessness of yours. We don't have such a desire to get involved in disputes with Hrafnkel that we feel like risking our honour any more.) Thus concludes Þorgeirr, who refuses to pursue further the development of Sámr's original undertaking, on the folly of which the latter himself had commented upon his commencement of the project.⁶¹ He offers Sámr and his family resettlement and protection with them in Þorskafjǫrðr, but Sámr's foolish pride, which is key to his essential "*gæfuleysi*" (lucklessness), will not permit him to accept, and he departs in an unfriendly mood, despite all they have tried to do for him and Þorbjǫrn.

* * *

While the proverb, "Illt er heimskum lið að veita" (It's bad to give help to the foolish), is never explicitly formulated in the narrative of *Hrafnkels saga*, its paroemial force is clearly present in Sámr's allusion to it at the start, and it comes to inform the thematic unity of the plot. Hrafnkell loses power because he exercises it foolishly, and Sámr wins only because he has the benefit of the cunning and wisdom of the Þjóstarsynir. He regains his position because he is clever and has a mind suitable for a *goði*, and Sámr loses, in the first place because he has foolishly granted life to his opponent, but more crucially because he lacks the character to support the challenges of the *goði*'s office.

Thus, we see that much of the misfortune in the story results from the foolishness of those who experience it and that Hrafnkell's redemption is only accomplished when he discovers a sufficient flexibility of vision to recognize the nonproductive arrogance of his ways and rather cunningly adopts more effective modes of behavior. Those who would emphasize a moralistic lesson in the correction

---

60. ÍF 11:132, ch. 10; *CSI* 5:281.
61. ÍF 11:133, ch. 10; *CSI* 5:281.

of Hrafnkell's pride fall short in explaining how a chieftain whose pride is reformed could nevertheless undertake the killing of Eyvindr. Most would acknowledge that the hero's initial overweening pride is foolish, but it seems reasonable that this last killing is more closely related to the stark practicality of his desire to regain his position than to the pride or a rigid adherence to the maintenance of heroic honor. A more persuasive common denominator would thus seem to lie in reference to the paroemia of foolishness than to the moral flaw of pride.

The difficulty of resolving this reading is reflected in the number of participant voices in the critical discussion of *Hrafnkels saga*. For example, was there any justification for the killing of Eyvindr? And if one decided so affirmatively, then the light thus cast on the accepted necessities of *goðar* leadership is not flattering. It is in this sense, finally, that this saga could not be seen as positively supportive of this traditional mode of leadership, whatever the other options of governance might have been thought of as having been. And here we might ask whether the composer even went so far as to envisage a solution, whether the point of his narrative extended itself in any way beyond the senselessness of helping foolish people in a society so brutally inimical to their innate vulnerability.

CHAPTER 7

Proverbial Echoes and the Point of *Hœnsa-Þóris saga*

"Ek ætla þar vándum manni at duga sem þú ert"

🙞

Shared phraseological similarities and commonalities of narrative structure in *Hœnsa-Þóris saga* and *Hrafnkels saga*, as well as shared preoccupations with the fundamentals of power, suggest affinities of composition between these two products of later thirteenth-century Iceland that would justify further investigation.[1] In this chapter, the former saga will be examined not only against its paroemial background but also with reference to the particular qualities of its apparent closeness to *Hrafnkels saga*.

The Generic Protagonist of *Hœnsa-Þóris saga*: Tungu-Oddr

Theodore M. Andersson notices what is easily missed in *Hœnsa-Þóris saga*—namely, that while the figure for whom it is named elicits much attention on account of his unalloyed evil nature and egregiously churlish ways, the saga itself, to judge by generic expectations, can be thought of as having the leading figure of the district as its main subject. Oddr Ǫnundarson breiðskeggs of Breiðabólstaðr, who is known in this story as Tungu Oddr, "has the highest standing among the characters and the most precipitous fall."[2] Just as with *Hrafnkels saga*, the story begins and ends with a discussion of a primary leading district figure. His genealogical background is outlined, here through five generations, and his character is then described with a device favored elsewhere by this composer, in

---
1. See chapter 6 for a discussion concerning the sagas of wealth and power.
2. Theodore M. Andersson, *Growth*, 163.

which the repetition of a word or a phrase is humorously used for derogatory, ironic effect: "Hann var kallaðr Tungu-Oddr; engi var hann kallaðr jafnaðarmaðr" (He was called Tungu-Odd; by nobody was he called a fair-minded man).³

The chieftain whose character is of interest in this saga is therefore, like Hrafnkell, flawed in a most unattractive way—here he has an utter lack of regard for people under his power and for whom he has at least some responsibility. Unlike Hrafnkell, who was "linr ok blíðr við sína menn, en stríðr ok stirðlyndr við Jǫkulsdalsmenn" (mild and gentle with his own people, but stiff and stubborn with the people of Jokulsdal), Tungu-Oddr practices no such favoritism, preying wherever he can on the weak and vulnerable, and revealing a rapacity of spirit that finds no abatement as his story progresses.⁴

The Nebulous Origins of Hœnsa-Þórir, *Óvinsæll* and *Vǫndr*

It is in a society controlled by such traditional figures of power that the lowly Þórir, whose father is never specified and who leaves no descendants at the end of the saga that is named for him, first makes his remarkably unprepossessing appearance, having once been "snauðr at fé ok eigi mjǫk vinsæll af alþýðu manna" (poor and not very well liked by most people).⁵ Of an obviously impoverished and unpromising background, he nevertheless amasses some wealth by trading between districts, making a profitable trip north at one point with chickens. When the composer remarks that his uncomplimentary nickname was derived from this enterprise, he is most likely implying that it arose from the inspiration of those who were jealous or otherwise resentful of his success.

Although Þórir's unpopularity, based on the composer's description of him, could well have been earned at a personal level, socioeconomic theorists have for some decades seen it as arising, in the simplest of terms, from his having started very poor and from his having created his wealth by trading in an unregulated market, a practice ill regarded in old societies where ruling classes engaged in trade to strengthen their social activities and connections rather than purely for profit.⁶ Even if, as seems unlikely, the composer was

---

3. *Hœnsa-Þóris saga*, in ÍF 3:3–4, ch. 3.
4. ÍF 11:99, ch. 2; CSI 5:262.
5. ÍF 3:6, ch. 1; CSI 5:240.
6. E. Paul Durrenberger, Dorothy Durrenberger, and Ástráður Eysteinsson, "Economic

sympathetic to this conservatively disapproving view of the new merchant class, however, Hœnsa-Þórir's position in the emerging economic structure cannot be taken as the sole reason for his eventual misfortune.

It instead becomes clear as the story progresses that he is an ill-disposed individual with no real concern for, or commitment to, the interests of the society in which he gains his wealth and with no kind regard for its members. Becoming so well off that he is able to buy a farm—and here the composer interjects that "hann átti undir vel hverjum manni stórfé" (he had large sums of money lent out to almost everyone)—he still does not enjoy the approval of his community.[7] At this point, even more than anywhere in *Hrafnkels saga*, there is a growing emphasis on the importance of popularity as a desirable if not indeed necessary concomitant of power, whether that power is financial or political in its origins. In this respect, despite Þórir's material success, his life is not universally happy: "En þó at honum grœddisk fé mikit, þá heldusk þó óvinsældir hans, því at varla var til óþokkasælli maðr en Hœnsa-Þórir var" (Even though he had accumulated a great deal of money, his lack of popularity continued, so that there was scarcely a man more detested than was Hen-Thorir).[8] Such extreme and explicitly noticed unpopularity as this left an individual at a strategic disadvantage among peers in the saga world, as well as in medieval Icelandic society itself.

Oddr Ófeigsson: Acceptable New Wealth

At this point, a contrastive comparison of his character with that of Oddr Ófeigsson, the merchant hero of *Bandamanna saga*, may be helpful to an understanding of how the composer intends his audience to interpret Hœnsa-Þórir's nature. Oddr comes from what would seem to have been at one point a family of substance, his father, Ófeigr Skíðason, owning "lendur miklar, en minna lausafé"

Representation and Narrative Structure in *Hœnsa-Þóris saga*," *Saga-Book of the Viking Society*, 22.3–4 (1987–88): 143–64; Helgi Þorláksson, "Social Ideals and the Concept of Profit in Thirteenth-Century Iceland, in *From Sagas to Society: Comparative Approaches to Early Iceland* , ed. Gísli Pálsson (Enfield Lock: Hisarlik Press, 1992), 241.

7. ÍF 3:6, ch. 1; *CSI* 5:240; Marina Mundt, "Pleading the Cause of Hoensa-Thorir" (paper presented at the Alþjóðlegt fornsagnaþing, Reykjavik, Iceland, August 2–8, 1973), http://www.sagaconference.org/SC02/SC02_Mundt.pdf. Mundt examines sympathetically Hœnsa-Þórir's lack of popularity, although her arguments do not seem persuasive.

8. ÍF 3:6, ch. 1; *CSI* 5:240.

(extensive lands but not so much cash).⁹ Ófeigr maintains his social standing according to old traditions, however, with universal hospitality: "Hann sparði við engan mann mat" (he denied no one hospitality).¹⁰ Between him and his son the composer sets a distinct and cool distance, perhaps with a phraseological echo of the coal biter about the young man: "Ekki hafði hann ást mikla af feðr sínum; ekki vann hann ok heima nema þat, er hann vildi" (he got little affection from his father; he didn't work around home except as he wanted to).¹¹ Oddr, like Þórir, acquires much wealth; indeed, "svá er sagt, at engi var jafnauðigr maðr í kaupferðum þann tíma sem Oddr" (it is said that no other trader sailing at that time was as rich as Odd).¹² His accomplishment, however, is accompanied by the approbation rather than resentment of his community, as can be seen, for instance, from the fact that when he visited Hrútafjǫrðr, intending to stay the winter there, "var hann beðinn af vinum sínum at staðfestask hér, ok gerði hann þat at bœn þeira" (he was urged by his friends to settle down here and he did as they asked).¹³

Any resentment his good fortune arouses becomes apparent only when he makes the mistake of placing his trust, his property and by then newly acquired *goðorð*, in the hands of Óspakr, a nephew of Grettir Ásmundarson who possesses a few of his outlaw uncle's less attractive traits. Their enmity and a faultily pursued case against Óspakr for manslaughter stemming from that enmity eventually put Oddr in the power of chieftains who are jealous of his wealth and his success and who are knowledgeable in the workings of the law of which he, though now a *goði*, is damagingly ignorant. Styrmir, his father's chieftain, urges Óspakr's father-in-law Þórarinn to sabotage the suit against Óspakr as a way of gaining access to Oddr's wealth, and in doing so makes explicit the grounds for their resentment of his wealth and position:

Er þat ok mála sannast, at vel væri, þótt Oddr vissi, at fleiri eru nǫkkurs verðir en hann einn; treðr hann oss alla under fótum ok þingmenn vára, svá at hans eins er getit; sakar eigi, at hann reyni, hversu lǫgkœnn hann er.

---

9. ÍF 7:294, ch. 1.
10. ÍF 7:294, ch. 1; *CSI* 5:283.
11. ÍF 7:294, ch. 1.
12. ÍF 7:297, ch. 1; *CSI* 5:284.
13. ÍF 7:297–98, ch. 2; *CSI* 5:284.

(The fact of the matter is that it would also do Odd good to realise that there are others of consequence around. He tramples over all of us and our thingmen, so that he gets all the attention. It will do him no harm to discover just how skilled in law he really is.)[14]

Ófeigr, who is poor and improvident and yet far more cunning and learned in law than his son, the newly elevated *goði*, comes to his rescue and thus brings them together against the threat to Oddr's welfare that, in this saga, emanates from the arrogant but impoverished and greedy *goðar* rather than, as with Hœnsa-Þórir, from a more generally inimical community. Although Styrmir's speech may represent the jealousy of some leaders and their resentment of his success and purchased office of leadership, the fact is that Oddr has offended none by his behavior in his rise to wealth. The composer makes clear that "Hann var betri af fé en flestir menn aðrir ok góðr órlausna við alla þá, er honum váru næstir . . ." (he was more generous with his money than most, good at helping out people who needed it in his neighbourhood).[15] It is only with his acquisition of a *goðorð* through his wealth, a position for the exercise of which he has no experiential background or training, that he finally makes himself vulnerable to the greedy attentions of the jealous *goðar*. His case, then, is very different from that of Hœnsa-Þórir, whose chronic unpopularity is, as we have seen, a factor of his essential personality.

Hœnsa-Þórir Seeks Protection by Contract

Seeking to protect himself through relatively formal association with the powers of the establishment by which he is rejected personally, Hœnsa-Þórir offers to foster Helgi, the son of Arngímr goði, the local chieftain priest of Norðrtunga, whose initial reaction to such an arrangement is unenthusiastic: "Svá lízk mér, sem lítill hǫfuðburðr muni mér at þessu barnfóstri" (It seems to me that there's very little honour to me in this fostering arrangement).[16] Arngrímr goði's judicious hesitance here to enter into a protective agreement with Þórir, perhaps of legally binding

---

14. ÍF 7:317–18, ch. 5. This passage is taken from the version in "M", that is, AM 132, fol.
15. ÍF 7:298, ch. 2; *CSI* 5:284.
16. ÍF 3:7, ch. 2; *CSI* 5:240.

friendship, as a result of the fostering arrangement, is grounded, first, in the proverbial wisdom of communal perception. It also reflects, however, the customary treatment of people who were in some sense touched by *ógæfa*, by a lack of popularity, and therefore also by tendencies to be involved in situations where there was potential for conflict.[17]

Hávamál describes such views in verse 123, in continuing its preceding warning, "Orðum skipta / þú skalt aldregi / við ósvinna apa" (you should never bandy words / with a stupid fool), and in including, along with fools, others whom it was undesirable to support through an association burdened with potential social or legal obligations: "því að af illum manni / mundu aldregi / góðs laun um geta. / En góður maður / mun þig gjörva mega / líknfastan að lofi" (for from a wicked man you will never get / a good return; / but a good man will make you / assured of favour of his praise).[18] While custom accorded to the parent of the fostered child a superior standing over the individual undertaking the fostering, in these unfavorable circumstances it is remarkable that Arngrímr should be persuaded by any means to engage in the transaction.[19] An examination of the dialogue later in this story will further clarify the composer's purpose in creating this relationship between local *goði* and neighborhood pariah—that is, by exploring the damage an *illr maðr* like Þórir can inflict on his community in the pursuit of his predictably ignoble ends.

Ironically Rationalized Greed: "neita eigi því, er svá er vel boðit"

When Þórir adds the incentive, however, of giving the boy half his wealth in return for support and defense of his rights, Arngrímr readily agrees, justifying doing so by observing in near proverbial terms that it is wise for a person "at neita eigi því, er svá er vel boðit" (not to turn down that which is well offered).[20] Seeming

---

17. For the best description of this unfortunate condition, see Einar Ól. Sveinsson, *Masterpiece*, 192, quoted above, in chapter 5, the section Order and the Triumph of Chaos: "Eigi má við ǫllu sjá", along with the commentary and sources found there.

18. ÍF 36, 1:346–47, sts. 122 and 123; Larrington, *Poetic Edda*, 29.

19. See the note there in the fornrit edition regarding the traditional transaction of fostering, including citations of the custom's observance in several other places in saga literature. Noticed also by JGF 161; TPMA 7.42. See also above, chapter 2, the section "The Fostering of Hǫskuldr Þráinsson: 'Oft er úlfr í ungum syni,'" for fostering customs.

20. ÍF 3:7, ch. 2; JGF 602; TPMA 1.110.

unable to admit that he is simply succumbing to the financial pressure of half Þórir's wealth, Arngrímr retreats to this proverbial wisdom regarding the astute acceptance of gracious offers, wisdom that is also referred to in a couple of other sagas, in situations where its force must surely be ironic.

In Ǫrvar-Odds saga, for example, the eponymous hero is offered aid in his adventures by Rauðgrani, or Red-Beard, who asks if he would like to become his blood brother. "Vant er því at neita, sem vel er boðit" (It's hard to refuse a generous offer), he answers proverbially, unaware that he has just entered into a pact with Óðinn.[21] This blood brotherhood proves of dubious value, and the composer remarks on Rauðgrani's final disappearance as follows, "Var þá sem oftar, at hann hafði sik sjaldan í mannhættu, en var inn harpasti í öllum tillögum" (It was as true this time as any other that he never risked his own life, though when it came to giving advice he was the toughest of men).[22]

Perhaps even more tellingly, in Grettis saga, as its hero declines Þorbjǫrn ǫngull's offer to let him leave Drangey with a false assurance of his safety, the latter's sorceress foster-mother, Þúríðr, scolds, "Þessir menn munu vera hraustir ok hamingjulausir; verðr yðvar mikill mannamunr. Þú býðr þeim marga kosti góða, en þeir neita ǫllum, ok er fátt vísara til ills en kunna eigi gott at þiggja." (These men are brave but luckless. There is a great difference between you. You have made them many fine offers but they turn them all down, and there are few more certain ways to court trouble than to refuse what is good.)[23] Grettir and presumably the audience of Hœnsa-Þóris saga are more sensitive to the dangers of well-made offers than is Arngrímr, whose polite acquiescence leads to his undoing. The composer places this proverb in a situation where its generally ironic implications could not be lost on the audience; and with Arngrímr's rationalizing misapplication of this wisdom, he embraces his tragic fate.

Although this first instance of the aristocracy's yielding to Þórir's financial blandishments enables him to assert his legal rights among his neighbors, the composer, relishing again the repetition of phrases descriptive of his unchanged social circumstances, observes that

---

21. FSN 2:280, ch. 19; Arrow-Odd, 75
22. FSN 2:296, ch. 23; Arrow-Odd, 62.
23. ÍF 7:247, ch. 78; CSI 2:169, slightly modified; JGF 660; TPMA 1.110.

he "grœðisk honum nú stórmikit fé ok gerisk inn mesti auðmaðr; helzk honum enn óvinsældin" (made money hand over fist. He became a very wealthy man, but was still considered unpopular).[24] In an overtly mean and petty social environment governed by powerful competitive impulses and where there was a dwindling of wealth available for accumulation, his success was accompanied by dangers—whether arising from quarrels about the daily inconveniences and humiliations of life in an abrasive community, or from maliciously planned physical harm from those most irritated by what they would have seen as his ill-gained and therefore ill-placed wealth.

Óvinsæld as Liability

That the thematic structure of *Hœnsa-Þóris saga* is informed by the importance of popularity to the maintenance of power is evident in several episodes, two of which are examined here. In the first of these episodes, Tungu-Oddr, whose immoderate behavior was noted above, becomes momentarily entangled in conflict with Blund-Ketill, "manna auðgastr ok bezt at sér í fornum sið" (one of the richest men and well versed in heathen lore), who had thirty tenants and was "inn vinsælasti maðr í heraðinu" (the most popular man in the district), and whose personal qualities are described by the composer in the most ideal terms.[25] Here Qrn, a Norwegian trader, is prohibited by Tungu-Oddr from selling his goods in the district when he clashes with the latter over his determination to exercise the powers of the *heraðstjórn* (district government), which gives him the privilege of legal responsibility for controlling the price at which goods are to be sold in his district.[26] The Norwegian is not willing to engage in commerce under this old custom but demands instead the advantages of modern unhindered market trading, presumably a reflection of practices in his own country by that time.

Blund-Ketill, hearing of this, now chooses to take Qrn under his protection, thereby challenging Tungu-Oddr's local authority. And so a dangerous animosity comes to pervade the neighborhood—Qrn

---

24. ÍF 3:7, ch. 2; CSI 5:240.
25. ÍF 3:5, ch. 1; CSI 5:240.
26. Helgi Þorláksson notices that *goðar* in seven of the *Íslendingasögur* reserve to themselves this right of the *heraðstjórn*. See "Social Ideals," 241,

himself stays with Blund-Ketill but disperses his men about the district as a way of protecting them from concerted attack. The composer makes the standoff clear: while Blund-Ketill is explicitly warned of the instability he is creating by this exercise of hospitality, Tungu-Oddr must admit that, in the end and though he has lost face, he can do nothing: "þar er sá maðr, er bæði er vinsæll ok kappsamr; þó vil ek um sinn vera láta." (He is a man who is both well liked and ambitious. For now I'll just let things stand as they are.)[27] Despite his occupying a traditional position of power, he lacks the popular backing required for its exercise. Communal support is therefore also of crucial importance to the maintenance of Blund-Ketill's security in this charged environment.

On the other hand, the latter's popularity-based victory is embedded in and encourages a background of resentment that has been nourished by his blatantly pragmatic disregard for the traditionally held power of Tungu-Oddr. When his son, Hersteinn, warns him of the consequences of this enmity, he merely observes, with that misplaced optimism typically exhibited by victims soon to be annihilated in the saga world, the following: "Þar sem vér berum eigi verra mál til en Oddr, þá kann vera, at oss falli þat létt" (Since our case isn't any worse than Odd's, it could be that it will turn out well for us).[28] It is from such smoldering hostilities, whether arising from insults or minor injuries, and whether real or perceived, that full-fledged feud actions are brought to fruition; indeed, the composer has used this early incident of his narrative to prepare the way for the demise of Blund-Ketill, the much loved and respected *stórbóndi* (great farmer) of the district.

In this hostile communal environment a second series of scenes, which leads to the death of Blund-Ketill and his family, is also fraught with the notion of unpopularity and the vulnerability it entails. Having imbued the district with the tensions of competitive friction between the wealthy farmer and Tungu-Oddr, the composer tells how in a winter when hay is in short supply, Blund-Ketill's tenants come to see him for help on three occasions, each succeeding one more dire in its urgency. This narrator's quaint predilection for things in threes becomes gradually apparent to the audience, and the third time for anything becomes ever more unnerving for

---

27. ÍF 3:11, ch. 3; *CSI* 5:242.
28. ÍF 3:10, ch. 3; *CSI* 5:241.

the likelihood of its portending misfortune.[29] On this last occasion, Blund-Ketill is persuaded to support his tenants in a visit to Hœnsa-Þórir to purchase hay from him: "þat er sannligt, at þeir seli, sem til hafa" (it is fair that those who have extra should sell), says Blund-Ketill, echoing views associated with a controversial change in law regarding the forced purchase of hay in time of need, effected in 1281 with the acceptance in Iceland of *Jónsbók*, the royal Norwegian code of law. A great deal of earlier critical scholarship was expended on the significance of this innovation to the composer and audience of *Hœnsa-Þóris saga*, but it is probably safe to assume that the topical allusion was only incidental to the point of the saga, even though authorial sympathy so obviously favors the spirit of the new law.

In a painfully prolonged scene where Blund-Ketill attempts to buy hay from the impossibly reluctant and surly merchant-farmer, the composer uses his foster-son Helgi Arngrímsson, with his engagingly honest ways, to put Þórir in an even worse light, if indeed that is possible to do. Helgi tries, unsuccessfully, to get his foster-father to come to the door and talk with the visitors; he assures Blund-Ketill of Þórir's abundance of hay; and he even leads him to where it is stored. When Blund-Ketill takes what he needs for his tenants, with due regard for the owner's own requirements and leaving payment, as specified by the new law of the 1280s, the latter chooses to term the event a case of *rán* (robbery), as it would indeed have been according to the older law of that commonwealth the composer attempts to describe in his narrative saga world—though it would not, of course, have been so at the time in which he and his audience presumably lived.

The bitterness of this scene is exacerbated by Þórir's insistently resentful harping on the socioeconomic differences between himself and his more than gracious supplicant. When Blund-Ketill offers to

---

29. ÍF 3:13, ch. 5; *CSI* 5:243; Andersson, *Saga*, 120. Andersson notices the "epic triads" of this saga. See Axel Olrik, "Epische Gesetze der Volksdichtung," *Zeitschrift für Deutsches Altertum* 51 (1909): 1–12. This article has been translated into English as "Epic Laws of Folk Narrative," in *The Study of Folklore*, ed. Alan Dundes (Englewood Cliffs, NJ: Prentice-Hall, 1965), 129–41. For an exhaustive review of the data for threes in saga literature, see Alfred L. Bock, "Die epische Dreizahl in den Islendinga sögur," *Arkiv för nordisk filologi* 37, 38 (1921, 1922): 263–313, 51–83. For proverbial recognition of this tendency, see JGF 665–66 and TPMA 2.300. The composer makes use of the rhetoric and devices of epic style composition perhaps humorously, in several other ways as well.

buy hay from him, he responds, "Eigi er mér þitt fé betra en mitt" (your money isn't any better to me than mine), cynically referring to the differing respective economic modes by which each has gained his wealth.[30] He taunts him, "Hví ertu í heyþroti, auðigr maðr" (How come a rich man like you is in need of hay)? When his visitor explains the problem as resulting not from his own improvidence but from that of others, he rejoins, "Þat muntu eiga allra heimilast, at veita ǫðrum þitt, en eigi mitt" (Then you are most welcome to give others what is yours, but not what is mine).[31]

And finally, when Blund-Ketill has offered him not only financial payment but additional gifts for his honor, he continues his partly coherent objections, concluding, "enda vil ek eigi selja" (besides, I don't want to sell).[32] As negotiations disintegrate he complains of the socially based political inequality that enables Blund-Ketill to ignore his objections and take what he likes: "en veit ek, at er sá ríkismunr okkar, at þú munt taka mega hey af mér, ef þú vill" (Still, I know that there is such a big difference in power between us and that you can take hay from me if you want to).[33] Although Blund-Ketill professes distaste for the situation, he concludes their discussion with a reluctant determination to take what has become an unavoidable action: "Þá mun fara verr, ok munu vér allt at einu hafa heyit, þó at þú bannir, en leggja verð í staðinn ok njóta þess, at vér erum fleiri." (Then it'll be so much the worse. Even though you forbid it, we'll take the hay right now and leave payment in its stead—since we have the advantage of numbers.)[34] Only at the end of their discussion, when all reasonable negotiation has failed, does Blund-Ketill take explicit notice of the present inequality of numbers that enables his imposition of the one-sided transaction. It is not, however, to a difference in numbers that Þórir refers when he remarks on the difference in power between them. Rather, it is to a moral power derived from Blund-Ketill's superior, socially

---

30. ÍF 3:14, ch. 5.
31. ÍF 3:14, ch. 5; *CSI* 5:243.
32. ÍF 3:15, ch. 5; *CSI* 5:243. Hœnsa-Þórir's response here signals the "verbal casuistry" of his arguments; see Andersson, *Saga*, 117. A similar quality of argument has been remarked on in the exchange of the Þjóstarsynir in *Hrafnkels saga*, where logically supported dialogue comes to an abrupt end when Þorgeirr threatens to leave his brother if he does not get his support to Þorbjǫrn and Sámr. Bolton, "Heart," 42–44. See, in support of this observation by Bolton, above, chapter 6, the section The Sophistry of Persuasion.
33. ÍF 3:15, ch. 5; *CSI* 5:244.
34. ÍF 3:16, ch. 5; *CSI* 5:244.

secure position. Like Tungu-Oddr in this respect, Hœnsa-Þórir articulates his lack of effective popularity—namely, that communal support which would be required to stave off Blund-Ketill's demand successfully.

Arngrímr's Belated Regret: *"illt ódrengjum lið at veita"*

Consistent in his narrative form, the composer then tells of three attempts by Hœnsa-Þórir to get what he claims he conceives of as justice. Readers familiar with Þorbjǫrn's persistent search for help with his errand of litigation against Hrafnkell might see a studied contrast between the pitiably simple, foolishly proud sincerity of his endeavor and the cynical malignity of Þórir's attempts at destructive manipulation.

In the first attempt, while visiting Norðrtunga, Hœnsa-Þórir asks Arngrímr, his *goði*, whose son Helgi he is, after all, fostering, for help. He begins by responding to the ritual query about district news with this statement: "Ekki hefi ek nú nýligra spurt en ránit" (I haven't heard of anything more recent than the robbery).[35] On questioning, Helgi puts straight Þórir's version of the purchase, adding "fór Blund-Ketill vel með sínu máli" (Blund-Ketil behaved very well in the matter). The *goði*'s sympathies are left in no doubt: "betr er þat hey komit, at hann hefir, en hitt, er fúnar fyrir þér" (It's better that he has the hay than that it should rot in your hands). When Þórir complains that he is ill protected by Arngrímr despite their earlier agreement, the latter expresses renewed discomfort and regret over the fostering and the obligations it entailed: "Þat var þegar ófyrirsynju, því at ek ætla þar vándum manni at duga, sem þú ert" (It was really lacking in foresight, . . . for I think to help a man like you is to help an evil man).[36] As he alludes to the proverbial wisdom of avoiding associations with bad men, it is clear that by now he has come to understand the gravity of the situation in which he placed himself by succumbing to the lucrative arrangement about the fostering of Helgi.

The syntactic structure of the phrasing of Arngímr's response to the urgings of Hœnsa-Þórir will immediately remind the reader

---

35. ÍF 3:17, ch. 6; *CSI* 5:244.
36. ÍF 3:17, ch. 6; *CSI* 5:245, slightly modified. For warnings against association with evil persons, see JGF 290–94.

of Sámr's comment in *Hrafnkels saga* as he undertakes Þorbjǫrn's foolish business of seeking redress through litigation for the killing of his son. There, in a scene in which the composer first begins alluding to the proverbially informed thematic pattern of *Hrafnkels saga*, Sámr, the prosperous young farmer with a proudly fancied knack for litigation, gives in to the importuning of his uncle Þorbjǫrn to help in taking up a case against Hrafnkell for the killing of his son Einarr with the glum observation, "Ófúss geng ek at þessu. Meir geri ek þat fyrir frændsemi sakar við þik. En vita skaltu, at mér þykkir þar heimskum manni at duga, sem þú ert." (I go into conflict with Hrafnkel unwillingly. I do this mainly for the sake of my relationship with you. But you ought to know that I think I'm helping a fool.)[37] The proverb to which the composer alluded here, as we noticed above, was "Illt er heimskum lið at veita" (It's bad to help the foolish), and indeed the folly of his ill-considered acquiescence to his uncle's foolish ambition is immediately reinforced when "Hrafnkell spyrr þetta ok þótti hlœgiligt, at Sámr hefir tekit mál á hendr honum" (Hrafnkel heard about this and found it ridiculous that Sam had taken on a case against him).[38] In this way the composer of *Hrafnkels saga* tells his story of an overbearing chieftain's learning to dispense with foolishly cherished pride by confronting it with a situation where helping the foolishly proud is demonstrated to be singularly unproductive.

But here—in a comparable narrative approach in which, however, the similarly structured allusive phrase uses a form of *vándr* (evil) rather than *heimskr* (foolish)—Arngrímr is commenting regretfully on the obvious inadvisability of his having helped one of the most wretched figures of the saga world. His expression of regret, as is the case in *Hrafnkels saga*, alludes to a wisdom text that similarly admonishes disadvantageous alliances of the sort in which he has placed himself. The proverb is very close to one used by Grettir when he realized that blame for the accidental conflagration caused when he fetched fire for the merchants would bring him to harm, claiming, "kvað nú þat fram komit, er hann grunaði, at þeir

---

37. ÍF 11:108, ch. 3; *CSI* 5:267. The syntactic construction of this statement of reluctance is paralleled in the *Íslendingasögur* only once—in Arngrímr's complaint over his unwise involvement with Hœnsa-Þórir. This phraseological coincidence, if that is what it is, might be included among the verbal and conceptual affinities of the two sagas.

38. ÍF 11:108, ch. 3; *CSI* 5:267; *JGF* 240; *TPMA* 8.380.

myndi honum illa eldsóknina launa, ok segir illt ódrengjum lið at veita" (what he suspected had come true, that they would reward him badly for fetching the fire and said it was a bad thing to help dishonourable men).[39]

Such an observation, which is made by Grettir in a peculiarly localized situation, is surely meant, like the warning that is echoed in *Hrafnkels saga* against helping the foolish, to encourage more generally the consideration of wisdom regarding what sorts of people make suitable objects of support and legally burdened association. As Þórir's unpopularity, which has presumably arisen in large part from the hostility with which he treats people, as well as his disdain for the niceties of traditional commerce, weakens him in his political dealings, so too those who become involved with him also make themselves subject to the destructive forces he arouses in the community. And they share with him in his unenviable demise in this way. Arngrímr wisely withholds support in this circumstance where so little recommends Þórir's obviously manufactured cause.

Tungu-Oddr: "mynda ek svá hafa gǫrt, ef ek þyrfta"

On his second attempt to gain justice Hœnsa-Þórir proves no more successful in his approach to Tungu-Oddr than he was with Arngrímr. He repeatedly informs the district leader, "Ekki hefi ek nýligra frétt en ránit" (I haven't heard of anything more recent than the robbery), and he again recounts in his maliciously distorted fashion Blund-Ketill's attempt to reach an amicable deal with him over the hay. Again, Helgi, when he is asked, sets the record straight: "Hann sagði, at Þórir affœrði stórmjǫk; greinir nú allt, hversu fór" (He said that Thorir was way off the mark and then told everything that had happened). Unimpressed, Oddr is also decidedly unsympathetic: "mynda ek svá hafa gǫrt, ef ek þyrfta" (I would have done the same thing if I had been in need), comments the chieftain who, it will be remembered, was "kallaðr jafnaðarmaðr" (called a fair-minded man) by no one. The composer now places

---

39. ÍF 7:131, ch. 38; CSI 2:111; JGF 433. The sentiment is echoed allusively in *Reykdœla saga*, where Áskell "kallar þat óvitsamligt at gefa slíkum óvendismanni mat sinn sem Þorgeirr var" (said it was unreasonable to provide for a wretch like Thorgeir). ÍF 10:182; CSI 4:272, ch. 12.

in Hœnsa-Þórir's mouth two proverbs that here carry the hostile weight of imprecations: "Satt er þat, er mælt er, at spyrja er bezt til váligra þegna" (It is true, as is said, that it is best to only hear about bad company), by which he means Tungu-Oddr.[40] And, he continues, "án er illt um gengi, nema heiman hafi" (you don't have bad company unless you bring it from home), referring to the foster-son and his irritatingly truthful nature.[41] In his wrathful frustration, Þórir misses the dramatic irony of the moment—both texts could be used meaningfully of himself in these circumstances. He is sufficiently bad so that it is better to hear of him than to have dealings with him, and his foster-son Helgi, who his from his own household, will die because of his mischief.

Þorvaldr Tungu-Oddsson: "Eigi mun ek neita fjarviðtǫkunni"

The third and tragically successful attempt to gain support for action against Blund-Ketill over the *rán* (robbery) is directed at Þorvaldr Tungu-Oddsson, who is newly returned from a sojourn in Norway and who perhaps still feels comfortably distant from the dealings of local Icelanders as he enjoys a visit with Arngrímr goði at Norðrtunga.[42] Þórir, who is overjoyed to hear of his arrival and apparently assumes that something about him that is not clear to the reader will make him a softer touch than others, also comes to visit. The composer presents Þorvaldr keeping himself above the petty prevailing tensions as Hœnsa-Þórir paces about the hall floor, not having been offered a seat. When Þorvaldr questions this negligence of hospitality, Arngrímr "kvað hann eigi varða" (said that he didn't need one), which could mean that it wouldn't make any difference to Þórir if he were seated or that seating Þórir was simply not Þorvaldr's concern.[43]

Possibly assuming an objectivity not expected of those more closely involved, Þorvaldr insists that Þórir sit by him and

---

40. ÍF 3:18, ch. 6; *CSI* 5:245, slightly modified; JGF 659; *TPMA* 6.191–92.
41. ÍF 3:18, ch. 6; *CSI* 5:245; JGF 188; *TPMA* 5.452.
42. Sverrir Jakobsson. "Strangers in Icelandic Society 1100–1400," *Viking and Medieval Scandinavia*, 3 (2007): 141–57. Interestingly Frederik J. Heinemann, "Analysis," 107, identifies Eyvindr as "a type of returning hero," but one who is typically and insultingly vain rather than naïve. See above, chapter 3, the section titled "Fate and Gísli's Character" for discussion of the naïve returnee.
43. ÍF 3:19, ch. 7; *CSI* 5:246.

predictably learns the news, "Raun var þetta, er Blund-Ketill rænti mik" (It was rough when Blund-Ketil robbed me).⁴⁴ "Lýgr hann mestan hlut frá, ok er alllítit til haft" (He's lying about most of it, . . . and there's precious little to the rest of it), warns Arngrímr. But Þorvaldr persists and, learning that Blund-Ketill did indeed take the hay, comments with a proverb supportive of the old law, "Bærr er hverr at ráða sínu" (To each, his own).⁴⁵ When he tells Þórir that he has no power to undertake a suit, however, the latter makes him a by now familiar offer of half his wealth, "til þess, at þú réttir málit ok hafir annathvárt sekðir eða sjálfdœmi, svá at óvinir mínir siti eigi yfir mínu" (if you settle the case with a verdict of outlawry or an award on my terms, so my enemies no longer sit on my possessions). As he did previously with Arngrímr, Þórir settles for buying his way into the power structure of the establishment that despises him. Arngrímr warns Þorvaldr, again in the same language that alludes to that proverbial wisdom regarding the situation: "Ger eigi þetta . . . því at eigi er góðum dreng at duga, þar sem hann er" (Don't do it, . . . you are not helping a decent man in that one).⁴⁶ As Þórir speaks temptingly of his wealth, Arngrímr warns a second time, "Letja vil ek þik enn . . . at þú takir við máli þessu . . . uggir mik, at mikit hljótisk af" (I would advise you one more time, . . . against taking on this case. . . . I suspect that there will be grave consequences). But Þorvaldr, like Arngrímr before him, gives in because of the money: "Eigi mun ek neita fjarviðtǫkunni" (I won't say no to getting the money).⁴⁷

The Summons and the Pretext for Killing Blund-Ketill: "illt mun af þér hljótask"

His mistake becomes immediately apparent to him when Þórir, although he professes his intentions of seeking advice first from his father Tungu-Oddr as to how to proceed, demands that he instead go to Ǫrnólfsdalr, Blund-Ketill's farm, and take instant action: "Þetta mun vera reyndar, at þú munt vera engi gæfumaðr, ok illt mun af þér hljótask; en svá mun nú vera verða." (It might be

---

44. ÍF 3:19–20, ch. 7; *CSI* 5:246.
45. ÍF 3:20, ch. 7; *CSI* 5:246; *JGF* 461; *TPMA* 2.394.
46. ÍF 3:20, ch. 7; *CSI* 5:246; *JGF* 433.
47. ÍF 3:20–21, ch. 7; *CSI* 5:246; *JGF* 293–94.

indeed, ... that you are not a man of good luck, and that something bad will happen because of you. But now that's the way it has to be.) This is how he complains, expressing through proverbial allusion his immediate regret about the obligations under which he is placed by the interests of the malevolently wealthy peasant.[48] Not only does he echo the phrases of Arngrímr's ignored warning; he also uses the language of those in other sagas who are inveigled into or forced to undertake a lethal errand, expressing foreboding but with all power of decision now given over to fate. In this we see yet another narrative signal of the disaster that is likely to result from his acquiescence to Þórir's demands.

In a relatively short saga such as this one, where character is rarely developed with any complexity beyond the necessities of plot, it is impossible to fathom with much certainty Þorvaldr's pliability under pressure from Hœnsa-Þórir. The reader must wonder, for instance, why the latter is pleased beyond our understanding when he learns of Þorvaldr's return from abroad and hastens to meet him to seek his support. And the blunt opacity of Þorvaldr's refusal to heed the warnings of Arngrímr about the danger of association with an individual who is distinctly not a *góðr drengr* (good fellow), which is annoying in its neglect of motivation, must also puzzle the audience to no end. Clearly, however, the point of the episode is all that concerned the composer—namely, that whatever induced Þorvaldr to help an undeniably *illr maðr* (bad man), the proverbially reinforced traditional expectations of such a decision will soon be fulfilled. The psychological development of characters' motivations is never a high priority in this story.

The composer emphasizes the contrast between Blund-Ketill's good spirit and attendant, if not directly resultant, popularity, on the one hand, and Hœnsa-Þórir's utter self-isolation in his wretched state, on the other, when, meeting the next day for the journey to Ǫrnólfsdalr, Arngrímr and Þorvaldr come with a company of thirty men, whereas Hœnsa-Þórir is accompanied by only two men—his unpleasant relative Viðfari, and his foster-son Helgi. Riding through Þverárhlíð toward their destination, they are seen by farmers along the ridge who, understanding the purpose of their visit, immediately hasten to the support of Blund-Ketill against such hostile forces:

---

48. ÍF 3:21, ch. 7.

"þykkisk sá bezt hafa, er fyrst kemr" (each of them thought it best for him to be the first). Blund-Ketill's welcome of his adversaries is typically gracious, since he offers hospitality where it would be least appreciated. Þorvaldr's surly refusal seems out of character for him, at least in terms of the annoyingly little we in fact know about it, reflecting in its tone the gratuitous hostility of Þórir, the malicious instigator of the venture: "Annat er ørendi hingat en eta mat" (Our business here isn't to eat food).[49] Blund-Ketill seeks to make peace with Þorvaldr, offering the same compensation he had made to Hœnsa-Þórir, but with gifts: "því betri ok meiri sem þú ert meira verðr en Þórir" (more and better ones since you are of a higher station than Thorir). This offer is of course a reminder for the audience of the complainant's social or perhaps individual inferiority, and yet it is at the same time an offer that Þorvaldr, who is silenced by the gesture, is at a loss to refuse. Indeed, he "þótti vel boðit" (thought it a good offer), the composer asserts, using a phrase normally descriptive of terms that proverbially should not be turned down. Spurred by Þorvaldr's silent yet understandable hesitation, Þórir again complains that the gift of half his wealth is badly spent if there is no better deal than was offered in the first place; and Þorvaldr, still without plausible motivation, responds perversely to Blund-Ketill's admirable generosity of spirit by proceeding to serve him with a summons: "Svá lízk mér sem engi sé annarr á gǫrr en at stefna" (It looks to me as if there's no other recourse but to summon you to court).[50]

Ǫrn, the Norwegian stranger, who was used earlier by the composer as the initiating cause of feud-based hostilities between the two factions of the narrative, once again becomes the catalyst as the story progresses toward its tragic sequence. Moved by his magnanimous host's humiliation in the process of the summons, he impulsively shoots an arrow into the crowd as they prepare to leave, and it finds a mark with lethal effect. Since the victim is the young Helgi, the son of Arngrímr, a *goði*, the consequences are potentially most dire, and the quick-thinking demagogue in Hœnsa-Þórir immediately takes advantage of the killing. Although Helgi is already dead, his foster-father pretends he has lived long enough

---

49. ÍF 3:21, ch. 8; *CSI* 5:247.
50. ÍF 3:22, ch. 8; *CSI* 5:247. The social obligations of "vel boðit" are evident here as well.

to say "Brenni, brenni, Blund-Ketill inni" (Burn, burn / Blund-Ketil inside), and despite the obvious ruse, the mere claim of such words leads quickly to the burning itself.

The evil intentions of Þórir and his duplicity are remarked proverbially in a text where Arngrímr goði, when he learns of the killing, comments even as the tragedy proceeds:

> Nú fór sem mik varði, at opt hlýtr illt af illum, ok grunaði mik, at mikit illt myndi af þér hljótask, Þórir, ok eigi veit ek, hvat sveinninn hefir sagt, þó at þú fleiprir eitthvert; en þó er eigi ólíkligt, at slíkt verði gǫrt; hófsk þetta mál illa; kann ok vera, at svá lúkisk.

> (Now things have gone as I expected. Bad things come from bad people, and I suspected that you would bring great evil, Thorir. I don't know what the boy said, despite what you babble about. It's not unlikely, though, that evil will be done. This matter started off badly, and it could be that it will end that way.)[51]

While proverbial observation is primarily didactic in nature, most often being of ethical bent and used to exert indirect control, here such paroemially based rhetoric is not meant to change decisions or the course of events but rather to inform them with the encoded wisdom that imbues the narrative with its moral value.

The Conflagration

Editors of this saga notice, in commenting on the burning of Blund-Ketill and his household, the strikingly cold cruelty with which the undertaking is conducted. Both in the *Íslendingasögur* and in the contemporary events reported in *Sturlunga saga* at least some exceptions to this form of execution are universally granted. Women, some children, the elderly, servants, and others whose neutrality or political harmlessness render their killing superfluous tend to be spared. In the remarkably few lines devoted by the composer to the burning itself we learn simply that Blund-Ketill "frétti, ef nǫkkut skyldi ná sáttum" (asked if there were any way to reach an

---

51. ÍF 3:23, ch. 8; *CSI* 5:248. See Hermann Pálsson, trans., *The Confederates and Hen-Thorir* (Edinburgh: Southside, 1975), 32: "One of the essential themes of Hen-Thorir is epitomised in the saying 'Evil comes of evil men.'" *JGF* 293–94; *TPMA* 10.138.

agreement). Þórir's brief and heartless response must leave even the most sensitive social theorist less than enthusiastic in his defense: "Þórir sagði, at engi er kostr annar en brenna" (Thorir said that there was no other choice than to burn).[52] Such a strangely laconic treatment of this remarkable atrocity, a treatment that, after all, describes one of the few events of the story deriving from historical sources creates a particularly harsh impression. Þórir's refusal of mercy to any is the most extreme example of what might be seen as his neglect of the niceties of the old social economy, or more accurately of his brute unconcern for those from whom he never could expect unpurchased support. In any case his complete lack of mercy should render him undeserving of any sympathy readers might have been tempted to profess for him on account of his unfortunate origins or his being ostracized by the traditional elements of the society from which he gained his wealth.

Compensation and Resolution

In the morning, with smoke and some flames still rising from the ruins, Blund-Ketill's son Hersteinn is inveigled against his better judgement by his foster-father Þorbjǫrn stígandi into seeking *ráð* (advice and support) from Tungu-Oddr, about whom readers were informed earlier, "engi var hann kallaðr jafnaðarmaðr" ("By nobody was he called a fair-minded man"). Justifying Hersteinn's reservations about approaching Tungu-Oddr for help, the chieftain, when he accompanies them to the scene, takes a burning timber, rides around the homestead, claims it for his own, and abruptly departs, giving them no help or support whatever, affirming by these actions once again his unpleasant reputation.

Þorbjǫrn proves to be more effective in arranging, through an intricate and unsurprisingly tripartite campaign, the support of three influential figures for the project of gaining retribution for the burning. The conflict moves in two different ways toward a resolution: privately with Hersteinn's beheading of Hœnsa-Þórir back at the farm, while publicly his newly acquired allies use their power to bring about sentences for the primary figures in the

---

52. ÍF 3:24, ch. 9; CSI 5:248.

burning—for Arngrímr a life sentence, and for Þorvaldr, three-year outlawry.

The Last Campaign of Tungu-Oddr

Unpacified, Tungu-Oddr resets his sights on Ǫrnólfsdalr, Blund-Ketill's farm, which has now been taken over by the powerful champion, Gunnar Hlíðfarsson, one of those men whose aid was enlisted in taking up the case for the burning. When Tungu-Oddr sets out to retake the property, however, he finds himself opposed by his second son Þoroddr, who has become enamored of his enemy Gunnarr's other daughter Jófríðr. This woman is made by the composer to demonstrate an engaging sensitivity when she is visited by her admirer, and she expresses a concern lest their meetings should become known: "vilda ek gjarna, at eigi hlytisk illt af mér" (I wouldn't want anything bad to happen because of me).[53] Here again, through proverbial allusion, the composer draws a contrast between her and Hœnsa-Þórir, the bad man because of whom so many bad things happen. In any case it marks her positively as a person who is admirably considerate and careful in behavior. Although Gunnarr is at first unreceptive to Þoroddr and his intentions, the latter brings about his marriage as well as the end of the feud conflict when his father descends on Ǫrnólfsdalr with a troop of followers who are ready for murder, mayhem, and of course confiscation.

The unredeemed coarseness of Tungu-Oddr's rapacity, which is as repellent in its way as Hœnsa-Þórir's universal negation of humanity, makes itself felt most damningly in the last paragraphs of the saga when he reacts to news of Þóroddr's betrothal to his enemy's daughter: "Heyr hér á endemi, . . . væri þér þá verra at eiga konuna, þótt Gunnarr væri drepinn áðr, er mestr var várr mótstǫðumaðr" (This is outrageous, . . . Would you be any worse off by marrying the woman after the death of Gunnar, who has been our worst enemy)?[54] In this fairly humorously developed scene of urgent betrothal and foiled callous aggression the composer distinguishes explicitly between those like Jófríðr, concerned as she is to avoid letting bad things result from her actions, and people of

---
53. ÍF 3:43, ch. 16; *CSI* 5:257.
54. ÍF 3:46, ch. 17; *CSI* 5:259.

evil intention, like Tungu-Oddr and Hœnsa-Þórir before him, who are utterly unconcerned about the bad effects of their despicable behavior.

The goði's Decline

His second son's marriage having been happily accomplished, the account of the feud reaches its end, and the next sentences in the text turn immediately to the brief steps of Tungu-Oddr's decline. Þóroddr learns that his brother Þorvaldr has been taken as a slave in Scotland and sets off to free him. Neither of them is heard from afterward, and Tungu-Oddr ages swiftly, dying with the realization that he has lost both his sons. As his story ends, he leaves directions for his friends to "flytja hann upp á Skáneyjarfjall, þá er hann væri dauðr, ok kvazk þaðan vildu sjá yfir tunguna alla." (Carry his body up to the mountain Skaneyjarfjall when he was dead. He said that he wanted to look over the entire tongue of land from there.) He thus maintains, even after his death, surveillance of the district he has so harshly controlled.[55]

* * *

When Þóroddr was persuading Gunnarr to agree to his betrothal to Jófríðr it proved necessary for him to respond to the latter's fears of appearing to have allowed himself to be threatened into consent. He did this by citing the likely opinion of *góðgjǫrnum mǫnnum* (men of good will), using a phrase related to those noticed elsewhere for their conscious reference to well-disposed men of influence whose presence in society works toward the moderation that preserves order, in opposition to those whose interests are less benign.[56] It must be admitted, however, that only a handful of men answer this description in *Hœnsa-Þóris saga*, and that its composer expresses limited optimism about the efficacy of their influence until reaching his sudden, brief, and unconvincingly happy end regarding the evil fruits of Þórir's evil plans. The *illr maðr* (bad man), a figure of *gæfuleysi* (lucklessness) and an object of general disdain, succeeds in

---

55. ÍF 3:46, ch. 17; CSI 5:259.
56. Jesch, "'Good Men,'" 64–82, considers references to varieties of public opinion in saga argumentation. In this passage, it seems to be Þóroddr's reference to the approval of *góðgjǫrnum mǫnnum* (men of good will) that makes Gunnar's decision possible.

spreading the effects of his destructive resentment over his district, and in doing so he is aided by the corrupt greed of its leaders. In the end, Þóroddr, as a son of Tungu-Oddr and of inexplicably good will considering his origins, brings about a final reconciliation of the opposing forces whose mutual animosity had been so inflamed by the manipulative schemes of Hœnsa-Þórir.

This pervasiveness in society of the flaw explicitly illustrated in some individuals in this story is similarly obvious in *Hrafnkels saga*, offering perhaps another example of evidence regarding the two works' closeness of composition. As Sámr's is by no means the only foolishness of that saga, where Hrafnkell goði himself learns to eschew his former arrogance—namely, the foolish assumption that his power resided in the structure of tradition rather than in his judicious public behavior and the immediate approval of his subjects—so, too, the evil meant to be avoided in *Hœnsa-Þóris saga* turns out to be spread far wider than the unpleasant figure of Hœnsa-Þórir. The voracious greed and heartless rapacity of the chieftains who wreak havoc on the very social order they should support and protect makes them far less attractive and more generally dangerous than the eponymous subject of the saga. As Gunnar Hlifarson remarks to Þórðr gellir Óláfsson, a chieftain upset about having just allowed himself to be duped into enlistment in the campaign against the burners of Blund-Ketill, "nú er vel, at þér reynið eitt sinn, hver yðar drjúgastr er hǫfðingjanna, því at þér hafið lengi úlfsmunni af etizk" (it is well now that you test which of you chieftains is greatest, since you have long been devouring each other with a wolf's mouth).[57] The implied comparative reference to the feeding behavior of wolves, which could possibly even echo the mythic hunger of Fenrir at Ragnarǫk, forms a fitting description of the evil and the greed the composer intended to convey through his story. Just as Þorbjǫrn is by no means the only fool in *Hrafnkels saga*, so too in *Hœnsa-Þóris saga* its subject is not the only *illr maðr* (bad man) whom one would do best to avoid.

---

57. ÍF 3:33, ch. 11; JGF 594, cites Låle 1148.

CHAPTER 8

Fóstbrœðra saga, Sverris saga, and Narratives of the Will

"Jafnan segir inn ríkri ráð"

In his paper for the First Saga Conference in 1971, on "The Sagas of Icelanders as Dramas of the Will," Robert Cook spoke of saga figures' chronic obsession with asserting and maintaining the right to decide, to have control over their social environment.[1] "Borrowing the medieval division of the soul into three faculties—reason, emotions, will—we can say that the saga treatment of character centers almost exclusively on the will, to the neglect of the other two faculties."[2] Cook studied several types of scenes in the sagas—whetting, requests for aid, trickery, persuasion of reluctant persons, warnings, obstinacy, and wise refusals—showing how "saga characters express themselves, and relate to each other primarily on the level of will."[3] The development of feud theory in the years shortly after the publication of this paper would resituate his observations, which were apt in their original context, in order to refer to the incessant competition between individuals in a society where resolution of conflict was sought in those traditional processes.

---

1. This section incorporates themes and (modified) text from my paper, "'*Jafnan segir inn ríkri ráð*': Proverbial Allusion and the Implied Proverb in *Fóstbrœðra saga*," in *New Norse Studies: Essays on the Literature and Culture of Medieval Scandinavia*, ed. Jeffrey Turco, Islandica 58 (Ithaca, NY: Cornell University Press, 2015), 61–97.

2. Robert Cook, "The Sagas of Icelanders as Dramas of the Will," in *Proceedings of the First International Saga Conference, University of Edinburgh, 1971*, ed. Peter Foote, Hermann Pálsson, and Desmond Slay (London: Viking Society for Northern Research, 1973), 91. http://www.sagaconference.org/SC01/SC01_Cook.pdf

3. Cook, "Sagas of Icelanders," 94.

245

This pervasive social urge to assert control over territory, geographical or political, would understandably be expressed in personal terms by one's insistence on having one's way, in small matters as well as in larger ones. Within that segment of the paroemial inventory of Old Norse society that encoded the axioms of feud a proverb pertinent to such imposition of will, "Jafnan segir inn ríkri ráð" (The more powerful always decides), predicts, in terms having resonance with beliefs in fate, the outcome of such conflict.[4] First attested for Old Norse in line 89 of "Málsháttakvæði," a proverb poem usually attributed to Bishop Bjarni Kolbeinsson and composed around the year 1200, this paroeme's force is often implicitly celebrated in the *Íslendingasögur*.[5] It is used, too, in the thirteenth-century "Sólarljóð," a mystical dream-vision poem that is at the same time an example of medieval Icelandic wisdom literature. Its style is similar to that of *Hávamál*, and it is generally analogous in its imagery to continental poetry of this genre.[6] The cleric Jón Halldórsson, writing *Klári saga* while a student in Paris around the year 1300, used the proverb in that text, though whether he rendered it from the now lost Latin original or drew it from his native cultural background is uncertain.[7] Its use is attested further by Peder Låle in East Norse, and *TPMA* cites it in Middle High German too.[8] Modern Icelandic compilations also include it in their inventory, and it has universal application, though with various nuances of interpretation, in narratives of the will from any place or age.[9] In *Fóstbrœðra saga* this proverb can be identified by

---

4. JGF 473; *TPMA* 4:460.

5. Bishop Bjarni Kolbeinsson, "Málsháttakvæði," in *Den norsk-isländska skjaldedigtning*, ed. Finnur Jónsson, vols. B$_{1-2}$, Rettet tekst (Copenhagen: Gyldendal, 1912–15), B2:138–45 See also Axel Kock, ed., *Den norsk-isländska skaldediktningen*, 2 vols. (Lund: Gleerup, 1946–49), 1:308–16.

6. "Sólarljóð," in *Den norsk-isländska skjaldedigtning*, ed. Finnur Jónsson, vols. B$_{1-2}$, Rettet tekst (Copenhagen: Gyldendal, 1912–15), B1:635–48. See also *skaldediktningen*, 2:73–78. See also the recent edition by Carolyne Larrington and Peter Robinson of "Sólarljóð" in *Poetry on Christian Subjects, Part 1: The Twelfth and Thirteenth Centuries*, ed. Margaret Clunies Ross, Skaldic Poetry of the Scandinavian Middle Ages 7 (Turnhout: Brepols, 2007), 287–357.

7. Jón Halldórsson, *Klári saga*, ed. Gustav Cederschöld, Altnordische saga-bibliothek 12 (Halle an der Saale: Max Niemeyer, 1907), 47. For discussion of this matter, see Shaun F. D. Hughes, "*Klári saga* as an Indigenous Romance," in *Romance and Love in Late Medieval and Early Modern Iceland: Essays in Honor of Marianne Kalinke*, ed. Kirsten Wolf and Johanna Denzin, Islandica 54 (Ithaca, NY: Cornell University Press, 2008), 135–16.

8. Låle, "Forndanska", 111; *TPMA* 4.460.

9. FJ Proverb word 334, 181; Jónsson, *Málsháttasafn*, proverb word 74, 76. Vilhjálmsson, *Málshættir*, 268.

allusion, illustrated by action, and placed in a context of Christian interpretation where its earlier, secular meaning is elevated to a spiritual plane.

And finally, included primarily as a conceptual rather than a phraseological appendix to the last study, is an investigation of *Sverris saga konungs*. In its overtly Christian setting, the force of the same proverb as that which allusively informs the text of *Fóstbrœðra saga* is brought to bear by the composer on political implications regarding the moral quality of this usurping king's right to the throne. The reader familiar with *Fóstbrœðra saga* will immediately see the conceptual associations between it and *Sverris saga konungs*, the story of a king who ultimately justified his rule in terms of God's exertion of his will, rather than in terms of his own rather insecure claim to the throne by paternal linkage.

The Composition of *Fóstbrœðra saga*

Over the last eighty years textual discussion of this saga has revealed a most complex set of problems regarding the history of its composition. Whereas a simpler and somewhat shorter version, dating from perhaps the early thirteenth century, in *Hauksbók* (ca. 1300) had been thought the more original, studies in the 1930s and 1940s suggested that the fuller, oddly floreate passages in the saga found where it is combined with *Óláfs saga helga* of *Flateyjarbók*, while once thought to be interpolations, were in fact part of the early text.[10] The *Hauksbók* version thus came to be seen as derivative. Jónas Kristjánsson, in *Um Fóstbrœðru* (1972), argued for a later thirteenth-century date of composition, the saga's peculiar stylistic features not being inconsonant with the learned style in Old Icelandic prose, which in the fourteenth century became marked by more florid adornments.[11]

In this work he also established that chapter 1 of *Fóstbrœðra*, whose contents are found also in chapter 52 of *Grettis saga*, was original to the former work, and derived from its text in the latter.[12] The story is omitted from the otherwise longer *Flateyjarbók*

---

10. Vera Lachmann, *Das Alter der Harðarsaga*, Palaestra 183 (Leipzig: Mayer & Müller, 1932), 222–23. Sigurður Nordal, "Handrit. Aldur. Höfundur," in *Vestfirðinga sögur*, lxxii–lxxiii.

11. Jónas Kristjánsson, *Um Fóstbrœðrasögu*, 251–91.

12. Kristjánsson, *Fóstbrœðrasögu*, 81–82.

redaction but it occurs in its related manuscript, *Membrana Regia Deperdita*, as well as in *Mǫðruvallabók*, whose text, alongside that of *Hauksbók*, is seen by Jónas Kristjánsson as deriving from a source different from that of the former two books. Up to this time the passage had been regarded as an inexplicable interpolation from *Grettis saga*, but it was now given undisputed textual authenticity in *Fóstbrœðra saga*.

Grettir Ásmundarson and the Thematic Prelude in *Fóstbrœðra saga*

In this episode, Grettir Ásmundarson, whose appearance otherwise in the saga is quite minimal, is saved from summary execution at the hands of some poor farmers he has annoyed in Ísafjǫrðr by the intervention of the aristocratic Þorbjǫrg digra Óláfsdóttir pá, who rules the district when her chieftain husband, Vermundr inn mjóvi Þorgrímsson, is absent from home. A "vitr kona ok stórlynd" (wise and magnanimous woman) and learning Grettir has been captured and is in danger, she arrives at the place where preparations have been made for the hanging.[13] When the farmers explain their plans, she advises them not to kill him: "hann er ættstórr maðr ok mikils verðr fyrir afls sakar ok margrar atgørvi, . . . ok mun frændum hans þykkja skaði um hann, þótt hann sé við marga menn ódæll." (He comes from a high-ranking family and is greatly respected for his many physical accomplishments. His kinsmen will take his death badly, even though he is regarded as overbearing by many.) They point out the legal justification for what they are doing, considering him "ólífismaðr" (rightly condemned to death), . . . since "því at hann er skógarmaðr ok sannr ránsmaðr" (he is an outlaw and a proven thief). Nevertheless, Þorbjǫrg will not allow them to hang him: "Eigi mun hann nú at sinni af lífi tekinn, ef ek má ráða" (His life will not be forfeit on this occasion if I have any say in the matter). They submit to this assertion of her authority with a grudging qualification; "Hafa muntu ríki til þess, at hann sé eigi af lífi tekinn, hvárt sem þat er rétt eða rangt" (Right or wrong, you have the power to prevent him from being executed). The composer uses the farmers' concluding comment to ensure the audience is aware that while the wrongness of this imposition of her will on

---

13. ÍF 6:121, ch. 1; CSI 2:329.

her men is not altogether just, she nevertheless has the power to enforce it. In fact, he is explicit about the point of the episode: "Í þessum atburði má hér sýnask, hversu mikill skǫrungr hon var" (It can be seen from this incident that Thorbjorg was a woman of firm character).[14]

The characters in this episode are of no particular significance otherwise to the rest of the saga, and its action might at first reading seem irrelevant to the narrative as a whole. However, the test of narrative consistency or coherence in medieval Icelandic literature has been shown to rely on more than merely linear progression. Ian Maxwell, in his study of *Njáls saga*, formulated a critical concept that can be usefully applied in cases such as this—namely, "the principle of the integrity of episodes." "Sagas," Maxwell argues, "prefer to deal with whole episodes, not pieces or aspects or reflections of them."[15] Thus the composer has included the entire story of Grettir's brush with ignominious death at the hands of these farmers, who are weak as individuals but who, as a group, have brought him within their power. And countering their power is that of Þorbjǫrg, the *goði*'s wife, on whose authority they are forced to relinquish their captive. As a corollary of this first concept, Maxwell introduced a second, the "partial interdependence" of episodes: Even though scenes are recounted in a way that renders them whole in themselves, they should also be read as part of the extended composition in which they occur. "Is there not also a rhetoric of narrative by which, without explicit comment, the author may keep his readers on track?" he asks.[16] Our reading of such seemingly irrelevant episodes, then, requires our seeking their thematic unity with the text in which they are embedded rather than attempting to place them within a logical and linear progression of the narrative.

Proceeding on such grounds, Giselle Gos sought for the value of the story as a prelude in a thematic rather than a linear sense. She studies how some women in *Fóstbrœðra saga* are presented by the composer as wise mediators between outlaws and society— Grettir in this first, introductory segment, and the *fóstbrœðr* in the

---

14. ÍF 6:122, ch. 1; CSI 2:330. Readers may be reminded here of the authorial comment on Unnr in djúpúðga Ketilsdóttir in *Laxdœla saga*, following her ingenious and courageous escape from Scotland: "má af því marka, at hon var mikit atbragð annarra kvenna" (It shows what an outstanding woman Unn was). See ÍF 5:7, ch. 4; CSI 5:3.
15. Maxwell, "Pattern," 25.
16. Maxwell, "Pattern," 26.

remaining body of the narrative. For Gos, the purpose of chapter 1 lies in "the comparison between the foster-brothers and Grettir, their relationships to the communities, and the need for mediators in those relationships, as well as the large part women play in that social mediation in Iceland."[17] Gos views the point of the saga as in part "the degree to which the women's roles in mediation parallel King Óláfr's."[18] There can be no doubt that her discussion touches on a theme of interest to the composer of the saga, but shifting the emphasis of our reading of this first episode indicates that he may have had concerns of a broader or more comprehensive nature, and that these concerns are more clearly traceable through a wider range of the narrative as a whole.

In the derivative version of this story in *Grettis saga* Þorbjǫrg's assertion of authority is couched in her and Grettir's shared aristocratic status and the fact that Grettir is more than the farmers can handle, both physically and socially. In *Fóstbrœðra saga*, however, the outlaw's privileged family background is less pronounced. Þorbjǫrg does observe that his kinsmen would take his death badly, alluding to likely repercussions for the poor farmers of Ísafjǫrðr extending beyond their control if they hang him. Besides this, however, her concern seems to be that his life is in her hands, not theirs, and that her position and character imbue her with the power to decide his fate. Gos sees as most important here the fact that "the verb used to describe Þorbjǫrg's actions is 'ráða' (judge/counsel/advise)"[19] We might add to that the term "ríki," which is used by the farmers to describe their mistress's advantage, which exists because of her power to control the situation and its denouement. There are many instances in this saga where reference is explicitly made to characters' possession and assertion of their power to exercise their will to judge, to decide issues, to control others. This is frequently done by using the terms *ráð*, or *ráða*, and sometimes

---

17. Giselle Gos, "Women as a Source of *heilræði*, 'Sound Counsel': Social Mediation and Community Integration in *Fóstbrœðra saga*," *Journal of English and Germanic Philology* 108 (2009): 288. Interestingly, Margaret Clunies Ross, in her thoughtful discussion of this puzzling introductory episode in *Fóstbrœðra saga*, observed in a similar fashion that "the narrating voice shows a considerable interest in Þorbjǫrg's position and represents the whole episode as a vindication of her superior qualities of wisdom and magnanimity." See Margaret Clunies Ross, *Prolonged Echoes: Old Norse Myths in Medieval Northern Society*, 2 vols. (Odense: Odense University Press, 1998), 2:70.

18. Gos, "Women as a Source," 298.

19. Gos, "Women as a Source," 285.

a form of *ríki* in the text, or by presenting a situational description in which that power is implied or contested.

Þorgeirr and Þormóðr

In *Fóstbrœðra saga* the force of the proverb "Jafnan segir inn ríkri ráð" (The more powerful always decides) intrudes on the reader's consciousness, especially in the earlier passages of the story. The second chapter develops this very theme when introducing its two heroes and then a local chieftain, Þorgils Arason, who is described with alliterative phrases in Old Icelandic, as "vitr ok vinsæll, ríkr ok ráðvandr" (wise and well liked, powerful and honest). The latter term, *ráðvandr*, is defined by Guðbrandur Vigfússon as "'heeding one's ráð,' honest, upright."[20] Opposing this figure of wisdom and maturity, the composer describes the unwholesome dynamic in the relationship between Þorgils's cousin Þorgeirr, and Þormóðr, both of whom are "í mǫrgu skapglíkir" (alike in temperament).[21] The violence of their lives leads them to conclude they will die fighting, and so "tóku þeir þat ráð með fastmælum, at sá þeira skyldi hefna annars, er lengr lifði" (they thus swore that whoever survived the other would avenge his death). The narrator explicitly disapproves of this *ráð* from a Christian perspective: "En þó at þá væri menn kristnir kallaðir, þá var þó í þann tíð ung kristni ok mjǫk vangǫr, svá at margir gneistar heiðninnar váru þó þá eptir ok í óvenju lagðir" (Though people called themselves Christians in those days, Christianity was a new and very undeveloped religion and many of the sparks of heathendom still flickered, manifesting themselves as undesirable customs).[22]

After this they become even more obnoxious in their neighborhood, and Vermundr, the authority of whose position was already established in chapter 1, has to intervene. Using his power to banish Þorgeirr's family from Ísafjǫrðr, where they had in any case settled without permission, he expresses the hope, "at minni stormr standi af Þormóði, ef þeir Þorgeirr skiljask" (that Thormod will be less

---

20. ÍF 6:124, ch. 2. C-V, 487b.
21. ÍF 6:124, ch. 2; CSI 2:331.
22. ÍF 6:125, ch. 2; CSI 2:331. A similar observation is found in *Grettis saga*, chapter 88: "Yet although Christianity had been adopted in Iceland, many vestiges of heathendom remained." (En þó at kristni væri á landinu, þá váru margir gneistar heiðninnar eptir.)

unruly if he parts company with Thorgeir). When Þorgeirr's father Hávarr submits to this decision, he speaks in terms recalling the proverb whose kernel is under discussion as he complains, "Ráða muntu því, Vermundr, at vér munum ráðask í brott ór Ísafirði með fé várt, en eigi veit ek, nema Þorgeirr vili ráða vistum sínum" (Vermund, you have the power to make me leave Isafjord with all my belongings, but I expect Thorgeir will want to decide for himself where he stays).[23] Although Vermundr has the local power to force Hávarr and his household to leave Ísafjǫrðr, the wayfarings of Þorgeirr are another matter, for him to *ráða* as he wishes, and beyond anyone's control: "var hann mǫrgum mǫnnum nǫkkurr andvaragestr, þar sem hann kom, þó at hann væri á ungum aldri" (despite his youth, he was an unwelcome guest at most places he visited).[24]

In the episode after this Jǫðurr of Skeljabrekka, "ríkr í heraðinu ok stórráðr, vígamaðr mikill" (powerful in the district, but was ambitious and slew many men) and who "bœti menn sjaldan fé, þótt hann vægi" (rarely paid men compensation for the lives he took), asks to borrow a horse from Þorgeirr's father to fetch flour. His personal description does not bode well for amicable dealings with Hávarr, who also lacks flexibility and, even though he allows him to take a horse, demands, "vil ek, at þú látir hestinn hér eptir, er þú ferr aptr, ok hafir þú eigi lengra" (I'd like you to return the horse to me on your way back and take it no farther). On returning, Jǫðurr decides to renege despite his companions' warning: "Gera máttu þat, ef þú vill, en eigi hefir Hávari jafnan líkat, ef af því væri brugðit, er hann vildi vera láta" (You can do that if you wish, but Havar has never looked kindly on broken agreements). As expected, Hávarr is adamant: "Eigi vil ek, at nú fari hestrinn lengra" ("I don't want the horse to go any further"). Here Jǫðurr asserts his own will, declaring "Þó munu vér hafa hestinn, þótt þú vilir eigi ljá" (we shall have the horse with or without your consent). "Svá mun vera, at þat sé" ("That remains to be seen"), says Hávarr, who, after attacking Jǫðurr, is swiftly killed by him.[25]

When the youthful Þorgeirr comes to seek redress from his

---

23. ÍF 6:126, ch. 2; CSI 2:332. See above, chapter 1, the section titled "The Contribution of Linguistically Based Approaches to Paroemiological Investigation," for Neal Norrick's concept of a proverb's kernel.
24. ÍF 6:126, ch. 2; CSI 2:332.
25. ÍF 6:127, ch. 2; CSI 2:332.

father's killer, Jǫðurr reminds him that he is not in the habit of paying compensation for his slayings. Þorgeirr, saying he knows nothing of this, nevertheless points out "þá kømr þetta til mín, at leita eptir þessum vígsbótum, því at mér er nær hǫggvit" (it is my duty to seek compensation from you now since the stroke was close to me).[26] When Jǫðurr proves unmoved from his discouraging custom, Þorgeirr challenges him: "Þér munuð ráða, hvern sóma þér vilið gera, en vér munum ráða þykkju várri" (It's for you to decide how much you pay, and it's for me to decide whether I accept it or not).[27] Þorgeirr then kills Jǫðurr in vengeance for his father's death, and, when he reports back to his mother Þórelfr, she, while pleased with him, can only allow him to stay one night before he has to leave to seek protection with Þorgils, since "Hér munu menn koma á morgin at leita þín, ok hǫfum vér eigi ríki til at halda þik fyrir fjǫlmenni" (Tomorrow, men will come here looking for you and we don't have the strength to protect you against a large party).[28]

Free Will and Þorgeirr's Choice

Conflicts over the horse and compensation are discussed in terms of *vilja*, *ráða*, and *ríki*, as we might expect from the rhetoric of feud and its literary expression in what Cook called dramas of the will. As he notices the skill and bravery of Þorgeirr, who is only fifteen years old, the composer employs the ecclesiastical rhetoric that has been noticed in a number of passages in this saga. He comments thus:

> En þó var eigi undarligt, því at inn hæsti hǫfuðsmiðr hafði skapat ok gefit í brjóst Þorgeiri svá øruggt hjarta ok hart, at hann hræddisk ekki, ok hann var svá øruggr í ǫllum mannraunum sem it óarga dýr. Ok af því at allir góðir hlutir eru af guði gǫrvir, þá er ørugglekir af guði gǫrr ok gefinn í brjóst hvǫtum drengjum ok þar með sjálfræði at hafa til þess, er þeir vilja, góðs eða ills, því at Kristr hefir kristna menn sonu sína gǫrt, en eigi þræla, en þat mun hann hverjum gjalda, sem til vinnr.

---

26. ÍF 6:130, ch. 3; CSI 2:334, slightly modified.
27. ÍF 6:130, ch. 3; CSI 2:334.
28. ÍF 6:132, ch. 3; CSI 2:335.

(And yet it was no great wonder since the Almighty Creator had forged in Thorgeir's breast such a strong and sturdy heart that he was as fearless and brave as a lion in whatever trials or tribulations befell him. And as all good things come from God, so too does steadfastness, and it is given unto all bold men together with a free will that they may themselves choose whether they do good or evil. Thus Jesus Christ has made Christians his sons and not his slaves, so that he might reward all according to their deeds.)[29]

In representing the significance of Þorgeirr's indulgence in violence as a matter of choice, the composer directs the attention of his audience to the ensuing narrative of the two *fóstbrœðr*, rendering clear the purpose of his story. In making choices, people exercise the will that God gave them, and in doing so they are self-defined and will themselves be judged on the basis of their choices. The composer calls God the *hǫfuðsmiðr* (a chief workman, the architect), the most powerful being, who allows people free will so that they in turn may choose good or evil for themselves.[30] For these choices they will be rewarded accordingly.

Parodic Humor and the Moral Implications of Free Will

Preben Meulengracht Sørensen studies the composer's narrative intentions at this moral level, remarking that these oddly learned, ecclesiastically flavored passages exhibit ironic humor. Admittedly, he remarks, the satirization of the saga in the 1952 novel by Halldórr Laxness changed irreversibly the reading public's perspective: "It can be said that since the appearance of *Gerpla* it has been difficult not to see parody in *Fóstbrœðra*."[31] Yet that style had of course been in the narrative long before it was critically noticed. It was probably in the first layers of the saga's written form, since it appears occasionally at various points throughout the whole work. Just as "Fjarlægð gerir fjöllin blá og mennina mikla" (Distance makes mountains blue and people large), so too the distorting effects

---

29. ÍF 6:133, ch. 3; CSI 2:336, slightly modified.
30. C-V, 308b.
31. Preben Meulengracht Sørensen, "On Humour, Heroes, Morality, and Anatomy in *Fóstbrœðra saga*, in *Twenty-Eight Papers Presented to Hans Bekker-Nielsen on the Occasion of his Sixtieth Birthday*, ed. Michael Barnes, E.W. Hansen, H.F. Nielsen, and R. Schützeichel (Odense: Odense University Press, 1993), 396 of 395–418.

of cultural distance make humor difficult to recognize, let alone interpret.³² The qualities of this parodic humor in *Fóstbrœðra saga*, however, do remind one of passages in *Grettis saga* where the hero's lines might have seemed noble in the mouths of his ancestors of past generations and yet are easily and humorously deflatable when he speaks them himself—that is, in the context of the saga world he inhabits. His visit to Auðunn Ásgeirsson, for example, the good-natured farmer to whom he returns in order to match his strength as a way of retrieving the honor he imagines he lost in a boyhood confrontation, begins with this challenge: "Ek vil berjask við þik" (I want to fight you). This, in turn, is answered with what seems a humorous laconism: "Sjá mun ek fyrst ráð fyrir mat mínum" (I have to see to the food first).³³ Putting the misfit hero and his literary heroic stance in their place, Auðunn affirms the practical necessities of his own world—namely, the storing of food. He responds in this way not only to his old friend's unrealistic aspirations but also more generally, at least for the composer's audience, to the lack of viability of a heroic commitment where there are, after all, only farmers—and merchants, for whom Grettir, as the composer makes clear elsewhere, also shows little respect—trying to make a living in a rather difficult world.

Not only does the humor of *Grettis saga* repeatedly puncture the outlaw hero's attempts to impose the heroic mode on an Iceland whose rather ordinary, hard-working, domestically inclined inhabitants have undertaken to live Christian lives; it seems also to indulge in Twain-like jabs at the antiquated ideals of nobility in such behavior. The composer uses humor as a weapon, belittling the values of that heroic ideal according to which old pre-Christian heroes of the saga world lived, admired and praised as they were in the country's literary culture. Similarly, the violence of the *fóstbrœðr* is out of place in their world, just as Grettir's gratuitous aggression is in his narrative, and this conflict between peaceable Christian communities and chaotic ruffians ostracized for their violent ways seems to be a thematic thread common to both works. As Vésteinn Ólason remarks of *Grettis saga*, touching on his sense of a Christian background in the morality of that saga's vision: "The stories about Grettir highlight more general truths about man and

---

32. Vilhjálmsson, *Málshættir*, 86, quoting from Sigurjónsson, *Rit*, 1, 117; JGF 151.
33. ÍF 7:96, ch. 28; CSI 2:94.

his society; about man's place in the natural order, and about his relationship to those forces which lie beyond everyday reality, and not least, about man as one of God's most remarkable creations, who nevertheless misuses his maker's gifts."[34] The humor, which is derived from the stark contrast in the respective behavior of the two groups, effectively neutralizes the value of the old literary heroism.

Thus, in his high parodic style, using medical texts from the continent but placing their erudition ludicrously in the service of explaining Þorgeirr's outrageously chaotic violence, the composer questions, with ironically implied criticism, the morality of the pre-Christian heroic mode. Although God has given him heroic strength and courage, Þorgeirr becomes ever more amoral in his unrestrained violence, especially after this leads to his estrangement from his *fóstbróðir*. Þormóðr's behavior, on the other hand, is controlled, if not ameliorated, with time and the influence of his idol, King Óláfr. Twice the king observes that Þorgeirr is not in all respects a lucky man, and this could be interpreted as having spiritual implications when he seems not quite dead after he has been killed.

Preben Meulengracht Sørensen sees traditional Germanic heroism reinterpreted and valued in Christian terms at the same time that the violence of pre-Christian times is ridiculed: "Þorgeirr serves demonic powers after his death, and that is the saga author's final judgement on his conduct in this life."[35] The ancient pagan wisdom of feud, whereby the more powerful decides, while remaining true in the secular, physical world, is translated into the Christian reality of God in his spiritual kingdom, rendering the decision—that of the "*hǫfuðsmiðr*," with vastly greater impact than that *ráð* that was of concern in the old communal wisdom of the North—final. While *Fóstbrœðra saga* has no Norwegian prelude, as happens elsewhere among the *Íslendingasögur*, its narrative up to and culminating in this stylistically remarkable and critically much noticed passage on free will acts as a prelude in a thematic sense.

Parodies of the Heroic Ideal

Much of the rest of *Fóstbrœðra saga* studies this test of the human reaction to the good or evil impulse, and for this test the composer uses his interestingly subversive humor that we have already noticed

---

34. Ólason, *Dialogues*, 190.
35. Meulengracht Sørensen, "*Fóstbrœðra*," 411.

in passages where power is tried or challenged. An example of this is seen in the "huglauss í hjarta" (rather fainthearted) Þorkell of Gørvidalr's home, where he must provide hospitality to Þorgeirr as well as to Vermundr's unpleasant kinsman, Butraldi, "einhleypingr, mikill maðr vexti, rammr at afli, ljótr í ásjónu, harðfengr í skaplyndi, vígamaðr mikill, nasbráðr ok heiptúðigr." (A loner of no fixed abode. He was a large, powerfully built man with an ugly face, quick-tempered and vengeful, and he was a great slayer of men.)[36] The very presence of two such aggressive figures in the home of a timid host suggests humorous possibilities for the narrative. Butraldi crosses himself before supper, but "Hvárrgi þeira vildi deila við annan kníf né kjǫtstykki. En þó at þeim væri lítt verðr vandaðr, þá fóru þeir þó eigi til sjálfir at skepja sér mat, því at þeim þótti þat skǫmm sinnar karlmennsku." (Neither of them would share either the knife or the food with the other. Though the meal was not good, they did not bring out their own provisions for fear that it would be seen as a sign of weakness.)[37]

The tension in the scene between the men's ridiculous preoccupation with their aggressive masculinity and Þorkell's timid apprehension of their potential violence in his household prepares the audience for the ensuing heroic battle between them. In a scene echoing Skarpheðinn's nimble feats at Markarfljót, Þorgeirr slides down a snowy slope, axe raised, toward Butraldi, who "lítr upp ok finnr eigi fyrr en Þorgeirr hjó framan í fang honum ok þar á hol; fellr han á bak aptr" (looked up, but before he knew what was happening Thorgeir struck him full on the chest with his axe and cut right through him and he fell back down the slope).[38] Þorgeirr's superior power having been conclusively demonstrated and celebrated in verse, the composer then adds humorously that no vengeance will be taken for Butraldi by his fearful relatives: "því at þeim þótti illt at eiga nátthól undir vápnum Þorgeirs" (since they had no desire to be sent off to rest for the night by his weapons).[39]

Any sympathy the audience might have for the *fóstbræðr* is strained beyond tolerance by their last killing episode before their mutual estrangement. Here they challenge a respected member of the community, and they do so in a situation where the righteousness

---

36. ÍF 6:142 and 142–43, ch. 6; CSI 2:340.
37. ÍF 6:145, ch. 6; CSI 2:341.
38. ÍF 6:146, ch. 6; CSI 2:342
39. ÍF 6:147, ch. 6; CSI 2:343.

of their involvement cannot be defended. Þorgils Másson, who is related to Grettir's father, is a "mikill maðr ok sterkr, vápnfimr, góðr býþegn" (a big, strong man, skilful in the use of weapons and a good farmer).⁴⁰ He refuses to share with them a stranded whale that he is carving up. Þorgeirr observes that he has already taken quite a lot of it. When Þorgils won't give in, however, Þorgeirr reacts in his typically aggressive way: "Þat munu þér þá reyna verða, hversu lengi þér haldið á hvalnum fyrir oss" (Then you will have to see how long you can hold us away from it).⁴¹ The ensuing fight ends predictably, with Þorgeirr triumphant and Þorgils dead, since " Þorgeirr var þeira meir lagðr til mannskaða" (Thorgeir was the deadlier of the two).⁴² After this the two *fóstbrœðr*, Þorgeirr and Þormóðr, range freely over Strandir, "ok gengu þeir einir yfir allt sem lok yfir akra" (and they prevailed over all things like weeds overtaking a field).⁴³

The Separation of the fóstbrœðr

The composer uses the term *ofsi* (overbearing, tyranny) of both *fóstbrœðr* in the next scene, where he forms a distinction between the two both personally and morally: "Svá segir sumir menn, at Þorgeirr mælti við Þormóð, þá er þeir váru í ofsa sínum sem mestum: 'Hvar veiztu nú aðra tvá menn okkr jafna í hvatleika ok karlmennsku, þá er jafnmjǫk sé reyndir í mǫrgum mannraunum, sem vit erum?'" (People say that at the height of their tyranny, Thorgeir spoke these words to Thormod: "Do you know of any other two men as eager as we or as brave, or indeed anyone who has stood the test of his valour so often?")⁴⁴ Addressing the proverbial wisdom situated in the rhetoric of *mannjafnaðr* in his culture, Þormóðr responds with care: "Finnask munu þeir menn, ef at er leitat, er eigi eru minni kappar en vit erum" (Such men could be found if they were looked for who are no lesser men than us).⁴⁵ And here Þorgeirr voices

---

40. ÍF 6:148, ch. 7; CSI 2:343.
41. ÍF 6:148–49, ch. 7; CSI 2:343
42. ÍF 6:149, ch. 7; CSI 2:343.
43. ÍF 6:149–50, ch. 7; CSI 2:344.
44. ÍF 6:150, ch. 7; CSI 2:344. (C-V 464b.)
45. ÍF 6:150, ch. 7; CSI 2:344. The proverb alluded to here, "that no one is boldest of all" (at engi er einna hvatastr), is found in *Hávamál* 64 and *Fáfnismál* 17; JGF 275; TPMA 12.326. See above, chapter 2, the section titled, "'Engi er einna hvatastr'—Some Dangers of Mannjafnaðr," for a discussion of the custom of *mannjafnaðr*.

the hypothetical challenge that ends the path of their life together: "Hvat ætlar þú, hvárr okkarr myndi af ǫðrum bera, ef vit reyndim með okkr" (Which of us do you think would win if we confronted each other)?

Þormóðr's response is surprisingly abrupt: "Þat veit ek eigi, en hitt veit ek, at sjá spurning þín mun skilja okkra samvistu ok fǫruneyti, svá at vit munum eigi lǫngum ásamt vera." (I don't know, but I do know that this question of yours will divide us and end our companionship. We cannot stay together.) When Þorgeirr realizes he has gone too far, he tries to backtrack: "Ekki var mér þetta alhugat, at ek vilda, at vit reyndim með okkr harðfengi" (I wasn't really speaking my mind—saying that I wanted us to fight each other). But the ideation has been voiced, as Þormóðr observes: "Í hug kom þér, meðan þú mæltir, ok munu vit skilja félagit" (It came into your mind as you spoke it and we shall go our separate ways).[46] Þorgeirr has thus isolated himself even from his *fóstbróðir* with his aggressive exuberance. The challenge, whether whimsical or serious, differentiates his worldview from Þormóðr's, since he considers his most trusted friend as a possible competitor. His amorality as revealed in this incident initiates a divergence from the fate of Þormóðr. They now head down spiritually differentiated paths, having chosen to exercise their power in opposing ways. After this we first see the results of Þorgeirr's choice; then we see Þormóðr's exaggeratedly robust vengeance for his fallen associate, which is justified in its assignment by King Óláfr himself.

Þorgeirr's Will

The composer represents Þorgeirr's behavior as becoming more extreme after Þormóðr separates from him. He makes his way among the communities of Strandir, an "andvaragestr" (unwelcome guest), while his cousins, Þorgils Arason and Illugi, purchase a share in a ship so he can leave for his outlawry.[47] Stories about the time before his departure for Norway have gathered in the written text here. One of them, involving a horse conflict, was obviously intended by the composer to form a parallel with the horse-borrowing incident that led to the death of Þorgeirr's father. Yet at the

---

46. ÍF 6:151, ch. 7; CSI 2:344.
47. ÍF 6:151, ch. 7; C-V 21a.

same time readers today at least are reminded by it of the initial tragedy of *Hrafnkels saga* and its hero's foolish arrogance in killing Einarr Þorbjarnarson. Since the actual crime of stealing a horse was not a part of either episode in *Fóstbrœðra saga*, the gravity of both these situations in which killings occur is questionable. The humorous distortion of the concepts of honor and the exaggeration of violence thus both become matters for consideration. Þorgeirr discovers that Bjarni Skúfsson has taken his horse to catch some sheep. With understated menace he advises him, "Þat sýnisk mér nú ráð, at þú stígir af baki ok látir hestinn koma í hendr eiganda" (I think it would be a good idea for you to get down off that horse and give it back to its owner). And he persists, when Bjarni will not cooperate: "Þat vil ek, at þú stígir nú þegar af baki" (I want you to get down from the horse immediately). Bjarni observes that the horse won't be hurt by being ridden, but for Þorgeirr that is irrelevant: "Ek vil þessu ráða, at þú ríðir eigi lengra at sinni" (I must insist that you ride it no farther at this present time).[48] Affirming his power to decide, he thrusts a spear through Bjarni's middle, ending the conflict; he regains his horse and then kills the servant Skúfr, for whom Bjarni had been collecting the sheep.

The theologically trained composer continues with these stories of Þorgeirr's last deeds in Iceland, seemingly intent on illustrating the unbalanced, perhaps demonic, lack of restraint in his determination to exercise his power. His behavior continues to be indefensible and it affirms beyond doubt the judgment of Icelandic society as well as of the ecclesiastical institution from whose culture these stories emerge. In the former episode he kills Torfi bǫggull for not answering his greeting, never realizing his victim could not hear him. Þorgeirr "reiddisk hann við, er honum var áðr skapþungt. Hann ríðr þá yfir ána at Torfa ok leggr spjóti í gegnum hann. ([Þorgeirr's] already bad mood turned to anger. He rode across the stream at Torfi and plunged his spear through him.)[49] Such recklessness is matched in a succeeding passage, in which he kills a resting shepherd while riding down to the ship: "var hann nǫkkut bjúgr, steyldr á hæli ok lengði hálsinn. En er Þorgeirr sá þat, reiddi hann up øxina ok lét detta á hálsinn. Øxin beit vel, ok fauk af hǫfuðit ok kom víðs fjarri niðr." (He was rather hunched over, with his tired legs bent and his neck sticking out. When Thorgeir saw this he drew his axe

---

48. ÍF 6:155, ch. 8; *CSI* 2:346.
49. ÍF 6:153, ch. 8; *CSI* 2:345.

in the air and let if fall on the man's neck. The axe bit well and the head went flying off and landed some distance away.) In explaining his brutality, he speaks utterly without feeling: "Eigi hafði hann nǫkkurar sakar til móts við mik, en hitt var satt, at ek mátta eigi við bindask, er hann stóð svá vel til hǫggsins." (He had committed no wrong against me. If you want the truth I couldn't resist the temptation—he stood so well poised for the blow.) To his blunt description of the situation of the killing his cousin responds, "þat mun sýnask í því, . . . at þú munt óhandlatr reynask" (One can see from this, . . . that your hands will never be idle).[50] Once Þorgeirr and Þormóðr are no longer together, Þorgeirr's violent deeds are scarcely motivated by anything at all, are senselessly destructive, and are beyond even his own ability to control them.

This general trend in his behavior seems curbed, or at least more rationally channeled, when he arrives in Norway and enters the court of King Óláfr, since there his actions are under the control of his royal host. Óláfr assigns him a mission of vengeance against Þórir of Hrófá, who has mistreated one of his men. When the king explains, "Því býð ek þér um þetta mál, at ek hygg, at þú munir minn vilja gera í þessu verki" (I am asking you because I believe you will do my will in this matter), Þorgeirr responds appropriately: "Skyldr em ek til þess at gera þat, sem þú vill" (I am obliged to do as you bid me).[51] For once, Þorgeirr's will gives place to another's. The king, who appears to be divinely guided, exerts his will through Þorgeirr's strength and courage, so that his violence has the approbation of society. At the scene of vengeance itself there is humor in Þórir's arrogant response to Þorgeirr's demand for compensation: "Vera má, at svá sé, at þú hafir hans umboð, en varla virðisk mér svá, sem ek heyra orð konungsins, þó at þú mælir" (It may well be that you are here as the king's representative, but I seriously doubt that these are the king's words you speak). Before impaling him on his spear, Þorgeirr jokes, "Satt er þat, at þú heyrir eigi hann sjálfan mæla, en þó má vera, at þú reynir nǫkkurt sinn hans ríki" (It is true that you do not hear him speak personally, but it may well be that you feel his power).[52] Here the violence is Þorgeirr's, but the will to its application is the

---

50. ÍF 6:157, ch. 8; CSI 2:347.
51. ÍF 6:183, ch. 13; CSI 2:358.
52. ÍF 6:185, ch. 13; CSI 2:359.

king's, for it is done at his bidding, and the king thanks Þorgeirr for the deed when they next meet.

The placement of the scene following this one draws attention to how Þorgeirr's will can be directed when it comes from his own impulses. At the same time, it also reminds us of the earlier episode with Grettir, where Þorbjǫrg imposes her wishes on the farmers of Ísafjǫrðr. Here Þorgeirr uses his will quite arbitarily to save the life of a smith, Veglágr, who has proved to be a thief and a forger of keys. To the demands that he be hanged, Þorgeirr, echoing Þorbjǫrg, exclaims, "Hvat sem yðr sýnisk rétt vera um þetta mál, þá mun yðr þó verða maðrinn dýrkeyptr í þessu sinni, ok eigi mun hann af lífi tekinn, ef ek má því ráða." (Despite what you think is the right course of action, in this instance the man's price will be too costly for you. He will not be executed if I have any say in the matter.)[53] Here the same words as Þorbjǫrg's are used in a bullying manner. Þorgeirr uses the threat of his physical power for unequivocal injustice, and the audience must recall again the explanation of his behavior and character after he has taken vengeance for his father's killing. The power itself is God-given; the will to use it is his own; and by its use he defines himself. When he returns to the Norwegian court, King Óláfr thanks him for carrying out his will in Iceland.

When Þorgeirr wants to leave for Iceland, the king tries to discourage him, saying he will receive greater favor by remaining with him. He relents, however, but reminds him of his earlier observation about his character, perhaps even about his spiritual flaw: "Nú mun at því koma, sem ek sagða in fyrsta tíma, er þú komt á várn fund, at þú myndir eigi vera gæfumaðr í ǫllum hlutum" (What I said to you the first time we met will now come to pass—you will not be fortunate in all you do). When the king tells him they will not meet again if they part now, Þorgeirr, with his usual determination, counters, "þat ætla ek, at fara á yðvarn fund at sumri" (I fully intend to return to meet you next summer). The king understands that in spite of Þorgeirr's own will and the power with which he is capable of exercising it, a will beyond his by now has other designs for him, and he insists on the following: "Vera má, at svá sé, at þú ætlir þat, en eigi mun svá verða" ("You

---

53. ÍF 6:188, ch. 13; CSI 2:360.

may well intend it, but it will [not] come to pass").⁵⁴ Like other Norwegian kings in their sagas, King Óláfr sees further than his subjects, and just as he later predicts that he and Þormóðr will be together after death, here he sees Þorgeirr's death, but with a different spiritual outcome.

It is, in the end, the unjustified killing of Þorgils Másson over the stranded whale that results in Þorgeirr's death. Gautr Sleituson, a relative of the victim, tries to create a lethal confrontation as they wait for the ship to Norway, but he himself dies in that confrontation. As Þormóðr comments in verse, "opt verðr ríkr, þeims rœkir, / raun" (he who does such deeds / often reaps a just reward).⁵⁵ Then a relative of Gautr's, Þórarinn ofsi Þorvaldsson, together with the Greenlander Þorgrímr trolli Einarsson, takes up the familial burden of vengeance for Gautr, even though he had previously made a truce with Þorgeirr. There is a gruesome battle, and the tragic hero is beheaded. The composer reminds us again of God's having given him the courage that was such a significant part of his character: "Almáttigr er sá, sem svá snart hjarta ok óhrætt gaf í brjóst Þorgeiri; ok eigi var hans hugprýði af mǫnnum gǫr né honum í brjóst borin, heldr af inum hæsta hǫfuðsmið" (It was the Almighty who touched Thorgeir's heart and put such fearlessness into his breast, and thus his courage was neither inborn nor of humankind but came from the Creator on high).⁵⁶ The tragedy is of his life, rather than his death, and of the choices that he made in his uses of God's gifts.

Þormóðr, the King's Will, and God's Will

Following Þorgeirr's killing, Þormóðr visits the court. There King Óláfr has a second assignment of vengeance—this time, for his *fóstbróðir*'s death. The mission takes him to Greenland, where Skúfr Bjarnarson lives. There he stays at the home of Þorkell Leifsson, at Brattahlíð, in Eiríksfjǫrðr. He arouses the antipathy of his host by his unfortunate ways with and competition over women, and he thus creates an atmosphere among Greenland's people of power that

---

54. ÍF 6:194, ch. 14; CSI 2:362.
55. ÍF 6:201, ch. 15, st. 13, ll. 7–8; CSI 2:365, st. 13. Guðni Jónsson renders the passage into modern Icelandic as follows: "sá kemst oft í harða raun, sem rækir slíkt" (CSI 2:365, st. 13n).
56. ÍF 6:208, ch. 17; CSI 2:368.

is averse to his pursuit of vengeance. In this alien and unfriendly atmosphere, Þormóðr takes on the roles of trickster and assumer of disguise, with humor attached to incidents where he gets the better of the Greenlanders. Although he kills far more people than King Óláfr intended for him to do, this happens without the apparent disapproval of the composer. Cloaked and hooded, he cleaves off the head of Þorgrímr trolli at the Garðarþing in Einarsfjǫrðr, where the latter, in a moment that may anticipate Gunnarr Lambason's beheading by Kári Solmundarson in *Njáls saga*, has been telling a slanted story of his triumph over Þorgeirr.

The continuing presence of King Óláfr and his royal power with Þormóðr are felt when the king appears in a dream to Þorgrímr í Vík í Einarsfirði, alerting him to the hero's plight—stranded on a skerry, badly wounded, and exhausted from swimming to escape forces roused to avenge his slaying of Ljótr, one of several of Þorgrímr's nephews whom he dispatches in an extended pursuit of vengeance. Telling Þorgrímr to save Þormóðr, the king in the dream confirms his identity by revealing that a person named "Gestr," who is staying with Þorgrímr, is really the Icelander Helgu-Steinar, who has also come to Greenland seeking vengeance for the killing of Þorgeirr. Þormóðr receives eventual recognition for his robust pursuit of his *fóstbróðir*'s killers, although he has gone to lengths that might seem immoderate to the modern reader were it not for the fact that King Óláfr, whose wishes are just, had initiated the process in the first place. Commending him for his enthusiastic execution of the task, the king comments, "Seint mun sá díli gróa, er þú hefir þar brennt" (It will be a long time before the ground you have scorched begins to grow again).[57] The phrasing echoes and is no doubt from an immediately preceding boasting verse by Þormóðr, and it indicates the king's approval of this exaggeratedly extended spate of bloody vengeance.

King Óláfr's divinely derived power to impose his will is emphasized for the last time in the closing scenes of the saga, where, when he asks why Þormóðr, who is by now his faithful skáld, has become despondent, he is told, "Því, herra, at mér þykkir eigi víst vera, at

---

57. ÍF 6:260, ch. 24; CSI 2:392. For a discussion of the proverbial phrase, "Brenna e-m díla," see Halldór Halldórsson, *Íslenzk orðtök* (Reykjavík: Ísafoldarprentsmiðja, 1954), 151–52 and 156, as well as Halldór Halldórsson, *Íslenzkt Orðtakasafn*, 2 vols. (Reykavík: Almenna bókafélagið, 1968–69), 2.109, s.v. "díli."

vit munim til einnar gistingar í kveld. Nú ef þú heitr mér því, at vit munim til einnar gistingar báðir, þá mun ek glaðr." (Because, my Lord, I am not certain that we shall be resting in the same place tonight. Promise me now that we shall be and I will be glad.)[58] The king's reassurance must be qualified, for such things are not really in his own power: "Eigi veit ek, hvárt mín ráð megu um þat til leiðar koma, en ef ek má nǫkkuru um ráða, þá muntu þangat fara í kveld, sem ek fer" (I don't know whether it is within my power to decide, but if it is, then tonight you shall go where I go).[59] But Óláfr is struck and dies in battle, and Þormóðr is still alive, bereft of his king. "Þat ætla ek nú, at eigi muna ek til þeirar gistingar, sem konungr í kveld, en verra þykki mér nú at lifa en deyja" (Since I shall not be resting in the same place as the king tonight, living seems worse than dying), he laments.[60] But at that moment, "fló ǫr at Þormóði ok kom fyrir brjóst honum, ok vissi hann eigi, hvaðan at kom" (an arrow flew towards him and struck him in the chest. He knew not whence it came). The episode has Þormóðr addressing the deceased king as follows: "Hvárt muntu nú, inn heilagi Óláfr konungr, eigi ætla at enda við mik þat, sem þú hézt mér, at þú myndir mik eigi fyrir róða láta, ef þín ráð mætti standa?" (Will you not, King Olaf, grant me the end you promised? You said you would not forsake me, if it were within your power?) He then rejoices at the subsequent arrow shot, claiming that he is "þessu sári feginn harla" (greatly pleased at being wounded thus).[61] By a miracle, his death is now certain, and King Óláfr's *ráð* has indeed proved to be consonant with that of *inn ríkri*, God himself.

* * *

The moral distinction in the conduct of the two heroes of *Fóstbrœðra saga*, as envisaged by Meulengracht Sørensen, is more clearly recognizable and defined in the light of our awareness of the underlying proverbial allusion that is operative at those moments in the text examined above. The drama of the will that Robert Cook described and that is present in many of the *Íslendingasögur*, essential as it was to social interactions from the beginning of Icelandic

---
58. ÍF 6:263, ch. 24; *CSI* 2:392.
59. ÍF 6:263–64, ch. 24; *CSI* 2:392.
60. ÍF 6:268–69, ch. 24.
61. ÍF 6:269, ch. 24; *CSI* 2:399. The version in *Flateyjarbók* recounts this episode at greater length.

culture, is studied from a Christian point of view by the composer, or one of the composers, of *Fóstbrœðra saga*. It is worth noticing that in the part of the narrative that could be called *Þorgeirr's saga* the paroemial subtext is more frequently alluded to than it is in the portion devoted to Þormóðr. Of the two, Þorgeirr is the spiritual *ógæfumaðr*. His unrestrained will to gratuitous violence is eventually in conflict with the divine will itself. It is this conflict that is examined in his story. Þormóðr, by contrast, in subjecting his will to that of the divinely appointed King Óláfr, ultimately exercises his free will by applying those powers given him in accordance with the intentions of the giver, or at least not in direct opposition to them.

Sverris saga and the Divine Will

Robert Cook's conception of the sagas as dramas of the will is not in fact limited to the *Íslendingasögur* with their stories of family feuds and the competitive ways of champion warriors. The observations that he makes about that genre have wider applications in the Old Norse world and indeed almost universally account for the underlying motivations of conflict in any narratives about its various communities. Among the *konungasögur*, *Sverris saga* tells of King Sverrir's nearly lifelong struggle to establish and maintain his controversial right to the Norwegian throne, and in doing so it presents significant paroemially informed similarities to the passages of *Fóstbrœðra saga* discussed above. In particular, it will be seen that in this narrative, also, the same proverb, "Jafnan segir inn ríkri ráð" (The more powerful always decides), is the subject of allusion and that its interpretation is, again, twofold, pertaining as it does to the power both of men and of God.

The Origins of *Sverris saga*

While the dating of this saga's composition is less problematic than that of *Fóstbrœðra saga*, its composership is debated, and there is textual as well as external evidence of there having been more than one narrator in its background. The prologue to *Sverris saga* in AM 327 4to, a Norwegian manuscript from around 1300, confirms its at least partial authorship by Abbot Karl Jónsson of Þingeyraklaustur (1135–1213), with the king himself overseeing its composition:

"upphaf bókarinnar er ritat er eftir þeiri bók er fyrst ritaði Karl ábóti Jónsson, en yfir sat sjálfr Sverrir konungr ok réð fyrir hvat rita skyldi" (The beginning of the book is written according to the one that Abbott Karl Jonsson first wrote when King Sverri himself sat over him and settled what he should write).[62] The first part of the saga, then, telling of the battles by which Sverrir came to power, was composed under the king's eye—"Kǫlluðu þeir þann hlut bókar fyrir því Grýlu" (They therefore called this part of the book Gryla)—and the prologue vaguely observes, "er sú frásǫgn eigi langt fram komin" (The story has not come far [from its source]).[63] Composition of the remainder of the book is said to be drawn from "þeira manna frásǫgn er minni hǫfðu til svá at þeir sjálfir hǫfðu sét ok heyrt þessi tíðendi, ok þeir menn sumir hǫfðu verit í orrustom með Sverri konungi" (those who remembered what happened, having actually seen or heard it, and some of them have been with King Sverri in battles).[64] This account is augmented, and perhaps confused, by its version in the fourteenth-century *Flateyjarbók*, which adds, "en eftir þeiri bók skrifaði Styrmir prestr inn fróði, en þessa Sverris sǫgu ritaði þar eptir þeiri bók [of Styrmir's] Magnús prestr Þórhallsson [one of the writers of *Flateyjarbók*]" (Priest Styrmi, the historian, followed that book [Karl's] when he wrote, and Priest Magnus Thorhallsson wrote this Saga of Sverri following that book [Styrmi's]).[65] Presumably, the writer is reporting that Styrmir fróði first copied the biography and that afterward the same copy was used when *Sverris saga* was included in *Flateyjarbók* by Magnús Þórhallsson. Despite critical uncertainty over the interpretation of this passage, Guðbrandur Vigfússon's view—namely, that the entire work was Abbot Karl's—has become the dominant one, with a general but not unanimous agreement that *Gryla* ends with chapter 100, following the death of King Magnús and its aftermath.[66] A single hand, then, that of Abbot Karl Jónsson of Þingeyraklaustur, is perceived to be at work, at least intermittently, through the entire text, but with the voice of the king intruding on or combining with the writing of the

---

62. *Sverris saga*, ed. Þorleifr Hauksson, Íslenzk fornrit 30 (Reykjavík: Hið Íslenzka fornritafélag, 2007), 3, "Prologus"; John Sephton, trans., *The Saga of King Sverri of Norway*, Northern Library 4 (London: David Nutt, 1899) (henceforth Sephton), 1.
63. ÍF 30:3; Sephton, 1.
64. ÍF 30:3; Sephton, 1.
65. ÍF 30:285 (Appendix: first prologue to *Flateyjarbók*), Viðauki; Sephton, 239.
66. Guðbrandur Vigfússon, *Sturlunga*, I, Prolegomena, lxxi, I.

abbot. In this collaborative process a narrative was created whose depths have yet to be analyzed definitively.

Sverrir Unásson's Journey to the World's Stage

Born in Norway in 1151 to a comb maker or smith, Sverrir Unásson, as he was first known, was taken to the Faroes at the age of five to be fostered by his paternal uncle, Bishop Hrói of Kirkjunes, in whose care he was clerically educated and ordained to the priesthood. Aggressive by nature, "óeirinn" (rather unruly), says the writer, and not suited to the priesthood, he must have found it some relief to receive from his mother Gunnhildr the news that he was in fact the son of King Sigurðr Munn.[67] Her revelation came about ostensibly as the result of a confession she had made to that effect while in Rome, in response to which the pope had enjoined on her the necessity of informing her son of his royal paternity. Meditation on this discovery, and supposedly also on several peculiarly contrived dreams that he interpreted to portend his royal entitlement, sent him at the age of twenty-five to Norway on a violent path that led to his defeating in combat and slaying, three years later, first Erlingr jarl in 1179, and then, five years after that, the jarl's son, King Magnús, in 1184. His victory was succeeded by the almost immediate challenges of other claimants, and when these were quelled, his energies were taken up with the defense of the crown's rights of power against the encroachments of the church, an endeavor in which Sverrir, as a son of that institution, made an unusually knowledgeable and articulate royal opponent. Although we know that his reign brought about significant legal and administrative improvements, which set Norway on the path toward a European modernity, a path that was to be completed by his grandson Hákon Hákonarson inn gamli (1204–63), these improvements are not mentioned in his saga. That saga is instead devoted from start to finish to the heroic narrative of his ascent to the throne and his subsequent struggles to maintain his kingship and its powers against both secular and ecclesiastical adversaries.

Sverrir's Dreams of God's Will

This story of Sverrir's contentious life is composed of a chaotic

---

67. ÍF 30:5, ch. 1; Sephton, 2.

assortment of episodes: prophetic dreams; political maneuvers; but mostly action—strenuous marches through Norway seeking support for the throne; naval expeditions; battles on sea and on land against his royal opponents; the building and subsequent loss of ships and fleets and fortresses. Loyalty to his clerical background is stressed in scenes such as those showing his Christian magnanimity with defeated enemies and his demonstrations of piety even in the heat of battle. His speeches, which are attributed by the saga's most recent editor to the invention of its primary composer, are so authentic in tone and so incisive in argument that some scholars have taken them for interpolations of the king's own writing. Since both men were educated ecclesiastics in the first place, it is not surprising that the king's purported speeches demonstrate remarkable rhetorical skill and theological training, which, on Sverrir's part, should have promised a good future in the church had it not been for the secular career he claimed to have had divinely thrust on him.

The combative rhetoric with which Sverrir was execrated by his enemies in the church identifies in theological terms that institution's political objection to his reign. Calling him a *"guðníðingr"* (a perpetrator of sacrilege) because, as an ordained priest he should never have undertaken the secular office of kingship, let alone given up his sacerdotal duties, his ecclesiastical enemies made it clear that, whatever his claim to the Norwegian throne, he had discarded prior and more urgent spiritual commitments. It is in the light of such ideologically based opposition that the polemical intent of his dreams, as he and his biographer have constructed them, becomes clearer.[68]

Thus chapter 42 reports a complicated dream Sverrir had before the Battle of Nidaróss, in which Erlingr Jarl was killed. In the dream a man leads him to a roasted male corpse and tells him to eat. Regarding the meal as unclean, the hero demurs; his dream man, however, commands him to obey, for it is God's will: "Þú vilt eta ok þú skalt eta; svá vill sá er ǫllu ræðr" (Thou wilt eat and shalt eat, for so wills He who governs all things).[69] Finding the meal unexpectedly enjoyable, he is admonished by his guide to stop as he comes to the head of the corpse, "ok varð þá við at skiljask"

---

68. For a discussion of Sverrir's dreams, see Lars Lönnroth, "Sverrir's Dreams," *Scripta Islandica: Isländska Sällskapets Årsbok* 57 (2006): 97–110.

69. ÍF 30:66, ch. 42; Sephton, 53.

(and with that they parted).⁷⁰ Sverrir's interpretation of his dream includes the death in battle of Erlingr Jarl and his most powerful barons, but also the escape of King Magnús, the leftover roasted head, in this instance. The import of this passage for the audience, however, is best understood in the context of the proverbial allusion established in the reference to God as one who rules or decides all—that is, the Christian spiritual reading of the traditional Old Norse proverb, "Jafnan segir enn ríkri ráð" (The more powerful always decides).

The allusion, which again is operative in this work, is invoked to emphasize Sverrir's contention throughout his biography that he has undertaken the pursuit of monarchy in deference to God's will rather than following his own. The sensitivity of the English translator, John Sephton, to this issue is apparent in his loose rendering of "varð þá við at skiljask" with an explicit allusion to this proverb, "the stronger man had his way." Thus, at the same time as this dream engagingly admits Sverrir's joy in conquest, it supports his contention that he was not in fact a *guðníðingr* but an initially reluctant follower of God's overwhelming will, a point that is often reiterated in the course of the narrative. The biography, or autobiography, of King Sverrir, no doubt in partial response to the church's criticism of him, emphasizes consistently the monarch's adherence to the principles of his ecclesiastical background. He prays on his knees before battle—and in the midst of one where the results are crucial but uncertain he ceases fighting, falls on his knees and prays heroically for divine intervention. To the defeated and to those who throw themselves voluntarily on his mercy he is unfailingly forgiving. He is described, then, as a very Christian king, no doubt in response to the church's characterization of him as a *guðníðingr*.

Norway's *Grýla*

In accordance with what were meant to be viewed as signs of respect for his training and faith, however, critics have remarked

---

70. ÍF 30:66, ch. 42. Sephton translates the phrase "but the stronger man had his way" with an inaccurate rendering, of course, while making clear his interpretation of the situation in terms of relative power, and thus his awareness of the informing cognitive patterning we are discussing here.

the presence of a dark and malicious humor—whether exercised by the nebulous biographer or represented by him as coming from the king's own mouth, or perhaps resulting rather from the collaborative dynamic of king and abbot in recounting the adventure. The very idea of titling the account of Sverrir's ascent to power "Grýla," after a monster—a traditional and personified embodiment of that which threatens accepted social order, and perhaps even, mythologically, the order of the universe—casts a viciously humorous light on his long journey to power.[71]

Humorous references to the overwhelming effect of his assaults on his enemies stress their aggressive nature to the point of their being troll-like. On three occasions the threat of the Birkibeinar is compared to that of "trolls at the door" or "between outhouse and home," emphasizing the chaotically destructive potential of the insurgent forces. Interestingly, the phrase, "*troll/trǫll fyrir durum,*" (troll/trolls at the door), which rarely occurs elsewhere in Old Icelandic literature, is found twice in *Fóstbrœðra saga*. For its humorous context, we might notice that it is used of Grettir's depredations on the Ísafjǫrðr countryside in chapter 1, though it is not found in the corresponding chapter 52 of *Grettis saga* itself. It appears also in chapter 9, where Þórdís's mother, Gríma, complains to Þormóðr about his importunate attentions to her daughter, saying that he may frighten more serious suitors away: "þeir menn, er til hafa gǫrzk at biðja hennar, ef þeir vissi, at þú ert nǫkkut riðinn við hennar mál—má vera, at þeim sýnisk troll standa fyrir durum, þar sem þú ert" (those men, who might be thinking about proposing marriage to her, if they knew that you are somewhat involved with her—could be that it will seem to them as if a troll stands at the door, where you are).[72]

An example of this humorous yet threatening rhetoric is found in his boisterously triumphant speech over the new corpse of Erlingr jarl, in 1184. At twenty-eight years of age and victorious after his long struggles, he stands, according to the composer, before Erlingr's defeated host at Niðaróss to deliver a funeral oration over the jarl's corpse. "Aldaskipti er mikit orðit, . . . sem þér meguð sjá, ok er

---

71. For useful information on *Grýla*, see Árni Björnsson, "Tröll og forynjur—Grýla," in *Jól á Íslandi* (Reykjavík: Ísafold, 1963), 139–46; Terry Gunnell, "Grýla, Grýlur, 'Grøleks' and Skeklers: Medieval Disguise Traditions in the North Atlantic?" *Arv: Nordic Yearbook of Folklore* 57 (2001): 33–54.

72. ÍF 6:161, ch. 9.

undarliga orðit er einn maðr er nú fyrir þrjá: einn fyrir konung ok einn fyrir jarl, einn fyrir erkibiskup, ok em ek sá" (Times are greatly changed, as you may see, and have taken a marvellous turn, when one man stands in the place of three—of King, of Earl, of Archbishop—and I am that one).[73] He continues by ironically deriding the promises of Erlingr's henchman, the archbishop Eysteinn, that "allir þeir menn er berðisk með Magnúsi konungi ok verði land hans ok létisk með því, at sálur þeira manna allra væri fyrr í Paradísu en blóðit væri kalt á jǫrðunni" (all those men who die fighting for King Magnus and defending his land, that their souls will enter Paradise before their blood is cold on the ground).[74] Remarking that he sees "margan hér hryggan standa yfir þessum grefti er fullkátr myndi vera ef svá stœði yfir mínum grefti" (many now present here at this grave sorrowing who would have been filled with joy if they so stood over my grave), he pretends to find their sorrow senseless.[75] "Nú megum vér allir fagna hér svá margra manna heilagleik sem hér munu helgir hafa orðit ef þetta er svá sem erkibiskup hefir sagt" (We may therefore rejoice at the sanctity of many men who have become saints, if what the Archbishop said is true).[76] He notices slyly that while "vér megim eigi fagna þeira jartegnum þá mun þó gott orðit til kyksettra í bœnum í þessi hríð" (we cannot yet rejoice at any miracles wrought by them, there must be an abundance of glorified saints in the town at this moment).[77]

And here the ascendant king's mood turns to somber admonition: "En ef svá illa er sem mér segir hugr um" (But if . . . there should be any danger, as my heart tells me there may be), that the archbishop's promises were empty, then better to "biðja fyrir þeim er fram eru farnir af þessum heimi ok biðja til Guðs at Erlingi jarli sé fyrirgefnar allar þær syndir er hann gerða meðan hann var í þessa heims lífi." (Pray for those who have departed. Pray God that Earl Erling may be forgiven and all the sins which he committed in this life.) Let us, he continues, "biðja fyrir allra manna sálum, þeira er látizk hafa í þessu inu rangliga vandræði bæði nú ok fyrr" (pray too for the souls of all those who have come by their death, now and aforetime, in

---

73. ÍF 30:61, ch. 38; Sephton, 49–50.
74. ÍF 30:61, ch. 38; Sephton, 50.
75. ÍF 30:62, ch. 38; Sephton, 50.
76. ÍF 30:61, ch. 38; Sephton, 50.
77. ÍF 30:62, ch. 38; Sephton, 50.

this wrongful trouble).[78] By this point he has made explicit his accusation that Erlingr jarl would need God's forgiveness, since "hann tók svá mikla dirfð til, einn lendr maðr, at hann lét gefa konungs nafn syni sínum, en á þat ofan reisti hann flokk ok merki á móti konunga sonum, Hákoni konungi ok Eysteini konungi, ok felldi þá báða frá ríkinu" (he, a mere baron, caused the title of King to be given to his son; and more than that, collected a force and raised his standard against kings' sons, King Hakon and King Eystein, both of whom he deprived of their realm).[79] This abrupt shift toward a seriousness of spiritual bent but with a political import in the sense of the righteousness of his cause reflects much on the origins and background and intentions of the speaker.

On his deathbed in 1202 Sverrir observes, "Hefi ek meira starf, ófrið ok vandræði haft í ríkinu en kyrrsæti eðr mikit hóglífi. Er svá at minni virðingu sem margir hafi verit mínir ǫfundarmenn, þeir er þat hafa látit ganga fyrir fullan fjándskap við mik, sem nú fyrirgefi Guð þeim þat ǫllum. Ok dœmi Guð milli vár ok allt mitt mál." (The kingdom has brought me labour and unrest and trouble, rather than peace and a quiet life. But so it is that many have envied me my rank, and have let their envy grow to full enmity. May God forgive them all; and let my Lord now judge between me and them, and decide all my cause.)[80] Even at his death, as he contemplates the many voices that doubt his paternal right to the throne, he leaves the question in the hands of "sá er ǫllu ræðr" (him who decides all).

The exercise of power in association with God's gift of free will, which is of primary concern in *Fóstbrœðra saga*, is thus also a matter of interest in *Sverris saga*, one of whose composers at least means to represent the priestly usurper's ascendence as the result of God's will. In addition, such striking phraseological similarities between the two texts, as well as their stylistic sharing of a humor derived from situations of violence, might lead us to consider whether they share also, at some point in their respective literary development, a common compositional hand. While this is not the place for a detailed study of such matters, it is interesting to recall the connections of Abbot Karl Jónsson to Þingeyraklaustr as well as the conjecture of Guðni Jónsson, in an admittedly earlier critical

---

78. ÍF 30:62–63, ch. 38; Sephton, 50 and 51.
79. ÍF 30:63, ch. 38; Sephton, 51.
80. ÍF 30:66, ch. 42; Sephton, 231–32.

era, that *Fóstbrœðra* "Líklega hefir ... verið skrifuð upp oftar en einu sinni af Þingeyramunkum milli 1210 og 1380" (has probably been written more than one time by the monks of Þingeyraklaustur between 1210 and 1380).[81] The composition of both works was imbued at some point with a transcendent spiritual vision of the ultimate source of the power to decide, the one wielded by "*sá er ǫllu ræðr*," and that vision is clearly conveyed through the process of proverbial allusion.

* * *

Far more than we ordinarily realize in our daily lives of communication with one another, we rely on allusion, on a variously and unevenly shared cognitive world of recognition of what we have experienced, and of what has gone before. So, too, the saga world of the thirteenth-century Icelandic composers was made up of such shared memories, on which narrative and dialogue were built in ways far too complicated ever to be sorted out to completion. Our study of the Icelandic saga at microstructural levels, however, conducted with care, can help us to understand the conceptual backgrounds in which such stories were placed and what their composers' purposes were in doing so. The resultant possibilities, therefore, of enhanced and illuminating interpretations of texts are as endless as they are tantalizing.

---

81. ÍF 7. Formáli, lxxv–lxxvi.

CHAPTER 9

Concluding Discussions and Directions of Research

As will be obvious to the reader by now, the chapters of this book have been intended to provide background for the study of how proverbs were used in the composition of medieval Icelandic literature. I hope that students of this subject will feel encouraged by its contents to approach medieval Icelandic literature with an active awareness of the possibilities of its shaping as well as its interpretation with reference to the paroemial cognitive background of the culture in which the sagas originated. Up to this point, as we noted above, the proverbial content of sagas has received little attention from those seeking to understand them. Torfi Tulinius, for instance, in establishing a frame of reference for such an understanding, suggested seven components: law, scientific learning, history, mythology, heroic literature, religion, and the everyday life of the saga composers.[1] My primary purpose here has been to demonstrate, with a few carefully chosen examples, the breadth and potential impact of another component: the application of the paroemiological discipline to our literary critical appreciation and understanding of the sagas.

Further to the Theory of Paroemiological Cognitive Patterning

As we consider the potential and the future of proverb studies in the area of medieval Icelandic literature we may benefit in particular from paying further attention to the developing theory of paroemial

---

1. Tulinius, *Matter*, 220–26.

cognitive patterning. This should not be confused with the individual intellectual and artistic processes of an ultimately conscious composer, who lays the groundwork of his narrative, its ethical assumptions, or its intended moral against established proverbial patterns to which he knows his audience will respond. Rather, this phenomenon has to do with a vast, pervasive, amorphous, body of wisdom communally shared in preliterate culture—not, as Larrington, Deskis and Shippey have noted, fully articulated in formula and yet lying nevertheless at the roots of thought about the world and how best to behave in it. This store of common sense has about it a fragility not readily apparent, one only partly revealed as a culture succumbs to literacy. Plato has Socrates recount for Phaedrus in his dialogue how Theuth, a god of the Egyptian city of Naucratis, an inventor of many arts, told Thamus, the king of Egypt, that of all the skills he had given to the people he prized literacy most, claiming it would "make the Egyptians wiser and give them better memories; it is a specific both for the memory and for the wit." Thamus, instead of applauding, expressed reservations, concerned about the intellectual loss resulting from this powerful convenience:

> This invention will produce forgetfulness in the minds of those who learn to use it, because they will not practice their memory. Their trust in writing, produced by the external characters which are no part of themselves, will discourage the use of their own memory within them. You have invented an elixir not of memory, but of reminding; and you offer your pupils the appearance of wisdom, not true wisdom, for they will read many things without instruction and will therefore seem to know many things, when they are for the most part ignorant and hard to get along with, since they are not wise, but only appear wise.[2]

The point that Plato's Thamus makes thus pertains directly to the theory we consider here. The preliterate mind remembers in ways that the literate mind does not. In fact, the actual cognitive activity of preliterate humans, it will be remembered, was, in Walter J. Ong's view, dependent on such memory. Speaking specifically of

---

2. Plato, *Phaedrus*, in *Plato Euthyphro, Apology, Crito, Phaedo, Phaedrus*, trans. Harold North Fowler, Loeb Classical Library 36 (Cambridge, MA: Harvard University Press, 1914), 274e–275b.

remembered wisdom texts, he comments, "Thought in any extended form is impossible without them, for it consists in them."[3] For us, as members of a culture separate from these earlier modes of thinking, having come to rely on the resources of knowledge derived from literacy, the internalized, readily accessible inventory of which such writers as Larrington, Deskis, and Shippey speak has dwindled to a point where it is barely conceivable, let alone readily detectable in our intellectual competence.

And yet this sensitivity can still be consciously cultivated by us. Students in my proverb seminars have repeatedly risen with success to the challenge of finding in *Beowulf* passages indicative of paroemial cognitive patterning once that phenomenon was explained to them. And they have on occasion found in proverb compilations, particularly *TPMA*, explicit paroemiological justification for the passages so identified. Interestingly, the particular texts that they found there have proved to be very much the same as a group of such texts examined by Susan Deskis in *Beowulf and the Medieval Proverb Tradition*. There, in chapter 5, "Warnings and Advice," she addresses as "sententiae" wisdom passages that in their surface form did not satisfy traditional standards for true proverbiality.

For example, she cites, in the early lines of *Beowulf*, in a passage praising Hrōþgār's grandfather Bēow, the observation, "Swā sceal ġe(ong) guma gōde ġewyrċean, / fromum feoh-ġiftum on fæder (bea)rme, / þæt hine on ylde eft ġewuniġen / wilġesīþas, þonne wīġ cume, / lēode ġelǣsten; lofdǣdum sceal / in mǣġþa ġehwǣre man ġeþēon" (In this way a young man ought by his good deeds, by giving splendid gifts while still in his father's house, to make sure that later in life beloved companions will stand by him, that people will serve him when war comes).[4] Although the advantages for a prince of early generosity in the interests of acquiring loyal followers are not specifically expounded here, or perhaps anywhere, by perceivable traditional proverbial formula, the meaning is clear, and its more general sense is partly articulated by several of those lines in *Hávamál* that offer advice on reciprocal generosity in friendship, affirming thus Norse-Anglo-Saxon cultural affinities while attesting to the desirability of such magnanimous behavior.

---

3. Ong, *Orality*, 35.
4. *Beowulf*, ll, 20a–26b; *Klaeber's* Beowulf, 3. *Beowulf*, trans. Donaldson, 1.

In this poem are several stanzas that recommend the reinforcement of friendship through the exchange of gifts. For instance, *Hávamál* 42 advises "Vin sínum / skal maðr vinr vera / ok gjalda gjǫf við gjǫf; / hlátr við hlátri / skyli hǫlðar taka / en lausung við lygi" (To his friend a man should be a friend / and repay gifts with gifts; / laughter men should accept with laughter / but return deception for a lie).[5] A subsequent stanza emphasizes furthering the intimacy of friendship through gifts: "Veiztu, ef þú vin átt, / þann er þú vel trúir, / ok vill þú af honum gott geta, / geði skaltu við þann blanda / ok gjǫfum skipta, / fara at finna opt" (You know, if you've a friend whom you really trust / and from whom you want nothing but good, / you should mix your soul with his and exchange gifts, / go and see him often).[6] The firm acceptance of these standards of gift giving in friendship is sufficiently established so that, in cautioning the audience regarding a negative relational situation, the speaker uses the word *gjǫf* (gift) in a metaphorical sense as he suggests the reciprocity of treachery where such danger is suspected: "Þat er enn of þann / er þú illa trúir / ok þér er grunr at hans geði, / hlæja skaltu við þeim / ok um hug mæla; / glík skulu gjǫld gjǫfum." (Again, concerning the one you don't trust, / and whose mind you suspect: / you should laugh with him and disguise your thoughts: / a gift should be repaid with a like one.)[7] In these wise admonitions we see a glimpse of some aspects of the significance of gift giving in the paroemial cognitive patterning that was current in the preliterate Germanic North, and from this parallels are discernible in the thinking of the *Beowulf* poet and his audience.

Although intending not to stray too far from the direction of our concluding remarks, we will consider for a moment wider parameters of paroemial cognitive patterning than those we considered in chapter 2. As an example, first, of how layers of meaning in the sagas may be revealed through the alert reading of texts, we might examine two brief passages from *Hœnsa-Þóris saga* that also seem to draw on the passively maintained yet expansively influential reservoir of wisdom in the ethical area under discussion. First, when Blund-Ketill decides to help Ǫrn the Norwegian merchant after the latter has fallen out with the local chieftain, Tungu-Oddr, he does so by recalling the kindness of Ǫrn's father with whom he had once

---

5. ÍF 36, 1:330, st. 42; Larrington, *Poetic Edda*, 18.
6. ÍF 36, 1:330, st. 44; Larrington, *Poetic Edda*, 18.
7. ÍF 36, 1:330, st. 46; Larrington, *Poetic Edda*, 19.

stayed in Norway as a child: "ek var með fǫður hans, þá ek var barn, ok hefi ek eigi nýtra dreng fundit en hans fǫður ... ok þat myndi faðir hans ætla, at ek mynda nǫkkut líta á hans mál, ef hann þyrfti þess við." (I spent time with his father when I was a child, and I have never met a man with more integrity than his father. . . . His father would want me to lend him a hand if he needed it.)[8] His decision to help Ǫrn, which the magnanimity of his character might in any case seem to dictate, is thus motivated by the composer in terms of a sense either of gratitude or possibly of obligation for a former kindness on the part of Ǫrn's father.

In the second passage of interest here, Gunnarr Hlífarson, seeking support among powerful men for Hersteinn Blund-Ketilsson's campaign to gain compensation for the burning of his father, approaches the chieftain Þórðr gellir Óláfsson, ostensibly owing to an innocent motive to gain his close involvement in Hersteinn's marriage to Gunnarr's daughter, which, however, would then place him among those responsible for legal action. Although he seems to sense the plot, even without yet knowing of Blund-Ketill's death, he recognizes an obligation to the kind and wealthy farmer:

> Vel er mér við Blund-Ketil, því at einn tíma, ... fór ek at heimta í foraðs-illu veðri ok vér þrír saman, ok kómum um nótt til Blund-Ketils, ok var oss þar all vel fagnat, ok þar váru vér viku. Hann skipti við oss hestum, en gaf mér góð stóðhross. Slíkt reynda ek af honum, en þó lízk mér svá á, at eigi muni því misráðit, þó at eigi sé þessu keypt

> (I like Blund-Ketil, ... I went to collect [a penalty payment] in treacherous weather with a couple of other men, and we came to Blund-Ketil's place during the night. We were treated very well there and stayed a whole week. He traded fresh horses for ours and gave me good stud-horses. So that was my experience with him, but I can't help feeling nevertheless that it wouldn't be a bad idea if this deal didn't come about.)[9]

And he allows his justified suspicions to be overridden by a sense, again, of gratitude or of obligation—or perhaps of both. The passages are so brief, and the character is so short in development,

---

8. ÍF 3:10, ch. 3; CSI 5:241.
9. ÍF 3:31, ch. 11; CSI 5:252.

that it is difficult to distinguish with certainty the precise motivations behind the positive response of both speakers. Certainly, the noble quality of their observations is otherwise out of place in the unpleasant society depicted by this saga.

Our objectivity in the study of these readings may be enhanced, however, by referring to a couple of passages in *Beowulf*. In the first passage Hrōþgār speaks, early on during the hero's visit to Heorot, of how Bēowulf's father Ecgþēow had come to the Danish king for help after starting a feud with the Wulfings. Hrōþgār arranged the settlement: "'Siððan þā fǣhðe fēo þingode, / sende iċ Wylfingum ofer wæteres hrycg / ealde mādmas; hē mē āþas swōr'" (Afterwards I paid blood-money to end the feud; over the sea's back I sent the Wylfings old treasures; he swore oaths to me).[10] In this context, Bēowulf's visit at the court of Hēorot to provide Hrōþgār with his support against Grendel could acquire in its motivation an element of obligation, of repayment for a great favor given to his father. As with the scenes in *Hœnsa-Þóris saga*, the sentiments as they are expressed are admirably noble, especially within the heroic ethical framework.

And this motivational obligation may also be sensed at the end of Bēowulf's visit to the Danes, after saving Hrōþgār's court by killing Grendel and his mother. The old king expresses his gratitude in terms of the political impact of these deeds: "'Hafast þū ġefēred þæt þām folcum sceal, / Ġēata lēodum ond Gār-Denum, / sib ġemǣnu, ond sācu restan, / inwitnīþas, þē hīe ǣr drugon'" ("You have brought it about that peace shall be shared by the peoples, the folk of the Geats and the Spear-Danes, and enmity shall sleep, acts of malice which they practiced before").[11] Although heroes live, typically, for the acquisition of personal honor, Bēowulf's accomplishments are described by Hrōþgār as having healed and bonded the relationship of Geats and Danes. The resolution of one feud is paid for by the resolution of another, and Bēowulf can be seen as having returned, or paid for, the favor Hrōþgār did for his father.

Although there are obviously no direct literary connections between the late thirteenth-century Icelandic saga and the much earlier Old English poem, the two works share common sentiments and apparently common ethical assumptions, which again can be interpreted as arising from the common paroemial cognitive patterning of the respective cultures from which they originate.

---

10. *Beowulf*, ll. 470a-72b. *Klaeber's Beowulf*, 18. *Beowulf*, trans. Donaldson, 9.
11. *Beowulf*, ll, 1855a–1858b; *Klaeber's Beowulf*, 62; *Beowulf*, trans. Donaldson, 32.

Such processes of thought, which I have tried to begin describing in this volume, and of which others before me have already indicated their awareness, deserve much further attention. Comparative studies within the Germanic cultural areas could provide us with a useful understanding of those patterns of ethical thought that came to inform the literatures we read. And on a much broader field, the cognitive mechanisms discovered in these investigations could in turn prove to have an eventual impact on linguistic as well as psychological disciplines.

Suggestions for Further Research

Each of the sagas I chose to examine in this volume was of interest for some particular reason in paroemiological terms, as I explained in my preface and in chapter headings and introductory passages.

1. Of the more than forty *Íslendingasögur*, however, readers will by now surely have thought of some I might have included but did not. A perfect candidate for attention is *Laxdœla saga*, which I did discuss briefly, examining the influence of the Vǫlsung-Niflung cycle on its characters and their actions. Someone reading this saga with the perspicacity, say, of an A. Margaret Arent Madelung might find evidence of structural thematic signaling in its paroemial usage.[12] In fact, nearly any of the more carefully written examples of the saga genres offer data that could be useful for paroemiological investigation.

2. In addition, as the Skaldic Poetry Project makes its way toward completion, large quantities of data become available there that may provide us with significant evidence in our pursuit of a more detailed understanding of the paroemial cognitive patterning that informs, as I have shown above, the texts of Old Icelandic literature. Russell Poole, for example, has already studied such material, in his chapter, "The 'Sentential Turn' in Sigvatr Þórðarson."[13]

---

12. A. Margaret Arent Madelung, *The Laxdœla Saga: Its Structural Patterns*, University of North Carolina Studies in Germanic Languages and Literatures 74 (Chapel Hill: University of North Carolina Press, 1972).

13. "The 'Sentential Turn' in Sigvatr Þórðarson," in *Proverbia Septentrionalia: Essays on Proverbs in Medieval Scandinavian and English Literature*, ed. Michael Cichon and

3. Much lies beyond the parameters of internal investigation that I have described while introducing the pursuit of my subject. External to the purely literary critical focus of this work, many other things of interest also invite study:

   a. To return momentarily to *Laxdœla saga*, readers will notice the marked imagery of Iceland's flora and fauna in its paroemial inventory.
   b. A number of sagas display elements of riddling or apparently nonsensical commentary, not specifically proverbial in character but close enough to be of interest to paroemiologists and others concerned with phraseological matters. Among those sagas are: *Víga-Glúms saga*, *Víglundar saga*, *Króka-Refs saga*, *Bósa saga*, and *Gísls þáttr Illugasonar*. Saxo Grammaticus uses riddling also in his story of Ericus disertus, which occurs in book 5 of his *Gesta Danorum*.[14]
   c. Punning on personal names occurs in phrases that could come to have a proverbial turn in *Hallfreðar saga vandrœðaskálds*, *Bjarnar saga Hítdœlakappa*, and *Svarfdœla saga*.
   d. While it would also be acknowledged as among the areas of investigation external to the purposes of paroemiology as that is defined in this volume, the limited and concentrated presence of Wellerisms, especially in texts of Norwegian rather than of Icelandic origin, would make a suitable subject for an extensive study. Wellerism is a term used for a hybrid proverbial format that creates a humorous or ironic effect; it derives from the conversational style of Charles Dickens's character Sam Weller in *The Pickwick Papers* (1837). The form itself seems ageless if not universal, occurring as early as Greek and Roman literature, and yet it is quite unevenly distributed in later European cultures. Wolfgang Mieder has defined the Wellerism's triadic structure as consisting of (1) An often-proverbial statement, (2) identification of its speaker, which can be an animal, and (3) a phrase placing the statement in an unexpected situation. An example would be

---

Lin Yiu, Medieval and Renaissance Texts and Studies 542 (Tempe: Arizona Center for Medieval and Renaissance Studies, 2019), 119–38.

14. See Arthur Hruby, *Rätselreden in den altnordischen Sagas* (Vienna: Stanzell, 1932).

"'Everyone to his own taste,' said the farmer when he kissed the sheep."[15] Archer Taylor remarked that while Wellerisms were popular in northern medieval Germany they were much less so in its southern areas, to judge by extant sources. And while the form flourished in continental Scandinavia, its occurrence in Iceland in such texts as *Sverris saga* and *Morkinskinna* probably derives from continental sources; its recorded native presence is certainly sparsely attested.[16]

Of the four Wellerisms in *Morkinskinna*, two or three occur within a few lines of each other, and they are uttered by Sveinki Steinarsson in a heated public debate with King Magnús's man, Sigurðr ullstrengr, who has been sent to enforce the farmer's departure from his ancestral lands. This passage is remarkable for the rhetoric displayed in Sveinki's speeches. As he inveighs against King Magnús's henchmen, he soars into a series of comparative proverbial phrases. The rhetoric of Sveinki gains momentum and power, with the Wellerisms forming part of the gradual escalation to this urgent passage. We cannot be sure of their origin; nor can we find them elsewhere in Norse literature. But if they do not come from an unusually sophisticated orally transmitted episode about Sveinki's defiance of Magnús and his campaign against the men of Elfr, then they are certainly a tribute to the eloquence of the composer to whom we owe them and the story in which they are embedded. The clustering of this material, if it is not of a purely literary origin, seems likely the result of an episode having been composed orally and preserved intact—the Wellerisms, like other paroemial material, acting in a mnemonic as well as a dramatic function. The passage deserves much further attention.

e. What would also be external to the study of proverbs themselves are formulaic phrases by which these texts are sometimes introduced, in conversation as well as in literature. Hugo Gering collected a large number of such phrases that he includes in his augmentation of Finnur Jónsson's collection. From a traditionalist point of view, certainly, such introductions confirm the authenticity of a proverb. It could be useful to

---

15. Mieder, *Proverbs*, 15.
16. Taylor, *Proverb*, 207–8, 211–13.

consider what other purposes they might serve in the narratives in which they occur.[17]

f. We have spoken earlier of the cultural context of paroemial allusion, of that extensive communal repository of wisdom to which composers, and for that matter anyone using the Icelandic language, might refer, even today. Finnur Jónsson, in a section following his compilation of medieval proverbs, observes, "I ethvert tilfælde synes ordsprogene at måtte gå tilbage til tiden för reformationen" (In each instance the proverb seems as if it must go back to the time before the Reformation).[18] His following list is comprised of currently used proverbs from mythology as well as saga narrative, including, for example, "viða koma Hallgerði bitlingar (pytlingar)" (From far and wide morsels come to Hallgerðr).[19] Another such proverb, "Fáir eru Kára líkir" (Few are like Kári), refers of course to the last hero of *Njáls saga*, Kári Solmundarsson, and his inimitably great courage and strength.[20]

"Phrases and sentences from this saga become apothegms," observes Einar Ól. Sveinsson, "which go flying out through town and countryside to become proverbs quoted by all Icelanders. It has been said of Horace that scarcely any event occurred on which he could not be quoted. For Icelanders *Njáls saga* has become a similar storehouse of quotations."[21] This paroemial legacy, though primarily indebted to that saga, derives not only from other major works like *Grettis saga* but also from less-widely read stories, such as *Svarfdœla saga* and *Vatnsdœla*, as Finnur Jónsson records in his list: "Fra historiske sagaer hæntede ordsprog."[22] Again, we have in such data another subject awaiting attention, and much could be revealed from it regarding the legacy of the saga world in the language by which Icelanders still communicate with one another today.

---

17. Gering, "Sprichwörter," 2–6.
18. FJ 206.
19. FJ 208; JGF 52.
20. FJ 209; JGF 358.
21. Einar Ól. Sveinsson, *Masterpiece*, 75.
22. FJ 208–11.

* * *

A list of the possibilities of inquiry is not endless, but it is long, and by now it will be clear to readers that this discipline of paroemiology and its use in saga criticism has much room for research and consideration. When I was a student in Iceland, the phrases of wisdom must have struck me quite incidentally, but without inspiring more than youthful conversational attention on my part. Today, that is a very different matter. My reading of medieval Icelandic literature against its proverbial background has led me to realize how very important this element of the narrative is to our understanding of the point of the sagas, the intentions of their composers, and the purposes of the lives and actions of those characters with which they are peopled.

* * *

In conclusion, I must add that it would be impossible to say how many times, in my recent years working with this book, I have thought of Ásta Jónsdóttir, whose hospitable kindness and that of her friends in my youthful days so long ago in Iceland may well have been guided, at some level, by the advice of the early stanzas of *Hávamál*. As one of them once told me, in his generation people still looked to that poem for direction in the conduct of their lives.

Bibliography

Primary Sources

Almanak Hins íslenzka þjóðvinafélags. Reykjavík: Ríkisprentsmiðjan Gutenberg, 1899, 1903–5, 1907, 1913.

Alter, Robert. *The Wisdom Books: Job, Proverbs, and Ecclesiastes; a Translation with Commentary*. New York: W. W. Norton, 2010.

Andersson, Theodore Murdock, and Kari Ellen Gade, trans. *Morkinskinna: The Earliest Icelandic Chronicle of the Norwegian Kings (1030–1157)*. Islandica 51. Ithaca, NY: Cornell University Press, 2000.

Aristotle. *The "Art" of Rhetoric*. Translated by John Henry Freese. Aristotle 22. Loeb Classical Library 193. Cambridge, MA: Harvard University Press, 1926.

Aristotle. *Metaphysics X–XIV*. Translated by Hugh Tredennick. Aristotle 28. Loeb Classical Library 287. Cambridge, MA: Harvard University Press, 1935.

Ármann Jakobsson and Þórður Ingi Guðjónsson, eds. *Morkinskinna*. 2 vols. Íslenzk fornrit 23–24. Reykjavík: Hið íslenzka fornritafélag, 1968.

Aðalheiður Guðmundsdóttir, ed. *Úlfhams saga*. Rit 53. Reykjavík: Stofnun Árna Magnússonar, 2001.

Bjarni Aðalbjarnarson, ed. *Heimskringla*. 3 vols. Íslenzk fornrit 26–28. Reykjavík: Hið íslenzka fornritafélag, 1941–51. Abbreviated as ÍF 26–28.

Bjarni Kolbeinsson. "Málsháttakvæði." In *Den norsk- isländska skaldediktningen*, edited by Ernst Albin Kock, 1:308–16. 2 vols. Lund: Gleerup, 1946–49.

———. "Málsháttakvæði." In *Den norsk-isländska skjaldedigtning*, edited by Finnur Jónsson, B.2:138–45. 2 vols. Copenhagen: Gyldendal, 1912–15.

Bjarni Vilhjálmsson and Óskar Halldórsson. *Íslenzkir málshættir*. 2nd ed. Reykjavík: Almenna Bókafélagið, 1982.

Björn K. Þórólfsson and Guðni Jónsson, eds. *Vestfirðinga sögur*. Íslenzk fornrit 6. Reykjavík: Hið íslenzka fornritafélag, 1943. Abbreviated as ÍF 6.

Blake, Norman Francis, ed. and trans. *Jómsvíkingasaga. The Saga of the Jomsvikings. Translated from the Icelandic with Introduction, Notes and Appendices*. London: Thomas Nelson and Sons, 1962.

Brandl, Alois, and O. Zippel, eds. "The Proverbs of Alfred." In *Mittelenglische Sprache- und Literaturproben. Ersatz für Mätzners Altenglische Sprachproben. Mit etymologischem Wörterbuch zugleich für Chaucer*. Berlin: Weidmannsche Buchhandlung, 1917.

Byock, Jesse, trans. *The Saga of King Hrolf Kraki*. London: Penguin Books, 1998.

———. *The Saga of the Volsungs: The Norse Epic of Sigurd the Dragon Slayer*. London: Penguin Books, 1999.

Chaucer, Geoffrey. *The Riverside Chaucer*. Edited by Larry Benson. 3rd ed. Oxford: Oxford University Press, 1987.

Clarke, D. E. Martin, ed. *The* Hávamál: *With Selections from other Poems of the* Edda, *Illustrating the Wisdom of the North in Heathen Times*. Cambridge: Cambridge University Press, 1923.

Cleasby, Richard, and Guðbrandur Vigfússon. *An Icelandic-English Dictionary*. 2nd ed. Oxford: Clarendon Press, 1957. Abbreviated as C-V.

Coogan, Michael D., ed. *The New Oxford Annotated Bible with the Apocryphal/Deuterocanonical Books*. Edited by Michael D. Coogan. 3rd ed. Oxford: Oxford University Press, 2001.

Cook, Robert, trans. *Njals Saga*. London: Penguin Books, 2002.

De Boor, Helmut, ed. and trans. *Das Nibelungenlied: Zweisprachig*. Cologne: Parkland Verlag, 2004.

Dennis, Andrew, Peter Foote, and Richard Perkins, trans. *The Laws of Early Iceland*. Grágás: *The Codex Regius of Grágás with Material from other Manuscripts*. 2 vols. Winnipeg: University of Manitoba Press, 1980.

Donaldson, Ethelbert Talbot, trans. *Beowulf: A New Translation*. New York: W. W. Norton, 1966.

Ebel, Uwe, ed. *Hœnsa-Þóris saga: Mit Anhang, Skizzen und Nachwort*. Metelen: Dagmar Ebel, 1989.

Edwards, Paul, and Hermann Pálsson, trans. *Arrow-Odd: A Medieval Novel*. London: University of London Press, 1970.

Einar Ól. Sveinsson, ed. *Brennu-Njálssaga*. Íslenzk fornrit 12. Reykjavík: Hið íslenzka fornritafélag, 1954. Abbreviated as ÍF 12.

———. *Laxdœla saga*. Íslenzk fornrit 5. Reykjavík: Hið íslenzka fornritafélag, 1934. Abbreviated as ÍF 5.

———. *Vatnsdœla saga*. Íslenzk fornrit 8. Reykjavík: Hið íslenzka fornritafélag, 1939. Abbreviated as ÍF 8.

———. *Verzeichnis isländischer Märchenvarianten: Mit einer einleitenden Untersuchung*. Folklore Fellows Communications 28, no. 83. Helsinki: Helsinki Suomalainen Tiedeakatemia Academia Scientiarum Fennica, 1928.

Einar Ól. Sveinsson and Matthías Þórðarson, eds. *Eyrbyggja saga*. Íslenzk fornrit 4. Reykjavík: Hið íslenzka fornritafélag, 1935. Abbreviated as ÍF 4.

Erasmus, Desiderius. *The Collected Works of Erasmus*. Vol. 31, *Adages Iiı to Iv100*, translated by M. M. Phillips, annotated by R. A. B. Mynors. Toronto: University of Toronto Press, 1982.

Evans, David Anthony Howell, ed. *Hávamál*. Viking Society for Northern Research Text Series 7. London: Viking Society for Northern Research, 1986.

Finnur Jónsson. *Íslenskt málsháttasafn*. Copenhagen: Gyldendal, 1920.

———. "Oldislandske ordsprog og talemåder." *Arkiv för nordisk filologi*, 30 (1913–14): 61–217. Abbreviated as FJ.

Finnur Jónsson, ed. *Brennu-Njálssaga (Njála)*. Altnordische Saga-Bibliothek 13. Halle an der Saale: Max Niemeyer, 1908.

———. *Den norsk-islandske skjaldedigtning*. 4 vols. Copenhagen: Gyldendal, Nordisk forlag, 1912. Reprint Copenhagen: Rosenkilde and Bagger, 1967, 1973.

Fox, Denton, and Hermann Pálsson, trans. *Grettir's Saga*. Toronto: University of Toronto Press, 1975.

Fulk, R. D., Robert E. Bjork, and John D. Niles, eds. *Klaeber's Beowulf and the Fight at Finnsburg*. 4th ed. Toronto: University of Toronto Press, 2008.

Gering, Hugo. "Altnordische Sprichwörter und sprichwörtlische Redensarten." *Arkiv för nordisk filologi* 32 (1915–16): 1–31.

Grimstad, Karen, ed. *Vǫlsunga saga. The Saga of the Volsungs. The Icelandic Text According to MS Nks 1824 b, 4o*. Bibliotheca Germanica. Series Nova 3. Saarbrücken: AQ-Verlag, 2000.

Grundtvig, Svend, comp. and ed. *Gamle danske minder i folkemunde: folkeæventyr, folkeviser, folkesagn og andre rester af fortidens digtning og tro, som de endnu leve i det danske folks erindring*. Copenhagen: C. G. Iversen, 1854–61.

Guðbrandur Vigfússon. *Origines Islandicae. A Collection of the More Important Sagas and Other Native Writings Relating to the Settlement and Early History of Iceland*. 2 vols. Oxford: Clarendon Press, 1905.

———. *Sturlunga Saga: Including the Islendinga Saga of Lawman Sturla Thordsson and Other Works*. 2 vols. Oxford: Clarendon Press, 1878.

Guðmundur Jónsson. *Safn af íslenzkum orðskviðum, fornmælum, heilræðum, snilliyrðum, sannmælum og málsgreinum: Samanlesið og í stafrófsröð sett af Guðmundi Jónssyni prófasti í Snæfellsnessýslu og presti í Staðarstaðarsókn*. Copenhagen: Hið íslenzka bókmenntafjelag, 1830. Abbreviated GJ.

Guðmundur Ólafsson. *Gudmundi Olaui Thesaurus adagiorum linguæ septentrionalis antiquæ et modernæ: Utgiven med parallellhänvisningar och register*. Edited by Gottfrid Kallstenius. Skrifter utgivna av Vetenskaps-Societeten i Lund 12. Lund: C. W. K. Gleerup, 1930.

Guðni Jónsson, ed. *Fornaldar sögur norðurlanda*. 4 vols. Reykjavík: Íslendingasagnaútgáfan, 1954, 1959. Abbreviated as FSN.

———. *Grettis saga Ásmundarsonar*. Íslenzk fornrit 7. Reykjavík: Hið íslenzka fornritafélag, 1936. Abbreviated as ÍF 7.

Halldór Halldórsson. *Íslenzk orðtök*. Reykjavík: Ísafoldarprentsmiðja, 1954.

———. *Íslenzkt orðtakasafn*. 2 vols. Reykjavík: Almenna bókafélagið, 1968, 1969.

Halldór Hermannsson, ed. *The Hólar Cato: An Icelandic Schoolbook of the Seventeenth Century*. Islandica 39. Ithaca, NY: Cornell University Press, 1958.

Hallgrímur Scheving. *Bodsrit til að hlýda á þá opinberu yfirheyrslu í Bessastada Skóla þann maí 1843: Islendskir málshættir; safnaðir,*

útvaldir og í stafrofsrød færdir. Reyjavík: Reykjavíkur skóli, 1843.
Hatto, Arthur Thomas, trans. *The Nibelungenlied*. London: Penguin Books, 1969.
Hermann Pálsson, trans. *The Confederates and Hen-Thorir*. Edinburgh: Southside, 1975.
Hock, Ronald F., ed. *The Infancy Gospels of James and Thomas: With Introduction, Notes, and Original Text featuring the New Scholars Version Translation (Scholars Bible)*. Sonoma, CA: Polebridge Press, 1996.
Jakob Benediktsson, ed. *Íslendingabók: Landnámabók*. 2 parts. Íslenzk fornrit 1. Reykjavík: Hið íslenzka fornritafélag, 1968.
Jakobsen, Jakob, ed. *Austfirðingar sǫgur*. Copenhagen: Samfund til udgivelse af gammel nordisk litteratur, 1902–3.
Jóhann Sigurjónsson. *Rit*. 2 vols. Reykjavík: Mál og menning, 1940, 1942.
Johnston, George, trans. *The Faroe Islanders' Saga*. Ottawa: Oberon, 1975.
———. *The Saga of Gisli*. Toronto: J. M. Dent & Sons, 1971.
Jón Árnason. *Íslenzkar þjóðsögur og ævintýri*. 6 vols. Reykjavík: Bókaútgáfan Þjóðsaga, 1954–61.
Jón Geir Friðjónsson. *Mergur málsins: Íslensk orðatiltæki; Uppruni, saga og notkun*. Reykjavík: Örn og Örlygur, 1993.
———. *Orð að sönnu. Íslenskir málshættir og orðskviður*. Reykjavík: Forlagið, 2015. Abbreviated JGF.
Jón Halldórsson. *Klári saga*. Edited by Gustav Cederschöld. Altnordische Saga-Bibliothek 12. Halle an der Saale: Max Niemeyer, 1907.
Jón Jóhannesson, ed. *Austfirðingar sǫgur*. Íslenzk fornrit 11. Reykjavík: Hið íslenzka fornritafélag, 1950. Abbreviated as ÍF 11.
Jón Jónsson Rugmann. *Jonas Rugmans Samling af isländska talesätt; med inledning, översättning, kommentar och register*. Edited by Gottfried Kallstenius. Skrifter utgivna av Kungliga Humanistiska Vetenskaps-Samfundet i Uppsala 22:8. Uppsala: Almqvist & Wiksell,1927.
Jónas Kristjánsson, ed. *Eyfirðinga sǫgur*. Íslenzk fornrit 9. Reykjavík: Hið íslenzka fornritafélag, 1956. Abbreviated as ÍF 9.
Jónas Kristjánsson and Vésteinn Ólason, eds. *Eddukvæði 1–2*.

Íslenzk fornrit 36. Reykjavík: Hið íslenzka fornritafélag, 2014. Abbreviated as ÍF 36.

Karl Jónsson. *Sverris saga*. Edited by Þorleifur Hauksson. Íslenzk fornrit 30. Reykjavík: Hið íslenzka fornritafélag, 2007. Abbreviated as ÍF 30.

Kock, Ernst Albin, ed. *Den norsk-isländska skaldediktningen*. 2 vols. Lund: C. W. K. Gleerup, 1946–50.

Kålund, Kristian. "En islandsk ordsprogsamling fra 15de århundrede." In *Småstykker 1–16*, 131–84. Samfund til udgivelse af gammel nordisk litteratur 13. Copenhagen: S.L. Møllers bogtrykkeri, 1884–91.

Larrington, Carolyne, trans. *The Poetic Edda*. Oxford: Oxford University Press, 1996, rev. 2014.

Larrington, Carolyne, and Peter Robinson, eds. "Sólarljóð." In *Poetry on Christian Subjects, Part 1: The Twelfth and Thirteenth Centuries*, edited by Margaret Clunies Ross, 287–357. Skaldic Poetry of the Scandinavian Middle Ages 7. Turnhout: Brepols, 2007.

Lichtheim, Miriam. *Ancient Egyptian Literature. A Book of Readings*. Vol. 2, *The New Kingdom*. Berkeley: University of California Press, 1976.

Låle, Peder. "Forndanska och latinska ordspråk." In *Östnordiska och latinska medeltidsordspråk: Peder Låles ordspråk och en motsvarande svensk samling*, edited by Axel Kock and Carl af Pedersens, 5–250. Samfund til udgivelse af gammel nordisk litteratur 20/4. Copenhagen: Berlingska boktryckeri-och Stiljuteri-Aktiebolaget, 1889–94.

———. *Östnordiska och latinska Medeltidsordspråk: Peder Låles Ordspråk och en motsvarande svensk samling*. Edited by Axel Kock and Carl af Petersens. Copenhagen: Berlingska boktryckeriet, 1889–94.

———. *Parabolae*. Copenhagen: Gotfred af Ghemen, 1506.

Magnús Gíslason. Kvällsvaka: En isländsk kulturtradition belyst genom studier i bondebefolkningens vardagsliv och miljö under senare hälften av 1800-talet och början av 1900-talet. Acta Universitatis Upsaliensis. Studia ethnologia Upsaliensis 2. Uppsala: Almqvist & Wiksell International, 1977.

Magnus Magnusson and Hermann Pálsson, trans. *Laxdæla saga*. London: PenguinBooks, 1969.

McConnell, Winder, trans. *The Lament of the Nibelungen* (*Div Chlage*). Columbia, SC: Camden House, 1994.
Ólafur Halldórsson, ed. *Færeyinga saga. Óláfs saga Tryggvasonar eptir Odd munk Snorrason*. Íslenzk fornrit 25. Reykjavík: Hið íslenzka fornritafélag, 2006. Abbreviated as ÍF 25.
Plato. *Phaedrus*. In *Plato Euthyphro, Apology, Crito, Phaedo, Phaedrus*, translated by Harold North Fowler. Loeb Classical Library 36. Cambridge, MA: Harvard University Press, 1914.
Powell, F. York, trans. *The Tale of Thrond of Gate, Commonly Called Færeyinga saga*. Northern Library 2. London: D. Nutt, 1896.
Saxo Grammaticus. *Gesta Danorum: The History of the Danes*. 2 vols. Edited by Karsten Friis-Jensen. Translated by Peter Fisher. Oxford: Oxford University Press, 2015.
———. *The History of the Danes. Books I-IX*. Translated by Peter Fisher. Edited with Commentary by Hilda Ellis Davidson. Cambridge: D. S. Brewer, 1979–80. Reprint Woodbridge: BOYE6, 1996, 2002.
Sephton, John, trans. *The Saga of King Sverri of Norway*. Northern Library 4. London: David Nutt, 1899.
Sigfús Blöndal. *Íslenzk-dönsk orðabók*. Reykjavík: Verslun Þórarins B. Þorlákssonar, 1920–24.
Sigurbjörn Einarsson, Guðrún Kvaran, and Gunnlaugur Ingólfsson, eds. *Íslensk Hómilíubók: Fornar stólræður*. Reykjavík: Hið íslenska bókmenntafélag, 1993.
Sigurður Nordal, ed. *Egils saga Skalla-Grímssonar*. Íslenzk fornrit 2. Reykjavík: Hið íslenzka fornritafélag, 1933. Abbreviated as ÍF 2.
Sigurður Nordal and Guðni Jónsson, eds. *Borgfirðinga sǫgur*. Íslenzk fornrit 3. Reykjavík: Hið íslenzka fornritafélag, 1938. Abbreviated as ÍF 3.
Sijmons, Barend J., and Hugo Gering, eds. *Die Lieder der Edda.*. 3 vols. in 4. Germanistische Handbibliothek 7. Halle an der Saale: Buchhandlung des Waisenhauses, 1888–1931.
Singer, Samuel, ed. *Thesaurus Proverbiorum Medii Aevi: Lexikon der Sprichwörter des romanisch-germanischen Mittelalters*. 13 vols. Berlin: De Gruyter, 1996–2002. Abbreviated as *TPMA*.
Snorri Sturluson. *Edda*. Translated by Anthony Faulkes London: J. M. Dent, 1998.
———. *Edda Snorra Sturlusonar. Nafnaþulur og skáldatal*. Edited by Guðni Jónsson. Reykjavík: Íslendingasagnaútgáfan, 1954.

———. *Heimskringla*. Translated by Alison Finlay and Anthony Faulkes. 3 vols. London: Viking Society for Northern Research, 2011–15.
"Sólarljóð." In *Den norsk-islandska skjaldedigtning*, edited by Finnur Jónsson, B1:635–48. 2 vols. Copenhagen: Gyldendal, 1912–15.
"Sólarljóð." In *Den norsk-isländska skaldediktningen*, edited by Ernst Albin Kock, 2:73-78. 2 vols. Lund: C. W. K. Gleerup, 1946–50.
Synesius. *In Praise of Baldness*. Translation from the Greek with introduction and notes by George H. Kendal. Vancouver: Pharmakon Press, 1985.
Syv, Peder. *Aldmindelige danske ordsproge og korte lærdomme, med foregaaende underviisning om dennem; samt efterfølgende tilhæng af nogle sære, som fordom have været oc endeel endnu ere brugelige i disse tre nordiske riger. Saa og et register paa titlerne og et andet paa de gamle og sielden forekommende ord*. Copenhagen: Sl. Corfitz Luftis paa C. Geertzens bekostning, 1682, 1688.
Tacitus. *Germania*. Translated by M. Hutton. Revised by H. E. Warmington. Loeb Classical Library 35. Cambridge, MA: Harvard University Press, 1914. Rev. ed., 1970.
Thorsen, Peder Goth, and Konráð Gíslason, eds. *Sagan af Hrafnkeli Freysgoða*. Copenhagen: Trykt hos B. Luno, 1839.
Turville-Petre, E. O. G., ed. *Víga-Glúms saga*. 2nd ed. Oxford: Clarendon Press, 1960. Reprint, 1974.
Tuvestrand, Birgitta, ed. Hugsvinnsmál: *Handskrifter och kritisk text*. Lundastudier i nordisk språkvetenskap, series A, no. 29. Lund: Carl Bloms boktryckeri, 1977.
Vilhjálmur Finsen, ed. *Grágás: Islændernes Lovbog i fristatens tid*. 2 vols. Copenhagen: Brødrenes Berlings bogtrykkeri, 1852.
Viðar Hreinsson, ed. *The Complete Sagas of Icelanders*. 5 vols. Reykjavík: Bókaútgáfan Leifur Eiríksson, 1997. Abbreviated as *CSI*.
Vrátný, Karel. "Noch einiges zu den altisländischen Sprichwörtern." *Arkiv för nordisk filologi* 33 (1917): 58–63.

Secondary Sources

Aðalheiður Guðmundsdóttir. "The Werewolf in Medieval Icelandic Literature." *The Journal of English and Germanic Philology* 106 (2007): 277–303.

Aguirre, Manuel. "Narrative Composition in *The Saga of the Volsungs*." *Saga-Book* 26 (2002): 5–37.
Alexiou, Margaret. *The Ritual Lament in Greek Tradition*. Rev. ed. Cambridge: Cambridge University Press, 2002.
Allen, Richard F. *Fire and Iron: Critical Approaches to Njáls saga*. Pittsburgh: University of Pittsburgh Press, 1971.
Alster, Bendt. "Proverbs from Ancient Mesopotamia: Their History and Social Implications." *Proverbium. Yearbook of International Proverb Scholarship* 10 (1993): 1–20.
Anderson, Sarah M. "Introduction: 'og eru köld kvenna ráð.'" In *Cold Counsel: Women in Old Norse Literature and Mythology*, edited by Sarah M. Anderson and Karen Swenson, xi–xvi. New York: Routledge, 2002.
Anderson, Sarah M., and Karen Swenson, eds. *Cold Counsel: Women in Old Norse Literature and Mythology*. New York: Routledge, 2002.
Andersson, Theodore Murdock. "The Displacement of the Heroic Ideal in the Family Sagas." *Speculum* 45 (1970): 575–93.
———. *The Growth of the Medieval Icelandic Sagas (1180–1280)*. Ithaca, NY: Cornell University Press, 2006.
———. *The Icelandic Family Saga: An Analytic Reading*. Cambridge, MA: Harvard University Press, 1967.
———. *A Preface to the Nibelungenlied*. Stanford, CA: Stanford University Press, 1987.
———. *The Problem of Icelandic Saga Origins: A Historical Survey*. New Haven, CT: Yale University Press, 1964.
———. "Some Ambiguities in *Gísla saga*: A Balance Sheet." *Bibliography of Old Norse-Icelandic Studies* 1968 (1969): 7–42.
———. "The Textual Evidence for an Oral Family Saga." *Arkiv för nordisk filologi* 81 (1966): 1–23.
Árni Björnsson. *Jól á Íslandi*. Reykjavík: Ísafold, 1963.
Arora, Shirley. "The Perception of Proverbiality." *Proverbium. Yearbook of International Saga Scholarship* 1 (1984) 1–38.
Bax, Marcel, and Tineke Padmos. "Two Types of Verbal Dueling in Old Icelandic: The Interactional Structure of the Senna and the Mannjafnaðr in *Hárbarðsljóð*." *Scandinavian Studies* 55 (1983): 149–74.
Beckman, Gary. "Proverbs and Proverbial Allusion in Hittite." *Journal of Near Eastern Studies* 45 (1986): 19–30.

Bjarni Guðnason. "The Icelandic Sources of Saxo Grammaticus." In *Saxo Grammaticus: A Medieval Author Between Norse and Latin Culture*, edited by Karen Friis-Jensen, 79–93. Copenhagen: Museum Tusculanum Press, 1981.

Bock, L. Alfred. "Die epische Dreizahl in den Islendinga sögur." *Arkiv för nordisk filologi* 37, 38 (1921, 1922): 263–313, 51–83.

Bolton, W. F. "The Heart of *Hrafnkatla*." *Scandinavian Studies* 43 (1971): 35–52.

Bonner, Maria. "Grettir's First Escapades: How To Challenge Your Father And Get Away With It: A Case Study In Historical Dialogue Analysis." In *Frederic Amory in Memoriam: Old Norse-Icelandic Studies*, edited by John Lindow and George Clarke, 184–212. Berkeley, CA: North Pinewood Press, 2015.

Bouman, Ari Cornelius. *Patterns in Old English and Old Icelandic Literature*. Leidse Germanistische en Anglistische Reeks van de Rijksuniversiteit te Leiden. Deel 1. Leiden: Universitaire Pers Leiden, 1962.

Bredsdorff, Thomas. *Chaos and Love: The Philosophy of the Icelandic Family Sagas*. Translated by John Tucker. Copenhagen: Museum Tusculanum Press, 2001.

Broussard, Jonathan Mark. "Waging Word Wars: A Discourse Analysis of the Patterns of Norse Masculinity Presented through Mannjafnaðr in the Icelandic Sagas." Master's thesis, McNeese State University, 2003.

Bryce, Glendon F. *A Legacy of Wisdom: The Egyptian Contribution to the Wisdom of Israel*. Lewisburg, PA: Bucknell University Press, 1979.

Bultmann, Rudolph. *History of the Synoptic Tradition*. Translated by J. Marsh. Oxford: Basil Blackwell, 1963.

———. "The Study of the Synoptic Gospels." In *Form Criticism. Two Essays on New Testament Research*, translated by Frederick C. Grant, 7–76. Chicago: Willett, Clark, 1934. Reprint, New York: Harper Torch Books, 1962.

Byock, Jesse. *Feud in the Icelandic Saga*. Berkeley: University of California Press, 1982.

Bååth, Albert Ulrik. *Studier öfver kompositionen i några isländska ättsagor*. Lund: Fr. Berlings Boktryckkeri och Stiljuteri, 1885.

Carnes, Pack, ed. *Proverbia in Fabula: Essays on the Relationship of the Fable and the Proverb*. Sprichwörterforschung, vol. 10. Bern: Peter Lang, 1988.

Chomsky, Noam. *Syntactic Structures*. The Hague: Mouton, 1957.
Clark. David. *Gender, Violence, and the Past in Edda and Saga*. Oxford: Oxford University Press, 2012.
Clark, George. "*Beowulf* and *Njálssaga*." In *Proceedings of the First International Saga Conference, University of Edinburgh, 1971*, edited by Peter Foote, Hermann Pálsson, and Desmond Slay, 66–87. London: Viking Society for Northern Research, 1973.
Clover, Carol. "Cold are the Counsels of Women: The Tradition Behind the Tradition." In *The Sixth International Saga Conference 28/7–2/8 1985. Workshop Papers*. 2 vols. I:151–75. Copenhagen: Det arnmagnæanske Institut, 1985.
———. "*Hárbarðsljóð* as Generic Farce." *Scandinavian Studies* 51 (1979): 124–45.
———. "Hildigunnr's Lament." In *Structure and Meaning in Old Norse Literature: New Approaches to Textual Analysis and Literary Criticism*, edited by John Lindow, Lars Lönnroth, and Gerd Wolfgang Weber, 141–83. The Viking Collection 3. Odense: Odense University Press, 1986.
———. "The Long Prose Form." *Arkiv för nordisk filologi* 101 (1986): 10–39.
———. *The Medieval Saga*. Ithaca, NY: Cornell University Press, 1982.
———. "Scene in Saga Composition." *Arkiv för Nordisk Filologi* 89 (1974): 57–83.
Clunies Ross, Margaret. *The Cambridge Introduction to The Old Norse-Icelandic Sagas*. Cambridge: Cambridge University Press, 2010.
———. *Prolonged Echoes. Old Norse Myths in Medieval Northern Society*. 2 vols. Odense: Odense University Press, 1998.
Condren, Edward I. "On Civilizing Hrafnkell." *Modern Language Notes* 88 (1973): 517–34.
Cook, Robert. "The Reader in *Grettis saga*." *Saga-Book* 21 (1984–85): 133–54.
———. "The Sagas of Icelanders as Dramas of the Will." In *Proceedings of the First International Saga Conference, University of Edinburgh, 1971*, edited by Peter Foote, Hermann Pálsson, and Desmond Slay, 88–113. London: Viking Society for Northern Research, 1973.

Davis, Craig. "Cultural Assimilation in *Njáls saga*." *Oral Tradition* 13 (1998) : 435–55.
De Looze, Laurence. "The Outlaw Poet, the Poetic Outlaw: Self-Consciousness in *Grettis saga Ásmundarsonar*." *Arkiv för nordisk filologi* 106 (1991): 85–103.
Deskis, Susan E. *Alliterative Proverbs in Medieval England: Language Choice and Literary Meaning*. Columbus: Ohio State University Press, 2016.
———. *Beowulf and the Medieval Proverb Tradition*. Tempe: Arizona Center for Medieval and Renaissance Texts and Studies, 1996.
———. "Proverbs and Structure in Maxims I.A." *Studies in Philology* 110 (2013): 667–89.
Driscoll, Matthew. *The Unwashed Children of Eve: The Production, Dissemination and Reception of Popular Literature in Post-Reformation Iceland*. Enfield Lock: Hisarlik Press, 1997.
Dronke, Ursula, Gudrun P. Helgadottir, Gerd Wolfgang Weber, Hans Bekker-Nielsen, eds. *Speculum Norrœnum: Norse Studies in Memory of Gabriel Turville-Petre*. Odense: Odense University Press, 1981.
Dundes, Alan. "On the Structure of the Proverb." *Proverbium. Yearbook of International Proverb Scholarship* 25 (1975): 961–73. Reprinted in *The Wisdom of Many: Essays on the Proverb*, edited Wolfgang Mieder and Alan Dundes, 43–64. Madison: University of Wisconsin Press, 1994.
Durrenberger, E. Paul, Dorothy Durrenberger, and Ástráður Eysteinsson. "Economic Representation and Narrative Structure in *Hœnsa-Þóris saga*." *Saga-Book of the Viking Society for Northern Research* 22 (1987–88): 143–64.
Ebel, Uwe. *Der Untergang des isländischen Freistaats als historischer Kontext der Verschriftlichung der Isländersaga: Zugleich ein Beitrag zum Verständnis der "Hœnsa-Þóris saga."* Wissenschaftliche Reihe 2. Metelen: Dagmar Ebel, 1989.
Einar Ól. Sveinsson. *Á Njálsbúð: Bók um mikið listaverk*. Reykjavík: Ískenzka bókmenntafélag, 1943.
———. *The Age of the Sturlungs: Icelandic Civilization in the Thirteenth Century*. Translated by Johann S. Hannesson. Islandica 36. Ithaca, NY: Cornell University Press, 1953.
———. "Celtic Elements in Icelandic Tradition." *Béaloideas* 16 (1957): 3–24.

———. Njáls saga: *A Literary Masterpiece*. Translated by Paul Schach. Lincoln: University of Nebraska Pres, 1971.

———. *Sturlungaöld: Drög um íslenzka menningu á þrettándu öld*. Reykjavik: Nokkrir Reykvíkingar, 1940.

———. *Um íslenzkar þjóðsögur*. Reykjavík: Sjóður Margrétar Lehmann-Filhés, 1940.

Evans, David Anthony Howell. "Hugsvinnsmál." In *Medieval Scandinavia: An Encyclopedia*, edited by Phillip Pulsiano and Kirsten Wolf, 306a. New York: Garland, 1993.

Falk, Hjalmar. *Altwestnordische Kleiderkunde mit besondere Berücksichtigung der Terminologie*. Kristiania: Jacob Dybwad, 1919.

Falk, Oren. "The Vanishing Volcanoes: Fragments of Fourteenth-Century Icelandic Folklore." *Folklore* 118 (2007): 1–22.

Foote, Peter G. "An Essay on *The Saga of Gisli* and its Icelandic Background." In *The Saga of Gisli*, translated by George Johnston, 93–134. Toronto: J. M. Dent & Sons, 1971.

Fox, Denton. "*Njál's Saga* and the Western Literary Tradition." *Comparative Literature* 15 (1963): 289–310.

Fulk, Robert Dennis. "The Moral System of *Hrafnkels saga Freysgoða*." *Saga-Book* 22 (1986): 1–32.

Fulk, Robert Dennis, Robert E. Bjork, and John D. Niles, eds. *Klaeber's* Beowulf *and the* Fight at Finnsburg. Toronto: University of Toronto Press, 2008.

Gerstein, Mary R. "Germanic Warg: The Outlaw as Werewolf." In *Myth in Indo-European Antiquity*, edited by Gerald James Larson, C. Scott Littleton, and Jan Puhvel, 131–56. Berkeley: University of California Press, 1974.

Gísli Sigurðsson. *The Medieval Icelandic Saga and Oral Tradition: A Discourse on Method*. Translated by Nicholas Jones. Cambridge, MA: Milman Parry Collection of Oral Literature, Harvard University, 2004.

———. *Túlkun Íslendingasagna í ljósi munnlegrar hefðar: Tilgáta um aðferð*. Reykjavík: Stofnun Árna Magnússonar á Íslandi, 2002.

Gordon, E. V. *An Introduction to Old Norse*. 2nd ed. Rev. Arnold R. Taylor. Oxford: Oxford University Press, 1957.

———. "On *Hrafnkels saga Freysgoða*." *Medium Ævum* 8 (1939): 1–32.

Gos, Giselle. "Women as a Source of heilræði, 'Sound Counsel': Social Mediation and Community Integration in *Fóstbrœðra saga*," *Journal of English and Germanic Philology* 108 (2009): 281–300.

Gunnell, Terry. "Grýla, Grýlur, 'Grøleks' and Skeklers: Medieval Disguise Traditions in the North Atlantic?" *Arv: Nordic Yearbook of Folklore* 57 (2001): 33–54.

Hallberg, Peter. "The Concept of *gipta-gæfa-hamingja* in Old Norse Literature." In *Proceedings of the First International Saga Conference, University of Edinburgh, 1971*, edited by Peter G. Foote, Herman Pálsson & Desmond Clay. London: Viking Society for Northern Research, 1973.

———. "Hunting for the Heart of *Hrafnkels saga.*" *Scandinavian Studies* 47 (1975): 463–66.

———."Några anteckningar om replik och dialog i *Njals saga.*" In *Festschrift Walter Baetke, dargebracht zu seinem 80. Geburtstag am 28 März 1964*, edited by K. Rudolph, R. Heller, and E. Walter, 130–50. Weimar: Hermann Böhlaus nachfolger, 1966.

Halleux, Pierre. "Hrafnkel's Character Reinterpreted," *Scandinavian Studies* 38 (1966): 36–44.

Hamer, Andrew J. "*Grettis saga* and the iudicium dei." In *Northern Voices: Essays on Old Germanic and Related Topics, Offered to Professor Tette Hofstra*, edited by Kees Dekker, Alasdair MacDonald, and Hermann Niebaum, 19–40. Mediaevalia Groningana, New Series, 11/Germania Latina; 6. Leuven: Peeters, 2008.

———. *Njals Saga and its Christian Background: A Study of Narrative Method*. Mediaevalia Groningana New Series, 20/ Germania Latina 8. Leuven: Peeters, 2014.

Haraldur Bessason. "Mythological Overlays." In *Sjötíu tirgerðir helgaðar Jakobi Benediktssyni, 20. Júli 1977*, edited by Einar G. Pétursson and Jónas Kristjánsson, I: 273–92. 2 vols. Reykjavík: Stofnun Árna Magnússonar, 1977.

Harris, Joseph. "A Nativist Approach to *Beowulf*: The Case of the Germanic Elegy." In *Companion to Old English Poetry*, edited by Henk Aertsen and Rolf H. Bremmer Jr., 45–62. Amsterdam: VU University Press, 1994.

Harris, Richard L. "Concordance to Proverbs and Proverbial Materials in the Old Icelandic Sagas." University of Saskatchewan, Department of English. https://research-groups.usask.ca/icelanders/concordance.php.

———. "The Deaths of Grettir and Grendel: A New Parallel." *Scripta Islandica* 24 (1973): 25–53.

———. "The Eddic Wisdom of Hreiðarr the Fool: Paroemial

Cognitive Patterning in an Old Icelandic *þáttr*." In *Literary Speech Acts of the Medieval North: Essays Inspired by the Works of Thomas A. Shippey*, edited by Eric Bryan and Alexander Vaughan Ames, 3–27. Tempe: Arizona Center for Medieval and Renaissance Studies, 2020.

———. "'The Hand's Pleasure in the Blow is Brief,' Proverbs Escalating Danger in the Revenge Pattern of *Njálssaga*." *Proverbium. Yearbook of International Saga Scholarship* 18 (2000): 149–65.

———. "'Jafnan segir inn ríkri ráð': Proverbial Allusion and the Implied Proverb in *Fóstbrœðra saga*." In *New Norse Studies: Essays on the Literature and Culture of Medieval Scandinavia*, edited by Jeffrey Turco, 61–97. Islandica 58. Ithaca, NY: Cornell University Press, 2015.

———. "Odin's Old Age: A Study of The Old Man in The Pardoner's Tale." *Southern Folklore Quarterly* 33 (1969): 24–38.

———. "The Proverbial Heart of *Hrafnkels saga Freysgoða*: 'Mér þykkir þar heimskum manni at duga, sem þú ert.'" *Scandinavian-Canadian Studies* 16 (2006): 28–54. https://scancan.net/pdf/harris_1_16.pdf. Accessed 24 November 2021.

———. "The Proverbs of *Vatnsdœla saga* and the Sword of Jǫkull: The Oral Backgrounds of Grettir Ásmundarson's Flawed Heroism." In *The Hero Recovered. Essays on Medieval Heroism in Honor of George Clark*, edited by Robin Waugh and James Weldon, 150–70. Kalamazoo: Medieval Institute Publications, Western Michigan University, 2010.

Heinemann, Frederik J. "*Hrafnkels saga Freysgoða* and Type-Scene Analysis." *Scandinavian Studies* 46 (1974): 102–19.

Helgi Þorláksson. "Historical Background: Iceland 870–1400." In *A Companion to Old Norse-Icelandic Literature and Culture*, edited by Rory McTurk, 136–54. Oxford: Blackwell, 2005.

———. "Social Ideals and the Concept of Profit in Thirteenth-Century Iceland." In *From Sagas to Society: Comparative Approaches to Early Iceland*, edited by Gísli Pálsson, 231–41. Enfield Lock: Hisarlik Press, 1992.

Heller, Rolf. *Die literarische Darstellung der Frau in den Isländersagas.* Untersuchungen zur nordischen Literatur- und Sprachgeschichte 2. Halle an der Saale: Max Niemeyer Verlag, 1958.

Hermann Pálsson. *Hávamál í ljósi íslenskrar menningar.* Reykjavík: Háskólaútgáfan, 1999.

———. *Oral Tradition and Saga Writing*. Studia Medievalia Septentrionalia 3. Vienna: Fassbaender, 1999.
———. *Sagnaskemmtun Íslendinga*. Reykjavík: Mál og Menning, 1962.
———. *Siðfræði Hrafnkels sögu*. Reykjavík: Heimskringla, 1966.
———. "Um gæfumenn og ógæfu í íslenzkum fornsögum." In *Afmælisrit Björns Sigfússonar*, edited by Björn Þorsteinsson and Sverrir Tómasson, 135–53. Reykjavík: Sögufélag, 1975.
———. *Úr hugmyndaheimi Hrafnkels sögu og Grettlu*. Reykjavík: Bókaútgáfa Menningarsjóðs, 1981.
Heusler, Andreas. *Die Anfänge der isländischen Saga*. Abhandlungen der königlichen preussischen Akademie der Wissenschaften. Philosophische-historische Klasse, no. 9. Berlin: Verlag der königlichen Akademie der Wissenschaften, Georg Reimer, 1914.
Hill, Thomas D. "Njáll's Comforting Words: *Brennu-Njáls saga*, Chapter 129," *Saga-Book of the Viking Society for Northern Research* 41 (2017): 71–78.
Honeck, Richard P. *A Proverb in Mind: The Cognitive Science of Proverbial Wit and Wisdom*. Mahwah, NJ: Lawrence Erlbaum, 1997.
Hruby, Arthur. *Rätselreden in den altnordischen Sagas*. Vienna: Stanzell, 1932.
Hughes, Shaun F. D. "*Klári saga* as an Indigenous Romance." In *Romance and Love in Late Medieval and Early Modern Iceland. Essays in Honor of Marianne Kalinke*, edited by Kirsten Wolf and Johanna Denzin, 135–63. Islandica 54. Ithaca, NY: Cornell University Press, 2008.
Hume, Kathryn. "The Thematic Design of Grettis Saga." *Journal of English and Germanic Philology* 73 (1974): 469–86.
Jesch, Judith. "'Good Men' and Peace in *Njáls saga*." In *Introductory Essays on* Egils saga *and* Njáls saga, edited by John Hines and Desmond Slay, 64–82. London: Viking Society for Northern Research, 1992.
Jochens, Jenny. "The Female Inciter in the Kings' Sagas." *Arkiv för nordisk filologi* 102 (1987): 100–119.
———. "The Medieval Icelandic Heroine: Fact or Fiction?" In *Sagas of the Icelanders: A Book of Essays*, edited by John Tucker, 99–126. New York: Garland, 1989.
———. *Old Norse Images of Women*. Philadelphia: University of Pennsylvania Press, 1996.

Johansen, Jan Geir. "The Hero of *Hrafnkels saga Freysgoða*." *Scandinavian Studies* 67 (1995): 265–84.
Jónas Kristjánsson. *Um Fóstbræðrasögu*. Rit. 1. Reykjavík: Stofnun Árna Magnússonar á Íslandi, 1972.
———. "Learned Style or Saga Style?" In *Speculum Norrœnum. Norse studies in memory of Gabriel Turville-Petre*, edited by Ursula Dronke, Guðrún P. Helgadóttir, Gerd Wolfgang Weber, and Hans Bekker-Nielsen, 260–92. Odense: Odense University Press, 1981.
Jónas Kristjánsson and Vésteinn Ólason, eds. *Goðakvæði*. Vol. 1. Íslenzk fornrit 36. Reykjavík: Hið íslenzka fornritafélag, 2014.
Kanerva, Kirsi. "*Ógæfa* (Misfortune) as an Emotion in Thirteenth-Century Iceland." *Scandinavian Studies* 84 (2012): 1–26.
Ker, William Paton. *Epic and Romance. Essays on Medieval Literature*. London: MacMillan, 1908.
Kinck, Hans Ernst. "Et par ting om ættesagen, skikkelser den ikke forstod." In *Til Gerhard Gran: 9. december 1916 / fra venner og elever*, edited by Anders Krogvig, 32–58. Kristiania: Aschehoug, 1916.
Kolb, Eduard. *Alemannisch-nordgermanisches Wortgut*. Beiträge zur schweizerdeutschen Mundartforschung, vol. 6. Frauenfeld: Verlag Huber, 1956.
Kratz, Henry. "*Hrafnkels saga*: Thirteenth-Century Fiction?" *Scandinavian Studies* 53 (1981): 420–46.
Lachmann, Vera. *Das Alter der Harðarsaga*. Palaestra 183. Leipzig: Mayer & Müller, 1932.
Larrington, Carolyne. "Hávamál and Sources outside Scandinavia." *Saga-Book of the Viking Society* 23 (1992): 141–57.
———. *A Store of Common Sense: Gnomic Theme and Style in Old Icelandic and Old English Wisdom Poetry*. Oxford: Clarendon Press, 1993.
Lethbridge, Emily. "Dating the Sagas and *Gísla saga Súrssonar*." In *Dating the Sagas. Reviews and Revisions*, edited by Else Mundal, 77–105. Copenhagen: Museum Tusculanum Press, University of Copenhagen, 2013.
———. "*Gísla saga Súrssonar*: Textual Variation, Editorial Constructions and Critical Interpretations." In *Creating the Medieval Saga: Versions, Variability and Editorial Interpretations of Old Norse Saga Literature*, edited by Judy Quinn and Emily

Lethbridge, 123–34. Odense: University Press of Southern Denmark, 2010.

———. "Who Says What in *Gísla saga Súrssonar*? Speaker Attribution in the Three Versions of the Saga." *Quaestio Insularis* 5 (2004): 42–61.

Lindow, John, Lars Lönnroth, and Gerd Wolfgang Weber, eds. *Structure and Meaning in Old Norse Literature: New Approaches to Textual Analysis and Literary Criticism.* The Viking Collection 3. Odense: Odense University Press, 1986.

Lionarons, Joyce Tally. "The Otherworld and its Inhabitants in the *Nibelungenlied*." In *A Companion to the Nibelungenlied*, edited by Winder McConnell, 153–71. Columbia, SC: Camden House, 1998.

Lönnroth, Lars. *Njáls saga: A Critical Introduction.* Berkeley: University of California Press, 1976.

———. "The Noble Heathen: A Theme in the Sagas." *Scandinavian Studies* 41 (1969): 1–29.

———. "Rhetorical Persuasion in the Sagas." *Scandinavian Studies* 42 (1970): 157–89. Reprinted in an abridged version in *Sagas of the Icelanders: A Book of Essays*, edited by John Tucker, 292–322. New York: Garland, 1989.

———. "Sverrir's Dreams." *Scripta Islandica: Isländska Sällskapets Årsbok* 57 (2006): 97–110.

Madelung, A. Margaret Arent. *The* Laxdœla Saga: *Its Structural Patterns.* University of North Carolina Studies in Germanic Languages and Literatures 74. Chapel Hill: University of North Carolina Press, 1972.

Maxwell, Ian R. "Pattern in *Njáls saga*." *Saga-Book of the Viking Society for Northern Research* 15 (1957–59): 17–47.

McCreesh, Bernadine. "Grettir and Glámr—Sinful Man Versus the Fiend: An Allegorical Interpretation of a fourteenth-Century Icelandic Saga." *Revue de l'Université Ottawa/University of Ottawa Quarterly* 51 (1981): 180–88.

———. "How Pagan Are the Icelandic Family Sagas?" *Journal of English and Germanic Philology* 79 (1980): 58–66.

———. "Structural Patterns in *Eyrbyggja saga* and Other Sagas of the Conversion." *Mediaeval Scandinavia* 11 (1978): 271–80.

Messenger, John. "The Role of the Proverb in a Nigerian Judicial System." *Southwestern Journal of Anthropology* 15 (1959): 64–73.

Meulengracht Sørensen, Preben. "On Humour, Heroes, Morality, and Anatomy in *Fóstbrœðra saga*." In *Twenty-Eight Papers Presented to Hans Bekker-Nielsen on the Occasion of his Sixtieth Birthday*, edited by Michael Barnes, E.W. Hansen, H.F. Nielsen, and R. Schützeichel, 395–418. Odense: Odense University Press, 1993.

Mieder, Wolfgang. "Popular Views of the Proverb." *Proverbium* 2 (1983): 109–43.

———. *Proverbs: A Handbook*. Westport, CT: Greenwood Press, 2004.

———. *Wise Words: Essays on the Proverb*. Edited by Wolfgang Mieder. New York: Garland, 1994.

Mieder, Wolfgang, and Alan Dundes, eds. *The Wisdom of Many. Essays on the Proverb*. Madison: University of Wisconsin Press, 1981.

Miller, William Ian. *Bloodtaking and Peacemaking: Feud, Law, and Society in Saga Iceland*. Chicago: University of Chicago Press, 1990.

———. "The Central Feud in *Njáls Saga*." In *Sagas of the Icelanders: A Book of Essays*, edited by John Tucker, 292–322. New York: Garland, 1989.

———. "Choosing the Avenger." *Law and History Review* 1 (1983): 159–204.

———. "Justifying Skarpheðinn: of Pretext and Politics in the Icelandic Bloodfeud." *Scandinavian Studies* 55 (1983): 316–44. Reprinted in an abridged version as "The Central Feud in *Njáls saga*," in *Sagas of the Icelanders: A Book of Essays*, edited by John Tucker, 292–322. New York: Garland, 1989.

———. *"Why is Your Axe Bloody?" A Reading of* Njáls saga. Oxford: Oxford University Press, 2014.

Milner, G. B. "Quadripartite Structures." *Proverbium. Yearbook of International Saga Scholarship* 14 (1969): 379–83.

———. "What is a Proverb?" *New Society* 332 (1969): 199–202.

Mitchell, Steven A. *Heroic Sagas and Ballads*. Ithaca, NY: Cornell University Press, 1991.

Mundal, Else. "Kǫld eru kvenna ráð." In *Kvinner og Bøker: Festschrift til Ellisiv Steen På hennes 70-årsdag 4. Februar 1978*, edited by Edvard Beyer, 183–93. Oslo: Gyldendal, 1978.

Mundt, Marina. "Pleading the Cause of Hoensa-Thorir." Paper presented at the Alþjóðlegt fornsagnaþing, Reykjavik, Iceland,

August 2–8, 1973. http://sagaconference.org/SC02/SC02_Mundt.pdf. Accessed 24 November 2021.

Netter, Irmgard. *Die direkte Rede in den Isländersagas.* In *Form und Geist: Arbeiten zur germanischen Philologie,* edited by Lutz Mackensen in collaboration with K. Kaiser, B. Markwart, F. R. Schröder, H. Teuchert, and K. Wesle. Vol. 36. Leipzig: Hermann Eichblatt Verlag, 1935.

Norrick, Neal R. *How Proverbs Mean: Semantic Studies in English Proverbs.* Trends in Linguistics. Studies and Monographs 27. Berlin: Mouton, 1985.

North, Richard. *Pagan Words and Christian Meanings.* Costerus New Series 81, edited by C.C. Barfoot, Hans Bertens, Theo D'haen, and Erik Kooper. Amsterdam: Rodopi B. V., 1991.

O'Donohugue, Heather. *Skaldic Verse and the Poetics of Saga Narrative.* Oxford: Oxford University Press, 2005.

Old Norse-Icelandic Literature: A Critical Guide. Edited by Carol J. Clover and John Lindow. Islandica 45. Ithaca, NY: Cornell University Press, 1985.

Olrik, Axel. "Epische Gesetze der Volksdichtung." *Zeitschrift für Deutsches Altertum* 51 (1909): 1–12, translated into English as "Epic Laws of Folk Narrative," In *The Study of Folklore,* translated by Jeanne P. Steager, edited by Alan Dundes, 129–41. Englewood Cliffs, NJ: Prentice-Hall, 1965.

Ong, Walter J. *Orality and Literacy. The Technologizing of the Word.* 2nd ed. London: Routledge, 2002.

Permyakov, Gregori L. *From Proverb to Folktale. Notes on the General Theory of Cliché.* Moscow: Nauka, 1979.

Perry, Theodore A. "Quadripartite Wisdom Sayings and the Structure of Proverbs." *Proverbium. Yearbook of International Saga Scholarship* 4 (1987): 187–210.

Podles, Leon J. "*Njals saga*: Pagan Myth and Christian History." PhD. diss., University of Virginia, 1975. ProQuest (AAT 7600026).

Poole, Russell. "Myth, Psychology, and Society in *Grettis saga.*" *Álvissmál* 11 (2004): 3–16.

———. "The 'Sentential Turn' in Sigvatr Þórðarson." In *Proverbia Septentrionalia: Essays on Proverbs in Medieval Scandinavian and English Literature,* edited by Michael Cichon and Yin Liu, 119–38. Medieval and Renaissance Texts and Studies 542.

Tempe: Arizona Center for Medieval and Renaissance Studies, 2019.
Quinn, Judy. "From Orality to Literacy in Medieval Iceland." In *Old Icelandic Literature and Society*, edited by Margaret Clunies Ross, 30–60. Cambridge Studies in Medieval Literature 42. Cambridge: Cambridge University Press, 2000.
Quinn, Judy, and Emily Lethbridge, eds. *Creating the Medieval Saga: Versions, Variability and Editorial Interpretations of Old Norse Saga Literature*. Odense: University Press of Southern Denmark, 2010.
Richmond, Velma Bourgeois. *Laments for the Dead in Medieval Narrative*. Pittsburgh: Duquesne University Press, 1966.
Rudolf, K., R. Heller, and E. Walter, eds. *Festschrift Walter Baetke. Dargebracht zu seinem 80. Geburtstag am 28 März 1964*. Weimar: Hermann Böhlaus, 1966.
Russom, Geoffrey. Beowulf *and Old Germanic Metre*. Cambridge: Cambridge University Press, 1998.
Ryding, William W. *Structure in Medieval Narrative*. De proprietatibus litterarum. Series Maior 12. Edited by Cornelis H. van Schooneveld. The Hague: Mouton, 1971.
Saussure, Ferdinand de. *Course in General Linguistics*. Edited by Charles Bally and Albert Sechehaye. Translated by Albert Riedlinger. With introduction and notes by Wade Baskin. New York: Philosophical Library, 1959.
Sayers, William. "Gunnarr, His Irish Wolfhound Sámr, and the Passing of the Old Heroic Order in *Njáls saga*." *Arkiv för nordisk filologi* 112 (1997): 43–66.
Schach, Paul. *Icelandic Sagas*. Twayne's World Authors Series. Scandinavian Literature. Edited by Leif Sjöberg. Boston: Twayne Publishers, 1984.
———. "Some Observations on the Generation-Gap Theme in the Icelandic Sagas." In *The Epic in Medieval Society. Aesthetic and Moral Values*, edited by Harold Scholler, 361–81. Tübingen: Max Niemeyer Verlag, 1977.
———. "The Use of the Simile in the Old Icelandic Family Sagas." *Scandinavian Studies* 24 (1952): 149–65.
Schorn, Brittany Erin. "'How Can His Word Be Trusted?': Speaker and Authority in Old Norse Wisdom Poetry." PhD diss., University of Cambridge, 2012. ProQuest (AAT U594596).

———. *Speaker and Authority in Old Norse Wisdom Poetry*. Trends in Medieval Philology 34. Berlin: De Gruyter, 2017.
Schott, Christine. "Footnotes on Life. Marginalia in Three Medieval Icelandic Manuscripts." Master's thesis, Háskóli Íslands, 2010.
Shippey, Thomas A. "Foreword: Awareness of Immanence." In *Literary Speech Acts of the Medieval North: Essays Inspired by the Works of Thomas A. Shippey*, edited by Eric Bryan and Alexander Vaughan Ames, 3–27. Tempe: Arizona Center for Medieval and Renaissance Studies, 2020.
———. *Old English Verse*. London: Hutchinson, 1972.
Sigurður Nordal. "Handrit. Aldur. Höfundur." In *Vestfirðinga sögur*, edited by Björn K. Þórólfsson and Guðni Jónsson, lxiv–lxx. Íslenzk fornrit 6. Reykjavík: Hið íslenzka fornritafélag, 1943.
———. *Hrafnkatla*. Studia Islandica 7. Reykjavík: Ísafoldarprentsmiðja, 1940.
———. *Hrafnkels Saga Freysgoða: A Study*. Translated by R. G. Thomas. Cardiff: University of Wales Press, 1958.
Sigurður Sigurðsson frá Arnarholti and Jónas Guðlaugsson. *Tvístirnið*. Reykavík: Prentsmiðjan Gutenberg, 1906.
Sijmons, Barend J., and Hugo Gering, eds. *Kommentar zu den Liedern der Edda*. 3 vols. in 4. Germanistische Handbibliothek 7. Halle an der Saale: Buchhandlung des Waisenhauses, 1888–1931.
Silverman-Weinreich, Beatrice. "Towards a Structural Analysis of Yiddish Proverbs." *Yivo Annual of Jewish Social Science* 17 (1978): 1–20. Reprinted in *The Wisdom of Many: Essays on the Proverb*, edited by Wolfgang Mieder and Alan Dundes, 65–85. Madison: University of Wisconsin Press, 1981.
Somerset, FitzRoy Richard (Lord Raglan). *The Hero: A Study in Tradition, Myth and Drama*. London: Methuen, 1936.
Sommer, Bettina Sejbjerg. "The Norse Concept of Luck." *Scandinavian Studies* 79 (2007): 275–94.
Spiess, Gisela. "Die Stellung der Frau in den Sprichwörtern isländischer Sprichwörtersammlungen und in isländischen Sagas." *Proverbium. Yearbook of International Saga Scholarship* 8 (1991): 159–78.
Springer, Otto. "The Style of the Old Icelandic Family Sagas." *Journal of English and Germanic Philology* 38 (1939): 107–28.
Stefán Einarsson. *A History of Icelandic Literature*. Baltimore: Johns Hopkins Press, 1957.

Sverrir Jakobsson. "Strangers in Icelandic Society 1100–1400." *Viking and Medieval Scandinavia* 3 (2007): 141–57.
Swenson, Karen. *Performing Definitions: Two Genres of Insult in Old Norse Literature*. Studies in Scandinavian Literature and Culture 3. Columbia, SC: Camden House, 1993.
Taylor, Archer. *The Proverb*. Cambridge, MA: Harvard University Press, 1931.
Taylor, Jon. "The Sumerian Proverb Collections." *Revue d'assyriologie et d'archéologie orientale* 99 (2005): 13–38.
Tucker, John, ed. *Sagas of the Icelanders: A Book of Essays*. New York: Garland, 1989.
Tulinius, Torfi. *The Matter of the North: The Rise of Literary Fiction in Thirteenth-Century Iceland*. Translated by Randi C. Eldevik. Viborg: Odense University Press, 2002.
Turville-Petre, E. O. G. "Gisli Sursson and His Poetry: Traditions and Influences," *Modern Language Review* 39 (1944): 374–91. Reprinted in *Nine Norse Studies*, 118–53. London: Viking Society, 1972.
———. *Nine Norse Studies*. London: Viking Society, 1972.
Van den Toorn, Maarten Cornelius. *Ethics and Moral in Icelandic Saga Literature*. Assen: Van Gorcum, 1955.
Vésteinn Ólason. "Concentration of Power in Thirteenth-Century Iceland and Its Reflection in Some Íslendingasögur." Paper presented at the Alþjóðlegt fornsagnaþing, Reykjavik, Iceland, August 2–8, 1973. http://sagaconference.org/SC02/SC02_Vesteinn.pdf. Accessed 24 November 2021.
———. *Dialogues with the Viking Age: Narration and Representation in the Sagas of the Icelanders*. Translated by Andrew Wawn. Reykjavík: Heimskringla, 1998.
———. "Gísli Súrsson—A Flawless or Flawed Hero?" In *Die Aktualität der Saga. Festschrift für Hans Schottmann*, edited by Stig Toftgaard Andersen, 163–75. Berlin: De Gruyter, 1999.
Von See, Klaus. "Die *Hrafnkels saga* als Kunstdichtung." *Skandinavistik* 9 (1979): 47–56.
Walcot, Peter. *Hesiod and the Near East*. Cardiff: University of Wales Press, 1966.
Waltke, Bruce K. "The Book of Proverbs and Ancient Wisdom Literature." *Bibliotheca Sacra* 136 (1979): 211–38.
Ward, Donald. "The Wolf: Proverbial Ambivalence." *Proverbium. Yearbook of International Saga Scholarship* 4 (1987): 211–24.

Whiting, Bartlett Jere. "The Nature of the Proverb." *Harvard Studies and Notes in Philology and Literature* 13 (1931): 47–80. Reprinted in *When Evensong and Morrowsong Accord: Three Essays on the Proverb*, edited by Joseph C. Harris and Wolfgang Mieder, 51–85. Cambridge, MA: Harvard University Press, 1994.

———. *When Evensong and Morrowsong Accord: Three Essays on the Proverb*. Edited by Joseph C. Harris and Wolfgang Mieder. Cambridge, MA: Harvard University Press, 1994.

Wilson, Frank Percy. "The Proverbial Wisdom of Shakespeare." Presidential address to the Modern Humanities Research Association. Cambridge: Modern Humanities Research Association, 1961.

Þórbergur Þórðarson. *Í Suðursveit*. Reykavík: Mál og menning, 1975.

Þórður Ingi Guðjónsson. "'Köld eru kvenna ráð': Um gamlan orðskvið." In *Brageyra léð Kristjáni Eiríkssyni, sextugum, 19. Nóvember 2005*, edited by Guðvarður Már Gunnlaugsson, Margrét Eggertsdóttir, and Þórunn Sigurðardóttir, 115–19. Reykjavík: Menningar- og minningarsjóður Mette Magnussen, 2005.

Örnólfur Thorsson. "Farið á hriflingabjörgum í *Grettlu*." In *Strengleikar slegnir Robert Cook, 25. Nóvember 1994*, edited by Margrét Eggertsdóttir, Sverrir Tómasson, Valgerður Brynjólfsdóttir, and Örnólfur Thorsson, 79–83. Reykjavík: Menningar og minningarsjóður Mette Magnussen, 1994.

———. "Orð af orði: Hefð og nýmæli í *Grettlu*." Master's thesis, Háskóli Íslands, 1993.

Ingram Content Group UK Ltd.
Milton Keynes UK
UKHW012235170423
420333UK00003B/103